Wild Food
Proceedings of the Oxford Symposium on Food and Cookery 2004

Wild Food

Proceedings of the Oxford Symposium on Food and Cookery 2004

Edited by Richard Hosking

Prospect Books
2006

First published in Great Britain in 2006 by Prospect Books, Allaleigh House, Blackawton, Totnes, Devon, TQ9 7DL.

ISBN 1-903018-43-9

The drawing reproduced on the cover was made in 1760 by the artist Hugh Douglas Hamilton and has been published in The Cries of Dublin edited by William Laffan (The Irish Georgian Society, 2003). The original is in a private collection. See the paper by Máirtín Mac Con Iomaire, below.

Design and typesetting in Gill Sans and Adobe Garamond by Lucy Baker-Kind. Printed and bound in Great Britain by The Cromwell Press, Trowbridge.

Contents

Preface

The 2004 Symposium on Wild Food: Hunters and Gatherers, held in September under the chairmanship of Paul Levy and Claudia Roden, attracted a great deal of attention, with a large number of excellent papers being presented. It was our first meeting at Oxford Brookes University and therefore involved much detailed planning and hard work to prepare for the new venue, both on the part of the staff of Oxford Brookes and the Symposium. The Symposium Organizer, Silvija Davidson, earned the deep gratitude of all for the outstanding job she did in bringing everything together, and for Brookes, Donald Sloan, Head of the Department of Hospitality, Leisure and Tourism Management, did all a good host should do in making us welcome and ensuring satisfactory arrangements for the success of the Symposium. Geraldene Holt, Chairman of the Trustees, championed and organized the move to Brookes, and all this involved much hard work.

On Friday night there was a wine and canapé reception to welcome new members and to celebrate the publication of The Oxford Encyclopedia of Food and Drink in America, edited by Andrew Smith, a regular symposiast.

On Saturday night, there was a champagne reception, generously organized by the Champagne Information Bureau, in honour of Theodore Zeldin, newly appointed a Patron of the Symposium. Following this, Paul Bloomfield, Visiting Fellow of Brookes University, with Scott Wilson, (both of the Fox Club in London's Mayfair), together with Richard Watson, Head Chef of Brookes Restaurant, prepared and produced the excellent Symposium Dinner, planned and overseen with flair, enthusiasm and serious effort by Caroline Conran with the help of Elisabeth Luard and Anissa Helou, and carved and served with the help of students from Brookes. All these deserve our hearty thanks.

On Saturday for lunch members picnicked in the grounds of Headington Hill Hall, the grand 1850s mansion now part of Oxford Brookes University. Sunday lunch was a Game Workshop, presented with great enthusiasm and insight by Nichola Fletcher, the game being generously provided by Rick Bestwick and the bread by Dan de Gustibus, to all of whom many thanks.

Richard Manning opened the Symposium with a provocative keynote speech on 'Wild Food and Civilization'. There was also, on Sunday, a panel discussion on Foraging, in which Richard Mabey, Roger Phillips and Sinclair Philip took part.

The symposium papers presented here cover a very wide range of topics on the theme of "wild food" and all those who presented them are to be thanked for their efforts spent in producing and delivering them. Those who used audio-visual materials in their presentation were greatly supported by the patience and professionalism of the Brookes' AV staff.

Once again Patsy and Phil Iddison are to be heartily thanked for raising valuable funds for the Symposium with their Bring and Buy stall. Moving to a new venue put a great strain on all aspects of organizing the symposium, and required the help of many people, all of whom are to be thanked for their part in making it such an enjoyable event.

Richard Hosking

Wild Food: The Call of the Domestic

Ken Albala

In the late Middle Ages wild foods were among the most esteemed items on banquet menus, primarily game and wild fowl but also fish, wild fruits and vegetables. By the 18th century we find domesticated meats, especially veal and even beef, cooped and fattened capons and cultivated vegetables as the focus of elegant dining. Some species had disappeared altogether from the dining room, many wild fowl and sea mammals in particular, but also smaller four-footed creatures. Something had changed during the intervening centuries. Among the factors that may have influenced this turn of fortune were a growing population, shrinking acreage of uncultivated land and the growth of cattle rearing that ultimately caused the range of wild foods to diminish. There may also have been a deeper cultural and intellectual shift that relegated a few wild animals to exclusive hunting and all other wild species to marginalization as control over nature, taming and even, to paraphrase Francis Bacon, bending her to our will, became the conceptual ideal.

There are very obvious economic reasons why the general food supply would have been more dependent on production of domesticated species. A rising demand for food due to demographic pressure can only have been met by increasing output and cultivating or grazing more land. There was also a greater percentage of the population living in cities, more legal restrictions on hunting and collecting food in the wild. Ultimately there was a more dependable supply of cultivated plants and domesticated animals, particularly in northern Europe. For wild fowl the reduction of nesting grounds due to agricultural sprawl imperilled their reproductive cycles. These factors cannot be discounted, but there are other equally interesting cultural reasons for a shift. The change in mentality may have been triggered by these material factors, or one could say conversely that a new relationship to nature and the willingness to subdue and master it for the benefit of humans is what ultimately led to the economic and social changes. This is a matter of ideological chicken or material egg. Whichever, there was a reduction of the number and variety of wild foods normally consumed by Europeans between the late middle ages and the 18th century. For some reason people came to prefer domestic animals and plants to wild ones.

This was also the case among élite diners, though certain wild species never lost popularity. It is nonetheless true that chefs and their patrons consciously chose whiter and lighter meats, blander vegetables, and generally more soft and delicate foods in smaller cuts over what they increasingly saw as rough food unperfected by art. Veal and capon were the rising stars in 16th- and 17th-century cooking. For many, to consume dark rough and gamey food, was in a sense to become wild and uncultivated. This may itself have been an exciting diversion from the normal order of courtly behaviour, not only running wild in the forest on the hunt, and satisfying one's primal urges, but sating the taste for blood. It seems that such a desire would only be pronounced in a culture where such food was somewhat of a transgression of the norm. This may explain why some hunted wild animals, boar and venison in particular, remained popular while others disappeared entirely.

Of course, in many places only the landed nobility were allowed to hunt venison; that had always been the case. Thus the de-emphasis on game may be due to the broadening audience of cookbooks, increasingly written for urban élites or, later, even bourgeois readers. These books would have necessarily offered fewer recipes for game. The social class of the intended reader thus played a major role in the frequency of recipes for wild foods. For the cookbooks examined here in the 16th and 17th century, the audience is still primarily courtly or landed gentry, people with access to untamed land and thus venison and many wildfowl remain.

Apart from the cookbooks and banquet management guides, there are also references to wild food in other types of culinary literature, most notably natural histories, dietary literature, and herbals. Expectedly, agricultural texts are relatively silent on the topic. These sources often reveal those species that were once common but have fallen from favour on élite tables, and are especially valuable because they write as outsiders and usually for an academic audience, and were primarily interested in relaying facts rather than impressing with elaborate recipes and descriptions of banquets. Thus sometimes the wild food that was once esteemed and had since gone out of fashion can only be found in this type of food literature.

Beginning with cookbooks, medieval sources show that people enjoyed an extraordinary range of wild species. Hunting was a favourite pastime of the leisured classes and various species of deer (roebuck, fallow deer and red deer), boar and wild fowl were served and even offered as presents to relatives or to gain political favour. Patronage networks were sustained by presents of this sort. Professional hunters were also employed to bring in fresh game and may have been kept permanently employed on a noble estate. From late-medieval menus, in England for example, we learn that venison with frumenty (boiled whole grain) was a regular centrally featured item as were swans, herons, cranes and the stereotypical boar's head.[1] At royal weddings and affairs of state such items were absolutely necessary. These were often served simply roasted or according to cookbooks such as the French *Viandier*, venison was parboiled, larded and then simmered in wine, or set in a pastry shell with plenty of spices and perhaps served with a cinnamon-based sauce.[2] In 14th-century English manuscripts roe deer or boar is parboiled, chopped into pieces, and boiled in water and wine, thickened with bread and blood, spiced and then finished off with vinegar and raisins.[3] In Italy Martino Rossi offers a civet of venison which is parboiled with vinegar, fried and served with a sauce of raisins, almonds, bread, wine, cinnamon, ginger and onion.[4] All these were typical medieval flavour combinations.

10

In the end though, there are not that many recipes for game in medieval cookbooks. Although the stereotype of the huge beast turning on a spit at every medieval feast is certainly overplayed, when a large animal was killed there would have been a desire to present it intact to show it off. This may account for the paucity of recipes, especially when compared to the lowly chicken which a chef would not hesitate to pound, reshape and disguise. Since roasting and simmering were fairly simple procedures a professional chef would not need a recipe.[5] Keeping in mind that medieval cookbooks were always written for professionals in a kind of culinary shorthand and rarely give explicit measurements or detailed instructions, this may be why simple venison recipes rarely appear. It does not reflect a lack of popularity.

The relative status of venison, which then meant any hunted large wild mammal, not just deer, did not change significantly from the late medieval period into the 16th century. In fact it may have increased in prestige because rarer and increasingly confined to enclosed parks. Recipes abound straight through the 17th century, especially where owning land remained the economic and cultural ideal, that is, practically everywhere in Western Europe.

But game animals were only one part of the entire category of wild foods. A few wild foods were associated with the lowest classes, gathered only by those at the margins of subsistence or during famine. Hence we find reference to vetches, darnel and lupins, normally considered weeds among grains, eaten by starving peasants. In some places there was a stigma against eating chestnuts, especially putting them into bread as was done in the Cévennes. Surprisingly, few wild foods were explicitly associated with poverty and at the start of the early modern period it is clear that there was no particular aversion to wild foods, a remarkably wide variety of which were eaten, especially wild fowl and fish which were among the most desirable and frequently offered menu items.

Many small wild animals were also considered viable food. References to such creatures can be found throughout cookbooks of the period; they absolutely abound in the dietary literature. Hare and rabbit are always mentioned, but so too are hedgehog and fox, especially those that have been fattened up on autumn grapes. The Paduan physician Antonio Gazius includes in his list of wild meats, even though he generally disapproves of them, wild donkeys, mountain goats and gazelle which are best cooked in oil to temper their heat.[6] Melchior Sebizius describes how bears are usually prepared: they are skinned, hung to tenderize, salted and seasoned with fennel cinnamon and cloves and served as an appetizer.[7] Martino of Como preferred them in pies, and Scappi admits that though uncommon, he has cooked them. The limbs roasted are the best part.[8]

Dormice, as we know, were a favourite among ancient Romans, but their descendants centuries later also enjoyed them. Messisbugo and others included dormice on their menus.[9] Bruyerin says in the Auvergne people eat squirrels and Poles serve them at banquets.[10] Porcupines were used in pâtés or roasted on a spit larded and stuck with cloves.[11] Sebizius commends the musky fragrant odour of the flesh of marten (a weasel-like creature), and definitely prefers it to fox.[12] In the Alps marmots were roasted or made into a black broth based on their own blood. Badgers (*Taxus*) are reported in in Savonarola; Gesner says they're cooked with pears. Beaver tail was also served in more elegant dinners, especially for Lent,[13] because 'Carnem comede Pontificos est concessum', that is, because always in water, this part of the animal could be considered fish.

One particularly perverse fashion among élites involved removing the unborn foetus of a deer and cooking it. 'This was invented either by gluttonous men or to be something elegant, not because it's pleasant or healthy, but uncommon and acquired at a high price', claimed Domenico Sala.[14] Petrus Castellanus attests to the same fashion and adds that young stags' horns have also become popular as delicacies on noble tables, just when they begin to poke through. Normally they were boiled and the soft interior removed and served, or they were grated and boiled to make hartshorn jelly.[15] Most of these references come from 17th-century dietary works, and they usually condemn practices they found aberrant or unhealthy. They do suggest however that these wild foods were disappearing or were only eaten in extremely remote places or by courtly gluttons with jaded palates and a taste for the perverse. They do not appear at all in élite banquets by the 17th century, but had in earlier cookbooks. That is, in the course of these centuries small furry wild creatures went from viable if rare menu items to strange and perverse foods.

The diminution of wildfowl species is even clearer. The range of wild fowl presented on élite tables in the late Middle Ages and 16th century was simply staggering. There were wild geese and ducks and many waterfowl such as cranes, swans, storks, herons (Sebizius says, 'Truly Princes and Magnates love to hunt them.[16]) The lists of small wild-fowl regularly served are seemingly endless. The familiar pheasant, partridge, wild doves appear and even starlings, quail, fig-peckers, sparrows, and tiny thrushes. Snipes would be roasted whole with guts intact, which were later squeezed out on toast.[17] By the 17th century fewer and fewer species were eaten, particularly the waterfowl. Swan's flesh was found to be dark and malodorous, even wild ducks and teals were thought to taste like the pond muck they consumed. The preference shifted toward whiter and lighter fleshed fowl, which could include pheasant but was more likely capon or turkey.

Wild herbs were another set of common ingredients in this cuisine. The term usually referred to anything not classified as a garden vegetable (*olera*) and included wild greens, cresses, skirrets (*Sium sisarum*), samphire (*Crithmum maritimum*), eringoes (sea holly roots), water caltrops, nettles whose red spring buds went into pottage,[18] mallows (*Malva sylvestris*), and wild onions. It also included herbs in our sense of the word, as culinary seasonings. It is difficult to tell when an herb was grown in a garden, but authors do sometimes specify wild thyme, or note where a certain herb can be found, denoting that it would not be in the kitchen garden. The use of herbs is not as important as it would become in subsequent centuries, but chefs did use parsley and mint extensively as well as flowers such as fennel, elder, borage and violets. Myrtle and bay could also have been collected wild. Wild thistles were used as a curdling agent for making cheese in place of rennet, and Englishman Thomas Cogan recommends blessed thistle leaves in the morning on bread and butter.[19] He also suggests many wild herbs for medicinal as well as culinary uses – the root of the herb avens was used in stew: although it turns it black, it gives it the taste of cloves.[20]

Gathering wild herbs for a salad seems to have been common among all social classes. Cardano mentions rustics and women gathering wild endive (Condrilla) and sow thistle. These were not eaten out of desperation but for pleasure. He also mentions mallow shoots as a first course. Naturally noblemen would have their servants do the actual gathering, sometimes with grave results. Cardano mentions a case he saw of a Bolognese nobleman whose female servant accidentally put hemlock in a tart instead of parsley. The following night the nobleman was dead.[21] When Europeans became so frightened of such mistakes that they turned away from gathering wild herbs that might be poisonous is difficult to determine, but clearly warnings like this would have helped to dissuade people from doing so.

Salvatore Massonio in his book on salads mentions the 'mescolanza rustica' which he explains is a popular wild salad among noblemen, so called either because the people who usually eat it are rustics or because the herbs themselves are rustic or wild.[22] The impetus to eat such things was much like dressing up as shepherds and playing at pastoral, piping and dancing among the woodland nymphs and other such nonsense. Eating rustic wild foods was one part of this whole diversion

With the popularity and availability of sugar, honey went almost completely out of fashion in 16th-century cooking. Not that honey was truly a wild product, but the relationship of these two sweeteners is revealing. It appears though that once sugar became ubiquitous and was used among ordinary people, honey regained a certain vogue, especially in 17th-century England where it was made into mead. Rarity of honey may have had something to do with this. Apparently many monastic bee-keeping operations disappeared during the Reformation and bee-keeping became one of those noble rustic pastimes, perhaps following Virgil's *Georgics*, the fourth book of which is about the topic. Among authors such as Kenelm Digby, recipes for mead and quasi-medicinal drinks, much like the ancient Hippocratic concoctions, were passed around and published as a nobleman's personal invention. At any rate, the rarity of a wild food, or in this case managed, since the honey itself was not taken from wild bees, can bring it into fashion.

Collecting wild fruit was also considered noble. Cultivating fruit was of course a popular pastime, but only those with substantial stretches of wasteland could march off into the forest for a rustic picnic, Bacchic revel, or a day picking berries. Wild fruits including cornel cherries, sorb apples, service berries, *mespila*, *arbutus* (Strawberry tree), *uva ursi*, *uva crispa* and especially tiny wild strawberries were very fashionable. *Vaccinia* (whortleberries) along with the others were gathered and usually made into conserves, syrups or 'sapori' which were sauces used as condiments. There is no way to tell who actually did the dirty work of making these confections, though recipe books are addressed to élite readers, they could have left the messy job of collecting and cooking to servants. In any case, there was something titillating and daring about eating such wild foods precisely because in the course of the early modern period they became increasingly out of the ordinary. Most meals would be made up of domestic plants and animals and for those cooped up at court and in the city, the rustic diversion on one's own estate or *villa suburbana* provided a pleasant but ultimately safe way to escape into the wild.

Without doubt the largest category of wild foods was fish. Nearly all fish had to be wild, with the exception of a few species that could be raised in ponds, eels and fresh water carp for example, although these were probably caught wild and then stocked in ponds rather than bred in captivity as hatchlings. Of course, most fish are still wild. What makes this cuisine so different is the incredible variety of fish that were eaten. In fact, many cookbooks and practically all dietary guides spend a great deal of energy just straightening out the various names for fish, whether ancient or alternate names in dialect.

In the late Middle Ages and into the Renaissance dolphins and whales were consumed, and were considered fish. At some point thereafter they disappeared from elegant tables entirely. It may be that their numbers dwindled in European waters and they became too difficult to bring home fresh. (Cogan says of 'porpuis' – 'Although for rareness they bee esteemed of great estates.'[23]) It seems unlikely that some sudden realization that these are intelligent mammals had anything to do with growing aversion. Many other intelligent mammals were eaten happily. But the fact remains that sea mammals did disappear from élite tables during the early modern period.

We must not forget other aquatic creatures which were among the dainties served at noble tables. Frogs, often eaten whole, turtles – which grew in popularity once they were brought back from the Caribbean, as well as snails must also be in the list of wild foods.

Admittedly, many of the stranger wild foods appeared rarely in élite cookbooks. Nonetheless, given the high proportion of recipes for wild birds and fish, it is undeniable that wild foods played a major role in aristocratic cuisine in the 16th century. For example in the summary of all foods that can be used in banquets, divided by lean and meat days, Domenico Romoli lists 169 recipes based on wild ingredients out of 301 specifically for lean days, which includes every main dish without meat, any pie, pastry, soup or pasta based on fish, vegetables, or fruit. Of those recipes containing meat, 68 of 360 are based on wild ingredients.[24] These numbers are based on the primary ingredient, and it is assumed that fish are captured and fruits are usually cultivated, unless specified. For many items it is specified, as with *oche salvatiche* (wild goose) or *piccioni casalenghi* (domestic pigeon). Mushrooms and truffles were necessarily wild. There are some items whose source can not be determined, so these numbers can not be precise. Nonetheless wild foods account for more than half of the dishes eaten in Lent and about a fifth of meals on meat days. The proportion among meats seems to be the result of a wide variety of dishes made from specific parts of domestic animals such as head, liver, tongue, etc., of veal.

Bartolomeo Scappi was a bit more enthusiastic about wild foods. His fish recipes are again, mostly wild, but he also offers far more recipes based on wild fowl. With 1000 recipes in his cookbook a statistical analysis would be impractical. Suffice to say, Scappi had no aversion at all to the idea of wild food. The are about 10 wild boar recipes, about twice the number for deer of various types, a handful of recipes specifying wild duck, four for porcupine and even a recipe for guinea pig.[25]

Rossetti in his list of all possible dishes for banquets offers 3 boar recipes, 11 for deer, 14 for crane, 26 for hare, 35 for wild duck, which he specifies (there is even a recipe for their tongues smoked),[26] 57 for pheasant and partridge together, and 4 for guinea pig: roasted, in a fricassee, baked in an oven, grilled and with French mustard. Mountain goat he says to cook like mutton (*castrato*)[27] On the other hand, peacocks did not interest him much. He says cook it like turkey or serve it resewn into its feathers, but that is a dish more antique than modern.[28] Among wild foods sturgeon takes precedence with no less than 202 recipes based on the flesh, milt, liver or caviar.[29]

In the early 17th century, Cesare Evitascandalo's enthusiasm for game is as strong as his predecessors. Although the actual menus he presents rarely specify game, he does have separate entries for many wild species. Rabbits are stuffed with fruits and roasted or stewed with the same, placed in a pie, either hot or cold, cooked or alive. The latter was an old trick, though how the rabbits jumping around the table could rouse laughter time and time again one can only guess.[30] Although the medical advice Evitascandalo includes is rarely very favourable toward wild animals, he still includes, along with 14 ways to cook boar and 9 for hare, entries for dormouse which sound very enticing stuffed with chestnuts, pine nuts and spices or roasted and served on toast.[31] There are also dishes featuring porcupine, hedgehog and guinea pig. As usual, wild fowl and fish are given prominence.

In Spain Francisco Martinez Montiño's *Arte de Cocina* (1611) while heavily dependent on domestic meats such as mutton, kid, sucking pig and ham, chicken, also makes extensive use of wild foods. Hare and rabbit are presented in numerous guises. Boar appears whole or in pieces roasted, the head is made into head-cheese, the flesh is also put into *empanadas* and other pastries.[32] Venison is served in just as many ways, roasted, its horns on a plate, breadcrumbs (*migas*) fried in venison fat, *empanadas*, salted and even a version of venison jerky (*tasajos*).[33]

Lancelot de Casteau also, writing in the early 17th century in Liège, has a *Heuspot de venaison* made from boar or stag, which is essentially the medieval standby of meat in a sauce of toast, pepper and nutmeg, sugar and cinnamon with red wine and onions fried in butter, all boiled together.[34] Even his English pie is made of goat or lamb or a piece of fat venison which is offered as an alternative rather than the standard ingredient.[35] The rest of the cookbook is almost completely dependent on veal, beef, pork and other domestic species, as would be expected from a highly urban audience. It is only at the grandest banquet served for the entry of the Prince-Archbishop in 1557 that a variety of venison, boar, hare, cranes and swans and other such wild foods appear with frequency.[36] This seems to be more of a historical curiosity for his audience and not something they would be likely to cook, judging from the actual recipes in the book.

Gradually, recipes for game diminish and by the latter half of the 17th century the dominance of domestic species is apparent in most cookbook authors. Some wild foods retain their noble status, but it appears that chefs and their readers were less inclined to cook or serve them.

Bartolomeo Stefani, in the later 17th century, says of wild boar that 'the meat of this animal is very much appreciated by grand Lords, and of this are made various dishes.'[37] These words imply that his readers would not be included in this category of grand lords, and that they would be unlikely even to have the opportunity to cook such animals. He does give a recipe for wild boar salami, just in case. Of deer he says that they are rarely found in Italy and proceeds to describe how they are prepared in England. This supports the idea that game was merely over-hunted. Hares, he says, go into many dishes, but he seems more interested in their fur and that many cooks appreciate it to keep warm in cold weather.[38]

At about the same time, Venantio Mattei offers menus of meals he planned for the Rospigliosi family in Rome through the 1660s. His first, a meal in January for 20 noble ladies and gentlemen, provides good evidence that although wild foods had not disappeared entirely, there were fewer offered. The banquet in five courses included 66 separate dishes (requiring 18 covered platters, 100 large plates and 400 small round ones) and is mostly made up of veal and kid, capon, pigeon or turkey, sturgeon and other fish. Wild foods appear here and there, perhaps thrushes as a garnish to fried sweetbreads, but few dishes feature wild food. In the first course there is hare in a black broth made of prunes, chicken livers, crushed biscuits and pear syrup served in little marzipan baskets touched with sugar glazing and gold – the eighth of 14 dishes in that course. In the second course there is a whole roast pheasant, roasted larks and thrushes. Some of these appear in the next course as well. The fourth course is all fish, presumably wild. Lastly came the fruit course, including vegetables, conserves, olives, cheeses and truffles. Nowhere to be seen are venison or boar, though we know the former was hard to find according to Stefani's testimony.[39]

The French authors of the later 17th century are a little more ambivalent. In La Varenne there are a good number of recipes for wild food and this may, ironically, betray his conservatism. Teal, larks and woodcocks appear. Even heron is still present. There are several recipes for boar and a few for stag, fawn and roebuck liver.[40] These dishes are mostly very simply roasted. He no doubt had the opportunity to cook such animals for his patron the Marquis d'Uxelles and anticipated that other chefs working for similar patrons would, too. In other French cookbooks of the later 17th century, wild game plays a smaller and smaller role. Pierre De Lune offers several recipes for stag deer and roe as well as three for roasted boar at the beginning of his *Le Cuisiner* of 1656, followed by a few boar pâtés,[41] but they are not mentioned elsewhere in the cookbook.[42] By 1674, in LSR, wild fowl are still present according to season, but far more dependable chicken, lamb, sucking pig, veal, and even beef, are the mainstays. Boar's head, served cold as in La Varenne, is still there as an *entremets*,[43] and a recipe for young boar or *marcassin*,[44] but he has no interest in venison whatsoever. Again, whether this has to do with a broader and more bourgeois audience or the increasing rarity of wild game cannot be determined, but it does appear that a cultural preference for domestic food may play a role.

Cookbooks, in their aim to be as comprehensive as possible, continue to include wild ingredients, especially the aristocratic deer, boar and wildfowl. But it is clear that the proportion of these foods had diminished and appeared in menus less frequently. There may be underlying cultural reasons for the shift, one of which is clearly discernible in the dietary literature. The relative merit of domestic versus wild meat was a standard topic. Many authors contended that exercise and fresh air rids an animal's body of superfluous humidity and thus makes it leaner, more digestible and ultimately better for you. This was the standard Galenic view: wild meats may be a little tougher but ultimately more nourishing. In the early 16th century this would have been considered medical orthodoxy.

Interestingly, in preceding centuries the opposite view usually held sway. For example, Antonio Gazius in the late 15th century, using Arab authorities, insisted that wild animals were too gross, which here implies dense and dark-fleshed, and therefore generated melancholy. Domestic animals taste better and are more nourishing. Their internal heat is tempered by being well fed, getting a moderate amount of exercise and leading a relatively easy life. The same is true of fowl: 'The domestic nourish more and are more tempered and generate better blood.'[45] Perhaps this reflects the classical ideal internalized among medieval Arab authors long before it had been in Europe.

In any case, by the early modern period, although lip service is paid to Galen and the Greeks, it is clear that game has diminished in physicians' estimation. Castellanus remarks that of course lamb and kid are easier to digest and preferable to deer and hare. Rather than any specific medical reasoning, the preference for lighter, whiter and softer foods appears to be more a cultural shift than any major theoretical reappraisal. It appears that somehow people lost interest in gamey tastes. Castellanus speaking of the roe deer says that 'the odour especially and noxious flavour of the woods causes nausea, such that it is hardly able to please unless cooked with artifice and condiments to remove the persistent wildness.'[46] In England, Thomas Cogan exclaims, 'A wonder it is to see howe much this unwholesome flesh in desired of all folkes. In so much that many men rashly will venture their credite, yea and sometime their lives too, to steale venison.' He also goes so far as to criticize nobles for wasting so much land for deer parks. 'I could wish (saving the pleasure of honourable and worshipfull men) that there were no Parkes nor Forestes in England. For a great parte of the best pasture in this Realme is consumed with Deer, which might otherwise be

17

better employed for a common-wealth.'[47] Of course, over the next few centuries his prayers would be answered as more and more land came under cultivation.

It appears that physicians in general came to prefer lighter, whiter and more easily digested meats and this was paralleled in culinary literature. Perhaps physicians influenced élite taste in some way or, more likely, the two developed in the same direction together. A cultural shift seems to play some part in the gradual disappearance of wild species in both genres.

Keith Thomas has argued that reduction of species of wild birds for food in England, although partly due to the reduction of wild space and extinction, has as much to do with the custom of keeping birds for pets. Italians never lost the taste for small birds, and perhaps keeping them as pets was never so widespread as it was in England. Keeping small furred mammals as pets was common in both places and may have some connection to the acquired aversion to eating similar wild animals. This is clearly the case in modern times.[48] However, it seems unlikely that concern for animal welfare played any major role in the diminishing use of wild foods *per se*. At least such sentiments are extremely rare in culinary literature, and were normally expressed by vegetarians whose aversion was to killing in general, not just wild creatures.

If anything, the preference for domestic foods occurred at a time when most people had less familiarity, domestically or otherwise, with animals rather than more. Fewer people would have had direct experience of untamed space, and it is interesting and odd that it is precisely when they stop killing and eating wild animals very often that they begin to grow fond of wild nature for its own sake. They even begin to plan gardens to look uncultivated. In other words, romanticizing nature in its wild state that begins at the end of the early modern period may be linked directly with ceasing to use wild nature as a resource for food. Only when one stops eating such foods can the idea of preserving them for their own sake develop. Presumably seasoned hunters have no such conceptions of nature. It is the urbane outsider who prefers to dote on swans rather than serve them up.

Notes

1. Gilly Lehmann, 'The Late-Medieval Menu in England', in *Food and History*, vol. 1 no. 1, 2003, 49-84.
2. *The Vivendier*, ed. Terence Scully (Totnes: Prospect Books, 1997).
3. *Pleyn Delit*, ed. Constance Heiatt, et al. (Toronto: University of Toronto Press, 1996), 85.
4. Maestro Martino, *Libro de arte coquinaria*, ed. Luigi Ballerini and Jeremy Parzen (Milan: Guido Tommasi 2001); *The Medieval Kitchen*, ed. Odile Redon, et al. (Chicago: University of Chicago Press, 1998), 82.
5. Melitta Weiss Adamson, ed, *Regional Cuisines of Medieval Europe* (N.Y.: Routledge, 2002).
6. Antonius Gazius, *Corona florida medicinae* (Venice: Ioannes and Gregorius de Gregoriis, 1491), fiii.
7. Melchiore Sebizius, *De alimentorum facultatibus* (Strasbourg: Johannes Phillipi Mulbii et Josiae Stedelii, 1650), 670-1.
8. Bartolomeo Scappi, *Opera* (Bologna: Arnaldo Forni, 2002), 42.

9. Cristoforo di Messisbugo, *Banchetti* (Ferrara: Giovanni de Buglhat and Antonio Hucher, 1549); Libro Novo (Bologna: Arnaldo Forni, 2001), 4.
10. Sebizius, 699.
11. Sebizius, 704.
12. Sebizius, 712.
13. Sebizius, 1044.
14. Giovanni Domenico Sala, *De alimentis* (Padua: Io. Bapt. Martinum, 1628 in *Ars Medica*. (Padua: Franciscum Bolzetta, 1641), 58.
15. Petrus Castellanus, Κρεωψαγια, *sive esu carnium* (Antwerp: Hieronymus Verdussius, 1626), 147
16. Sebizius, 926.
17. Sebizius, 933.
18. Thomas Cogan, *The Haven of Health* (London: Thomas Orwin, 1589), 87.
19. Cogan, 55.
20. Cogan, 68.
21. Girolamo Cardano, *De usu ciborum* in *Opera Omnia* (Lyon: Huguetan et Ravaud, 1663), 58
22. Salvatore Massonio, *Archidipno* (Venice: Marc'antonio Brogiollo, 1627, 390.
23. Cogan, 146.
24. Domenico Romoli, *La Singolare Dottrina* (Venice: Gio. Battista Bonfadino, 1593), 166-182.
25. Scappi, vol. II, 95.
26. Giovanni Battista Rossetti, *Dello scalco* (Ferrara: Domenico Mammarello), 479. Reprint Bologna: Arnaldo Forni, 1991.
27. Rossetti 470-1
28. Rossetti, 476.
29. Rossetti, 484-488.
30. Cesare Evitascandalo, *Libro dello scalco* (Rome Carlo Vulietti, 1609), 36.
31. Evitascandalo, 37-8.
32. Francisco Martínez Montiño, *Arte de cocina* (Barcelona: Juan Francisco Pifferer for Juan Sellent, n.d.), 167-178.
33. Montiño, 179-181.
34. Lancelot du Casteau, *Ouverture de cuisine*, reprint (Antwerp: De Schutter, 1983), 14.
35. Lancelot, 71.
36. Lancelot, fols. K2-K4.
37. Bartolomeo Stefani, *L'arte di ben cucinare*, (Bologna, Arnaldo Forni, 2000), 33.
38. Stefani, 35.
39. Venantio Mattei, 1-7.
40. Hymans' tr., boar 69, 73, 100-1, deer 70, 84, 110.
41. Pierre De Lune, *Le cuisinier* in *L'art de la cuisine française au XVIIe siècle* (Paris: Payot and Rivages, 1995), 365.
42. De Lune, 244-6.
43. L.S.R., *L'art de bien traiter* in *L'art de la cuisine française au XVIIe siècle* (Paris: Payot and Rivages, 1995), 112.
44. L.S.R., 48.
45. Gazius, fol. Eiiivo.
46. Castellanus, 152-3.
47. Cogan, 122.
48. Keith Thomas, *Man and the Natural World* (Oxford: Oxford University Press, 1983), 116, 275.

Umbles and the Eating of Humble Pie

Joan P. Alcock

Everyone at some time or other has had to eat humble pie, even if they did not realize they were doing this. The name is derived from umbles, numbles, numlys, ombles and owmlys – the names seemingly changing because it was spelt phonetically rather than precisely. The *Oxford English Dictionary* gives a first mention of umbles as 'owmlys' about 1500 commenting that it is of Middle English derivation.

Numbles or umbles seemingly first referred to the back and loins of a hart, being a diminutive of *lumbus*, the loin. This was an acceptable part of the animal but the term 'umbles' came to refer to the edible offal and lights of animals, usually deer or boar. The late Maggie Black, in a discussion with the author, suggested that the relevant parts of other wild or semi-wild animals would be covered by this term. Those of hare and rabbit might be acceptable to modern taste and the eating of squirrel is still promoted, but parts of badger, stoat, otter, wild cat and rat cannot be deemed acceptable to English taste, except in times of famine, and these times in Britain are restricted to the medieval period.

The parts mainly referred to are the soft organs of the animal including those referred to today as offal – heart, liver, kidneys – but they also include sweetbreads, spleen and lungs (the lights or the pluck). Dorothy Hartley (Hartley 1954, p. 131) believed that umbles were 'the stones, sweetbreads, and what (in a modern pig) we should call "the best parts of the fry", and as much a delicacy as the "lamb stones" of old sheep-farming days. Later the word seems to be used for a much coarser selection of "fry", including liver and lights.'

The term 'umbles' seems mainly to have become attached to deer. In 1616 umbles were defined as 'the ordinairie fee and parts of the deer given unto a keeper by a custome, who hath the skin, head, umbles, chine and shoulders'. By then, however, the shoulders had been deemed to be too important to bestow on a keeper, the skin was sold to be tanned as leather and the head became a prize to be mounted in the lord's hall, so the gift was whittled down to the umbles.

Hunting deer was always considered as an aristocratic pastime, especially in the medieval period when it was reserved to royalty and the aristocracy. Woodland areas were enclosed to preserve the game for their pleasure. Acts passed throughout the centuries prohibited the hunting of game, in particular deer, and anyone disobeying these did so at their own risk. As late as 1671 an act was passed prohibiting the killing of game except for members of the nobility and the gentry. A commoner, caught hunting, might have his bow fingers (the first two on his right hand) cut off; his dog would have the claws pulled out or a paw removed to prevent it chasing deer.

Once the kill had been made, the game became the preserve of the aristocracy. Haunches of venison were given as gifts to be consumed at aristocratic tables. A feast could include roasted venison accompanied by strong sauces, or boiled venison with frumenty, that is pounded wheat grains mixed with beaten eggs and spices. The less desirable pieces could be boiled, but the umbles, the entrails and the soft parts, rather than be discarded or sold, were given to the chief huntsman as his perquisite. He could pass these on to his helpers, the peasants, as unworthy of being eaten by anyone of noble birth. Hence the humble nature both of the gift and of the person receiving it and the deliberate intention that this gift should mark the inferior nature of the person receiving it.

The term could also be used satirically or light-heartedly as when Middleton and Dekker in their play *Roaring Girl* (1611) comment in scene 3 on 'a good well set fellow if his spirit be answerable to his umbles' In Sir Walter Scott's novel *Woodstock* (1826), set in the Commonwealth period of 1651, there is a long description (Chapter 3) of the royal lodge at Woodstock Park with a large fireplace where huge fires burned, consuming two cartloads of wood. Here monarchs had amused themselves 'with broiling the umbles, or dowsets, of the deer upon the glowing embers with their own royal hands, when happy the courtier who was invited to taste the royal cookery'. Later, (Chapter 18) umbles is used as an oath when the keeper, Jocelyn Joliffe, finds a gold ring at the bottom of a pitcher dropped by a gypsy. He goes to ask Colonel Everard's advice, 'And I'll give them leave to give mine umbles to the kites and ravens if they find me conferring my confidence when it is not safe.'

Nevertheless, these humble parts were appreciated. In the 14th century recipes for numbles appear in manuscripts mainly based on those in *The Form of Cury* compiled about 1390 by the master cooks of the household of Richard II. The Reverend Richard Warner published *The Form of Cury* in 1791 using a version printed by Samuel Pegge in 1780. Warner stated that that the manuscript had been lost, but this was not the case, and Constance Hieatt and Sarah Butler edited this manuscript in 1985. *The Form of Cury* contains three recipes for numbles or noubles. The first one entitled Bruce (Warner, *The Form of Cury*, 1791 p. 5, no. 11; Hieatt and Butler 1985, p. 100, no. 13) uses the numbles of swine and shredded whites of leeks. The numbles are parboiled in water and wine, shredded leeks are added and the mixture allowed to simmer. Crumbled bread, blood and vinegar, seasoned with 'powder-fort' give taste and colour to the mixture. 'Powder-fort', as the name suggests, is what were considered to be the warmer spices, such as pepper and ginger. Lastly, minced onions are added and the whole dish cooked until the mixture thickens.

A second recipe is for the numbles of calf, and sheep (Warner, *The Form of Cury*, 1791, p. 6, no. 12; Hieatt and Butler 1985, p. 100, no. 14). These must be parboiled and cut into dice. Chyballs (spring onions) are seethed until tender and mixed with '3olkes of eyren' (eggs). Saffron is added to colour the dish while verjuice and 'powder douce' (cinnamon, ginger and cloves) give taste. Verjuice was a staple during the

21

Middle Ages and was usually added with the spices at the end of the cooking process 'to form a covering or presentation sauce for the cooked dish' (Rose 1990, 208).

The third recipe deals with the numbles of deer (Warner, *The Form of Cury*, 1791, p. 6, no. 13; Hieatt and Butler 1985, p.100, no. 15). In this the numbles are again parboiled to soften them and then cut into dice. The water in which they have been soaked previously is mixed with crumbled bread, wine and vinegar. Cooked, minced onions are added, together with powder-fort and blood in order to give the broth more taste and a deeper colour. The broth is then well boiled before serving, presumably to thicken it. Lorna Sass gives a variation of this recipe, which is suitable to modern tastes (Sass 1975, p. 74), but she uses cubes of venison rather than offal. She does include spices – pepper, mace, cinnamon and ginger.

Much later in *The Form of Cury* manuscript there is a recipe entitled 'Newe Noumbles' (Warner, *The Form of Cury*, 1791, p.12, no. 54; Hieatt and Butler 1985, p.110, no. 55). This is merely an instruction to wash the numbles clean with water and salt, parboil and dice them. Parboiling was regarded as necessary to soften them, probably to reduce them to a mush so that those who had few teeth could eat them.

Warner's book printed two other manuscripts, both under the heading *Ancient Cookery*. The first is a collection of recipes then in the possession of Samuel Pegge and probably dated to about 1381. In this the recipe for Noumbles (Warner, *Ancient Cookery*, 1791 No. 2, p. 38, no. 12) is almost the same except that the pepper and bread is mixed with ale before being added to the stew. The second printed manuscript, containing 441 recipes, is entitled *A Collection of Ordinances and Regulations for the Government of the Royal Household*. This was loosely bound with several other documents dating between 1328 and 1399. Warner believed that these recipes were collected in the 15th century but were based on those circulating in the previous century. The numbles recipes are similar except that cloves are added to the dishes (Warner, *Ancient Cookery*, No 3, p.53, nos. 283, 284). Herbs in the calves' umbles (recipe p. 53, no. 282) are identified as parsley, sage and savoury.

Two other manuscripts containing variations of *The Form of Cury* were compiled in 1430 and 1450 (Ashton 1888). The numbles' recipes are basically the same, but the instruction for the dish is 'serve it forth for a good pottage' which implies that it should be served as a very thick stew. This would be more acceptable to peasant taste, which is confirmed by the fact that only three recipes for numbles are included in a collection made for the royal household, out of over 400. Numbles therefore are not on the list of highly regarded dishes for a medieval household.

With their hearty meat content they were not suitable for Lent, so *The Form of Cury* provides Noumbles in Lent as a fast-day version using fish (Warner, *The Form of Cury*, 1791, p. 22, no. 114; Hieatt and Butler 1985, p. 124, no. 117). This uses the blood of pike and conger eel, together with their 'paunches' and that of 'cod lyng' (an inferior form of cod). The fish are boiled until the pieces are tender, minced and mixed with the blood. White bread, strained through a cloth to make fine crumbs, and cooked, minced onions are added to the dish, together with pepper, wine, malt vinegar and cider vinegar. Saffron is used for colouring. The recipe seems to create a very stiff mixture and it is possible that the dish may have been served shaped into meat numbles.

Numbles cooked in this form provide a thick stew with a very strong smell. It continued to be made in this fashion until the 17th century when the term humble pie seems to come into use. This presumably meant that the ingredients were placed in a dish and baked with a cover of pastry. Sir Kenelm Digby (Macdonell 1910, p. 219) recommends 'Bake humble-pyes without chopping them small into a pye, season with Pepper and Salt adding a pretty deal of Parsley, a little Sweet-marjoram and Savoury, and a very little Thyme.'

Samuel Pepys ate both venison and humble pie. On 5 July 1662 he entertained Sir William Penn and his son, William, to dinner, 'I having some venison given me a day or two ago, and so I had a shoulder roasted, another baked, and the umbles baked in a pie, and all well done'. On 6 July 1663 he comments that 'I stepped to Sir W. Batten [Surveyor of the Navy] and there stayed and talked with him, my lady being in the country, and sent for some lobsters, and Mrs Turner came in and did bring an umble pie, hot out of her oven, extraordinarily good, and afterward some spirits of her own making (in which she hath great judgement), very good, and so home; merry with this night refreshed.' Later, on 17 June 1667, he dined at Sir William Penn's, with Mrs Turner and her husband, on a venison pasty, 'which stunk like the devil. However we did not know it until dinner was done. We had nothing but only this, and a leg of mutton and a pullet or two.'

On 13 September 1665 he had visited Sir William Hickes' house in Greenwich, 'a good seat with groves of fair trees but so let to ruin, both house and everything in and about it, so ill-finished and miserably looked after.' Here, Pepys had 'the meanest dinner of beef, shoulder and umbles of venison, what he [Sir William] takes away from the keeper of the forest [Epping Forest], and a few pigeons and all in the meanest manner that I ever did see to the lowest degree.'

Humble pie as a dish continued to be made in the 18th century. Eliza Smith (Smith 1753, A viii) as early as 1728 serves as part of a first course for August, Westphalia ham and chicken, haunch of venison roasted, venison pasties and humble pyes. *Frazer's Magazine* (1857, 61, 217) has a phrase, 'commend us to a venison pudding, composed of the numbles and trimmings from the joints and breast'.

Yet by the 19th century the implication is that umbles has a derogatory status and the term 'to eat humble pie' has come into being. W. M. Thackeray in his novel *The Newcomes*, 1853–55 (Chapter 14), refers to a dinner given by Colonel Newcome, at which Clive, the Colonel's son, gets drunk, behaves badly and throws a glass of wine into his cousin Baine's face. Next day, not surprisingly, Clive wakes up with a drunken headache. The Colonel reproaches him. '"You drank too much wine last night, and disgraced yourself, sir," the old soldier said. "You must get up and eat humble pie this morning, my boy." "Humble what, father," asked the lad, hardly aware of his words, or the scene before him. "Oh, I've got such a headache."'

According to the *Oxford English Dictionary*, humble pie as a derogatory reference continued. As early as 1830 the phrase 'eating Lincolnshire Rue Pie' indicated that the verb 'to rue' or 'repent' was presumably linked to rue being a bitter herb and therefore that the eater ate humble pie. Shakespeare indicated this when Ophelia says in her madness (*Hamlet* Act 4, Scene 7) that rue is a bitter herb. In 1871, T. C. Jeaffreson, writing in *Annals of Oxford* (14, p. 224), recording one of the numerous riots, stated, 'The town had to eat a considerable amount of humble pie'. Richard Lowell in *McClellan or Lincoln? Prose Works* (1890) stated, 'Disguise it as you will, flavor it as you will, call it as you will, umble pie is umble pie, and nothing else.' By 1895, it had become a phrase in general use, for *The Times* could assume that readers would understand what was meant when it wrote (9 January), 'To sue for peace when future resistance becomes hopeless is a kind of humble pie that fate has condemned all the vanquished nations to swallow from time immemorial.' This is also a reference to a person who is required to be very submissive and apologetic.

Before then, as recorded in cookery books, umbles were being served in their separate parts. Hannah Glasse (Glasse 1796) provided recipes for liver, kidney and sweetbreads, which included a liver pudding boiled for three hours and sweetbreads fricasseed and prepared 'en cordonnier', served with beetroot. Mrs Beeton, in 1861, published recipes for liver, lamb and beef kidneys (broiled and fried) and lambs' sweetbreads, indicating that by now umbles were regarded as separate items in the food area. Her sweetbreads are larded and served with asparagus tips or stewed, then baked with a glass of sherry, being intended as a savoury for a dinner party. Calf's liver was also larded and roasted, and liver and bacon have made their appearance. 'Calf's liver aux fines herbes and sauce piquante' suggests, however, an attempt to raise a humble dish into a gourmet category. Chicken livers, minced and served with the addition of either lemon or parsley, are used as a sauce for poultry. Pig's liver is stated bluntly to be 'a Savoury and Economical dish'.

Yet these umble parts of the animal provide some of the most nourishing food. In the medieval period they would have been used at once and therefore have been absolutely fresh. Today, offal, especially kidney and liver, are regarded as having protein content and containing several vitamins, but some items are water-soluble and easily leach into water or gravy. Hence the cooking liquid and the broth are valuable and need to be incorporated into the dish. A stew or pie would be ideal but, failing that, offal needed to be cooked quickly and served immediately to preserve its nutritious value. Hearts need to be treated as a lean, well-exercised muscle, and so should be cooked slowly for a longer period. Liver, because it contains little connective tissue, should either be heated gently, or cooked very quickly, less than a minute on both sides. Long cooking will dry it out and toughen it. The hierarchy for liver is calf's liver as the best, followed by sheep liver, ox liver and lastly pig's liver, although some people prefer that because it has a stronger taste.

Liver is rich in iron, protein, nicotinic acid, folic acid and vitamins A and B12; kidneys are a good source of protein, iron, and nicotinic acid and have a high retinal content. Liver also has Vitamin D, which can absorb calcium from the small intestines into bones and teeth. Lack of it can cause rickets and eating it is recommended for those with anaemia. Eating too much liver, however, may cause calcium to be deposited in the soft tissue causing loss of appetite and vomiting. Unfortunately, the vitamin A content of liver more than doubled in the 1980s and 1990s in Britain because of the over-fortification of animal feed. Thus children and invalids were advised not to eat liver, which until then had been a cheap and nutritious food.

There were other reasons for the decline in eating offal. First was the fact that the British developed a squeamishness about eating most forms of offal. Sweetbreads, in particular, because of their soft texture and their origin, were regarded with aversion and so the product is mainly exported to France. Until the 1950s sweetbreads were regarded as a delicacy. Now they are seemingly prized everywhere except in Britain as gourmet food. They need only be freed of their membranes before cooking to be edible. Coarsely chopped, mixed with soaked, pounded oatmeal and seasoned, they can be fried or cooked gently with a little stock. Recently, they have disappeared from most English menus though they can still be found in parts of Europe, especially in France. On a visit to Riga in Latvia in June 2004, the author consumed with relish a hot starter which included sweetbreads. What is interesting with regards to eating sweetbreads is the reaction of her dining neighbour. She had been consuming them without a qualm, but when asked what these objects were, on being told that they were sweetbreads, she put down her eating implements and said, 'I don't like sweetbreads'. Is this prejudice or ignorance?

Secondly, offal was dark meat, dense with capillaries and hence suffused with blood, which made it distasteful to many people. Thirdly, offal has negative connotations. Literally it means 'off falls', that is the part thrown off, the leavings. In the 19th century low-priced meat and even fish were included as offal when sold from a stall. Hence it became a cheap dish for the working class and only appeared in middle class households, as indicated by Mrs Beeton, as a savoury. The exception seems to have been the hearty dish of steak and kidney pudding or pie, but here the kidney was hidden within the pastry or dough covering. Fourthly it is now suspected that most offal is used for pet food and therefore should be placed on the dog's plate, not on the owner's. The result is that although offal contains as much protein as fish, it is the latter which is promoted as a healthy diet. It is unlikely that this promotion will ever occur with offal.

By 2000 the consumption of liver, for example, had declined to less than six grams per person per week (*National Food Survey*). But there was a greater problem, which was linked with the CJD crisis. The British Government, in response to European Union's regulations, issued a statutory instrument (No. 2051 *The Bovine Offal (Prohibition) Regulations 1989*) laying down strict and detailed regulations for the extraction, use and disposal of bovine offal, which was defined as 'the brain, spinal cord, spleen, thymus, tonsils and intestines'. At a stroke this cut out dishes such as brains on toast and brains added to stews. The regulations did not specifically include bovine kidney, hearts and liver but these were gradually removed from public sale. So great was the anxiety over the possibility of anyone contracting CJD that in 1996 there was a possibility that the ban would extend to the brain, spinal cord and spleen and, by implication, the kidneys, liver and hearts of sheep and pigs. *The Times* (23 July 1996) reported that the British government was 'poised to ban more animal products from the food chain amid fears that "mad cow" disease could be passed to sheep'.

The European Agricultural Commissioner, Franz Fischler, had demanded an extension of Europe's anti-BSE restrictions to all ruminants. This was interpreted as sheep, goat, deer and even pigs. After the resulting uproar a long debate followed. The Irish Minister for Agriculture, for example, alarmed at the possibility of Ireland losing a large export trade, declared roundly, 'Sheep and goats do not have BSE. I appeal to the public to use their common sense'. Luckily, common sense did prevail; otherwise there was a possibility that the sale of any animal offal would be banned.

In response, however, several organizations and institutions, including British schools, removed offal completely from their menus. The other parts, the spleen, lungs, hearts and most of the intestines, are allowed to be ground for sausages or used for pet foods. Ironically, the British consumption of sausages has not gone down and much of what was once referred to as umbles may be found in the British sausage. Liver, kidney and sometimes hearts may be found in butchers' shops, but to get the full variety of offal it is necessary to shop in a multinational area. This is also the case in the United States (Schwabe 1979), where in most areas there is a repugnance to see, let alone eat, offal. Refusal to eat offal has not been the case elsewhere. The French, in particular, like it both fresh and as charcuterie, and in other parts of the world it is eaten with enormous relish. The author has been informed that there is no problem about the consumption of these parts of any animal in the Far East. In China and Tibet, for example, the author saw every part of an animal cut up ready for sale. In the aptly named Yak Alley near the Jokhung Temple in the centre of Lhasa, offal and the soft parts of yaks, cows, and sheep were in great demand, while fierce-looking dogs were waiting hungrily round the stalls ready for tit-bits.

26

Appendix I

Recipes from *The Form of Cury*
   Noumbles

Take noumbles of deer oþer of a reþer (bullock); parboil hem and kerf hem to dyce. Take the self broth or better, take brede and grynde with the broth, and temper it up with a gode quantite of wyne and vyneger. Take oynouns and parboyle hem, and mynce hen smale and do þerto. Colour it with blode and do þerto powdor fort and salt, and boyle it wele and serve it fort.

   To make Noumbles in Lent

Take the blode of pyke, oþer of congur and nyme (take) the paunches (paunches) of pykes, of congur, and of grete codelyng (inferior cod) and boile hem tender and mynce hem smale, and do hem in þat blode. Take crustes of white brede, and strayne it thurgh a cloth, þenne take oynouns iboiled and mynced. Take peper, and safroun, wyne, vynegar oþer (either) aysell (cider vinegar) oþer alegur (malt vinegar), and do þerto and serue forth.

Appendix II

In 1996 Kingfisher TV contacted the author to ask if she would contribute to a ten-minute programme in their *Alphabet of Food*. This was for the letter U and the subject was umbles. With recipes provided by the late Maggie Black and the culinary help of Alan Melville, Chef of the Tower Restaurant of South Bank University, the programme was filmed for their series. Alan provided both a stew or pottage and a pie.

   For the stew, Maggie suggested that we needed the soft fleshy parts of the intestines and the lungs, freed of their membranes, coarsely chopped and mixed with soaked, pounded oatmeal or barley meal. These should be seasoned, fried a little and cooked gently in a little stock. If the dish was to be served cold, gelatine should be used. Heart could be added, but this might be a little tough.

   The same ingredients should be used for the pie, which could be a raised pie or one on a plate with a crust. Alan selected to do this one. A 12-inch diameter deep pie dish was lined with short crust pastry, half-baked blind and filled with the partly cooked meat mixture. This was pressed down in the centre, covered with chopped herbs and topped with thin pastry, slit to allow the air to escape and glazed with beaten egg.

   It was rather sad that after all the hard work put into this by Alan, both in obtaining what were, for him, rather unusual ingredients, and in making the dishes, that in the final recording only his hands were seen slicing the ingredients and arranging them for the stew and the pie. For the record, it has to be said, that both stew and pie were tasted but, with their strong, earthy, meaty taste, were not greeted with great enthusiasm.

Bibliography

Austin, T. ed., *Two Fifteenth-Century Cookery Manuscripts*, Original series, no. 91, 1888, reprinted 1964 (London: published for the Early English Text Society [87] by Oxford University Press , 1964).

Beeton, I., *Book of Household Management* (facsimile of the 1861 edition, London: Chancellor Press 1982).

Glasse, H., *The Art of Cookery Made Plain and Easy* (facsimile of the 1796 edition, Wakefield: S R Publishers 1971).

Hartley, D., *Food in England* (London: Macdonald, 1954).

Hieatt, C. B. and Butler, S. eds. *Curye on Inglysch: English Culinary Manuscripts of the Fourteenth Century* (including the *Forme of Cury*) (London: published for The Early English Text Society by Oxford University Press, 1985).

Macdonell, A. ed., *The Closet of Sir Kenelm Digby, Knight, Opened* (London: Philip Lee Warner, 1910).

Pepys, S., *The Diary of Samuel Pepys*, any edition.

Rose B., 'A medieval staple, verjuice in England and France', in *Staple Foods, Oxford Symposium on Food and Cookery, 1989*, pp. 205-12 (London: Prospect Books, 1990).

Sass, L., *To the King's Taste. Richard II's Book of Feasts and Recipes* (New York: Metropolitan Museum of Art, 1975).

Scott, Sir Walter, *Woodstock*, 1826 (reprinted London: Nelson 1950).

Smith, E., *The Compleat Housewife or Accomplish'd Gentlewoman's Companion* (facsimile of the 1753 edition, London: Literary Services and Production Ltd, 1968).

Schwabe, C. B., *Unmentionable Cuisine* (Charlottesville: University Press of Virginia, 1979).

Thackeray, W. M., *The Newcomes* (1854) (London: Everyman 1965).

Warner, R., *Antiquitates Culinariae or Curious Tracts Relating to the Culinary Affairs of the Old English* (facsimile reprint of the 1791 edition, London: Prospect Books, 1981?).

Fungi as Food

Josephine Bacon

Fungi are probably the wildest – in the sense of untameable – form of non-animal wild food, since they are not really grown but propagated. I use the term 'non-animal' because, strictly speaking, fungi are not plants or animals, they are in a separate phylum or super-family of their own. That is because some of them can move! The slime-fungi or *Myxomycetes* creep over the area they inhabit. Fungi bridge the gap between plants and animals.

By no means all the fungi eaten by humans are the so-called macrofungi, the ones that vaguely resemble a field mushroom. The best known edible microfungi are all around us in the air. These include the yeasts, or rather members of the *Saccaromyces* genus of yeasts, used in beer, bread and cakes as a raising agent, since it emits carbon dioxide as a waste product from eating sugar. There are many other yeast-type fungi, such as *Candida* that is parasitic including on humans (in the form of Thrush) and *Torula*, the 'dirt-eating' ingredient in biological washing powders. Then there is mycoprotein, the edible microfungus used to make the meat substitute that has been given the brand name of Quorn. This is actually a fungal mycelium, the real body of the fungus as opposed to the 'mushroom' part of the plant which is what we normally eat and which is, in fact, just the fruit or what passes for a fruit in a fungus (technically referred to as the fruiting body). All mycelia are a mass of threads that are often microscopic, and they look pretty much alike to the naked eye. Even under the microscope, they can fool the experts. It wasn't realized for more than ten years after Quorn had been cultured by the large animal-feed manufacturer, BOCM-Silcock, that it was not the species they had originally thought! The makers of the first widely eaten mycoprotein thought they were using *Fusarium graminearum*, in fact it was *Fusarium venenatum*. Both are parasitic on wheat. In fact, Quorn is derived from the mycelium in its asexual reproductive phase, the so-called conidial stage. This is where we come on to the reason why fungi are so elusive. As usual, it all boils down to sex.

Sex and the fungus

Fungi that reproduce sexually usually have four sexes (!) and many also reproduce asexually as well as sexually. Others have lost the sexual stage of their life cycle altogether. These are known as the *fungi imperfecti*. For this reason, they are extremely difficult to identify because at this stage in their life cycle they all look very much alike. Hence the problem with Quorn.

Gathering and eating wild mushrooms

While there are quite a number of common species that are to some degree poisonous – some deadly poisonous – there are certain rules of thumb that should be observed gathering fungi. Fortunately, almost all the species that are edible are all distinctive and easy to identify. The chanterelle, for instance, could be mistaken for a false chanterelle only by someone who is very short-sighted since the false chanterelle has true gills, not veins or ribs. The beefsteak fungus, *Fistulina hepatica*, and the parasol mushroom, *Macrolepiota procera*, are both unmistakable. On the other hand, so is the pretty red-capped toadstool with the white spots that features in so many children's story illustrations. *Amanita muscaria*, the fly agaric, is poisonous and hallucinogenic! The *Amanita* genus contains lots of deadly species, and only one edible fungus, *Amanita rubescens*, known as the blusher because the white gills and brown cap turn pink if damaged. I have never dared to eat it and furthermore it is hard to find specimens that are not ruined by insects or animals, but those who have eaten say it is really not worth the trouble.

There are some stringent rules to observe when gathering wild fungi:

• Always bring a field guide with you, preferably more than one, and be absolutely sure that you are picking what you think you are picking. There are quite considerable variations in the look of some fungi, especially depending on whether they are growing in moist or dry conditions.

• Never mix edible and poisonous fungi or those you are not sure of together in one basket, because the spores of the death cap, for instance, are also deadly poisonous.

• Do not pick specimens that are old and shrivelled or badly damaged by insects. Fungi, like meat, deteriorate quickly and you could get serious food-poisoning from fungi that are past their peak. For the same reason, do not pick fungi when it is raining heavily and they are waterlogged, as they will swell and disguise potential damage.

The tools for fungus foraying are simple: a sharp knife or, better still, a widger for digging a fungus out of the ground (do not cut them off at ground level, you need to see the bottom of the stem to identify the fungus for certain; you will not harm the mycelium); paper bags (not plastic) for storing the fungi while you are out and a wide, open basket, such as a Sussex **trug**. And wear wellies: fungi that grow on the ground like damp – but not sodden – places.

Remember that many field guides were not originally written for the UK. Two popular edible species that you may encounter in books do not grow here. They are Caesar's mushroom, *Amanita caesaria* and the poplar mushroom, *Agrocybe aegerita*.

Cultivated mushrooms

Several varieties of mushrooms are now cultivated. We are all familiar with *Agaricus bisporus*, the cultivated mushroom, known in the USA as the store mushroom, and its variations the chestnut mushroom, known in the USA as the portobello, portabella and various variations thereof. This mushroom is closely related to, but not microscopically the same as the field mushroom, *Agaricus campestris*. The Japanese have successfully cultivated shiitake, *Lentinellus edodes*, by inoculating logs and the Italians have done the same with the poplar fungus, *Agrocybe aegerita*, since Roman times. The oyster mushroom, *Pleurotus ostreatus*, is now likewise cultivated, as are several other species including blewetts, *Tricholoma campanatum*.

I would very much advise cooking with cultivated mushrooms rather than picking wild ones if you have a choice. All cultivated mushrooms have to be grown in a super-sterile atmosphere, and the mycelium (the threads of the actual fungus) is grown under conditions of greater sterility than even the cleanest hospital operating theatre! That is because there is such a danger of contamination by spores of moulds that are all over the place in the atmosphere.

This does not mean that you should not hunt for fungi. They grow in the UK from March (*Hygrophorus marzuolus*) to the winter frosts (some species of *Pleurotus*) and there is always somewhere in the world where it is high season for them. Good hunting!

Bibliography

Wiebe, M. G., Robson, G. D., Cunliffe, B., Trinci, A. J. P., Oliver, S. G., 'Nutrient-Dependent Selection of Morphological Mutanta of *Fusarium graminearum* A3/5 Isolated from Long-Term Continuous Cultures', in *Biotechnology and Bioengineering*, 40, 1181–1189, (New York: John Wiley & Sons, 1992).

Yoder, W.T. & Christianson, 'Species-specific Primers Resolve Members Of *Fusarium* Section *Fusarium*. Taxonomic Status of the Edible 'Quorn' Fungus Re-evaluated,' in *Fungal Genetics & Biology*, 23, 62–80, (New York: Academic Press, a division of Harcourt, 1998).

E. A. Ellis, *British Fungi, a fully illustrated introduction to some of the smaller species* (Norwich, Jarrold & Sons, 1976).

Lamaison, Jean-Louis & Polese, Jean-Marie, *Grand guide encyclopédique des champignons* (Chamalières, France: Artemis Editions,1998).

Capering About

Rosemary Barron

The fall and winter months on the Greek Cycladic islands can be quite different from the idyllic images on the pages of travel magazines. Sometimes windswept and cool, and invariably damp, they provide the ideal conditions to explore the islands' kitchens and tavernas. From my first visit to Thira (Santorini), in 1965, to my now-annual visits, capers have intrigued me. This wild food, or flavouring, is still on every traditional Santorini table, yet it is very time-consuming to gather and prepare. Why, on this most elegant and wealthy Mediterranean island, should anyone bother with the back-breaking and awkward work of their preparation for the table? It's obvious that capers have influenced the islands' kitchens, and the quantities that are sold outside the Cyclades prove them to be a prized ingredient elsewhere in Greece. But is their long popularity due only to their strange, slightly sour flavour, or is there another reason, too?

In this paper, I shall explore the way a native wild food has shaped the kitchens, and the lives, of some islanders in the Cyclades over thousands of years.

Santorini, Folgandros, Anafi, and Andros are the Cycladic islands renowned for the quality of their capers, and where capers are an integral part of the traditional table. As my interest in capers grew, it became clear to me that the information available on them did not entirely resonate with my own experiences in these Cycladic kitchens.

Capers, like olives, cannot be eaten without some kind of processing – salting, pickling, or drying. The wild capers of the Mediterranean are not easy to pick, as mature plants have sharp spikes along their trailing branches. So who were those first people to think of taking the trouble to preserve those tiny flower buds, and why?

Climate may play a part: The caper bush, or shrub (*Capparis spinosa*), loves dry heat (up to 105°F), intense sunlight, and some rain (but only in winter and spring). A temperature of below 18°F will kill the plant, just as it would kill a young olive tree, and for its growing season (June and July), it likes two hot dry months. Place is important too: the caper bush thrives when swept by a strong sea breeze (it is salt-tolerant), and loves the cracks and crevices of cliffs and stone walls – conditions that make capers calcium- and salt-rich. The rocky, arid Cycladic islands provide the perfect climatic and geographic conditions.

In the diet of Greek antiquity, capers may have enabled people living a distance from the coast to consume salt throughout the year, or those living near the coast to continue to eat salt when high seas and cold temperatures made salt impossible to collect. Their sharp, piquant flavour would certainly have made the taste of fermented fish more bearable, and would have added 'interest' to pulses, for those of the ancient Greek kitchen were very dull compared to those of the New World. With a fragrant, mildly spicy, and slightly sour (because of the processing) quality, and tart and pungent flavour, capers would surely have been highly valued by imaginative classical chefs, and have had a good price paid for them.

But are these reasons enough for the Cycladic islanders to have turned capers into an important cash crop over two thousand years ago? Dioscorides noted that they were a marketable product of the ancient Greeks and, later, Pliny the Elder mentioned them in his writings. However, the first record of capers seems to have been by the Sumerians around 2000 BC, and it was related to their medicinal use. Capers have been found in excavations at prehistoric Bronze Age sites on the island of Cyprus and at one of them, Marki Aloni, there is evidence that it was an economic crop. However, the volcanic eruptions on Thira have made it difficult to establish all the foods the Minoans enjoyed on the island.

Because of their cash value, the Greeks would undoubtedly have encouraged the cooks of ancient Rome to include capers in their repertoire, and they probably first found their way to England, and elsewhere in Europe, via the Roman occupation. We know that caper seeds have been found in medieval Bruges, in a ditch dated between AD 1200 and AD 1495 (Bruges was an important trade centre at that time), and that in the mid-17th century there was a flourishing trade in capers between southern Europe and England. But why would the English, and other northern Europeans, pay money for capers (for their climates didn't allow them to grow capers for themselves)? Was it because of their own flavourless foods, because they were 'trendy', or because of their reputed, and actual, medicinal value?

But what could be the attraction of the caper bush (a spiny shrub of the *Capparaceae* (or *Capparidaceae*) family), and its products, be for the early peoples of the Cycladic islands? On Thira, traditional settlements are built into the volcanic cliffs and have little or no airflow. The same heavy night mists that frequently blanket the island, and that are used to water the vines, wound into basket-shapes to cover the grey volcanic soil, provide too the perfect conditions for arthritis. Capers, the salted or pickled immature flower buds of the caper shrub, comprise 85% water. The dry matter of the caper shrub contains bitter flavonoid glycosides, the main one of which is a mustard oil glycoside (*glucocapparin*) which, when 'processed', causes an enzyme reaction, releasing methyl isothiocynate (the pungent principle of capers) from the plant tissues. In this, capers resemble their cousins in the cabbage family – cress, mustards, horseradish – all of which contain mustard oil glycosides. Another of its flavonoids is rutin (in generous quantity in all the parts of the plant – the leaves, stems, flowering buds, and fruits), and this could, in my opinion, be the reason for the caper's longevity in the Cycladic diet. Pharmacologically speaking, rutin improves capillary function. It's considered to be anti-rheumatic, and therefore an effective treatment for arthritis and gout, a diuretic and, in non-medical speak, a 'liver protec-

33

tor' and 'kidney disinfectant'. It's also a strong anti-oxidant. Interestingly, most rutin is found in dried capers, and only on Thira have I come across any mention of these. All these reasons would make the caper shrub highly valued in the Cyclades of the past, and even in northern Europe.

Luckily, for those of us who appreciate variety on our tables, the cooks of Greek antiquity were not slow to incorporate their wild foods into their dishes, especially those that had some medicinal value. But has their 'taste interest' ensured they have remained in the diet, or is it because of their perceived medicinal value that they are still on traditional tables? In the Cycladic kitchen today, capers are considered to be a tonic and digestive. Like olives, their flavour depends on how they are processed.

The best are stored in fine sea salt or in wine-vinegar brine. Capers harmonize beautifully with other native herbs and flavourings – rigani, basil, chervil, mint, parsley, thyme, and garlic – and are frequently combined with olives. Every island cook knows that capers are added to room-temperature or lukewarm dishes as their aroma and flavour are destroyed by higher temperatures.

Capers are named from the Greek, *kapparis*. The origin of this word is thought to be somewhere east of Greece, maybe in western Asia, for the Arabic for caper is *kabar*.

The deciduous *Capparis spinosa* grows well close to the sea throughout the Mediterranean basin, and eastwards through the Crimea and Armenia to the Caspian Sea. It's an expert water- and soil-conservationist for the mature plants have deep and extensive root systems and their leaves form a canopy over the surface of the soil. Drought-resistant and needing very little care (only good drainage), the wild caper has one serious disadvantage for the gardener – it's very difficult to grow from seed (though it's easily propagated). There are many varieties of caper, and *Capparis spinosa* (the name *spinosa* refers to the pair of hooked spines at the base of each leaf) is considered to have the best flavour.

Caper bushes, 2 to 4 feet high, with trailing branches, small (1 to 2 inches) leaves and large (2 to 3 inches) flowers, cover the cliffs and stone walls of Thira. All parts of the bush are used in the kitchen – the flower buds (capers), leaves, and shoots, are salted or pickled in red wine vinegar, and the semi-mature fruits (caperberries) are vinegar-pickled too. The exquisitely pretty and lightly fragrant flowers are, unfortunately, rarely seen, for even if a few of the hundreds of blossoms produced by each plant every year succeed in avoiding the eagle eye of the island gatherers, they live only 24 hours. Each fragile flower begins blossoming at sunset and, by dawn, has begun the process of shedding its creamy-white petals and purple stamina. During the 8 to 10 hours of its life between dawn and mid-afternoon, each flower attracts a hoard of pollinators.

In the markets of ancient Greece, the smallest capers had the highest value. Sieves with differently sized holes were used as a quick way to measure them. Until recently, a similar value has been put on our own commercial capers – those under one centimetre in diameter (*nonpareilles, superfines*) are more expensive than larger ones (*capucines*, *communes*, and *cappoles*). But 'wild' is an emotive marketing word, and it is these capers that now tend to have the premium label. Capers are commercially cultivated in Spain, Italy, and Morocco and, to a much lesser extent, in Algeria, Cyprus, Sicily, Iran, Greece, Tunisia, and Egypt. The best sources for wild capers are Greece, Turkey, Cyprus, and a few regions of Italy.

The subject of this paper has been the wild caper of the Cycladic islands, but it has many 'poor' cousins throughout the world. One in particular – the far less flavourful caper of central Asia – tends to support the idea that Cycladic capers could have been highly valued for their medicinal qualities, for it is an important component of traditional Himalayan medicine. So was it for medicinal reasons that the Romans bothered to take capers to the comparatively harsh climate of northern Europe, and that the 17th-century English paid money for such a strange food?

Kitchen notes

Cycladic dishes to taste
- Santorini fava with capers & caper berries
- Capers & green olive sauce
- Dried capers & tomato sauce
- Bread salad with capers & sheep cheese

Capers, and some great flavour combinations in early Greek kitchens, with:
- olives; in olive sauces
- vinegar; in vinegar-based sauces
- eggs; in egg sauces such as mayonaiza
- beans (dried pulses)
- artichokes
- wild greens, especially rocket
- fish & shellfish
- salted/preserved fish, especially anchovies

In modern Greek kitchens, with:
- tomatoes; in tomato sauces
- poultry

And a few European dishes:
- Vitello tonnato (Italy)
- Königsberger klopse (Prussia)
- Mutton with caper sauce (Britain)
- Tartare (France)
- Sauces – ravigote, remoulade, puttanesca, caponata

More recipes with capers in

Barron, R., *Flavours of Greece* (London: Grub Street, 2001).

Barron, R., *Meze: Small Bites, Big Flavors from the Greek Table* (San Francisco: Chronicle Books, 2002).

Key references

Bond E., Robert, 'The Caper Bush', in *The Herbalist*, 1990.

British Pharmacopoeia (London: Her Majesty's Stationery Office, 1993).

Cullen J., Alexander J.C.M., Brady A., *The European Garden Flora* (Cambridge: Cambridge University Press, 1992).

Facciola, Stephen, *Cornucopia – A Sourcebook for Edible Plants* (Vista, CA: Kampong Publications, 1991).

Reynolds, J.E.F., *Martindale, The Extra Pharmacopoeia*, 30th ed., (London: The Pharmaceutical Press, 1993).

Rodrigo, M., Lazaro, M.J., Alvarruiz, A., Ginerv, V., 'Composition of Capers (*Capparis spinosa*): Influence of Cultivar, Size and Harvest Date', in *Journal of Food Science*, 1992.

Turkoz, S., Toker, G., Sener, B., 'Investigations of some Turkish plants regarding of Rutin', in *Journal Faculty of Pharmacy Gazi*, 1995.

For information on caper bush propagation and growing:

Demetrios C. Kontaxis, Ph. D, University of California Pest Management Public Information Programs Advisor, Contra Costa County Co-operative Extension (+1) 415 646 6540

Caper seeds (but check they are *Capparis spinosa*):

Park Seed Company, Cokesbury Road, Greenwood, SC 29647-0001 (+1) 803 223 7333

Richters, PO Box 26, Goodwood, Ontario 1OC 1AO. (+1) 416 640 6677

Muskrats and Terrapins: The Forgotten Bounty of the Coastal Marshlands of New Jersey, Delaware, and Maryland

Fritz Blank

Although muskrats and terrapins are far-ranging, this paper will chiefly be concerned with these animals as a food source along the mid-Atlantic coastal seaboard of the USA, viz. New Jersey, Delaware, and Maryland.

Terrapins – *Testudo kleinmannii* and other species:

Terrapins are members of the turtle family in the genus *Testudo*, wherein are found a number of species which range worldwide in areas of temperate climate. Diamondback terrapins are the only of three species of aquatic turtles which live in brackish water. They are found chiefly in the saltwater marshlands of the eastern seaboard of the US, ranging from Cape Cod and around the Florida peninsula and across the Gulf coast to Texas. In particular, it is the diamondback terrapin which is most revered as a food source, especially during the late 1800s and early 1900s, when supplies and cooks were plentiful.

The diet of diamondback terrapins consists of a variety of fish, molluscs, crustaceans, and insects. They seem to be especially fond of fiddler crabs (*Uca pugnax*) and common periwinkle snails (*Littorina littorea*). At high tide these turtles often leave the tidal creeks and hunt among the salt marsh grass – known as spartina (*Spartina alterniflora*).

Diamondback terrapin was at one time considered a delicacy and served in the best restaurants and homes of the cosmopolitan cities of Baltimore and Philadelphia. Terrapin was a hallmark in élite social clubs and hotels such as The Union League, Le Coin D'or, The Philadelphia Club, and the Bellevue-Strafford Hotel in Philadelphia; and The Lobby Club, Maryland Club and the finer hotels in Baltimore; The Brook Club in New York City, and The Metropolitan Club in Washington D. C. also served terrapin, as did the very exclusive and posh Jekyl Island Club off the coast of Georgia. On separate and different occasions F. D. Roosevelt was served terrapin, as was Winston Churchill. Both statesmen were in fact very fond of the dish. Terrapin 'keeps' could be found in the cellars of aristocratic homes wherein terrapins were kept and fattened for special-occasion dinners prepared by live-in cooks, and domestic servants.

The butchering, dressing, and cooking of terrapins, or turtles of any sort, is not an easy task. It is time-consuming and requires skill. Most often terrapin was served in the form of soups or more commonly stewed. The flavour of terrapin is quite mild and delicate, often described as tasting like turkey. It is certainly not at all akin to the assertive strong flavour and character of freshwater snapping turtles, or common 'cooters'. Likewise the flavour of terrapin is quite different from sea-turtle soups or consommés which were also highly regarded by *bec fins* and *bonne fourchettes*.

Alas, over-fishing and diminution of habitat has rather quickly depleted the terrapin population; to the point that it is now listed as an endangered species. More recently, conservationists have mounted great efforts to rescue and propagate terrapins and preserve their habitat. Roadside billboards can be seen along the roadsides of America's eastern-shore backwaters, and such efforts have resulted in a gradual comeback, although terrapins are not yet available commercially.

Terrapin Recipes

Recipes for cooking terrapin abound, and various schools of thought are defended by their advocates almost religiously. Daniel M. Henry, a master terrapin-cook offers the following:

> Cooking terrapin is like making corn bread or curing and cooking ham, there is no receipt that is sufficient. Almost everybody uses the same formal directions, similar to those used at the Maryland and Baltimore Clubs, or the Rennert Hotel, but they are only a general guide. Just as one can watch carefully day after day a good cook make rolls or pastry but never is able to make them right one's [sic] self, so with terrapin, experience and the cook really make the dish…. The final flavor of the dish is almost as elusive as the shades of a delicate color and (even) the most skillful cooks at times miss it.

Even with this authoritative advice, debates regarding how to cook terrapin properly are frequent and opinionated. For example, two distinct schools exist regarding the method used for butchering: should one scald, skin, clean and cook, or simply cook and then skin and clean? Of course the real question is, which procedure produces the best ('authentic') terrapin? Like fried chicken, there are some very distinct regional styles of terrapin cookery. Thus, one can find recipes for Philadelphia-style terrapin, Eastern Shore-style terrapin, Baltimore-style terrapin, and Charleston-style terrapin. There are soups, stews and 'calapashe,' cooter pies, and even mock terrapin dishes made from muskrat!

Often found in older cookbooks or manuscripts are recipes simply stating 'turtle', which can mean turtle species other than terrapins, including sea turtles or freshwater snapping turtles. Likewise, the southern slang term 'cooter' is a nonspecific generic term and can mean any number of different species within the genus *Testudo*. In addition to the recipes common to the American east coast, I have included a terrapin recipe from South East Asia where turtle is popular food item and readily found alive in city street markets.

Rorer, S.T., *Mrs. Rorer's Philadelphia Cookbook* (Philadelphia: Arnold, 1886).

Terrapins are always sold alive, and in season from November to March. Diamond backs are best, but are very expensive, costing from thirty to thirty-six dollars per dozen for cows. The males are small and of inferior flavor. The common red-legs or freshwater terrapin [Junianna terrapins?] are very good, and only cost about two or three a dozen for the very best.

Stewed Terrapin:

> 2 Terrapins
> ½ pint of thick cream
> 6 eggs
> ½ pound of butter
> 1 gill of sherry or Madeira
> ¼ teaspoon of mace
> Salt and cayenne to taste

Put the terrapins alive into boiling water, and boil ten or fifteen minutes, or until you can pull off the outer skin and the toe nails [of the legs and tail]. Now put them back in fresh boiling water, add a heaping teaspoonful of salt and boil slowly [simmer] until the shells part easily and the flesh on the legs is quite tender. When done take out, remove outer shell [carapace], and let them stand until cool enough to handle. Then take them out of the upper shells; carefully remove the sand bags, bladders, the thick heavy part of the intestines, and the gall sacks, which are found imbedded in one lobe of the liver, and throw them away. ...cut the small intestine into tiny pieces and add them to the meat; now add the liver broken up, and the eggs found in the terrapins. Now put it into a stewing-pan with the juice or liquor it has given out while being cut. Roll the butter in flour, add it to the terrapin, and stand on a very moderate fire until heated. Boil the 6 eggs for fifteen minutes, take out the yolks, mash to a smooth paste with two tablespoonsful of the wine, then add this, the cream and seasoning to the terrapin, let boil up once, take from the fire, add the wine and serve. It must never be boiled after adding the wine. More or less wine may be added according to taste.

Farmer, Fanny, *The Original Boston Cooking-School Cook Book* (New York: H.L. Levin, 1896).

This expensive member of the turtle family is highly prized in Baltimore and Philadelphia, but seldom used in New England. Terrapin may be kept alive through the winter by putting them in a barrel, where they will not freeze [usually in a cool cellar or basement], and feeding them occasionally with vegetable parings. Before cooking, soak them in strong salt water. Put them alive into boiling water, and boil rapidly ten or fifteen minutes. Remove the black outside skin from the shells, and the nails from the claws. Wash in warm water;

then put them on again, in fresh boiling water; add a little salt, and boil about three quarters of an hour, or until the outer shell cracks. Open them over a bowl to save the gravy, remove the under shell, the sand bags, the head, and the gall bladder from the liver. If the gall bladder is broken in the process, the whole dish will be ruined by the escaping gall. Put the upper shells on to boil again in the same water, and boil until tender; watch them carefully, and take each out as soon as tender. Pick the liver and meat from the upper shell, and cut into several pieces. The intestines are used with the meat in winter, when the turtle is in a torpid condition; but in summer they should be thrown away. Boil the intestines by themselves one hour. This should be prepared the day before. Heat the meat in the gravy. To each terrapin add one wineglassful of cream, half a cup of butter, a little salt, cayenne, and one wineglassful of sherry. Use turtle eggs if there be any; if not, the yolks of two hard-boiled eggs to each terrapin. Rub smooth, mixing with raw yolk enough to make balls the size of turtle eggs. Add these and the wine just before you send the dish to the table.

Maryland's Way: Andrews, L.R., Kelly, J.R., *The Hammond-Harwood House Cook Book* (Annapolis: Hammond-Harwood House Association, 1963).

To Prepare And Cook Diamond Back Terrapin:

It is a question of choice whether the terrapin's head should be cut off, some claiming that it should be, that it may bleed, others that it should be put in the pot alive. If the head is cut off, place the terrapin with the neck down for a few minutes so the blood can run from it.

Have two vessels of boiling water, put them in one and let them remain for five or six minutes, then take them out, and a flaky skin can be easily removed from all the exposed meat by rubbing with the fingers. This cannot be done after the terrapin has been cooked and the meat has become soft.

Put them now in the other pot of boiling water and boil them until you can, with the forefinger and thumb easily press through the foot. For a five inch terrapin this takes about one hour, for larger ones of course longer. But, by taking it out of the pot and testing it in this way, a mistake cannot be made. The great success of the dish is this cooking, for unless this is properly done they are apt to be stringy or tough.

After the terrapins are done, take them from the pot and put in a vessel that will hold the liquor that runs from them. Remove the top shell; if it is inclined to stick, use a sharp knife to run up between the shell and the meat. Some little tidbits are apt to adhere to the shell. Save them. Sometimes the sand bags adhere too; these are one of the few things about terrapin you must throw away. After removing the upper shell you will find the sand bags or lungs, unless they have remained on the top shell, on top of the meat. Remove these with a fork; they are thin and leathery looking.

Webster, A.L., *The Improved Housewife*, 20th ed. (Boston: Phillips, Sampson, 1855).

To Dress Turtle: Cut off the head in the morning, in summer; at evening, in the winter; hang it up by the hind fins, and let it bleed well; with care, separate the bottom shell from the top, lest you break the gall bladder, which, with care, take out and throw away; throw the liver into a bowl of water; empty the chitterlings (guts,) and throw them into water; the eggs also, if any – have a separate bowl for each article; slice the meat from the under shell, and throw that in water; break in pieces the shell; wash and clean and put it in a pot, completely covering it with water, and add to it one pound of middling (or flitch of bacon) with flour and chopped onions, and set it on the fire to boil. Open the chitterlings; clean them thoroughly; take off the inside skin, and put them in the pot with the shell; let them boil three hours steadily; if the water boils away too much, add more.

The top: – Wash the top shell neatly, after cutting out all the meat; cover, and set it by. Parboil the fins; clean them perfectly, taking off all of the black skin, and throw them into water. Now cut the flesh taken from both shells, in small pieces; cut the fins in two, and lay them in a dish with the flesh; sprinkle over some salt, and cover up the dish.

When the shell, chittterlings, &c. are done, or have boiled three hours, take out the bacon, scrape the shell clean, and strain the liquor – about one quart of which must be put back in the pot; reserve the rest of the soup; pick out the chitterlings, and cut them into small pieces; select all the nice bits that were strained out, put them with the chitterlings in the gravy; add the fins, cut in pieces, to them and enough of the flesh to fill the upper shell; add to it, if a large turtle, one bottle of white wine, cayenne pepper, and salt to your taste; one gill of mushroom catsup, one gill of lemon pickle, mace, cloves, and nutmeg, pounded, to highly season it; mix two spoonfuls of flour with one pound and a quarter of butter; add, with it, marjoram, thyme, parsley, and savory, tied in a bunch; stew all these together till the flesh and fins are tender; wash out the top shell; place a high paste round the brim; sprinkle over the shell salt and pepper, then take the herbs out of the stew; if the gravy is not sufficiently thick, add a little more flour, and fill the shell. If no eggs in the turtle, boil six new laid ones for ten minutes; put them in cold water a few minutes; peel them; cut them in two, and place them on the turtle. Make a rich forcemeat; fry the balls nicely and place them also in the shell. Place the shell in a dripping pan, with something underneath the sides to steady it, heat the oven as for bread, and bake till a fine brown. Fry the liver, and send it hot.

41

Rhett, Blanche S., *200 Years of Charleston Cooking*, ed. Lettie Gay, (New York: J. Cape & H. Smith, 1930).

Calapash (Terrapin in the Back)

The rice field "cooter" or terrapin is first killed and allowed to drip, head down. In extracting the meat, remove the bottom of the shell. Care should be taken to get this out in as large pieces as possible. This then should be boiled for at least four to five hours over slow heat, depending upon [the] age of the terrapin, when a rich brown soup or stew is obtained. Seasoning should be added at time of boiling, such as salt, pepper (red and black) [I like to add allspice as well. F.C.B.]. Some prefer a small quantity of white or Irish potatoes and a little onion. When thoroughly cooked, the meat should be cut into small pieces with a sharp knife or scissors, across grain, for if cut otherwise, it will have a tendency to become stringy.

The back of the 'cooter,' having been cleaned thoroughly inside and out, is then used as the container for the stew, to which is added bread or biscuit crumbs and ample butter. This is placed in the upper part of the oven, a slow heat rather than a fast one being preferable, for about one-half hour, after which the top will form a brown and crispy crust. Particular care should be exercised to serve very hot..

This is a recipe which you may never use unless you have a most elaborate household and live in a neighborhood wherein terrapin is common. It is included here partially because of its historical interest. Of Indian [Native American] origin, refined by three hundred years of use in white households, it is rarely cooked now, perhaps once every five or ten years, when a most distinguished guest comes to South Carolina. The art of cooking calapash is preserved by a few Negroes, mostly very old. The recipe here given was obtained from Joe Robinson, an old colored man from the country, servant of Mr. Robert Harleston of Bossis Plantation, whose great dinners have slipped into history, but whose recipes appear from time to time in this book.

Blank, F.C., transcribed recipe dictated by Leuchai Buakhokrang (Jomtien, Thailand, July 2004).

Tdao Geng (Curried Turtle)

Ingredients:

1 lb of prepared cooked turtle meat in its juice.

For the curry paste: ¾ cup chopped and sweated onions, 2 tablespoons minced fresh garlic, $^1/_3$ cup Thai curry powder, 2 tablespoons dried turmeric powder, 2 tablespoons dried red chile pepper flakes (or 2 or 3 fresh Thai red bird's eye peppers), ¼ cup fresh coriander leaves, peelings from one or two fresh kaffir limes, 2 tablespoons vegetable oil.

For the curry sauce: 1 pint of fresh (or canned) coconut milk, 2 tablespoons of the above home made curry paste, 2 tablespoons commercial Thai fish sauce, q.s. salt and freshly ground black peppercorns.

Garnishes: Assorted baby cooked vegetables, Thai hot sauce, black sesame seeds, raw cucumbers, julienned sweet red bell peppers.

1. Prepare the curry paste: Place all paste ingredients into a large mortar-and-pestle, or a food processor, and puree until a smooth puree is achieved. Set aside.

2. Place the measured amount of curry paste, coconut milk, and fish sauce into a double boiler and stir and heat gently until well combined; add the turtle meat and cook until heated through.

3. Taste and season by titration with salt and freshly cracked black pepper.

4. Serve with the baby vegetables, cucumber, and cooked white rice on the side. Bottled Thai hot sauce should be offered at table for anyone who wishes their curry to be 'pet mak mak'.

Muskrats – *Ondatra zibethicus*

Along the American eastern seaboard, muskrats share the brackish and freshwater marshlands with terrapins. However, muskrats are far wider-ranging because they are not confined to brackish water and are quite at home in freshwater estuaries, streams, ponds and lakes. In addition they are able to tolerate a colder climate than are terrapins. Thus, muskrats are found throughout the United States and across all of Canada with the exception of the Arctic tundra. They are also found in much of Europe where they were introduced by man somewhere about 1905. Muskrats then spread to Asia, and parts of Africa, especially in the north-eastern bush areas where they are relished, and cooked rudely by simply heaping the carcasses onto an open fire.

Muskrats are rodents and although it is often assumed that they are related to the beaver or thought to be a large version of the common rat, in point of fact their closest relative is the field mouse. Muskrats weigh 1.5 kg (3¼ lb). They are excellent swimmers and can swim for more than 90 metres underwater, and remain submerged for more than 15 minutes.

They are omnivores and feed on a wide variety of marsh vegetation as well as freshwater shellfish, frogs and small turtles. They are hunted by minks, foxes, coyotes, and lynx, and are sometimes prey for larger snapping turtles and raptor species. In the manner of beavers, muskrats build mound-like 'houses' but theirs are constructed of bulrushes, weeds and packed mud, whereas beavers use tree branches and tree saplings and even full-grown trees to make their huts. Muskrats will also build dens in stream banks with an underwater entrance. Inside muskrat houses there are separate platforms for each member of a family or clan to sleep.

Muskrats are mean-tempered and quarrelsome even among themselves, especially in the spring during the mating season. They are vicious fighters when affronted and on occasion will attack humans without provocation. Muskrats are promiscuous and

43

do not form lasting pairings. Muskrats bear their young alive, after a gestation period of about one month. Thus a female may bear up to three litters, depending upon the duration of summer. Even when muskrats were hunted commercially for their fur, which brought fair prices, and now, as their habitat is diminishing, muskrats seem to be able to maintain their numbers, and have readily adapted to living and thriving in close quarters with human beings.

Indeed muskrats and their reed houses may be seen daily by commuters who use the high speed trains of Amtrak's North East Corridor between Boston, New York and Washington D. C. – the busiest rail line in the US. Of course few, if any, well-dressed businessmen ever take notice of, or are even aware of these thriving rodent communities which are especially observable just eight minutes south of New York City near Newark, New Jersey, where they are sandwiched between the petroleum storage tanks located in that swampy wetland area.

The present-day low price of muskrat pelts is a far cry from the handsome prices these brought when muskrat fur coats were popular for both men and women dandies. This shift of fashion has greatly reduced muskrat trapping as a viable occupation for hunters who once made a comfortable living. And so it is that in mid-March through the first two weeks in April, only a few older die-hards venture out to set traps along the muskrat runs of America's remaining wetlands.

Fortunately the tradition of community muskrat suppers as fundraising events for volunteer fire companies, churches, and VFW clubs still attracts hungry folk who are avid muskrat hunters and eaters. Such community events are especially popular in small villages and towns along the Delaware Bay and its tributaries in Salem County, New Jersey – a region affectionately called 'South Jersey' by locals.

The style and menu of these events depends upon the organization sponsoring the supper. A typical church-run evening usually has two sittings: one at 5:00 pm and a second at 7:30. Long tables set with folding chairs are laid with baskets of bread (or soft rolls) and butter, a fork, knife, and spoon, and a cup and saucer. The first course is often canned, chilled fruit cocktail in a short glass sorbet cup and, eaten or not, cleared quickly by a bevy of high-school student volunteers. Next, heaping platters of almost-whole deep-fried muskrats, home-made potato salad, coleslaw, cooked green beans, and corn arrive. Without hesitation, the 16 or more guests gathered at each table begin to help themselves, and literally dive into the bounty set before them. Most everyone knows each other, but strangers, with some reservation, are welcome and conversations proceed accordingly.

At church-run muskrat dinners, cold water and coffee-by-the-pot are the only beverages offered. V. F. W. and volunteer fire company events usually offer colas and/or beer. Desserts are often provided by the wives and daughters of the community, and range from 4-star home-baked goods to cakemix cakes, and sometimes store-bought ice-cream.

Muskrat Recipes

The flavour of muskrat, regardless of methods of cooking or seasoning, is perhaps best described as 'strong'. It is often politely labelled 'an acquired taste', but aficionados relish its assertive gamey qualities. [Personally, when asked, I describe it as a cross between snapping turtle and goose.] Its flesh is very dark, and there is no mistaking that it lives in marshy wetlands. 'Musk' is indeed a most appropriate modifier. Written recipes are elusive, except in rural 'community cookbooks' found in the small hamlets where muskrat dinners are still celebrated. The most usual cooking methods, not surprisingly, call for slow, low temperatures in stock – whether braised, simmered, or stewed. Occasionally muskrats are fried like chicken, but the pieces are commonly part- or fully-cooked before they are coated and fried. Seasonings vary, but stronger bold spices, such as fresh bay leaves, black pepper, and allspice predominate.

Richard Olney in one of his last books, *Reflections* (2000), recounts visiting an open market in Baltimore where 'marsh rabbits' were for sale. He asked the vendor what they were and how to prepare them, to which the vendor replied: 'Muscrats [sic] – boil'm to get rid of the taste and fry'm like chicken.' Olney decided to treat his new-found meat with more respect so he cut them up, marinated the pieces overnight with red wine, herbs and aromatic vegetables, and some olive oil, and prepared them like a *coq-au-vin*. He describes the results: 'the flavour was delicately gamey, the sauce the colour of bitter chocolate, glossy with a velvet texture. Everyone loved it until, as cheeses were being served, it was announced that we had been eating muscrat [sic]; two guests turned green and fled to the bathroom!'

45

Recipes Old and New of St. Thomas' Church [Garrison Forest, Maryland], (Baltimore, 1961).

Muskrat (Marsh Rabbit): Muskrat or Marsh Rabbit is one of the cleanest animals in America and its meat is deliciously edible. They eat vegetable food chiefly, feeding on the roots and stems of aquatic plants. They may be purchased cheaply as they are trapped for their fur. They are found in the markets of Washington, Baltimore, Wilmington, and Philadelphia.

Transcribed from a 1742 manuscript.
Smothered Muskrat

Soak [skinned gutted and cleaned] muskrat overnight; drain and parboil in water to cover for 20 min. Heat some bacon drippings in thick skillet [heavy cast iron spider] and sear meat in it. Season with salt and pepper and chopped onion [a lot]. Add water, and cover and allow to simmer until thoroughly done. [Some similar recipes call for sage as a seasoning and that the muskrat be floured before it is fried.]

A Cook's Tour of the Eastern Shore (Easton, Maryland: 1961).

Muskrat Tred Avon: Cut up 3 muskrats, place in crock or enameled pn and cover with the following marinade: 6 sprigs of parsley and 6 celery tops – brushed well. 1 carrot, 1 onion, 1 leek, 1 clove garlic all sliced fine. 6 peppercorns [black] 2 bay leaves, 2 tablespoons olive oil, pinch cayenne, enough red wine to cover meat. Leave in marinade about 12 hours, stirring 3 or 4 times. Take meat out, season [salt and pepper?], roll in flour and fry in ½ butter and ½ lard until brown and crisp. Meanwhile, cook marinade until vegetables are tender, strain, and make gravy. Just before serving add 1 teaspoon [or more] of [red] current jelly to gravy. Mrs. Carroll Elder. [Tred Avon is a river in Talbot County, Maryland and a tributary of the Chesapeake Bay.]

Curried Rabbit or Muskrat: Cut meat in serving pieces and soak in strong salt water for several hours. Dry, dredge with flour, salt and pepper and brown in bacon or salt pork fat. Put meat in covered saucepan with a little water to steam. Mix 2 teaspoons curry powder, 1 teaspoon sugar and one heaping tablespoon flour. Meanwhile put one large sliced onion into fat left in skillet. Add curry mixture to onion and brown together. Add slowly: 1 pint of water, 1 cup strained [tinned] tomatoes, a small handful of raisins [sultanas] and 1 cup chopped sour apple. Cook until smooth and pour over rabbit [or muskrat] and continue cooking until meat is very tender. When ready to serve add 1 cup hot milk. Pour rabbit on platter and surround with hot cooked rice. Mrs. Joseph A. Ross.

Ellis, Eleanor A., *Northern Cookbook* (Ottawa:1967).

[Batter] Fried Muskrat: 1 muskrat, 1 tablespoon salt, 1 quart water, 1 egg yolk, ½ cup milk, 1 teaspoon salt, ½ cup flour, 4 tablespoons cooking fat. 1. Skin and clean the muskrat, remove fat, scent glands and the white tissue inside each leg. 2. Soak muskrat overnight in a weak brine solution of 1 tablespoon of salt [non-iodized] to one quart of water. Disjoint and cut the muskrat into desired pieces. 3. Parboil for 20 minutes, drain and wipe with a damp cloth. 4. Make a smooth batter by beating the egg yolk and milk, then add the salt and flour. 5. Heat the fat in a heavy [cast iron] fry pan. 6. Dip the meat in the batter then sauté in hot fat until brown. 7. When brown, reduce the heat and cook slowly for about 1½ hours. Serves 4.

Muskrat Meat Loaf: 1½ pounds ground muskrat, 2 eggs beaten, 1/3 cup dry bread crumbs, 1 cup evaporated milk, 1 small onion, minced or grated, ¼ teaspoon thyme, 1 teaspoon salt, ¼ teaspoon pepper, 1 teaspoon Worcestershire sauce, ¼ cup catsup. 1. Follow first three directions for fried muskrat above. 2. Grind the meat. 3. Mix ground meat thoroughly with other ingredients. 4. Place in a greased loaf pan. 5. Place loaf pan in a shallow pan containing hot water. 6. Bake in a 350° F. oven for 1½ hours. Serves 6.

Cooking His Goose:
Gender in American Wild Game Cookbooks

Bronwen E. Bromberger

The conception of the 'universal asymmetry of sex roles'[1] has been documented in societies throughout the world and across recorded time. Since the beginning of human society, hunting has been delegated to men, while women are associated with the duties of child-rearing and household maintenance. Although strict labour division along gender lines is widely regarded in contemporary American society as regressive and therefore undesirable, hunting and cooking are two practices that remain strongly associated with gender. Even as of 2001, the vast majority of sport hunters – some 91% – were male.[2] Similarly, the task of food preparation is customarily delegated to women, and before the massive paradigmatic shifts of the 1960s and 1970s it was assumed that a woman's duty was to provide for a nurturing and comfortable domestic space.

The wild game cookbook, an instruction manual for preparing hunted game for presentation in a domestic setting, lies at the intersection of these highly gender-specific roles. The purpose of this paper is to examine the ways in which a selection of game cookbooks published in the United States between 1937 and 1989 support and challenge the so-called 'traditional' sexual roles, and to explore the factors that contribute to the authors' level of conformity to those patterns. Central to this discussion will be the cookbooks' commentary regarding the attributes of the hunter and the cook, models for the division of labour in hunting households, and analysis of how gender identity is reflected tacitly in the recipes themselves. The cookbooks provide a fascinating range of commentary regarding the roles of men and women in the journey of game from field to table in 20th-century America.

Support for Traditional Gender Roles

In American society and game cookbooks alike, the archetypal hunter is generally portrayed as the consummate male, regardless of whether he is a working-class 'good ole boy' who dedicates his weekends to getaways with his buddies or a well-heeled sportsman who takes guided hunting excursions at exclusive lodges.

'Uncle' Russ Chittenden's *Good Ole Boys Wild Game Cookbook* (1989) contains recipes developed at the author's hunting club, dubbed 'The Lair of the Ancient Hunter', where men escape 'to lie, drink a lot, and eat fattening foods',[3] activities presumably not encouraged in the feminine-dominated home. At the other end of the spectrum, Harry Botsford's *Fish and Game Cookbook* (1947) recounts his hunting and eating experiences as part of a gentlemen's hunting club that is no less exclusively male. His narrative is peppered with recipes for foods he has eaten along the way, having wrested these from the hostesses, chefs, and domestic cooks who prepared his dinners over the years. Several cookbooks pay lip service to the idea of female hunters, then go on to contradict themselves. John Willard's *Game is Good Eating* (1958) states in its dedication that 'in every man, and probably woman, too, is the basic spirit of the hunter,'[4] and goes on to suggest that game might be taken 'home to your wife (or *husband*)'.[5] However, later Willard reverts to the traditional gender stereotypes. The chapter entitled 'How America's Most Famous Sportsmen Like Their Wild Game' emphasizes the machismo of eight hunting men, while claiming that their recipes 'will please…the housewife',[6] and later the author observes that 'how good [venison] is depends more on the man in the field than on the woman at the range'.[7]

If many game cookbooks portray hunting as a way for men to express their wild, uncivilized side, they also depict cooking as an innately female activity. The cover illustration for *How to Cook His Goose*, written by Karen Green and Betty Black in 1973, is a cartoon of a smiling woman with a duck perched somewhat incongruously on her head. Behind her sit jars labelled 'spice' and 'everything nice', two of the three major components of feminine personality according to the classic nursery rhyme. The books encourage women to take pride in the preparation of game for consumption in the home. In her 1965 *Game Cookbook*, Geraldene Steindler tells her reader that she will 'be paying your mighty hunter a compliment when you match his skill in the field with yours in the kitchen.'[8] In *How to Cook His Goose*, women are told that cooking is their sport, and that a full complement of 'Kitchen Ammunition' (i.e., cooking utensils) will ensure their status as 'a Cook to Be Reckoned With'.[9] So internalized is their conviction that cooking their husbands' game is a privilege that they counsel their protegées to 'finagle…higher-priced items' like roasting pans and fish poachers from their husbands as gifts on special occasions.[10]

Wild game cookery depends upon a synergistic relationship between the hunter and the cook, and the dynamics of the transfer of authority from one party to the other are often portrayed as complex and problematic. In *The Derrydale Game Cookbook* (1937) Louis DeGouy philosophizes that 'without harmonious cookery there can be no symphonic living'.[11] Other authors echo his sentiments, sometimes in less refined ways. In *Good Ole Boys Wild Game Cookbook*, Chittenden bemoans the plight of hunters 'duped into marrying women with good legs…but whom they belatedly discovered could not or would not skin a coon or pick a goose,'[12] and Botsford kicks off his *Wild Game Cook Book* with the story of a newly-married hunter who murders his simpering wife after she presents him with a badly-prepared game dinner. Even when a wife's inability to cook game meat does not result in a loss of life, it can contribute to marital tension. In another vignette, Botsford tells of a 'crafty' wife who, upon hearing that her 'Nimrod' husband has bagged a huge deer, plans to dispose of it by pawning it off to friends rather than cooking it.[13] Numerous stories of 'crestfallen hunters whose wives wouldn't or didn't know how to cook their game'[14] led Steindler to publish her cookbook, and Botsford suggests that any man who reads his *Fish and Game Cook Book* might forestall an 'outrageous culinary crime' by 'presenting to [his wife] a copy of this valuable and instructive tome'.[15]

Even as many authors agree that a wife's incompetence with game can ruin a domestic scene, a properly-prepared feast of wild game is held up as the epitome of marital bliss. DeGouy introduces a wild turkey stuffing that has 'kept the intimate tone of a few households'.[16] John Willard echoes his sentiments in *Game is Good Eating*, promising that by following his recipes 'you can have both domestic bliss and meals that would delight a gourmet'.[17] By preparing his catch for dinner, a woman fulfils her traditional female role: she strokes her husband's ego, nurtures her family, garners recognition from her guests, and – if she is truly savvy – even manages to save money in the process.

The act of feeding a husband and family is central to the traditional female identity, and game cookbooks communicate this in myriad ways. Many outline a system in which the wife coddles her husband with good food. In *Game Cookery*, written in 1968 by E. N. and Edith Sturdivant, the husband professes that 'I was her guinea pig...and as a consequence I am somewhat overweight,'[18] while Steindler somewhat smugly confides that tasting is her husband's 'chore' in the kitchen. The concept of 'man-pleasers', foods that are prepared specifically to satisfy a husband, is also addressed in several books. In *How to Cook His Goose*, skillet sea bass is introduced as 'a real man-pleaser',[19] and an entire chapter of Steindler's *Game Cookbook* is entitled 'Man-Pleasers!' Even small touches are considered important. Steindler suggests a selection of garnishes that will dress up a plate 'without the gussied-up look most men detest'[20] and counsels readers that well-prepared vegetables will keep their husbands both happy and healthy.

The ability to cook game is also presented as a source of pride for women, who garner recognition outside their home for their mastery of a purportedly difficult art. In a society where meat usually enters the house on styrofoam slabs, the ability to break down a 'mass of horns, hide, fins, or feathers'[21] is regarded as almost magical. The Sturdivants wrote their cookbook to dispel 'a notion that there is some deep, dark secret' to game cookery,[22] which, say the authors of *How to Cook His Goose*, 'was [probably] started by some sportsmen's wives who wanted to keep a good thing to themselves.'[23] The idea that the ability to cook game should be part of a housewife's aura of mystique is echoed by Steindler when she admits that 'I shall probably ruin my reputation as a game cook by stating that it is simple.'[24] Nevertheless, both male and female authors stress the potential of game for entertaining guests and that an ability to cook game can win women praise outside their immediate family. The chapter on wild bird cookery in *How to Cook His Goose* is called 'A Feather in Your Cap', reinforcing the message about proper modes of female achievement and recognition. Game meat is ideal for company, whether 'a proud husband...call[s] you at five o'clock to impress his boss at seven'[25] or plans for a company luncheon call for delicate elk tongue rolls. Both wife and food are expected to be ornamental: Botsford fondly recalls how 'very delightful [a certain hostess] looks'[26] as she prepares breast of grouse for her husband's guests.

While many books place an emphasis on women's achievement in the context of altruistic caretaking, several also appeal to women by stressing the practical advantages of game cookery. First and foremost is its budget-mindedness (disregarding the money spent on the hunt itself, which can be considerable). With a little skill the ingenious housewife may serve dressed-up game meat – even leftovers – at special events and 'still be ahead on [her] budget'.[27] In a chapter entitled 'What to Do With All That Burger', Steindler suggests 18 ways to disguise copious amounts of ground game 'before the family rebels'.[28] Green and Black concentrate on ways to dress up game using everyday ingredients, as in the recipe for quail *en chex*, in which crushed breakfast cereal becomes a coating worthy of a French moniker.

Evoking Gender Through Food

Male and female roles in game preparation are stressed in a number of game cookbooks, but in many cases the recipes themselves also evoke a gender identity. Wild game meat is inherently untamed, uncivilized, and undisguised, while its transfer to a domestic sphere in many cases brings with it signs of domestication and feminization. Most game books carry a range of recipes intended for preparation in different venues, from basic camp cookery to gourmet entertaining. The identity of the cook also depends on the context, with men responsible for most wilderness cooking and women generally taking charge in the domestic sphere.

The recipes intended for preparation in the field retain characteristics that reflect the meat's wildness: they generally call for cooking over a fire and a minimal number of ingredients. The natural flavour of the meat is accentuated rather than disguised, and the recipes themselves are vague, open to interpretation depending on the circumstances.

There also exists a corpus of what might be called 'hunting lodge recipes' designed to be cooked by men at lodges without the supervision or interference of women. Many of these recipes are unorthodox, displaying a disregard for traditional cooking techniques that might horrify the sportsmen's wives (in the unlikely event that they were ever invited). *Good Old Boys Wild Game Cookbook* presents recipes from the so-called 'Lair of the Ancient Hunter'. Bubba's red game marinade is based upon a combination of beer and red wine (what would Master Chef DeGouy have to say about that?), while Billy Bob's mallard soup is an amalgamation of packaged seasoned wild rice, soup mixes, and *ramen* noodles with some duck meat thrown in. The men are aware that their methods are unorthodox, and poke fun at others' standards by suggesting that 'possum meat benefits from tenderizing with a pickup truck'. While these foods might be coarse, they share an emphasis on ease of preparation, heartiness, and lack of affectation that separates them from foods made by the 'real' (i.e. female) cooks at home.

Recipes for domestic everyday suppers form the core of most of the game cookbooks in this study. Many of these emphasize traditional preparations of exotic meats, disguising their wildness by serving them as pot-roasts, spaghetti with meatballs, or, in one recipe, by dipping meat in fruit-flavoured yogurt and rolling it in shredded coconut.[29] Side dishes like salads and baked fruit are also emphasized and go a long way toward changing the character of the dish on the plate. The very act of accompanying a main course of moose with a lemon Jello salad basically emasculates the wild meat. The one area where men continue to dominate domestic recipes is at the grill: Steindler says of her recipe for barbecued bear leg, 'This is where the men take over!'[30] and Sturdivant presents an elk rib roast barbecue 'for the man who likes outdoors cooking on a barbecue stand'.[31]

The final type of recipe presented in many game cookbooks deals with entertaining: civilized, feminized dishes that present game as a novelty through which a hunting family might impress or surprise (and ideally delight) their guests. Recipes for exotic game like beaver tail sliced thin and served on crackers and more traditional dishes like cold poached salmon fillet in glazed aspic bespeak fussiness and delicacy. Taking a wild product and using it to display refinement and control is perhaps the ultimate symbol for game cookery: the domination of nature and its consumption in a civilized setting.

51

Challenging Traditional Gender Roles

Despite evidence that many game cookbooks support traditional gender roles, a diversity of viewpoints can be found, both over time and between contemporaneous volumes.

First of all, not all game cookbooks assume that the hunter will be male. Several of the cookbooks are actually written by female hunters themselves. These women defy many of the traditional female attributes such as delicacy, squeamishness, and confinement to the home. Even while Geraldene Steindler writes chapters entitled 'Man-Pleasers!' and is tagged in her biographical statement as 'The Huntsman's Hostess',[32] she does not hesitate to give readers advice regarding guns and ammunition and accompanies her husband on forays into the field. Similarly, in *The Catch and The Feast* (1969), author Joie McGrail challenges the status quo by participating in a number of exclusive hunting expeditions with her husband. She delights in observing the shock of the guides as she accompanies them dressed in a leather miniskirt, and professes her pleasure when 'the guide allowed that, female or not, I had done some good shooting.'[33] Rather than waiting for their husbands to bring home meat for dinner, these women join them in the field, proving themselves more versatile than social stereotypes might suggest.

However, even women who hunt generally assume most of the responsibility in

the kitchen as well, hinting that their hunting husbands may not be willing to abandon their masculine role. A notable exception is Bill McGrail, who helps Joie mix up
a batch of wild strawberry jam alfresco and gives her the first shot at a charging boar.
Without exception in the books, the female hunters were introduced to the sport
by their husbands and persuaded to join in. 'I could imagine only blood and killing
and roughneck hunters,'[34] writes Joie of her response when her husband professed
his hobby, and Steindler was 'horrified'[35] when her husband suggested she become
a shooter. In a sport traditionally dominated by 'ole boys', it may be socially unac-
ceptable for women to take the initiative to hunt or to impose themselves on their
husbands' hobby unless they are pressed to do so.

Men perform traditionally female roles (such as domestic cookery) in several game
cookbooks as well. However, most of their work involves a wider audience than their
families and friends, consistent with the theory that when a 'culture distinguishes a
higher level of the same functions [performed by women], the higher level is restricted
to men.'[36] Louis DeGouy was a cook, not a hunter, but he was also a classically-trained
French chef and a professional. Timothy Manion's *Wild Game and Country Cooking*
(1983) contains recipes for everyday suppers and features a picture of the author in an
apron at a stove on its cover. Similarly, Bill 'The Hunter' Johnson is introduced in his
Wild Game Cookbook (1968) as an avid cook and hunter, and his book features homey
domestic recipes like partridge pie and rabbit with fruit gravy. However, both these
men were television personalities as well as cookbook authors. The prestige associated
with teaching 'thousands of men, women, and children viewers'[37] on a nationally
syndicated television show may have attenuated the social liability of performing a
traditionally female activity. It is worth noting, however, that Bill Johnson's nickname
was 'The Hunter' and not 'The Cook'.

Common Denominators and Trends

A discussion of gender roles presented in game cookbooks means little without a com-
mensurate look at what determines whether or not specific books conform to those
paradigms. What causes one set of authors to teach game cookery from the perspective of clearly divided stereotypical gender roles, while another consciously sets out to
undermine those expectations?

First of all, there is no correlation between the authors' gender and their views
regarding gender roles. Both the most traditional books (*How to Cook His Goose*) and
the most radical (*The Catch and the Feast*) were written by women. This is initially
a surprise, especially in the books supporting a narrow construction of gender roles:
why would a female author choose to pigeonhole herself in a role that constricts her
movement, authority, and choices? In the book *Woman, Culture, and Society*, Michele
Rosaldo posits that women's status is lowest in societies where gender roles are clearly
differentiated, but that within those systems, there are multiple ways for women to
gain power. One option is for women to enter the male sphere, becoming doctors,

lawyers, or – in this case – hunters, as does Joie McGrail. However, this is not an option for the majority of American women, and others find power 'by accepting and elaborating upon the symbols and expectations associated with their cultural definition.'[38] Whether by stroking their husbands' egos ('there isn't a sportsman alive who wouldn't swear his catch was the greatest he'd ever tasted'[39]), forming support networks with other women ('we would like to show you, step by step, how to prepare your sportsman's catch'[40]), or exercising control of foodstuffs (implicit in any household where the woman is responsible for cooking), the authors of *How to Cook His Goose* wield a very different kind of power. Even the title is a double-entendre, at once a superficial statement about preparing wild game and a metaphor for a woman's domination of her husband.

As one might expect, traditional gender roles are emphasized less in more recent books. The fifty years between 1940 and 1990 saw sweeping changes in American society and an increasing awareness that sharply defined sex roles tend to devalue women. References to 'the woman at the range'[41] or 'the Lady who presides in the kitchen',[42] while perhaps common mid-century, would raise eyebrows if published fifty years later, in a society where women constitute more than 60% of the workforce and almost half of all meals are consumed outside the home.[43] Accordingly, the standard in more recent game cookbooks is conscientious gender neutrality. While Chittenden (1989) goes out of his way to reinforce traditional stereotypes and initially appears to be an exception to this rule, his identity as a self-professed 'long-time male chauvinist'[44] is carefully calibrated to be humorous and contradict the politically-correct society he and his fellow hunters escape from on trips to the 'Lair'.

Gender bias is also linked to the socioeconomic status and education level of the cookbooks' authors. American hunters represent a wide range of income levels, both well below the national average and significantly above. Educationally, the same is true: in 2001 a full 14% of hunters had not completed secondary school, while 8% held graduate degrees.[45] In general, game cookbooks that challenge gender norms tend to be written by authors who were more affluent than their more traditional counterparts. The McGrails, who hunted and cooked together, were a high-income couple with several residences and white-collar jobs. Gertrude Parke, author of *Going Wild in the Kitchen* (1965) and an avid sportswoman, talks of domestic help as if a hired cook were an option for every woman. Geraldene Steindler, though she plays the role of the happy housewife, also spends a fair amount of time in the field bringing down big game with her ·270 rifle. In one of her recipes, she mentions luncheons with the Bryn Mawr Club, suggesting that she had gone east for university, a rare accomplishment for a woman of her era. The concept that higher education and greater income is linked to less traditional views and practices is well-established, and seems to hold true in many game cookbooks as well.

Traditional norms are also more emphasized in books from the Midwest and the South, regions that have a reputation for being rural, conservative, and concerned with 'family values'. Green and Black, as well as Chittenden, who express some of the strongest gender biases, hail from Oklahoma and Kentucky, while E. N. Sturdivant, who narrates his wife's cookbook and makes numerous generalizations regarding gender roles, grew up in rural Arkansas. Meanwhile, contemporaneous books written by authors in the north-eastern United States generally display less traditional attitudes, such as those espoused in *The Catch and the Feast* and *Going Wild in the Kitchen*.

It is important to remember that the extent of gender bias is a result of several factors: date of publication, socioeconomic status of the target audience, and regionality, as well as the individual characteristics of the author – for example, DeGouy and Botsford, who betrayed significant gender bias, were both affluent and eastern; however, their books reflect the dominant societal attitudes during the 1930s and 1940s, when they were published. Overall, however, traditional gender stereotypes are most prevalent in earlier cookbooks and those aimed at middle-class readers in rural, midwestern, or southern areas, while later books and those intended for affluent hunters and cooks in eastern and metropolitan areas betray a more progressive set of standards.

Conclusion

Like all cookbooks, the success of game cookbooks depends on a bond between author and reader. Both hunting and eating are intensely personal experiences, and whether or how one chooses to hunt, as well as what types of food one prepares and consumes, are reflections of both identity and values. Just as a homey dish like ''Coon in The Pot' might assault the sensibilities of a gourmet cook who wishes to prepare pheasant souvaroff, so very probably would the confident feminist discourse of a Manhattan magazine editor-cum-hunter offend a midwestern housewife who needs a reassuring guide to cooking the venison her husband wants to see on the table.

Hidden within the recipes and cooking tips in game cookbooks is a wealth of information regarding the values and evolving standards of a wide cross-section of mid-20th century American game cooks and hunters. These books reflect both the standards of their day and the mindset of their authors, and in doing so they provide an intimate picture of gender roles in a modern sport-hunting society.

Bibliography
Botsford, Harry, *Fish and Game Cook Book* (New York: Cornell Maritime Press, 1947).
Chittenden, Russ, *Good Ole Boys Wild Game Cookbook* (Paducah: Image Graphics, 1989).
DeGouy, Louis, *The Derrydale Game Cookbook* (New York: Greenberg, 1937).
Green, Karen and Black, Betty, *How to Cook His Goose* (Tulsa: Winchester Press, 1973).
Johnson, L. W., *Wild Game Cookbook* (New York: The Benjamin Company, 1968).
Manion, Timothy, *Wild Game and Country Cooking* (North Haven: O. F. Mossberg, 1983).
McGrail, Joie and Bill, *The Catch and the Feast* (New York: Weybright and Talley, 1969).
Nestle, Marion, *Food Politics* (Berkeley: University of California Press, 2002).

Ortner, Sherry, 'Is Female to Male as Nature is to Culture?', in *Woman, Culture, and Society*, ed. Michele Rosaldo and Louise Lamphere (Stanford: Stanford University Press, 1973).

Parke, Gertrude, *Going Wild in the Kitchen* (New York: David McKay Company, 1965).

Rosaldo, Michele, 'A Theoretical Overview', in *Woman, Culture, and Society*, ed. Michele Rosaldo and Louise Lamphere (Stanford: Stanford University Press, 1973).

Steindler, Geraldene, *The Game Cookbook* (South Hackensack: Stoeger Publishing, 1965).

Sturdivant, E. N. and Edith, *Game Cookery* (New York: Outdoor Life, 1967).

U. S. Department of the Interior, Fish and Wildlife Service and U. S. Department of Commerce, U. S. Census Bureau, *2001 National Survey of Fishing, Hunting, and Wildlife-Associated Recreation*.

Willard, John, *Game is Good Eating* (Helena: State Publishing Company, 1958).

Notes

1. Rosaldo, p. 22.
2. USFWS survey, p. 29.
3. Chittenden, p. 5.
4. Willard, introduction.
5. Willard, p. 3.
6. Willard, p. 9.
7. Willard, p. 27.
8. Steindler, p. 31.
9. Green and Black, p. 4.
10. Green and Black, p. 10.
11. DeGouy, p. 1.
12. Chittenden, p. 5.
13. Botsford, p. 57.
14. Steindler, p. 1.
15. Botsford, p. 10.
16. DeGouy, p. 144.
17. Willard, p. 3.
18. Sturdivant, p. 1.
19. Green and Black, p. 150.
20. Steindler, p. 119.
21. Willard, p. 3.
22. Sturdivant, p. 1.
23. Green and Black, p. 2.
24. Steindler, p. 25.
25. Green and Black, p. 21.
26. Botsford, p. 14.
27. Steindler, p. 110.
28. Steindler, p. 49.
29. Green and Black, p. 66.
30. Steindler, p. 30.
31. Sturdivant, p. 37.
32. Steindler, p. 209.
33. McGrail, p. 49.
34. McGrail, p. 1.
35. Steindler, p. 209.
36. Ortner, p. 80.
37. Johnson, p. 174.
38. Rosaldo, p. 37.

39. Green/Black, p. 4.
40. Green/Black, p. 5.
41. Willard, p. 27.
42. Botsford, p. 11.
43. Nestle, p. 19.
44. Chittenden, p. 119.
45. USFWS survey, pp. 30-1.

Some Notes on Seakale: *Crambe Maritima*

Lynda Brown

Seakale is a native of sea-cliffs, sands, and shingle around the coasts of Western Europe. It was formerly extensively cultivated in Britain but today it is a relatively uncommon vegetable. The blanched leaf-stalks are boiled, like asparagus. They have a nutty, slightly bitter flavour. The plants are grown usually from root cuttings, but sometimes from seed. They are blanched in winter and early spring either in the open or in hot- houses; a pot or box is placed over the crown and is covered with fermenting manure to create warmth for forcing early crops. Wild seakale is sometimes blanched where it grows, by covering the crowns with about 18 inches of shingle. The young shoots are cut when their cluster of blanched leaf -stalks is about 5 inches high.

Seakale belongs to the Wallflower family (*cruciferae*). The plant has broad, lobed and toothed, bluish-green leaves up to 1 foot long, and flowering stems up to 2 feet high, with white 4-petalled flowers. The roundish fruit contains a single seed.

The Oxford Book of Food Plants, Oxford University Press, 1969

Our See-keele …. Are very delicate

John Evelyn, *Acetaria*, 1699

These notes aim to give a brief resume of one of Britains's wild foods that is, in truth, often more talked and written about than eaten.

Along with symposiast and fellow seakale-devotee, Susan Campbell – who has seakale growing in her seashore garden and on the beach outside her back door – seakale has been part of my life for longer than I care to remember. As John Evelyn's quote hints at, it is a vegetable that has had its fair share of afficionados. These include William Curtis, founder of the *Botanic Magazine*; the 18th-century parson diarist Gilbert White; the American President and keen gardener Thomas Jefferson; Constance Spry; and cookery scholar and TV celebrity Clarissa Dickson Wright of BBC TV's *Two Fat Ladies* fame. Hugh Fearnley Whittingstall, a current TV food hero has just started growing it, too.

Alan Davidson in his *Oxford Companion to Food* states seakale was first forced in Italy in the Middle Ages and gradually spread to countries beyond. In Britain it has had a chequered but interesting history. First domesticated, we think, some time in the early 18th century, like the ebbing of the tides that lap its feet, it has fallen into and out of favour with regular monotony.

History

A perennial seashore plant of dry shingle beaches, wild seakale was once common along much of the south and west coastlines: entries for it appear in early herbals, notably that of Turner and Gerard, who write of locals heaping up pebbles or sand around the plants in early spring. The transition from seashore plant to vegetable happened presumably by gardeners digging up roots of the plant and transferring it to their own gardens. Gentlemen gardeners in Devon and Bath, apparently, were very partial to it.

The first professional interest in seakale came from Philip Miller, head gardener of the Chelsea Apothecaries' Garden (now Chelsea Physic Garden), in the 1731 edition of his *Gardener's Dictionary*. The man who did most to popularize it, however, and bring it to the attention of the wider public was William Curtis. He had been introduced to seakale by his friend and benefactor, Dr John Coakley Lettsom, who had discovered it on holiday in Southampton and grown it in his own garden in London. Curtis was so impressed he eventually grew seven acres of it adjoining his botanical garden and nursery at Brompton. He strove for many years to encourage its use, culminating in 1799 with the first (and as far as I am aware the only) pamphlet devoted to seakale, *Directions for Cultivating the Crambe Maritima, or Sea-kale, for the Use of the Table*, which he included in every box of seed.

58

The net result is that seakale thrived during Victorian times, especially in grand houses with their fine walled gardens, where it could be forced in vineries and mushroom houses, providing something choice during the lean late winter and spring time, and which came before asparagus. This popularity lasted until the Second World War. Since then, it has languished and become one of those 'unusual' vegetables that a few inquisitive gardeners and the odd enthusiastic box-scheme producer grow.

Well not quite. It had a brief moment of glory in the mid-nineties, in one of those periodic let's-discover-forgotten-wild-foods-and-vegetables moments in culinary history, thanks largely to Clarissa Dickson Wright who championed it, along with her beloved cardoons. A couple of chefs started to wax lyrical about it and Michael Paske (see below) grew it briefly for the Waitrose supermarket chain. I went to see it at the time, recording a piece for the *Food Programme* with Derek Cooper. It was just like being back in the forced rhubarb sheds: eerie. Alas, it didn't sell, and Waitrose moved on to speciality mangos.

Growing and cooking seakale

Seakale is easy to grow; and, as already noted, anyone with any interest in seeing what it tastes like, or cooking with it, will either have to go native, or grow it for themselves. Fortunately, seakale has a modern benefactor, Michael Paske, a leading grower whose father kept seakale alive for gardeners; Michael Paske has done the same. He is the man to buy your seakale thongs (pieces of root) from. Marshall's, the seed merchants, also sell it.

Plant the thongs in spring, let the plant grow, give it an annual dressing of sea-weed meal to make it feel at home and that's that. It will grow like a weed into a large sprawling bushy plant in the places it's happy, and struggle where it's not. Be warned that, like all crucifers, flea beetles and cabbage white butterflies love it. Unless the plants are really struggling, you can take your first taster crop the following year, covering the young shoots with a forcing pot (old Victorian chimney pots work well). Check regularly for slugs. The pale fleshy stalks are quite brittle, and need to be picked with care. Pull them as you would forced rhubarb, running your hands down to the base and breaking or cutting each stem off gently. The season is short, no more than a month. Remove the forcing pot, and let the plant grow on until next spring. It will eventually get large and spread, so make sure you allow for expansion.

Having got your seakale into the kitchen, the BIG question, of course, is what does seakale taste like, and how do you cook it?

Flavourwise, to liken it to asparagus, which it often is, is an exaggeration. At best its flavour is mild and nutty, at worst, plain bland. It also needs to be picked fresh: 'The sooner it is dressed after it is cut the better,' says William Curtis in his pamphlet. He's right. Seakale is not a vegetable that stores well, losing those delicate nuances of sweetness and flavour that John Evelyn clearly appreciated so much. Old seakale becomes a bit bitter and cabbage-like. It's actually nicest of all, I think, eaten raw (choose young shoots), the same way you would celery. My favourite recipe remains a simple seakale and hazelnut salad.

To cook it, think asparagus and cook it briefly, being mindful of the general cab-bage-family rule, no more than 5 minutes or so (it probably won't need this long), unless you want cabbage undertones. Whatever you do, take no notice of recipes that tell you to boil it for 20 minutes: that's positively Victorian. I cook mine with the stalks lying down in a single layer in a large covered pan with minimum water, and give them a hard boil for 3–5 minutes until the knife pierces easily (exactly how long depends on the age and thickness of the stem: moral, pick it young).

59

Search out old recipes and they all dress seakale the same way, namely boiled white sauce or cream. Or melted butter and hollandaise sauce, both of which are delicious. It's perfect dunked into soft-boiled eggs (real eggs also come into their own in spring-time); and is very tasty with finely grated Parmesan for a change.

And the fact that our 'see-keele' is not as much a gourmet eating experience as one would hope doesn't in the least detract from the thrill of having it, or eating it as a genuine and therefore fleeting springtime treat. Its history alone is a true whet. As one of the rare examples of domesticated kitchen garden vegetables that remain resolutely seasonal, I look forward to it as much as the asparagus that follows – which I also eat for a brief hedonistic 6 weeks a year.

Hunting in the Medieval Royal Forests 1066–1307

Reva Berman Brown

During the 12th and 13th centuries, a significant feature of the English landscape was the large number of royal forests protected by a special forest law. A vital distinction existed between land subject to the forest law and land which lay outside the boundaries of the king's forests. The law of the forest was a Norman innovation originating in the reason, firstly, that hunting was an activity that William I and his successors were passionate about, and secondly, that there was a constant need for meat to feed the king and his court. Although, for centuries, both forest and waste had been gradually encroached upon by cultivation, when the Normans came, England was still a well-wooded land. Whole villages with their arable land and pasture lay within the boundaries of royal forests and were subject to the law devised to protect the king's beasts of the chase. Despite its unpopularity, forest law was instrumental in curbing the intrusion of the plough, and protected the beasts of the forest for longer than would otherwise have been the case.

The word 'forest' derives from medieval Latin *forestem* (*silvam*), which in turn comes from Latin *foris*, meaning 'outside' and meant a place forbidden or protected by a barrier – the word 'foreign' is derived from the same source and denoted the stranger outside the royal territory, on the other side of the frontiers.

The concept of royal forest was defined by Henry II's treasurer, Richard fitz Nigel (the son of Nigel, Bishop of Ely), in the *Dialogus de Scaccario*:

> The King's forest is the safe dwelling place of beasts, not of every sort, but of the sort that dwell in woodlands, not in any sort of place, but in certain places suitable for the purpose … in wooded counties where the lairs of the beasts are, and very rich feedings. …In the forests are the secret places of the Kings and their great delight. To them they go for hunting, having put off their cares, so that they may enjoy a little quiet. There, away from the continuous business and incessant turmoil of the court, they can for a little time breathe in the grace of natural liberty, where it is that those who commit offences there lie under the royal displeasure alone.

Throughout England were forests preserved for the enjoyment of the king. The king's favourite hunting places lay in the south, south-west, the west, and the midlands. The beasts protected by the forest law were the red deer, the fallow deer, the roe, and the wild boar – although by the middle of the 13th century, there were few boars left. In Edward III's reign, the roe deer ceased to be protected by the forest law, because, it was believed that it drove away the other deer. The impression the records give of the forests of this period is that the English kings were trying desperately to cling to a rapidly vanishing past, when the forests were alive with game for their pleasure.

It was mainly for the purpose of protecting these cherished animals that the king assumed the right of allowing certain of his subjects the privilege of hunting other wild animals regarded as harmful to the beasts of the chase. The animals which were the subject of such grants were the fox, the wolf, the hare, the coney, the cat, sometimes the badger, and even the squirrel. The earliest grants of hunting rights of this nature do not specify the animals to be hunted, but merely state that the king is granting rights of warren. For his own reasons, the king was generous in his creation of warrens. He was much less willing to allow a subject to have a private forest, although grants by successive kings placed considerable stretches of country under the control of individual magnates as private forests. These were called chases.

To the people who lived within a chase, there can have seemed little difference in the severity of the rules which governed their contact with the country around them and the beasts that lived in it. The foresters who looked after a chase were responsible to a subject, not to the king, and the king's forest justices did not as a rule enter a chase to hear forest pleas. But when King John granted part of the forest of Huntingdonshire to Geoffrey fitz Peter, Earl of Essex, he promised that the local forest court should still take care of the offences against the forest for that part which he had given to Geoffrey and that Geoffrey should have the profits arising from it. In the north particularly, there were many woods put 'in defence' by their owners – the first step towards the assumption of full hunting rights and the exclusion of others from them.

The law of the forest was directed to the single end of protecting the wild beasts so that they might be found in abundance for the king's hunting. Any action whereby the beasts of the forest were harmed brought upon the perpetrator the king's displeasure. In a small country like England, deer would have become extinct within a few generations if hunting had been unrestricted. The breaking up of woodland, the making of assarts, would have accelerated the process of destruction, as indeed it did, despite efforts to regulate it. As Richard fitz Nigel stated, assarts resulted from the 'cutting down of forest, woods, and thickets suitable for feeding animals, ploughing the soil and cultivating it. ...If woods are so severely cut that a man standing on the half-buried stump of an oak or other tree can see five other trees cut down about him, that is regarded as waste. Such an offence, even in a man's own woods, is regarded as so serious that even those men who are quit of taxation because they sit at the king's exchequer must pay a money penalty all the heavier for their position.'

The private woods – 'a man's own woods' – referred to in this passage are those which lie within a royal forest, not those in a chase or in country outside forest law. In 1193, a searching forest-eyre was held, for Richard I was short of money for his

French war, and ten Berkshire villages were forced to pay for 'waste'. In each case, the amount charged was half a mark, and it was paid up in full.

The ultimate responsibility for administering the forest and preserving the law of the forest lay with the chief forester who, like his officials, was distrusted and disliked. Below the chief forester came the wardens, sometimes hereditary and sometimes appointed at the king's pleasure, responsible for the care of groups of woods. They often carried out their duties by deputy, but it was the wardens who were responsible for the actual administration of the forest. Below them were the verderers, generally four in each county, chosen in the shire court. They had no pay, but were freed from other unpaid local work, such as serving on juries. Their chief work was to attend the forest courts held every six weeks. These courts were called attachment courts, in which the offences against the forest were first of all dealt with. The ordinary work of the forest, the gamekeeping and all that went with it, was done by foresters, some riding and some walking, who sometimes had lads to help them.

For those who lived in or near the forests, there were many tempting delights – extra meat, though it had to be caught without the forester's knowledge, honey, acorns for pigs, dead wood for kindling, live wood for building. Those who lived out of the reach of the royal forests were free of the additional variety of offences and penalties that constrained forest dwellers.

It was not until the rebellion of the barons at the end of John's reign that any real concessions about the forests could be wrung from the King. The Charter of 1215 (Magna Carta) included certain general promises and, in 1217, the young King Henry III was forced by his Council to issue a long Forest Charter which dealt in some detail with the organization of the forests and provided remedies for the long-standing grievances which were most resented.

The Forest Charter clearly set out the courts and assemblies through which the business of the forest was to be done. It promised that the court assembly would be held as it was 'in the days of King Henry my grandfather and not otherwise', that is, once in every three years, conducted by twelve knights chosen for the purpose. The results of their enquiries were to be reported to the Justices of the Forest to be recorded in their rolls.

Of all the forest regulations perhaps the most hated was probably the ruling that dogs kept within the forest must be 'lawed'. The Forest Charter defined this as the cutting of three talons from the front foot. It declared that enquiry into dogs kept in the forest would be made only at these meetings held every three years, and 'by the view and witness of lawful men, that the owner of an unlawed dog shall pay three shillings, and that the lawing shall be done only in the places where it was done in Henry II's reign.'

The business of regulating the use of the woods in the forest was conducted in meetings known by the Old English name of swanimotes. The Forest Charter declared that only three should be held in the year – one a fortnight before Michaelmas, to arrange about the pasturing of pigs on the king's acorns, the second about St Martin's Day to collect the customary fees for the privilege, and the third about a fortnight before Midsummer, when the forest was closed for hunting because the beasts were supposed to be fawning.

In addition to these meetings, every six weeks throughout the year, the foresters and verderers met in the attachment court to review 'the attachments as well of the vert as the venison.' The 'vert' is the greenwood of the forest and the offences which could be committed against it were manifold. The cutting down of saplings, of branches, or of whole trees were all matters that were to be reported. Minor offences against the greenwood were dealt with by fine in this court and the perpetrators of serious offences were attached to appear before the Justices of the Forest. In other words, they were obliged to find pledges, who would vouch and ensure that they would appear when the court met.

Offences against the venison were the most serious of all forest offences, too serious for action on them to be taken in this attachment court. A forest beast found dead was dealt with in much the same way as a man found dead. A special inquest was held by the four neighbouring villages. The Forest Charter promised that

> in future no one shall lose life or limb for our venison. But if anyone shall be taken and convicted of stealing venison he shall redeem himself by a heavy payment, if he has that wherewith to do it. If he has nothing wherewith he can redeem himself, he shall lie in our prison for a year and a day. If after one year and one day, he can find sureties for good behaviour, he shall go out of our prison, but if he cannot, let him abjure our realm of England.

63

The new power of the Norman kings, exercized with equal force in every part of England, lay heavily on the countryside, and no aspect of their rule illustrates this more clearly than their assumption of tight control over the beasts of the forest and their hunting. There is no doubt that, even after the Conquest, men could hunt freely in wild country where the forest law did not run, and where royal grants of hunting rights to individuals did not limit ancient customs. But that area was constantly decreasing. Royal proclamation could put any stretch of countryside under forest law and, until the end of Henry II's reign, the royal forests were constantly expanding. When the growth of royal forests was checked, the hunting rights of barons still grew.

Although Richard I inherited the family passion for hunting, because he needed funds for his foreign campaigns, he was prepared to begin the practice of selling immunity from forest law to those of his subjects who were ready to pay enough for it. In the first year of his reign, 1190, the knights of Surrey offered him 200 marks that, 'they might be quit of all things that belong to the forest from the water of Wey to Kent, and from the street of Guildford southwards as far as Surrey stretches.' A large area of the county was thus freed from forest law. King John was offered large sums of money by the men of Essex, Surrey, Cornwall and Devon for the disafforestation of their shires.

Despite this extensive disafforestation in the reigns of Richard I and John, the Forest Charter promised further concessions. Afforestations made by Henry II were to be viewed by honest and lawful men, and only the king's own demesne woods were to be retained. Nevertheless, the forests; the law of the forests and the behaviour of forest officials remained standing grievances. The boundaries fixed by Henry III were a constant source of complaint and in 1277, and again in 1297, Edward I ordered fresh perambulations to be made. The honest and lawful men who made them were naturally more interested in disafforestation rather than in the preservation of the king's rights. The King's political difficulties, the French and the Scottish wars, forced him to agree in the Parliament held at Lincoln in 1300 to disafforestations, which he tried in vain to reverse.

Now that the forest law has long been forgotten, it requires imagination to comprehend the bitter feelings of resentment it roused in the most vocal classes of the community, men who owned woods which they could not freely hunt. It seems probable that the common people were less resentful of it. Everyone hated restrictions on hunting for food, for they seemed to rest on no moral basis. No one felt any guilt at poaching the king's deer any more than the Victorian villager at poaching the squire's pheasants. The surviving records of forest proceedings are full of poaching stories, and they often hint at the element of excitement and bravado felt by the poacher.

Certainly the men who lived near the forest found entertainment and profit in encouraging the king's deer to leave the protected area, for forest beasts found outside the forest could be freely hunted. It was the duty of the foresters to see that they did not stray and, if they did, to drive them back unharmed.

The forest proceedings show that all classes hunted in the forests despite the law. The Charter allowed the magnates of the land, 'archbishops, bishops and barons', as they passed through the forests to take one or two beasts by the view of the foresters if they were about. If they were not about, the hunters were to blow their horns so that they might not seem to be taking the beasts by stealth. All animals thus taken were reported so that the king's generosity was not abused. The king's own visits to the forest when 'he took beasts at his pleasure' were also reported. Ecclesiastical persons from archbishops down to unbeneficed chaplains hunted with zest. This delight in hunting united all classes below the aristocracy in a common dislike of the forest official. 'I'd rather go to my plough than serve in such an office,' a household officer of a Northamptonshire country gentleman is reported to have told a verderer in 1251. People were unwilling to give poachers away to the foresters. Sometimes this friendliness went even further than a refusal to answer questions.

The hatred felt by the countryside against the foresters was not caused merely by the check they kept on hunting for food. Many of the clauses of the Forest Charter were aimed at restricting the oppressions of the foresters. They were forbidden to hold 'scot ales', that is to brew ale, and force men who lived in the forest to come to buy and drink it, generally when they came to make payments to the forester either in kind or money. Nevertheless, throughout this period, unless foresters were definitely appointed as 'foresters in fee', which gave them certain rights and profits and enabled them to 'live at the expense of the lord King', they still preyed on the forest dwellers. Foresters in fee, who paid the king a rent for their charge, had certain rights in the taking of what was called 'cheminage', that is, toll, or payment for freedom to cut wood along roads within the forest. The Forest Charter sets out the rules which should guide foresters in making the charge:

> It is to be taken only at places where it has been taken from old time, and only from merchants who enter the forest by licence to buy wood or charcoal for sale elsewhere. Each cart shall be paid for at the rate of two pence a half year and each pack horse at the rate of a half penny a half year. Those who carry the wood on their back, although they get their living by selling it, shall pay nothing.

The English kings, by their forest law, were trying to preserve something that was bound to pass away. The forests were bound to yield to the encroachments of the farmer. Every English forest, even those wild areas such as the High Peak or the fells of Cumberland, had long before the beginning of this period been penetrated by men desiring land to plough and live by. But the shape of forest settlements was different from that of the villages in open country where for centuries the interest of the village had been centred on its arable fields. The windswept open fields and the close-set villages of the long-cleared and settled parts of England contrasted sharply with the scattered hamlets and farms of forest country. As time passed and the plough conquered the forest, many forest hamlets themselves grew into villages, but they rarely achieved a village street with the farm houses and yards lying cheek by jowl with one another. Even today, signs of the royal forests of Anglo-Norman England are present in a countryside of isolated farms, with patches of woodland here and there, and forest trees surviving in midfield or hedgerow.

The countryside was never static. Increasing population meant that an increasing area of land of necessity came under the plough. The king accepted the fact that encroachments must be made on his forests, but expected to receive a rent from the lands so ploughed up. One of the duties of the chief forester was to license assarts, that is to make a financial bargain on the king's behalf with those who wished to plough up forest land.

It was not only the king's forests that were being eaten into by the plough. Every village had, in addition to its arable fields, waste or common land where the village beasts could be pastured. Some of this common land was woodland, some, rough pasture as yet unploughed. Rights of common were as fertile a cause of quarrels in the villages of 13th-century England as they were of complaints when the open arable fields were enclosed in the 16th, 17th, or 18th centuries. All who had any arable land enjoyed rights of common on the village waste. These common rights made it very difficult for the acreage of ploughland in a village to be increased, since any individual commoner could bring an action and win it against the man who ploughed up the village waste. The necessity of increasing the acreage to feed a growing population meant that in 1236 the king's council declared as part of the Statute of Merton that the lord of a village could enclose waste land provided he left enough common land to provide pasture for those whose right it was. Before the Statute of Merton, the man who desired to 'plough up common land' was well advised to get the consent of all the commoners if he wished to avoid litigation in which he would probably be the losing side.

The Statute of Merton allowed the lord the right of ploughing up the common provided he left enough pasture for his own tenants. It did not consider the situation which arose when others besides the lord's own men had pasture rights. But in the Statute of Westminster of 1285, Edward I gave the lord the right of enclosing the common against others as well.

And finally, a short comment on the nutritional outcome of hunting in the royal forests. In addition to the joy provided by hunting, the products of the activity provided a great deal to the king's household – food, clothing, and tools and ornaments which could be fashioned from bone or antler. Tradition has it that game animals are not eaten on the same day as they are killed. Because of the chase, the animal will have secreted large quantities of lactic acid to nourish its muscles. This is reconstituted in the muscles as uric acid, a nitrogenous waste product. When the venison has been hung, most of these substances, though not all, evaporate, decreasing any risk of poisoning the consumer. Smaller game, and birds such as quails, partridge, wild duck or teal can be eaten at once, though woodcock, snipe, plover and pheasant should be hung in a cool place for one or two days and protected from flies before preparation. Hanging game has the advantage of tenderizing a wild meat which has none of the softness and fat of farmed meat – a fat game animal is a sick animal, and should not be eaten. Meats which might be tough, like that of the hare or wild boar, or large animals like red, roe or fallow deer were marinaded in wine and aromatic herbs to tenderize them. Cooking methods included roasting, boiling, and stewing and baking in pies.

Bibliography

Foster, C. W. (ed.), *Registrum Antiquissimum of Lincoln Cathedral*, Vol. I.

Toussaint-Samat, Maguelonne, *The History of Food*, translated by Anthea Bell (Oxford: Blackwell, 1994).

Pipe Rolls Henry I, Henry II, and Richard (London: Pipe Roll Society, London), but 31 Henry I, 2-5 Henry II, and 1 Richard I (London: Record Commission).

Plucknett, T. F. T., *The Legislation of Edward I* (Oxford: Oxford University Press, 1949).

Richard Fitz Nigel, *Dialogus de Scaccario*, in Charles Johnson (editor and translator) *The Course of the Exchequer* (London: Nelson's Medieval Classics,1950), pp. 59-60.

Stenton, Doris Mary, *English Society in the Early Middle Ages (1066-1307)* (Harmondsworth, Middx: Penguin Books, 1959).

Turner, G. J. (ed.), *Select Pleas of the Forest*, Selden Society, Vol. xiii. (1901).

The Hunting and Gathering of Wild Foods: What's the Point? An Historical Survey

Susan Campbell

Human beings like their food to be flavoursome, tender, sweet, and juicy, and they have been using the crafts of husbandry, the skills of technology and the art of cookery to enhance these qualities for thousands of years. Moreover, most 21st-century human beings, in our more affluent societies, like the procurement of their food to be swift and simple; ideally they will make a quick dash in the car to the nearest supermarket, get what they want with as little delay as possible, then dash home again, all the time staying well-coiffed, clean and tidily dressed – no fuss, no muss. Most of us like the preparation of our food to be swift and simple, too; some even prefer a meal to be ready without further ado, without using pots or pans, and eaten Roman-style, in the fingers, reclining on a couch, *sans* tables, crockery or cutlery.

None of this applies to the hunting and gathering of wild food, much of which, so far from being flavoursome, tender, sweet and juicy, is actually very nasty: tasteless and insipid, tough and/or stringy, sour and bitter, dry and mouth-puckering. The fact that it is wild, that is, growing or living as nature intended, means that it is 'unimproved'. It has had no human assistance, indeed its very resilience means that it thrives without it; it is therefore ostensibly 'free' for the taking, legal restrictions permitting. But finding it it means choosing the right season, or time of day; it might then take many hours to track down and, once found, many more hours to trap, shoot, catch, pluck or gather enough for a decent meal. It is quite likely, too, to be found in hostile habitats; on rocky mountains, in boggy marshes, in impenetrable woodland, on windswept moors or in overgrown, prickly thickets. On reaching home the hunter-gatherer may well be ragged, scratched, foot- and back-sore, covered in stains and insect bites, muddy, frozen stiff, soaked to the skin, or burnt scarlet by wind and sun. If he or she has been hunting with horse and hound they risk broken bones as well. If they have had a successful expedition, their trophies will have to be sorted at once: graded, gutted, skinned, trussed, scaled, hung, cleaned, hulled, shelled and made ready in a score of ways for cooking and eating. It is even possible, after hours of searching, to end the day with an empty basket.

So what's the point of wild food? Why bother to go out and collect it, especially today, when provisions are so easy to come by? The argument that wild food is free will scarcely wash, when the cost of getting it and preparing it to eat is calculated in terms of energy and time; nor have I yet met anyone who could convince me that modern man could subsist on wild food alone, legally or illegally, the year round, in a northern climate.

As it happens, it looks as if the questions of 'What's the point?' and 'Why bother?' have been asked only relatively recently. We presume that it is not a question that was asked by the earliest hunters and gatherers, those shaggy ancestors of ours who, clad in the skins of animals that they had themselves killed and eaten, scampered about in a boundless landscape, the men doing anything that needed killing – the hunting and fishing – the women and children carrying out the more peaceable gathering of wild berries, roots, seeds and nuts. Weapons and cooking methods were rudimentary and their way of life was nomadic, since once the resources of one spot were exhausted, it was time to move on to the next.

The point of their hunting and gathering is clear: it was survival, but for the Greeks and Romans it was seen as a pleasurable aspect of the Golden Age of legend, and for the Renaissance poets it was something that happened before the expulsion from Eden, in an age of innocence in which 'progress' has no place; as Shakespeare's madrigal has it:

> Who doth ambition shun
> And loves to live i' the sun,
> Seeking the food he eats
> And pleased with what he gets -
> Come hither, come hither, come hither!
> Here shall he see
> No enemy
> But winter and rough weather![1]

Winter and rough weather were actually two of the reasons that drove our shaggy ancestors to look for a less uncertain and more predictable method of staying alive. They had also discovered that the larger the group, the more efficient the hunting, but the drawback here was that larger territories were required. A better solution, the one seen by anthropologists as the beginnings of civilization, was for human beings to find a fertile spot and stay put, growing in it their own food and farming their own animals. The earliest apples, cabbages, cattle and pigs were all raised from plants and animals that people already knew well from the wild. They were selected for the most suitable characteristics regarding situation, nourishment and domestication – size, sweetness and tenderness in edible plants; docility, fatness and fertility in animals. But wild food still had a point, as a supplement to what could be farmed.

The domestication and improvement of plants and animals is a process aided not only by careful preparation of the soil, and generous feeding and watering, but also by judicious cross-fertilizing and breeding, as well as taking advantage of accidental, fortuitous mutations. Most commentators would agree that this is a benign activity;

Edward Hyams, a noted 20th-century strawberry-breeder and grower and author, writing at the height of the last war, hoped that, come Judgement Day,

> attention will be paid not to philosophers and scientists, priests, statesmen and soldiers and other such noisy and uneasy creatures, but to a certain quiet and laborious kind of men called gardeners. And if this order of men and women be bidden to speak up, it is to be hoped that they will overcome their customary and decent modesty and say: *we left the fruits of the earth finer than we found them.*[2]

As it happens, the strawberry provides a good example of how wild plants supply the building blocks for cultivated plants: several varieties of this wild, north-European woodland fruit, delicious enough to be eaten as it is but ripening at different seasons, at different altitudes, and different in flavour, were taken into gardens in the 14th century to extend the fruiting season and to suit different soils. The introduction, from the Americas in the 17th century, of two larger and better coloured, though not so well-flavoured Virginian and Chilean varieties led eventually, via a chance mutant or unexplained hybrid, to our large, juicy modern varieties of the cultivated strawberry.

Wild varieties are still looked for and used in plant breeding, when virtues in a cultivated plant are lacking, such as good flavour, good keeping qualities, an early, late or long fruiting season and immunity to disease. And yet the poets will have it that man cannot improve on nature – 'Lilies that fester smell far worse than weeds' (Shakespeare, *The Life without Passion*) – and that only man is vile:

> To her fair works did Nature link
> The human soul that through me ran;
> And much it grieved my heart to think
> What Man has made of Man.[3]

This mistrust of progressive man's ability to manage neither his own nor nature's resources, especially in times of war, natural disaster, depression, famine and disease, is a thread that runs throughout this paper. So too is the contrast between the gathering wild food for necessity, as a means of survival, and gathering, or hunting it, for pleasure. Historian Dorothy Hartley's description of famine at the time of the Black Death highlights how farming can slither into failure, and the unreliability of wild food when starvation looms:

> To realise how desperate was the famine you must know the seasons as the starving peasants knew them – close and vital knowledge. Autumn meant the end of all the green food from woods and commons, the last wild fruit was finished, and the corn had been gathered ... The geese and hens had eaten the fallen grain and been eaten in turn, and now the pigs were killed off for

70

winter, one by one. Winter came, and there were salt and dried meats, and some parsnips. After a good harvest these lasted well enough, but as the winter dragged out, the last of the fresh meat went: only the few beasts necessary for breeding in the spring remained… When necessity compelled the poor to eat those beasts, famine came since there was no possibility of fetching supplies from elsewhere. … now the shortage of labour ties men to their own ground, and summer sees them still there and still hungry. Autumn brings no extra food. Lacking plough beasts, no fields are tilled. So comes the terrible time when berries are gathered for food and wild roots of pig-nut and acorn are ground to make a miserable ash cake. Fish from the rivers, wild birds killed with sling stones, snakes, shellfish, braxy mutton – anything is food that will fill the belly. Then illness, and the desperate eating of the very last beast they kept for breeding! After that, no hope ahead, no future animals, no grain for seed – all gone.'[4]

It was the Crusades that had depleted the labour force on the land and, ironically, it was hunting that acted, as it has done since hunting began, as a preparation for those wars. To hunt successfully, human beings need to be warrior-like, that is, fit, strong, brave, good at horsemanship and skilful with weapons. Besides the development of lethal weapons, hunting has brought about the breeding and training of speedy, hardy horses and hounds, social rules as to behaviour on the hunting field, sociability in the sharing out of the kill and laws for the conservation of game. It has also shaped our landscape with its coverts, chases, rivers, decoy ponds, banks and hedges, and has brought about the sports of steeplechasing and racing. Skill at hunting was, from the earliest times, seen as a noble attribute; according to Rousseau, 'our rise from animality began … largely in the dietary shift towards meat … requiring the hunting of wild animals for food. … In addition hunting rewarded and selected for new virtues: moral virtues such as endurance, patience, tenacity, and boldness; intellectual virtues such as attentiveness, perspicacity, and cunning.'[5] It has inspired much fine music, sculpture and painting. But there are baser instincts at work as well; the urge to hunt is atavistic; the chase is thrilling, the risk and eventual kill is erotically charged and, as readers of Anthony Trollope will know, it is frequently used as a metaphor for courtship; it features in over twenty of his novels: '… too many no doubt, – but I have always felt myself deprived of a legitimate joy when the nature of the tale has not allowed me a hunting chapter.'[6] I often wonder what Trollope's reaction would be, were he to know that in 2004 his 'legitimate joy' in hunting was being threatened by a House of Commons which, in his day, would not even be sitting during the hunting season.

Part of the trouble with hunting is that it is seen by its opponents as an élitist, cruel sport and it is true that the nobility has always regarded hunting, fishing and shooting (on the whole) and the eating of venison, salmon and grouse (certainly), as an essential component of their way of life. In 1869 Trollope, challenged to defend hunting, held that it was God's will that animals, and man, should hunt each other, that it brought together all classes of society and encouraged the virtues of courage and persistence,[7] but game laws, besides allowing for a 'close season' to allow both game and vermin such as foxes to breed, also exclude participants who cannot pay for hunt subscriptions, permits or licence fees. Poachers were severely punished for taking something nourishing for the pot for free. Even so, little deterred them from trying their luck, partly I think because both poachers and licensed hunters are driven by the same primitive urges. The poacher may be driven more by hunger and financial gain than the legitimate hunter, who is seeking pure fun, but once again we can add the twin arguments of necessity and pleasure to 'the point' of foraging for wild food.

Financial gain might be seen as an important reason for seeking out exceptionally delicious wild foods and until very recently, as far as wild plants and seafood were concerned, the inhabitants of the locality in which they were found have had the freedom to make what profit they could from them, as long as they foraged on common land, or had the landowners' permission. Edward Hyams describes the gathering of wild strawberries in the US, 'as an article of commerce by the indigent and as a form of pleasure by the more fortunate natives.'[8]

To America's delicious wild strawberries one might add this country's bilberries, wild asparagus, sea kale, marsh samphire, laver bread, shrimps, cockles, field mushrooms and wild edible fungi. For centuries village communities have collected these commercially valuable wild foods, especially on beaches where sea kale grew. They heaped shingle over the crowns in winter, in order to blanch the stems as they pushed upwards in spring. When the tips showed through at the top of the heap they would gently remove the shingle and harvest the stems, taking these seasonal delicacies to market, where they would fetch a good price. The understanding was that the shingle mounds must not be disturbed while the sea kale was sprouting, but today on my local Hampshire beaches the practice is almost forgotten save by just one man, and his shingle mounds merely form targets for the local youths to kick at and destroy. This is just one example of a local custom being lost, and with it the 'point' of one of the most delicious of wild foods. However, sea kale can be grown in gardens; the same cannot be said of wild fungi, the recent gathering of which, in the New Forest at least, has led both to hostile behaviour and legislation.

As field naturalist W. P. K. Findlay writes in *Wayside and Woodland Fungi*, 'For some reason the English have always been suspicious of eating any fungi other than the common mushroom, but during the Second World War, when appetizing foods were scarce, many English people learnt with interest from Poles and other European immigrants that many toadstools are not only edible but even delicious.'[9] It strikes me that a wisp of suspicion still lurks over that particular sentence, and I confess that my own reason for buying this book in the first place, back in 1967, was the same as its author's in writing it, for 59 of the colour illustrations in it are by Beatrix Potter.

Our native caution is echoed five years later, in Richard Mabey's introductory words to his chapter on fungi: 'The thought of wild fungi raises a shudder in most people'.[10] Mabey's book has been described (by Peter Dunn in the *Observer*, 25 August 1996) as the seminal work on 'back to nature eating', but it was a series of television programmes ten years later, in the 1980s, and the consequent appearance of wild fungi upon the menus of every classy restaurant in the land, that suddenly brought hordes of fungi collectors into our native woods and commons. The shudders raised then were not of disgust for fungi, but of mercenary excitement, for a huge amount of money could be made by selling them to restaurants back in the metropolis. The point of gathering wild fungi had been, up till then, for the eccentric, solitary few that did it, not only the pleasure of cooking and eating them, but the enjoyment of their beauty and the places they best liked growing in; there were mysteries too, attached to how they came and went – some years prolific, other years barren – or how they would grow without fail in some places at exactly the same season, or turn up in a new spot quite unexpectedly. My patch was the New Forest, a place I live in and know well.

The commercial value of wild fungi ruined all that. As the season approached, people with large bags and baskets came by car from miles away; by mid-morning most of the edible fungi in our favourite haunts had been picked by 'outsiders', whisked up to London and sold. Whilst no one minded local restaurateurs picking and cooking their own hauls, we hated strangers doing it; here again our atavistic nature manifested itself; it was as if invading tribesmen were raping and pillaging our territory. Tyres were slashed and insults exchanged. The Forestry Commission, who controls the commercial use of the forest, got indignant too; people were making money out of one of their resources, admittedly one on which they had hitherto put no value, but now ... . Enquiries into the legality of the commercial picking of wild fungi reveal that forest by-laws are still vague on the subject; unlike many wild plants (and animals), British fungi have no legal protection. However, the Forest Rangers can now confiscate the haul of anyone taking home more than 1.5 kilos, and if they can catch anyone selling them, they can prosecute.

With the exception of samphire, which recently appeared to be going through the same fashionable craze as fungi, with detrimental effect to future stocks, the collection of other British wild foods seems to be in decline. It seems to me that the lanes and hedgerows have far fewer blackberry-pickers in them than they did when I was younger. Are people worried by the effect of petrol fumes of modern traffic? Or is it just that no one makes jam, or blackberry crumble any more? And out on the beach I no longer encounter my contemporary, old Charley Philips, with his shrimping net; he says the weed the shrimps lived in has all gone, and with it the shrimps. Another contemporary, Maurice Thomas, says he still likes seeking winkles among the rocks, but his son can't be bothered, and I don't actually feel too happy about cockling any more, after reports about the quality of the local seawater.

Even at the beginning of the Industrial Revolution in the late 18th century, when whole families migrated from the country to the towns, the links between town and country were still close enough for those uprooted people to retain their foraging habits, and these persisted into the next century. However, at the same time, an interest in natural history, including flower-pressing and the collecting of shells, ferns, birds' eggs and wild food, appears to have been taken up by the middle classes, as pleasant, amusing and mildly instructive pastimes.

I have not so far referred to the value and equal importance of wild plants in medicine, since I wanted to limit the subject of this paper to food, but it must be mentioned here. Medicines, salves and tonics – home-made versions of which had, up till now, been made from wild plants by wise women and the housewife, were now increasingly available as patent, manufactured commodities. With no need now to make them at home, herbal remedies became another piece of forgotten folklore, adding to the 19th and 20th century idea of wild plants being 'quaint' or fun to collect.

Florence White (founder of the English Folk Cookery Association), writing in *Flowers as Food* in 1934, admits that her collection of recipes began as an 'enchanting' and 'intriguing' literary hobby 'which proved full of unexpected interests. It brought the country into a town house or flat.' She encouraged her readers to experiment 'by making small quantities of flower syrups, vinegars, herb-teas, wines, confectionery etc.'[11] The knowledge of useful plants in Great Britain that had, hitherto, been passed down from mother to child, had become so much a thing of the past that Florence was keen that this knowledge 'should form part of the education of every child if we are going to make use of wild as well as cultivated herbs, salad plants and flowers; otherwise we shall run the risk of poisoning ourselves and others.'[12]

True neediness was actually still around; the Irish potato famine was a not-so-distant memory, and she wrote this book during the depression of the early 1930s. Most of her recipes are taken from cookbooks of the better-off, but she has an eye on the poor as well:

> English people are not sufficiently practical nowadays. We talk a great deal about poverty and trade depression and unemployment, but we neglect the things at our very door which might ease our burdens in many ways.[13]

I doubt if elderflower fritters or a cowslip cream (recipe from Joseph Cooper, cook to Charles I) would have much eased the burdens of an unemployed miner's family, but we can take her point.

A similar, ladylike attitude is found nearly fifty years later, in countless magazine articles and cookery books. I shared both their authors' and their readers' delight in 'tasting new tastes', in making the search for wild foods into 'the excuse to walk through peaceful, unspoiled countryside...a world away from the bustle of shopping'; I too sensed 'triumphant achievement' when I got home with my finds. 'Weed cookery' is certainly inventive, 'tasty, fun and free', but it scarcely counts as famine food, depending, as it does, on lashings of butter, cream, Parmesan cheese, brandy, sugar and egg-whites to make it enjoyable. [14]

Richard Mabey's *Food for Free* first appeared in 1972. In contrast to the stream of books on country foods and remedies that followed its publication, *Food for Free*, with its emphasis on social and natural history, is blessedly forthright. For Mabey, conscious of its toughness and resilience, and its value in times of crisis or famine, 'wild food use was anything but a frivolous pastime'. His enthusiasm for the history of wild food is one reason for bothering to search it out; the kinship to hunting is another. He enjoys, 'the search, the gradually acquired wisdom about season and habitats, the satisfaction of having proved you can provide for yourself,' but he has other reasons too. 'It is the flavours and textures that will astonish most, ... and the realization of just to what extent the cultivation and mass production of food have muted our taste experiences.' He also expresses the hope that his book 'helps deepen respect for the interdependence of all living things.'[15]

The first intimations of a concern for that interdependence had been published a decade earlier, in Rachel Carson's *Silent Spring*. Now, in the West at least, in an increasingly industrial and prosperous society, agriculture relied more and more on herbicides, pesticides and chemical fertilizers; cooking was becoming a hobby and convenience foods formed the staple diet. Cheap, nourishing meaty foods that often took hours to cook – the tougher cuts, offal, tripe, tails, feet and heads – were vanishing from the butchers' shops (the butchers were vanishing too, under a tide of supermarkets) and our humble, native, seasonal fruits and vegetables were being displaced by costly exotics from all over the world. Old varieties of fruits and vegetables were disappearing too, in obedience to EC regulations. Yann Lovelock published *The Vegetable Book* in the same year as *Food for Free*. His subject covers both wild and cultivated species from all over the world, but his message regarding 'the point' about wild plants is the same as Mabey's: we are in danger of losing knowledge about the very plants (and edible wild animals) that may one day make all the difference to our survival – the threat of nuclear war was another, very real concern in those days. He argues that,

> We are going to need all the knowledge we can find merely to survive: by encouraging self-sufficiency now, a greater respect for our hidden resources and less reliance upon a market whose guidance is steadily passing outside the control of the average individual, we can worry less about where our next meal is coming from ... and think more about where other people's meals are to come from.[16]

If Lovelock bemoaned the loss of the cheaper cuts of meat and offal in the '70s, those times seem now to have been a veritable age of innocence compared with the last thirty years, scourged as farming has been with the pestilence of salmonella, BSE and

75

foot-and-mouth. The sale of any meat connected to the spinal cord is now illegal and the buying of a chicken with its giblets in it, virtually impossible. Added to this we have confusing messages about intensively reared meat, farmed fish and the dangers of eating too much fat and sugar, and a rise in food allergies and food-related behavioural problems in a generation of young people who, deprived of cookery lessons both at home and in school, don't know what's best to eat, how to buy it or how to cook it – indeed, they are so divorced from the kitchen that raw materials are repugnant to them.

We are not starving, but the way many of us eat now does have an element of both social and aesthetic impoverishment. As Leon Kass points out:

> We face serious dangers from our increasingly utilitarian, functional, or 'economic' attitudes towards food. True, fast food, TV dinners, and eating on the run save time, meet our need for fuel, and provide instant gratification. But for these very reasons, they diminish opportunities for conversation, communion, and aesthetic discernment; they thus shortchange the other hungers of the soul. Disposable utensils and paper plates save labor at the price of refinement, and also symbolically deny memory and permanence their rightful places at the table. Meals eaten before the television set turn eating into feeding. Wolfing down food dishonours both the human effort to prepare it and the lives of those plants and animals sacrificed on our behalf. Not surprisingly, incivility, insensitivity, and ingratitude learned at the family table can infect all other aspects of one's life.[17]

Put another way, by the critic and essayist Jonathan Bate writing of Thomas Hardy:

> he values a world – for him vanishing, for us long vanished – in which people live in rhythm with nature. Presumably we value such a world because we are not entirely happy with our modernity, with speed, with noise. We sense that there is something wrong about our comfortable insulation against the rhythms of the seasons, something alienating about the perpetual mediation of nature through the instruments of culture, whether radio and canned food, which Hardy lived to see, or television and genetically modified crops, which he would have had grave difficulty in imagining.[18]

Like Trollope, Hardy would have found our present government's ignorance of country life, and its effect both on farming and hunting, quite baffling too.

Meanwhile, for those of us who buy food to cook, things have come to a pretty pass; there is less food that we will eat than there is that we will not. The popularity of farmers' markets, farm shops and genuinely organic food is cheering, but 'food avoidance', based on our childrens' fads and their fear of unknown foods; health anxieties about products – fed, fertilized, sprayed, dosed, processed or otherwise – that might lead to cancer, obesity and heart disease; the shame of revealing social inferiority or superiority by what we eat, and ethical considerations based on the avoidance of cruelty to animals, genetically engineered crops, diminishing resources, non-organic foods or unfair trading practices, leaves us searching the supermarkets at least, for the very few foods that do not belong to any of those categories. (See Stephen Mennell, *All Manners of Food* [Oxford, Basil Blackwell, 1985], p. 294, for a historical commentary on food avoidance.)

I shall remember all my life, the first time I ate a freshly caught native brown trout, but no one can pretend that eating food found solely in the wild is the only way to live – indeed my heart warms to Roger Phillips when he says of a very common plant called silverweed:

> I have had no joy eating this plant. The roots are generally too small to be worthwhile, so how whole populations of Scottish islanders lived on them I cannot imagine.[19]

Nor can Hugh Fearnley-Whittingstall, one of our younger champions of the wild larder, persuade me that I would really enjoy eating his fritters of morels and 'wood shrimps' (alias for woodlice).

So where wild food is concerned, some of you might still be asking 'What's the point?' It is actually Hugh who gives the most apposite answer to the question:

> Where once we selected our food directly from the land around us, now we are divorced from the process of food production by several removes. The result is that most of us know little or nothing about it. We don't know how the vegetables we eat are fertilized, or genetically altered. We don't know what chemicals are sprayed on our cereal crops, or even our breakfast cereals. And until the deaths of thousands of cattle, and several humans, how many of us knew that we were feeding dead sheep to our cows, and dead chickens to their own children? [he is writing here before the outbreak of foot and mouth] …Remember that every single plant and animal that is used for food is descended from a wild ancestor – and many of those wild ancestors are alive and well in our fields, forests and hedgerows. An understanding of wild food is therefore, in part at least, an education about food history, and food safety. Best of all, it is not a force-fed education, but one that both taps and nourishes inquisitiveness, a delight in the natural world, and a sense of adventure.[20]

References

1. William Shakespeare, verse 2 of *Under the Greenwood Tree* (in Palgrave's *The Golden Treasury*).
2. Edward Hyams, *Strawberry Cultivation* (London: Faber & Faber, 1943), p. 13.
3. William Wordsworth, verse 2 of 'Written in early Spring' (in Palgrave's *The Golden Treasury*), enjoying the sight of springtime primroses, bursting buds and hopping birds.
4. Dorothy Hartley, *Food in England* (London: Macdonald and Jane's, 1954), p. 231.
5. Leon R. Kass, *The Hungry Soul* (New York: The Free Press, 1994), p. 119.
6. Anthony Trollope, *An Autobiography* (Blackwood, 1883), quoted in Victoria Glendinning, *Trollope* (London: Pimlico, 1993), p. 126.
7. Glendinning, p. 402
8. Hyams, p. 19
9. W. P. K. Findlay, *Wayside and Woodland Fungi* (London: Frederick Warne, 1967), p. 3.
10. Richard Mabey, *Food for Free* (London: Collins, 1972), p. 37.
11. Florence White, *Flowers as Food* (London: Jonathan Cape, 1934), p. 17.
12. White, p. 16
13. White, p. 18
14. Rosamund Richardson, *Hedgerow Cookery* (London: Penguin Books, 1980), pp. xiii-xiv.
15. Mabey, pp. 11-15.
16. Yann Lovelock, *The Vegetable Book*, (London: George Allen & Unwin, 1972), pp. 18-19.
17. Kass, p. 229
18. Jonathan Bate, *The Song of the Earth* (London: Picador, 2000), p. 3.
19. Roger Phillips, *Wild Food* (London: Pan Books,1983), p. 155.
20. Hugh Fearnley-Whittingstall, *A Cook on the Wild Side* (London: Boxtree, 1997), p. 4.

La Ceuillette: Foraging for Edible Wild Plants in Southern France

Caroline Conran

The two old girls knew about walking. Best of all they liked taking a shortcut by a fallow, wooded rise, where according to the season, they gathered a very good harvest, whether it was wild asparagus and the shoots of wild hops – '*lous pares et lous aoberus*' – or *petit gris* snails or small snails called *cagarolettes*, or blackberries or rose-hips, '*les gratte-culs*', for jelly – we had no raspberries or wild strawberries where we lived of course – or simply mixed, wild salad-leaves including '*Rouquette*'.

> *Fourmiguetto, souvenirs, contes et recettes du Languedoc*, Albin Marty.[1]

The resourceful ladies described by Albin Marty were enjoying what is called in French *la ceuillette* – a term which describes the gathering of quite a wide range of wild foods, including mushrooms, nuts, berries, wild fruits, roots, snails, '*herbettes*' and '*saladettes*' and other wild plants; the equivalent English word would be foraging.

It is often stated that recounting such idylls is romanticizing a rural way of life that was, in reality, a tough and unromantic existence. But there was more to *la chasse*, *la pêche* and *la ceuillette* (hunting, fishing and foraging) than a pretty notion of life in the country; these activities had real importance to country dwellers in a variety of ways.

In many parts of France, *la cueillette*, along with *la chasse*, and *la pêche*, has long been seen as something of a democratic right, an activity bound up with a feeling of continuity with the past, however tough and unromantic that past may really have been, and with a sense of identity.[2] Historically, foraging has also been seen as an economy, a resource in hard times, an essential local form of medicine, an extension to a limited repertoire of ingredients and, of course, a pleasure. Some plants are still widely sought after and sold commercially, and it is interesting to look at some traditional and current ways of eating them.

In earlier times this universal pastime provided, and to some extent still provides, a particular satisfaction for women, partly because in the Midi *la chasse*, pursued fanatically throughout the region all through the autumn and winter, was strictly for men. As James Lehning points out, 'certain kinds of activities themselves carried gender implications, cementing the meaning, in rural culture of the categories "man" and "woman".'[3] He continues, 'The activities that were reserved for men were those that ... could lay claim to being the attributes of a full, active person, while women were portrayed as inherently limited and passive'.[4]

Hunting is definitely in the category of a culturally manly activity passed on through the generations, as fathers teach the boys how to be men. The *ceuillette*, however, is an occupation which can be enjoyed by both men and women.

Collective Rights to Hunting and Gathering

Taking the Languedoc and the Médoc as the focus of enquiry, it has been interesting to find out why the French regard this activity as an important right.

Since Neolithic times the inhabitants of the Languedoc have known every aspect of their land intimately. The Stone Age inhabitants roamed freely, and included as the main elements of their subsistence diet the fruits of their hunting, fishing and gathering expeditions. Robert Guiraud points out that from earliest times *la chasse, la pêche, et la ceuillette* were important supplements to resources, as early man struggled to grow crops, initially mainly grains, then, from Roman times, mainly wheat and vines.[5]

When the Romans arrived, in order to increase productivity they introduced irrigation – the remains of a Roman aqueduct can still be found in the alluvial plain of La Redorte in the Minervois. By the 12th century, irrigated market gardening was flourishing to such an extent that there was a population explosion, but subsequent harvest failures began to cause food shortages which 'afflicted this superabundant population with redoubled frequency and fury.'[6] In the 13th century we know that in order to help them survive, enlightened feudal lords such as the Count Roger-Bernard III in the Ariège, stated explicitly that the people were allowed, without paying any fees, 'complete and unimpeded freedom to use the woods according to their needs... People were free to gather food in the forests as well: hazelnuts, chestnuts, strawberries, raspberries, blueberries, various roots, mushrooms, snails, honey etc.'[7] The rights granted were far more extensive than any liberties, usages and customs granted further north.

Out of a period of forty-six years (1302–48) Languedoc was 'afflicted by famine and dearth for a total of twenty.'[8] I will take up the thread of the diet endured in famine years later, but for present purposes I would like to note that by the late 14th century the populations of the villages were so reduced by plagues and famines that the wilderness started to encroach into the villages and settlements. Deer, wild boar and other predators were so abundant that whole crops could be ravaged between dawn and dusk and the villagers had to stand guard at night. Hunting, then, was essential to protect their livelihood.

So, in the mid-14th century, a certain Monsieur Lannoy, the Superintendent of Waters and Forests in the Montagne Noir, in the Haut Languedoc, decreed, 'Go into the forests, cut the trees, assart (break ground ready for sowing), burn charcoal, break the soil to plough, make ash, plaster, lime, graze your sheep and cattle, hunt stags, partridges, rabbits, boars and other wild animals, fish...to your heart's content.'[9] It was open season for hunting and gathering in the forests.

In addition, grazing land in the Languedoc was often common land and had been so for centuries. Here the traditional practices of *vaine pâture* (sending cattle or flocks onto private fallow land or friches) and *droit de parcours* (allowing livestock access to forests across private land) were followed, while as late as the 16th century, they were practising *assolement*, a biennial harvest system in which fields were cropped every other year and allowed to lie fallow for a year in between to recover their fertility. It was on fallow land, untainted by artificial fertilizers and herbicides, and also in the *garrigues*, that an enormous number of species of edible wild plants grew in spring, emerging between January and the end of April. The season was over when they started to flower and became tough and stringy, or when the grasses grew up to smother them. These plants formed an important and cost-free element of the late winter and spring diet, particularly when other foods were scarce.

Understandably, then, the peasants' view was 'that wastelands, woodlands and water were in some way at their disposal, and that they could take what they liked at the times they deemed best and in reasonable quantities.'[10] However, by the beginning of the 16th century, the *seigneurs*, who had become distant and contemptuous of the peasantry, had started to see it very differently.

They held the notion that their vast lands belonged exclusively to them, including the water, the woods and the *garrigues*, and there were endless disputes and lawsuits, almost invariably ending in favour of the *seigneurs*. In addition, they hunted over cultivated and fallow land (the important site of animal fodder and springtime wild harvest) with complete impunity. This eventually became the most frequent complaint in the peasants' list of grievances compiled before the Revolution and called the *Cahier de Doléances*, in which the people were consulted about reform proposals.

In August 1789, as the Revolution took hold, the Assembly, by now in a panic, abolished feudal dues and seigneurial rights including hunting rights. By the end of that month the Declaration of the Rights of Man and of the Citizen was proclaimed. In order to get rid of feudalism and yet still keep the peasants on board, they stopped short of pure capitalism and allowed the peasants to keep many of their feudal privileges.[11]

The peasants hung onto the collective land rights and usages (and a large section of the population, descendants of those peasants, still cling tenaciously to their old rights and practices.) For example there were successive waves of rural protest aimed at local élites and representatives when the ruling Bourbon regime passed a new forest code in 1827. They were supplanted by the Orléanais, but things did not improve.

By the mid-19th century, the state and private owners of forests were closing them off in defiance of ancient customary rights, as wood was now a viable commercial product and could be sold at high prices to the iron industry. There were huge protests and defiance, and male peasants disguised as women invaded the forests. In the

81

end troops were sent in and the local landowners were supported in their attempt to control forest resources. In 1844 hunting laws were tightened to protect wildlife endangered by the democratization of hunting after 1789, and in 1846 a revised Forest Code further restricted access, limiting customary usage rights such as stock grazing and foraging by the poor. This enraged the peasants and they responded by taking the law into their own hands, and recently sold-off commons were taken back into collective control. To restore order 48,000 troops were sent out, particularly to the densely forested Pyrenees, with the brief of reinforcing the new restrictions.

In the first half of 20th century the peasants were still subject to recurring bad times and were boiling with rage against the restrictions and what they saw as interference of the centralized government. The *vignerons* of the South had to be suppressed by troops in 1907.

In the 1930s, 'an ever-deepening decline of farm prices ... lasted so long and plunged so low that even the most diligent efforts could barely keep a family alive.'[12] The city-dwelling French watched with dread as the village communities dwindled, farms went broke, children left, bakers and butchers shut down. They felt that the peasants were the keepers of some core values, that France without a peasant population would be a nation of urban individualism just like anyone else. National identity lay with the country *grandmères* and new agricultural policies were formed, based on the importance of preserving their way of life at any cost. *Paysan* was transformed from a pejorative word denoting thick and backward to one with noble connotations. Deliberately, France hung on to its small farms, the old traditions and rural ways of life were given a new importance. At last the rural communities had 'pride and a voice.' [13]

But rural communities continued to feel put upon by the state. They wanted the state's help but not its interference. They wanted to be allowed to continue their traditional practices and they would fight anyone who tried to interfere.

Today, as Christian Coulon states, *la chasse, la pêche* and *la ceuillette* are practices that still mean 'much more than mere material pleasures or sport; they are the symbols of a certain form of autonomy and of freedom'.[14]

So it can be seen that over the centuries, the collective right of the rural population to hunt and forage was a hugely important part of traditional life in these communities. This feeling still holds true in many parts of France, and particularly so in the parts that shared and lost a common language, Oc.

Examples of Collective Hunting Activities

One of the threads that drew the villagers closer together was the fact that they ran their own affairs collectively as far as possible, settling them by a popular or traditional code of law. Traditionally, and from earliest times, hunting animals was always a collective activity. To show the importance and scale of hunting even today, it is interesting to look at wild boar hunting. In 1994 there were an estimated 200,000 wild boar in the Midi.[15] Focussing on a typical individual, in 2002 Monsieur Galy, a semi-retired wine worker from the small village of La Livinière in the Languedoc, hunted, shot, and prepared for the freezer, together with the other members of his syndicate, over 200 boars between September and December of that year, which was not considered unusual.

The shooting of migratory doves, *la chasse aux palombes*, is also a very important tradition in the south-west, while in the Médoc there is the *chasse de printemps à la tourterelle* – the shooting of turtle doves – and there have been some quite serious disturbances caused by new regulations, following attempts by conservationists to get this sport banned. The Médoquins feel their traditions are being attacked, and they accuse conservationists of fundamentalism and of trying to wage war on a unique culture, even of attacking people's humanity.

This is seen as a deep sociological and cultural divide, with the local sportsmen, under the banner of the CPNT (Chasse, Pêche, Nature et Tradition) fighting to save the autonomy of their region as it is manifested in their right to continue with their traditional ways of *la chasse*, *la pêche* and *la ceuillette*, against the incursions of globalization and modernization.[16]

Famine

One of the many reasons why these activities are so important is a trace memory of the bad times in the past, when wild food has been crucial to survival.

The urge to obtain some free nourishment was often very pressing over the centuries, when peasants were driven hard and rewarded very badly, and when any foodstuff obtained for nothing had a real value as a contribution to a poor household's domestic economy. There is still, for many, an intrinsic pleasure in obtaining food that costs nothing, while others make a bit of money by gathering certain wild foods and selling them in the markets, or, until recently, by the side of the road.

But at times there were more pressing reasons for foraging. In the many lean or famine years, crop failures meant that what were normally subsistence diets became inadequate. Famines came almost one year out of two in the 14th century and have continued intermittently until the 20th century. At those times the ability to go foraging and a knowledge of wild plants that could be gathered and eaten, was one way of ensuring survival for your family, as can be seen from these historical references. For example, in the 13th century: 'In the hidden recesses of the Montagne Noir, famine took dramatic forms; they attempted to survive eating anything and everything.'[17] In the year 1333, a year of notoriously bad harvests, the town chronicle of Montpellier describes 'young men eating raw herbs.'[18]

An eyewitness account by Pierre Puech in 1586 states: 'Because of the misery of the present time caused by the extreme famine in the Languedoc countryside, even in Grabian, considering all these weeks when the local people have been forced to survive the famine and driven to looking for the decaying remains of dead livestock

83

and to eat them with bread made from ferns, and looking for the shrivelled figs that had dried on the trees, which they ate, and thanks to them survived the winter.' [19] (The fern used for bread-making was the *Fougère Aigle*, *Pteridium aquilum*, which was rich enough in *amidon* to form a starchy component of bread. NB this plant is poisonous if eaten raw.)

Another report, recounted by Pierre Goubert, tells us how they made soup in the hard times during the 17th century: 'Into water from the well, river or the pond (fortunately boiled), they put whatever they could find in the way of herbs and root vegetables from the garden or the open fields.' (It is interesting to note that until quite recently soup was often eaten two or even three times a day.[20]) To make bread in times of famine, 'They took barley, rye or oats and mixed them with all sorts of things; half-germinated seeds, which they dug up, crushed beans, vetches, acorns taken from the pigs, cabbage stumps, fern roots, every kind of leaf, even the bark of trees.'[21]

An account by Jean-Henri Haguenot states, 'During the big freeze of 1709 the towns suffered badly. There was even worse misery in the countryside, where even the strongest inhabitants were obliged to eat nothing but wild plants, for the most part eaten without bread or oil.[22]

One great staple in hard times was chestnuts. An enquiry of 1872 reported of 46 departments, 'A single low room is often the only lodging of a whole family. People eat rye, potatoes, maize, chestnuts. There are people who recount the important fact that they have eaten meat several times in their life'.[23] An account by B. Milhaud, secretary to the field workers' trade union in 1904 states: 'These wretches, look at them. After gathering wild leeks or snails in the hedgerows, or on the vine slopes or in the thickets, which are murderous to the hands, the fieldworker conjures up a frugal meal. He sets the snails on some dry grass, covers them with brushwood, sets this on fire, and the meal is ready, to be eaten with wine or bread from his pouch.'[24]

As late as in 1943, during the German occupation, a doctor reported that people were losing weight, particularly the elderly. The food shortages meant that various provisions came to the fore again such as,

> a much more frequent use of edible wild plants and wild fruits formerly despised. … hunger made many citizens resolve, in spite of their incompe-tence, to go in for *ceuillettes* of fungi and wild edible plants from the fields.[25]

It can be seen from this quote that to some people *la ceuillette* had become a despised occupation; these were the town-dwellers, who had presumably conceived a sort of snobbery about eating such things, connecting them with loutish country customs or with poverty. But they paid dearly for this, at a time when a traditional knowledge of plants was essential, for the same doctor reports a fatal meal, when an ignorant mother served her family with a salad of hemlock, a plant reputed to be even more toxic in the Midi than it is further north.

Health

In better times many of the *herbettes* and *saladettes* were favoured because they were given special status, almost revered by some, as health-giving, often for very specific ailments or for what we now call a de-tox. It is significant that the main season for picking *herbettes* is late winter and early spring, when not much is growing in the potager other than perhaps some roots and cabbage. How desperately one would long for salad and greenery, after sluggish months of an everyday winter diet, which in the Languedoc was simple and restricted, particularly during the fast-days of Lent, which were strictly adhered to.

The addition, therefore, of health-giving wild greenery, rich in vitamins and minerals, provided a badly needed supplement to such a diet. For example dandelions stimulate the bloodstream, liver, digestive organs, kidneys and bladder. They also provide copper, iron and vitamins A and C.

Apart from the salad plants, many of the edible wild plants on the accompanying list have specific medicinal properties of their own, and were used to cure illnesses.

Until very recently the countryside had two kinds of medicine, the medicine of the official doctors, and the medicine of the local healers, who used simples, plants gathered in the countryside, as part of their repertoire of cures. In the 1880s the official medical establishment,

> still had not won a social victory over their rural rivals, the variety of secular and religious healers (and, according to doctors, witches) who proliferated in the countryside... Moreover until the new epidemiological understanding of the 1880s their uses of herbal and spiritual remedies in which patients collaborated were at least as effective as the cures of professional doctors.[26]

As recently as the mid-1990s, at least one local healer was operating in the Montagne Noir, and he was frequently observed picking wild plants to make cures for his patients. These healers are referred to rather reverently and it is interesting to note what Fernand Braudel reports from *Le Berger Dans le Pays d'Aude* by René Nelli, published in 1952:

> The shepherds, known as *aultres*, in the Béarnais, the *mountagnols* in the Commingeois, know how to talk to animals, to dogs and sheep, they can foretell the weather by the sky and heal by means of plants.[27]

When I interviewed the proprietor of Hôtel d'Alibert in Caunes-Minervois, he stated that people eat wild herbs in spring because they regard them as necessary for the health; others disagree. Benoit Huppé, schoolteacher in the same village, forages regularly in spring and considerably enjoys the flavours of these wild plants. He and his wife make salads and soup from the harvest of their *ceuillettes* from mid-winter until the end of April. He is a fund of knowledge and has a large library on the subject.

One volume, *Guide des plantes sauvages comestibles et toxiques* by François Couplan and Eva Styner, describes eighty poisonous plants and two hundred edible wild plants. But it is clear that there are a few key plants which are still sold on local markets and enjoyed widely enough to remain part of the current *repertoire de cuisine*.

Some Wild Plants in Current Use

Wild leeks, dandelions, *raiponce*, wild garlic, *arroucat* or false dandelion and wild asparagus appear on the markets of Carcassonne, Narbonne, Lézignan and Perpignan, and I have recorded them. It must be emphasized that the season lasts from December or January to April, although one authority cites dandelions as being edible between September and April.[28]

Ail faux-poireau, wild leeks (*Allium polyanthum*), can be bought in quantity, tied in bundles, and are also to be found in the verges of old tracks. Many vineyards today are cultivated organically and the leeks have returned and are free of pesticides and weed-killers. They look like miniature versions of a normal leek and are strong in flavour, tasting like an earthy form of the garden vegetable. They are eaten cooked, dressed with a strong vinaigrette, and with chopped hard-boiled eggs on top, or they can be made into a soup of great finesse. In the Médoc they were once eaten in quantities, particularly with lampreys. They were also wrapped in damp greaseproof paper and cooked in the embers of a fire.

Pissenlit, dandelion (*Taraxacum officinale*): large quantities of a small variety, forming tight rosettes, are readily available on the markets of the Languedoc; they are eaten as a salad on their own, perhaps with bacon or torn or cut fine in a salad of mixed leaves (*mesclun*). An interesting recipe for cooked dandelion salad described as a *recette diététique* comes from Prosper Montagné,[29] and turns out to be a simple form of soufflé.

Raiponce, creeping bellflower (*Campanula rapunculus*), sold on Carcassonne market, is eaten before it flowers, when it turns out to be a very tall, blue campanula, lovely enough to pick and put in a vase. The white, crisp root is prized and eaten raw like a sweet, crunchy radish, or cooked, while the leaves are eaten in a mixed salad.

Ail des ours, wild garlic or ramsons (*Allium ursinum*): the young leaves, before the plant flowers and the hot, garlic-mustard flavour becomes too strong, are sold on Olonzac market at the end of March. The stall-holder picks them in the Montagne Noir and recommends them, first wilted in butter, in omelettes; she also puts them in soup and in meat and vegetable stews.

Arroucat, beaked hawksbeard (*Crepis vesicaria*), comes as rosettes of incredibly bitter, dark green, deeply cut, toothed leaves that fold back on themselves when picked and washed, like a parasol. They are sold on Carcassonne, Olonzac and Narbonne markets. One stall-holder gathers them on the Montagne de la Clape, beside the

Mediterranean, south of Narbonne. They are eaten in salads both for pleasure and for health reasons. If you cut them up very finely they can give a robust flavour to a bland salad.

Asperge sauvage, wild asparagus (*Asparagus acutifolius*), which is sold in quantity in several markets and gathered by many foragers for themselves and their families, is decidedly a shade or two more bitter than cultivated asparagus and has a subtle flavour considered superior to the cultivated vegetable by local pickers. It is highly appreciated in an omelette, or boiled and eaten with vinaigrette, or cut in small pieces and fried with fried eggs. On Easter Monday, young and old like to eat a wild asparagus omelette in the open air.[30]

Mixed Saladettes and Herbettes

If you want to collect a salad of mixed greens, you can find an enormous variety of edible leaves in the vineyards, banks, verges and uncultivated ground of the Languedoc in spring. Bitter greens can be made palatable when eaten fresh and raw, by introducing a sweetener in the form of such things as tomatoes, cheese or eggs. Often olive oil or walnut oil, vinegar, garlic or onion are introduced to tame the heat. Some are also eaten cooked, with the bitterness blanched out, and some are made into soups with garlic, tomatoes, potatoes and perhaps a ham bone, or cooked as a dish of greens, with olive oil, pork fat or goose fat or used to flavour omelettes and other egg dishes.

In her little book *Petit traité romanesque de cuisine*, Marie Rouanet suggests, for a winter salad, the very young leaves of daisies, poppies, valerian, sow thistle, milk thistle; wild watercress; all kinds of dandelions which she says taste of nuts; strong wild rocket or fausse roquette, which in spring grows in such profusion in the vineyards that when it flowers it looks like snow; wild lettuce or blue lettuce – *Lactuca perennis* – with its blue flowers; common richardia, called in the Languedoc *couscounille*; wild purslane; field scabious known picturesquely as *broute lapin* or *oreille d'âne*; and all kinds of land cress, including lady's smock, *Cardamine pratensis*.

Dress the salad with a traditional vinaigrette, adding fried lardons and croûtons rubbed with garlic and fried in olive oil and perhaps a chopped hard-boiled egg. You can crush Roquefort into the dressing or add hot goat's cheese.

As far as cooking less well-known wild plants is concerned, expert forager Benoit Huppé recommends *soupe de couscounille*, which he and his wife like to eat every week in spring. I have found much mention of the eating of burdock and of bistort. Black briony shoots, are boiled and eaten, and waterdocks and other docks, patiences, are cooked like rhubarb.

Huppé also recommends eating the small snails, *cargolettes* that feed on the roadside fennel plants, which he says have a wonderful flavour.

I have also come across recipes in current local cookbooks for nettle soup made with potatoes and watercress, and for nettle purée served as a vegetable. M. Huppé mentions delicious liqueurs made with juniper berries, thyme flowers or mulberries. With hawthorn berries he makes a strong-flavoured jelly to eat with meat, and I have come across a local jelly made with arbutus fruits.

Some people eat certain thistles, particularly the handsome *Silybum marianum* or *chardon marie*, whose tender stems taste deliciously of artichoke, and whose roots can also be eaten like salsify. Another prized edible thistle is the *Carlina acanthifolia* with a flower which looks like the sun, which appears as a motif on hand-blocked provençal fabrics.

There is also a wild salsify which is by all accounts excellent as is the wild scorzenera or black salsify. The roots can be eaten boiled, and the young leaves are good in salads, while Boulestin recommends enjoying the young buds in an omelette. Unfortunately there are too many edible plants in the Languedoc and the Médoc to recount them all here, with their culinary uses and their medicinal properties. So I will just give a few brief hints and a table of some of the more usual edible plants.

Wash wild greens very well in several waters. Shake dry and store rolled in kitchen paper inside storage boxes, in the fridge.

If the *herbettes* are to be cooked, they can first be blanched two or three times, or, if very bitter, soaked in salted water for an hour or overnight.[31]

You can cut up the greens and fry them in olive oil with crumbled sausage or lardons of streaky bacon and thyme.

Alternatively boil them until tender and serve with olive oil, or use for a *farci* (a patty containing breadcrumbs, egg, garlic and sausage meat or ham),[32] or an omelette. In the Vercors, a speciality is little pasta parcels, made in sheets, poached in broth, called *ravioles* – not ravioli strayed over the border, but a French dish in their own right. Today they use parsley, but the traditional filling was wild greens.

The sometimes savage, hot and bitter flavours of wild salads are genuinely quite addictive in spring; I am not surprised to find they are popular, when I remember our taste for radishes, mustard, horseradish and rocket. *La ceuillette* can be recommended, then, to all who like both unusual food and an exhilarating walk in the country. It offers a feeling of following a path that man has instinctively trodden, a very basic urge that can give us profound satisfaction.

But to the inhabitants of the Languedoc and the Médoc and other parts of south-western France, as we have seen, there is more to *la ceuillette* than a culinary interest or a fascinating walk. This activity is inherited and handed down; it stems from earliest roots and is bound up with history and with survival. It has been continuous since antiquity, gaining more or less significance with changing conditions, and coming into the fore in very hard times. A knowledge of edible and toxic plants and the ability to forage has frequently meant the difference between health and sickness, even, at times, the difference between life and death.

To some of those living in what is described as *la France profonde*, foraging still provides not just an occupation, but a form of work providing a commodity to sell on the markets as a food or a tonic, or both. The considerable quantity of such vegetables as wild leeks, dandelions and wild asparagus sold, together with snails, lime-blossoms for tisanes, chestnuts and wild mushrooms etc., shows that a taste for collecting and eating wild foods remains alive. People of the region value *la ceuillette* as part of their local identity; along with fêtes, local legends, folk tales, sayings and songs, it helps to define them as people of their *terroir*, as opposed to their identity as Frenchmen. It is seen as a right, like air or water, a common activity, like hunting, that they wish to retain and will indeed fight for. It is a manifestation of their autonomy and the freedom to enjoy their pays and of their connection with the land and with their roots.

Bibliography

Bonnaure, André, *Petit précis de cuisine occitane* (Portet-sur-Garonne: Loubatières, 1999).

Bournérias, Marcel; Pomerol, Charles; Turquier, Yves, *La Mediterranée de Marseilles à Banyuls* (Paris: Delachaux et Niestlé, 1992).

Braudel, Fernand, *The Identity of France*, Vol. 2 (Glasgow: William Collins, 1990).

Burnie, David, *Wild Flowers of the Mediterranean* (London: Dorling Kindersley, 1995).

Cabanaud, Laurent, *La Chasse à sanglier* (France: Editions Sud-Ouest, 1994).

Clason, W. E, *Elsevier's Dictionary of Wild and Cultivated Plant Names* (Oxford: Elsevier, 1989).

Coulon, Christian, *Le Cuisinier médoquin* (Bordeaux: Editions Confluences, 2000).

Creber G and Wrobel M, *Elsevier's Dictionary of Plant Names* (Oxford: Elsevier, 1998).

Dubourdieu, Françoise; Mouly, Hubert; Moynier, Michel, *Fleurs d'ici* (Narbonne: Graphisud, 1997).

Gray, Patience, *Honey from a Weed* (London: Prospect Books, 1986).

Grey-Wilson, Christopher, *Fleurs sauvages* (Paris: Bordas, 1995).

Ladurie, Emmanuel Le Roy, *The Peasants of the Languedoc* (Chicago: University of Illinois Press, 1974).

Ladurie, Emmanuel Le Roy, *The French Peasantry 1450-1660* (Aldershot: Scolar Press, 1987).

Lehning, James R., *Peasant and French* (Cambridge: Cambridge University Press, 1995).

Mabey, Richard, *Food for Free* (London: Harper Collins, 2001).

McPhee, Peter, *A Social History of France 1789-1914* (London: Palgrave Macmillan, 2004).

Paxton, Robert O., *French Peasant Fascism, Henry Dorgère's Greenshirts and the Crises of French Agriculture 1929-39* (New York: Oxford University Press, 1997).

Phillips, Roger, *Wild Food* (London: Pan Macmillan, 1983).

Reyerson, Katherine and Drendel, John, editors, *Urban and Rural Communities in Medieval France, Provence and Languedoc, 1,000-1600* (Leiden: Brill, 1998).

Valeri, Renée, *Le Confit et son rôle dans l'alimentation traditionelle du sud-ouest de France* (Lund: LiberLaromedal, 1997).

Villefranque, Josette, *Imagerie des Corbières* (Portet-sur-Garonne: 1987).

Wolfert, Paula, *Mediterranean Grains and Greens* (New York: Harper Collins, 1998).

Wolff, Philippe, *Documents de l'histoire du Languedoc* (Privat: L'Université de France, 1967).

French Edible Wild Plants

Latin	*French*	*English*
Aegopodium podagraria	Herbe St.Gérard, Pied de bouc Herbe-au-goutteux	Ground elder
Allium ampeloprasum	Ail faux-poireau, Poireau d'été, Pouragane, Poireau sauvage	Wild leek
Allium ursinum	Ail des ours	Ramsons, Wild garlic
Amaranthus acutifolius	Amaranthe réfléchie	Pigweed
Anchusa italica	Buglosse bleue, Azurea, Langue de boeuf	Italian bugloss
Arctium lappa	Bardane, La patience	Burdock
Asparagus acutifolius	Asperge sauvage, Repunchus	Wild asparagus
Bellis perennis	Pâquerette	Daisy
Beta vulgaris	Bette, Bette sauvage	Wild spinach beet
Borago	La bourrache	Borage
Bryonia dioica, Tamus communis	Tamier commun, Herbe aux femmes battues, Herbe du diable, Vigne blanche	Black briony
Campanula rapunculoides	Raiponce, Le repounchu,	Creeping bellflower
Capsella bursa-pastoris	Bourse à Judas	Shepherd's purse
Cardamine pratensis	Cardamine des prés, Cresson des prés	Lady's Smock
Centranthus ruber	Lilas d'Espagne, Barbe de Jupiter	Red valerian
Cichorium intybus	Chicorée sauvage, Lacheta	Chicory
Crepis versicaria	Arroucat, Faux pissenlit	Beaked hawksbeard
Diplotaxis ericoides	Fausse-roquette	White wall rocket
Eruca versicaria	Roquette	Salad mustard, rocket
Foeniculum vulgare	Fenouil	Wild fennel
Humulus lupulus	Houblon	Hop
Knautia arvensis	Oreille d'âne, Broute lapin	Field scabious
Lactuca perennis,	Laitue vivace, Escarola	Blue lettuce
Lathyrus tuberosus	Gesse tubéreuse, Gland de terre, Châtaîgne de terre	Earthnut peas
Lavatera arborea	Mauve royale	Tree mallow
Leontodon autumnale	Liondent d'automne	Hawkbit
Lepidium latifolium or Cardaria draba	Passerage	Hoary pepperwort
Malva sylvestris	Mauve	Common mallow
Mentha aquatica	Menthe aquatique	Watermint
Mentha arvensis	Menthe des champs	Corn mint
Mentha piperata	Menthe poivrée	Peppermint
Mentha pulegium	Menthe puliot	Pennyroyal
Nasturtium officinale, Rorippa nasturtium aquaticum	Cresson de fontaine	Wild watercress
Origanum vulgare	Origan, Marjolaine sauvage	Wild marjoram
Ornithogalum umbellatum	Bela de jour, Penitent blanc, Ornithogale en ombelle	Star of Bethlehem, Bath asparagus
Papaver rhœas	Coquelicot, Pavot, Ponceau	Field poppy
Phyteuma – see Campanula rapunculoides		

Picridium vulgaris	Couscounille, La terra grapia, Picridie	Common richardia
Plantago lanceolata	Plantain lancéolé	Ribwort plantain
Polygonum bistorta	Bistorte	Bistort
Portulaca oleracea	Pourpier sauvage	Common purslane
Rosmarinus officinalis	Romarin	Rosemary
Rumex acetosa	Oseille des prés, Surette	Sorrel
Rumex acetosella	Oseille des brébis, Petite oseille	Sheep's sorrel
Rumex hydrolapathum	Patience des eaux	Great Waterdock
Salicornia europaea	Passe-pierre, Salicorne	Marsh samphire
Sanguisorba minor	Petite pimprenelle, Petite sanguisorbe	Salad burnet
Satureja Montana	Sarriette	Winter savory
Scorzonera hispanica	Scorsonère	Scorzonera
Silene vulgaris	Silène enflée	Bladder campion
Silybum marianum	Chardon marie	Milk thistle, holy thistle
Sonchus arvensis	Laiteron	Sow thistle

Latin	French	English
Sonchus oleraceus	Laiteron potager	Smooth sow thistle
Symphitum officinale	Consoude	Comfrey
Tamus communis	Herbe aux femmes battues, Herbe du diable, Vigne blanche, Tamier commun	Black Briony (shoots only, the berries are poisonous)
Taraxacum officinale	Pissenlit	Dandelion
Thymus serpilloides	Thym serpolet	Wild thyme
Thymus vulgaris	Farigoule, Frigoula, Thym	Thyme
Tragopogon porrifolius	Salsifis à feuilles de poireau	Salsify
Tragopogon pratensis	Salsifis	Salsify
Urtica pilulifera	Ortie à pillules	Roman nettle
Urtica dioica, v. pubescens	Grande ortie	Stinging nettle

91

Notes

1. Marty, p. 55.
2. Lehning, p. 113.
3. Lehning, p. 128.
4. Lehning, p. 128.
5. Guiraud, p. 15.
6. Ladurie, p. 12.
7. Reyerson and Drendel, p. 178.
8. Ladurie, p. 12.
9. Ibid.
10. Goubert, p. 173.
11. Lefebvre, p. 162.
12. Paxton, p. 1.
13. Paxton, p. 77.
14. Coulon, p. 77.
15. traditionally the area south of a line between Bordeaux and Valence, see Alphonse Daudet's *N. Roumestan*, published in the late 19th century.
16. Coulon, p. 78.

17. Guiraud, p. 178.
18. Reyerson and Drendel, p. 269.
19. Guiraud, pp. 178/9.
20. Goubert, p. 86.
21. Goubert, p. 93.
22. Goubert, p. 250.
23. McPhee, p. 214.
24. McPhee, p. 353.
25. McPhee, p. 363.
26. Lehning, p. 214.
27. Braudel, p. 307.
28. Narbonne Environnement, p. 329.
29. Montagné, p. 112.
30. Villefranque, p. 43.
31. Wolfert, p. 4.
32. Rouanet, p. 71.

Ginseng: Taming the Wild

Andrew Dalby

Introduction

We know the difference between gathering and farming. If you're a hunter-gatherer, you go and get it from wherever it is. If you're a farmer, you plant it and help it to grow, and then you harvest it and store it.

So if you live in a farming economy, your selection of foods will depend on what the farmers chose to keep and grow, what's ready for harvesting now, what has come ripe previously and has been stored until now.

Farmers are specialists. They cultivate a far smaller range of foods than hunter-gatherers eat. There are good reasons for this. Persuading things to grow where we want and in the quantities we want, and then storing them till needed, are labour-intensive activities, especially since each potential farmed species has its own peculiarities. You have to devote your energies to a smaller range of species, and you have to strike a balance between species that you can persuade to flourish and species that are necessary to make up an adequate food supply. If farmers keep on specializing they can benefit from economies of scale. They can clear land, devote it entirely to human food species, focus on the work needed to keep a limited range of species in production, develop a food surplus, and watch the population grow. It will grow massively, but it will be at greater risk of famine: hunger and malnutrition flourish when people depend on a small range of species, some of which may fail in some years. It will be subject to new sicknesses, because the range of species farmed is inadequate for health and because some species, minor in food value but crucial medicinally, are not brought into cultivation and may eventually be forgotten.

The process that I have been describing is the Neolithic Revolution, which has been spreading across the world for the last ten thousand years and is now just about working itself out.

If you live in a hunter-gatherer economy, your selection of foods will depend partly on what the hunters and gatherers happened to find and partly on what they went out looking for. It's not random. In a sense, the hunters and gatherers are farming the whole earth, or at least the bit of it in which each community lives. They, too, have to specialize. Anthropologists have put some effort recently into identifying how, why, and with what results, hunter-gatherers do specialize. They have to remember from year to year, and from place to place, what foods will be available; they have to notice what kind of landscapes favour this or that species, and what seasonal variations may produce a good supply or a poor supply; they have to notice how species interact. Having made these observations, they have to pick and choose; they have to specialize in whatever will best repay their efforts. If they don't do this, they also are at risk of malnutrition and famine, just as are the farmers.

Up to now, I've pretended that you live either in a hunter-gatherer economy or in a farming economy. I've been oversimplifying.

Firstly, hunter-gatherers may well exert some control on the natural world. They don't, in the usual sense, farm it, but few of them are wholly innocent of practices that we link to farming. For example, if wild goats or buffaloes make a regular journey from winter pasture to summer pasture – or if fish such as tunny make an annual migration – and people take advantage of their knowledge to build fences or nets, channel the migrant animals, kill as many as they like, and preserve the meat, that's already moving from hunting in the direction of farming. How close is it to farming when you take young animals from the wild, quails for example, and keep them on a farm till they are good and fat for food? How close is it to farming when you spot young plants in the wild, herbs in Crete for example, and move them to where you can conveniently tend and water them?

Secondly, even people in farming economies continue to use wild plants and game animals that they especially value. Some go on seeking them out themselves, but, eventually, nearly everyone will come to rely on those few specialists who retain the knowledge of wild natural resources. Typically, the species concerned contribute to human survival not so much in terms of general nutrition, more as occasional luxuries, and medicines, and what we would now call food supplements.

In some cases, hundreds or thousands of years after farming has been introduced, additional species that must have been gathered from the wild since the very earliest times have been newly brought into cultivation. Like the Neolithic Revolution itself, this second revolution – if you consider it globally – goes in parallel with population growth. Valued spices and herbs and other plant and animal products, gathered from the wild, may travel far across the world in trade for hundreds or thousands of years, and then at last, with population growth, the world supply becomes insufficient. Then attempts will be made to farm these additional species. Yes, of course, there is an alternative outcome. If farming is impracticable or is not introduced in time, the value of the wild supplies will simply go on rising. Every last collector will seek out every last wild specimen. When the last specimen has been collected and sold and consumed, one more species has become extinct.

Introducing ginseng

Enough generalization. I want to focus on one group of examples. Ginseng, with its relatives and its analogues, might for all I know be humanity's oldest food supplement. Demand for it has grown; the wild supply has been, and still is, threatened; some species have quite recently been taken into cultivation; there are challenging questions of identification, genuineness, medicinal value.

'Might be our oldest food supplement': that's a vague claim, and necessarily so,

94

because in most cases it hasn't yet become possible to identify the prehistoric use of wild plants such as ginseng. It is likely, however, that its use has been widespread and has lasted a long time.

We're talking about a genus of plants that Linnaeus in 1753 named *Panax*. Incidentally, the fact that he chose the name *Panax* shows that he was fully aware of the health value attributed by the Chinese to ginseng root. In ancient Greek *panax* had been a name given to several Mediterranean plants that were multi-purpose healing agents or panaceas (*panax* means 'cure-all' in Greek). Since Linnaeus hadn't employed the generic name *Panax* for any of those Mediterranean panaceas, the word was hanging around unused, and that would never do. He applied it, therefore, to the genus to which China's favourite panacea belonged.

The genus *Panax* is represented both in eastern Asia and in eastern and central North America: as it happens, in each continent there is one highly important medicinal plant species belonging to the genus. *Panax ginseng*, Asian ginseng or Korean ginseng, is native to Manchuria (northeastern China) and Korea. *Panax quinquefolius*, American ginseng, is native from Quebec and Manitoba southward to Florida and Louisiana. There are other species which I will mention later. These two species are very similar and their nutritional or medicinal active constituents are also very similar.

Panax ginseng is important traditionally in Chinese nutrition and medicine: its use can be traced back at least 1,400 years in this tradition, to fragmentary Chinese herbals from which quotations survive in the well-known compilation by Li Shizhen, *Bencao gangmu*. Around that date, ginseng was a trade and tribute import from Manchuria and Korea to China (see sources quoted in Schafer 1963, p. 190). Earlier source texts may possibly be found, but claims that Chinese use of ginseng goes back 3,000 years, 5,000 years, 7,000 years and 10,000 years – all these claims will be found in serious recent publications and on serious scientific websites – are entirely speculative. In Chinese nutrition and medicine ginseng is taken both as a culinary ingredient – I have given a couple of recipes – and as a medicine. It is used to treat ailments of the digestive and respiratory systems, nervous disorders and diabetes, to keep the elderly warm in winter, to increase energy and sexual performance, and to improve memory. Koreans are said to feed ginseng to race horses to improve their performance.

95

> **Bird's Nest with Ginseng** (recipe by Amy Beh). Ingredients: 50g bird's nest; 20g sliced ginseng (*pau som*); 100–125g rock sugar; 500ml water. Method: Soak bird's nest in water until soft. Pick out any foreign matter such as twigs and tiny feathers. Wash nest in several changes of water until it is spotlessly clean. Place all ingredients in a tureen and double-boil for two to two and a half hours in a slow cooker. Serve the delicacy warm. (From *The Star Online*)

Chicken stuffed with Rice and Ginseng (*Samgyetang*). *Samgyetang* is a time-honored recipe of the Koreans. It is so traditional and consumed so widely that many regard it as the second national dish (behind *Kim Chi*). Using one of Korea's most famous products, ginseng, to give a unique flavor as well as medicinal value to the filling of glutinous rice, dried red dates (jujubes) and chestnuts.

Ingredients: 1 chicken approx 1 kg OR 2 spring chicken of 500 g each; 100 g glutinous rice, soaked in warm water for 30 min. and drained; 2 pieces dried ginseng each approx 5 cm long; 6 pieces dried red dates (jujubes); 2 pieces dried chestnuts, soaked in water for 30 min, coarsely chopped or halved; 2 slices fresh ginger, thinly sliced; 2 cloves garlic, halved; 1 stalk scallion (spring onion), finely chopped; 1 teaspoon salt (or as required); liberal sprinkle of white pepper; *Kim Chi* for accompaniment (optional).

Method: Wash and clean inside of chicken and let it dry. Combine the glutinous rice, 4 dried red dates, chestnuts and ½ teaspoon of salt in a bowl and mix well. If using one large chicken, put all the rice mixture inside. Take care not to pack the chicken too tightly as mixture will swell during cooking. Close the cavity of the chicken by threading a skewer in and out of the flap several times. Choose a sauce large enough to hold the chicken and add water to just cover, then add pepper, 2 dried red dates, ginger slices, garlic and scallion and bring to a boil. Cover, lower heat and simmer gently for 30 minutes. Turn and cook till very tender with the flesh almost falling off the bones. This will take another 30–40 minutes for a large chicken. Before serving, half or quarter the chicken and return the chicken with its fillings to the soup, then serve in a bowl. Can be accompanied by a small bowl of *Kim chi*. (From *Asian Recipes Online*.)

Panax quinquefolius, American ginseng, was widely used in the traditional nutrition and medicine of many peoples of central and eastern North America, notably speakers of Iroquoian and Algonquian languages, but also many others. This use can be traced back 300 years – not more, because there are no records. The herbal database at the University of Michigan, citing Hamel and Chiltoskey 1975, Taylor 1940, Swanton 1928, Tantaquidgeon 1972, Speck 1917 and 1941, Herrick 1977, Smith 1923, 1928 and 1933, Chandler and others 1979, Sturtevant 1954, indicates that American ginseng was used by Cherokee, Creek, Delaware, Houma (Louisiana), Iroquois, Menomini, Meskwaki, Micmac, Mohegan, Ojibwa, Penobscot, Potawatomi and Seminole Indians. It was used variously against convulsions, colic, 'weakness of the womb', thrush, gonorrhoea, palsy, vertigo, skin wounds, earache, sore eyes, fever, shortness of breath, poor appetite, rheumatism, vomiting, cholera, poor blood and laziness; they were used as expectorant, stimulant and tonic, in aromatherapy, as part of a compound medicine for various serious illnesses, and generally as a last resort when all other medicines failed. Ginseng was included by the Menomini and Seminole in supply packs for hunters and warriors (Smith 1923; Sturtevant 1954). It was used by the Pawnee apparently as a male aphrodisiac (Gilmore 1919). By the Iroquois the dried root of ginseng was smoked for asthma, weakness and as a panacea.

Now it is a generally accepted fact that North America's indigenous populations result from a series of migrations – possibly three or more at different periods – from eastern Asia across what we now call the Bering Straits. One such migration must have taken place around 20,000 years ago. This raises two questions.

1. Did any of these migrants carry with them from Asia, and perpetuate in North America, knowledge of the use of ginseng? 2. Did any of them carry living ginseng roots and plant them in North America: i.e. did the North American species arise out of a small supply of the Asian species in 'cultivation'?

The tentative answer to both questions is no, because the areas where ginseng is found are such a long way apart. It's several thousand miles from Manchuria to Manitoba, and it has to be supposed that the migrants who eventually populated North America took hundreds or thousands of years to cover such a distance, forgetting en route anything that their ancestors may once have known about ginseng. But, in this context, any information that the Chinese, a culture with many trade links, actually imported ginseng much earlier than about 1,400 years ago would be very important. If ginseng roots were already traded from prehistoric and protohistoric Korea towards China, that would mean that their value was already marketable outside the area where they grew; in that case, they might also have been traded northeastwards to Siberian peoples. Whereas, if they didn't reach China any earlier than that, they are also most unlikely to have travelled far towards the Bering straits.

97

Assuming that there was no direct transmission of information about ginseng, why, then, were the two similar species of ginseng prized in Chinese and in North American nutrition for similar purposes – essentially as a tonic and what some very recent researchers call an adaptogen, assisting human recovery from wounds and illnesses? The most obvious answer would be because ginseng really does offer benefits of that kind.

The cultivation of ginseng and the modern demand for it

The demand for and the price of ginseng rose so high in China in the course of the 17th century that the Koreans began to cultivate it; apparently this is the first time cultivation had been tried. A Jesuit priest, Petrus Jartoux, wrote a report from China in 1709 describing the plant and its value. As a result of this report, another Jesuit priest, Joseph François Lafiteau, successfully identified American ginseng, apparently with the help of Iroquois herbalists, in 1716. The Jesuits and other Europeans of North America never took seriously the opinions of Chinese or North American nutritionists: what they wanted was a source of income, and during the 18th century wild American ginseng was systematically over-harvested, first in Canada and then in the United States, for export to China. Fortunes were made. Finally, when the wild supply began to fail, the techniques of cultivation developed in Korea were borrowed (or stolen, some say) by United States growers in the mid-19th century. All this was still for the Chinese market: the North American market was shrinking and nobody else was interested. Even down to the 1950s the *Encyclopaedia Britannica* was still saying that the health benefits of ginseng were illusory.

The grower of American ginseng, I'm told, strives to approach forest conditions as nearly as possible. Plants begin to produce fruit (red berries) after the third year. Ripe seeds are gathered in autumn; some plants are not allowed to bear fruit so that the roots grow larger and faster. The seeds are washed and placed in barrels of slightly damp sand or forest soil for one year. In the following autumn seeds are planted. They germinate in the spring after the frosts end their eighteen-month dormancy. After pricking out, the plants eventually grow in hills 1 foot apart. It takes at least six years from seed-gathering to the production of a marketable root in the 'sang gardens' of the United States. Three tons of green ginseng roots will result in one ton of dried roots, the average amount harvested per acre; 30 or more roots make up one pound of dried ginseng.

The Far Eastern market, which is still the world's biggest, is therefore supplied by (very expensive) wild ginseng from Korea and Manchuria, by (cheaper) cultivated *Panax ginseng* from these places, by cultivated *Panax quinquefolius* from Illinois, Kentucky, Missouri, West Virginia, North Carolina, Georgia and Tennessee. In Chinese medicine American ginseng is classified as cold, Asian ginseng as hot, so the two are not wholly interchangeable. Very old roots of wild plants, now extremely difficult to find, fetch a far higher than average price. But this is essentially an unregulated market: many false claims are made, in China as elsewhere, about the origins of herbal medicines and food supplements. To an unknown but large extent, ginseng products in the Chinese trade contain, partly or wholly, substances that don't actually come from either of the two major species but from the other ginseng species and from other quite different plants.

Ginseng is mocked in older Western scientific sources. Because the roots are anthropomorphic, it was assumed without enquiry that ginseng was a piece of folk magic like mandrake. Thus it was not used in Western medicine until the 1950s, when scientists in the Soviet Union began studying its health benefits and concluded that it was an 'adaptogen', that is, something that helps the body adapt to outside stresses and ward off disease. Either Asian ginseng or the unrelated Siberian ginseng (see below), I am uncertain which, has been given to Soviet cosmonauts to reduce fatigue. It was perhaps under Russian rather than traditional Chinese influence that the Vietcong used ginseng to treat gunshot wounds during the Vietnam War. A good deal of scientific research is now being done on ginseng for various purposes, and the results are often positive. However, even the research is often vitiated by confusion over the plant source used. There is now a world market in ginseng, which has grown out of the traditional Chinese herbal market, but it, too, is beset by confusion and misinformation. A 1978 study of 54 ginseng products found that one quarter of them contained no ginseng at all.

Current names for ginseng in major languages are loanwords originating in Chinese *renshen*, though in everyday Chinese ginseng is usually called simply *shen*. In the longer, traditional name, *ren* means 'man'; clearly the root is so named because, with its single body extended into two legs, and often with a distinguishable head, it is remarkably anthropomorphic. This metaphor recurs: although the proper name of ginseng in Cherokee is *a'talikuli* 'the mountain climber', in Cherokee religious incantations ginseng was nicknamed 'the little man': in one of the formulas traditionally used when gathering ginseng the gatherer addressed the mountain as 'Great Man' and assured it that he had come only to take a small piece of flesh from its side.

Ginseng substitutes

First there are the related species. One of my sources in this section is the *Plants For a Future* website.

Panax japonicus, Japanese ginseng, is found in mountain forests all over Japan. It is strong in saponins, which are potentially toxic, but it is used medicinally as expectorant, febrifuge and stomachic.

Panax pseudoginseng, called Himalayan ginseng and Nepal ginseng, is the species native to the Himalayas (for an early report in Chinese medicine see Schafer 1963, p. 323 note 157). It has been widely collected in recent years, because of the demand on world markets rather than because of any local use; it is not part of the traditional Indian pharmacopoeia. It is threatened with extinction, and cultivation is being tried (Joshi 1991).

Panax notoginseng, called sanqi ginseng, is native to southern China and perhaps Burma. It has a separate identity in the Chinese pharmacopoeia: it is listed as anti-inflammatory, antiphlogistic, antiseptic, astringent, cardiotonic, discutient, diuretic, haemostatic, hypoglycaemic, styptic, tonic and vulnerary (Duke and Ayensu 1985, Yeung 1985).

Panax trifolius, sometimes called dwarf ginseng, is native to North America, with a range similar to that of American ginseng. It has been chewed as a treatment for headache, short breath, fainting and nervous debility (Foster and Duke 1990; Moerman 1998).

There are several other unrelated species which are named after ginseng in Chinese: these include 'red ginseng', also called red sage and Chinese sage, *Salvia miltiorhiza*; 'Dutch ginseng', which is actually saffron, *Crocus sativus*; and 'bitter ginseng', once identified as *Robinia amara*, but this is a long-superseded botanical name which I have not yet tracked down in modern sources.

Some quite different species have been discovered, relatively recently, in which similar active constituents are found. These are the most likely to be confused with ginseng in scientific literature and in trade, so I list them more fully.

Siberian ginseng, *Eleutherococcus senticosus*, sometimes nicknamed 'eleuthero' by herb enthusiasts, is a shrub native to mountain forests in northeastern China, Korea, Japan and Siberia. There is deep confusion in many statements made on this species. It is claimed by some to have the same active constituents as ginseng; others deny it, and I believe them. It is said by Duke and Ayensu 1985 to be commonly used in China in folk medicine as an alternative to ginseng, but perhaps this is a new development rather than a traditional practice. Duke and Ayensu add that it is similarly used in Russia, but Bown 2002 says that it is not known in Russian folk medicine. It is said to be cultivated in Russia and China. The Soviet Academy of Sciences' Ginseng Committee has certainly conducted extensive research on it. Athletes from the former Soviet Union are said to have used Siberian ginseng to improve their performance. After the Chernobyl nuclear reactor disaster, Russian and Ukrainian citizens are said to have been given Siberian ginseng to counter the effects of radiation poisoning, although there's no scientific evidence that it does so. There have been few studies of its safety or long-term effects. It now has a powerful reputation as a food supplement and performance enhancing drug.

A relative, *Eleutherococcus sessiliflorus*, is called Korean ginseng by the *Plants For a Future* website and some others, but this is a confusing or deceptive name. This species is native to moist woods, wooded riverbanks, forest edges and clearings in China, Korea and Manchuria. The root bark is analgesic, anti-inflammatory, antipyretic and diuretic according to Duke and Ayensu 1985 and Yeung 1985. Bown 2002 gives the Chinese name *wu jia pi* for this genus.

Codonopsis tangshen is known in Chinese as *chuandang* and has been called false ginseng. It is native to upland slopes in central western China (Shaanxi to Sichuan). The root is widely used as a substitute for ginseng; it is adaptogen, aphrodisiac and tonic (Yeung 1985). It is possibly the ginseng from Shaanxi that was already used in the Tang dynasty, according to sources cited by Schafer 1963: Schafer believes that this report demonstrates the cultivation in medieval China of real Asian ginseng, much earlier than any other reports of its cultivation, but I think he may be wrong. There is also *Codonopsis pilosula*, bellflower or bastard ginseng (across China, Tibet to Manchuria, plus Korea, Mongolia, Buryat, cultivated in southern China), known in Chinese as dangshen and commonly used as a culinary ingredient, and *Codonopsis tubulosa* (southwestern China and Burma), known as white dangshen.

Cooked Rice with Dangshen and Chinese Dates. (Source: Recipe of Xingyuan) *Ingredients*: Dangshen, *Radix codonopsis pilosulae* 10g; Chinese-date, *Fructus ziziphi jujubae* 20g; Polished long-grained glutinous rice, *Semen oryzae glutinosae* 250g; White sugar 50g. *Process*: Put dangshen and Chinese-dates in an earthenware pot, add water to make them expand. Decoct them in water for about 30 minutes and take out dangshen and Chinese-dates; wash the glu-

100

tinous rice clean, put it in a big porcelain bowl with just the right amount of water and steam until the rice is done. Turn the bowl upside down to put the cooked rice on a plate. Put dangshen and Chinese-dates on the rice. Add white sugar into the prepared extract of dangshen and Chinese-dates and concentrate it, then, pour it on the cooked Chinese-date rice. *Directions*: It can be taken for breakfast. *Efficacy*: Strengthening the spleen and nourishing *qi*. *Indications*: Deficiency of *qi* due to weak consititution, manifested as lassitude, palpitation, insomnia, loss of appetite, loose stool, dropsy, etc. (From *Sino Herb King*)

Pfaffia paniculata is native to central and south America. It is one of several plants known as *paratudo* (meaning 'for everything', i.e. panacea) in Brazil, and is also called Brazilian ginseng, *corang-acu* and *suma*. It is found in rainforests in Brazil, Ecuador, Paraguay and Peru; also in Panama, where perhaps it was not native and has been introduced; however, there are no reports that it is cultivated. It is claimed to have been 'used by Indians for centuries', or 'for 300 years', 'to fight numerous illnesses'; it may well be used currently in that way, though the historical claims are unlikely to be provable. It is said to be an adaptogenic, tonic, sedative, analgesic herb, with effects resembling those of ginseng. Like Japanese ginseng, it is rich in saponins. It is now much gathered and widely marketed; the supply is likely to be at risk, like the rainforests in which it is found.

Caulophyllum thalictroides is properly known as papoose root or blue cohosh or squaw root; among its other names are blue ginseng and yellow ginseng. It is native to eastern North America, from New Brunswick to South Carolina, Arkansas, North Dakota and Manitoba, and grows in rich moist soils in swamps, by streams and in woods. Papoose root is a traditional herb of many North American Indian tribes and was used extensively by them to facilitate child birth (Foster and Duke 1990). An Asian species, *Caulophyllum robustum*, has sometimes been considered a variety of blue cohosh. Native to Japan, Far Eastern Siberia, and perhaps China, it is used in Chinese medicine according to Bown 2002, but I have not been able to confirm this from Chinese sources.

101

Talinum triangulare is native from Mexico to Peru and is known as *cariru*, leaf ginseng, Surinam purslane, *bologi* and waterleaf. This plant has been naturalized in tropical African and Asian countries. The leaves are used as potherb, as in the recipe below; the roots are used in southeast Asia as a substitute for ginseng, according to Bown 2002, but I have not been able to confirm this. Another plant in this genus, *Talinum parviflorum* or sunbright, is used by the Navajo externally, to heal wounds, and as an aphrodisiac – not for people but for livestock (Vestal 1952).

Afang Soup, a soup made from *afang* leaves (a.k.a. *ukazi, okazi, Gnetum africanum*, a type of greens usually gathered from the forest), with meat, seafood, and palm oil – is from the Calabar and Cross-River region of southern coastal

Nigeria, near the border with Cameroon, which has long been a centre of the African palm oil industry.

What you need: water, broth or stock; one pound meat (some combination of stew meat, oxtail, tripe, or bushmeat); cleaned and cut into bite-sized pieces; one hot chile pepper, left whole (for mild soup) or chopped (for spicy soup); one onion, chopped; several periwinkles (sea snails or other edible snails – where snails are not available clams or muscles may be used); salt; one or two pieces dried fish (stockfish and/or other dried fish); skin and bones removed, soaked and rinsed in hot water; one to two pounds *afang* leaves (*ukazi* leaves, or similar – outside Africa, any other greens may be substituted); cleaned, stems removed, and torn into pieces or pounded with a mortar and pestle (or crushed with a rolling pin); one pound waterleaf (or spinach); cleaned, stems removed, and torn into pieces; one cup dried shrimp or prawns, crushed; one to two cups red palm oil (or canned palm soup base, cream of palm fruit, sauce graine).

In a large Dutch oven heat a few cups of water (or broth or stock) to a near boil. Add meat to pot. Cook for a few minutes on high heat. Add onion and chile pepper. Reduce heat, cover, and simmer. While meat is simmering: In a separate pan bring a few cups of lightly salted water to a boil. Place the periwinkles in the boiling water. Cover and cook for two or three minutes. Remove snails from water. Use a pick or small fork to remove the snails from their shells. Remove the inedible hard "foot" from each of the snails. Rinse the snail meat in cool water. Drain and sprinkle with lime or lemon juice. If using other shellfish, process in a similar fashion. Add the snails (or their substitute) and the dried fish to the pot with the meat. Cover and simmer for several minutes. Add the greens (afang and waterleaf, or their substitutes), and the crushed dried shrimp or prawns. Add more water, broth, or stock as needed. Pour palm oil (or canned palm soup base) into soup. Add salt (or other seasonings) to taste. Cover and continue to simmer until the greens – and everything else – is completely cooked and tender, half an hour or more, stirring occasionally. Serve with Fufu, or pounded (mashed) boiled yams. (From *The Congo Cookbook.*)

All these plant foods and supplements can substitute for ginseng, at least partially.

Forgetting and remembering

I said that as a farmer you have to devote your energies to a smaller range of species. In other words, you have to reject a huge number of species that hunters and gatherers knew where to find and how to use, and would use when they wanted them or if they found them. You set them aside because you haven't discovered how to grow them, and perhaps, in some cases, no one ever will. Rather more frequently, you set them aside because growing them will not repay the effort in terms of eventual food value. 'The effort' is not just sowing and planting, it's also clearing land, ploughing, weeding, irrigation, warding off predators, travelling to and from the field, building storage places, ensuring suitable conditions and guarding the stored food.

The Neolithic Revolution, through which we humans are still living, has been a process of forgetting. Six to ten thousand years ago the forgetting was necessary and unproblematic. Necessary because, as their population grew, humans needed to concentrate on the foods that were easy to farm and that brought economies of scale. Unproblematic because there were many, both in the farming communities themselves and among their neighbours, who still retained the knowledge of wild foods, their uses and their health benefits; and surrounding the farmed areas of the world there were many, at first far larger, wild areas wealthy in resources; sometimes forgotten, but not lost.

I said, too, that the Neolithic Revolution has now just about worked itself out. Food production of the farming kind now covers most of the sufficiently fertile land areas of the world. People who depend on that sort of food production for their survival now make up nearly all the human population. For the last couple of centuries, or even longer in some places, land clearances and water management schemes – necessary to find living space and farming space – have often led to the extinction of wild species. Ever-increasing demand for minor, specialized and medicinal species has also led to over-gathering and extinction. Such extinctions are rapidly gaining in frequency.

103

Those Neolithic revolutionaries, in the Near East six to ten thousand years ago, didn't foresee this. They thought the forests and mountains would always be there, always rich, always full of those less-used foods and medicines that farming peoples would continue to need. They assumed that the forest and mountain peoples, who knew how to exploit these rich resources, would also continue to be there, turning up regularly at markets, open to trade and exchange when not being conquered or colonized. A sort of symbiosis was established: why should it not continue?

We now know the danger we're in. These assumptions were valid for many millennia, but they are valid no longer. The symbiosis is almost at an end. Our economy is so powerful and so rapidly growing that there are not so many forests and mountains left outside it; it is so wondrously attractive that the few remaining peoples who still use wild resources are eager to forget their special skills. How many valuable, previously wild, species will become farmed species, like *Panax ginseng* and *Eleutherococcus senticosus*? How many risk being lost, like *Panax pseudoginseng* and *Pfaffia paniculata*, because the demand drives them towards extinction rather than towards farmed survival? How much local knowledge has already been forgotten, and how much more is on the way to oblivion?

Bibliography

Asian Recipes Online at www.asianrecipesonline.com

Chandler, R. Frank, Freeman, Lois, Hooper, Shirley N., 'Herbal remedies of the maritime Indians' in *Journal of ethnopharmacology* vol. 1 (1979) pp. 49-68. (*Panax quinquefolius*, p. 58.)

Congo Cookbook at www.congocookbook.com.

Court, William, in *Pharmaceutical Journal* vol. 263 no 7065 (1999) pp. 537-8.

Duke, J. A., Ayensu, E. S., *Medicinal plants of China* (Reference Publications, 1985).

Foster, S., Duke J. A., *A field guide to medicinal plants: eastern and central North America* (Boston: Houghton Mifflin, 1990).

Gilmore, Melvin R. , 'Uses of plants by the Indians of the Missouri River region' in *SI-BAE Annual report* no. 33 (1919) (*Panax quinquefolius*, p. 106).

Goldstein, B., 'Ginseng: its history, dispersion, and folk tradition' in *American journal of Chinese medicine* vol. 3 part 3 (1975) pp. 223-34.

Hamel, Paul B., Chiltoskey, Mary U., *Cherokee plants and their uses: a 400 year history,* Sylva, N.C.: Herald Publishing Co., 1975 (*Panax quinquefolius, Panax trifolius*, p. 36).

Herbal Database at herb.umd.umich.edu

James William Herrick, *Iroquois medical botany*. 1977 (*Panax quinquefolius*, p. 395).

Joshi, G. C., Tewari, K. C., Uniyal, R. N. and M. R., 'Conservation and large-scale cultivation strategy of Indian ginseng, *Panax pseudoginseng* Wall', in *Indian Forester* vol. 117 (1991) pp. 131-134.

Keller, Penny at www.siu.edu/~ebl/leaflets/ginseng.htm

Kim Young-Sik at www.asianresearch.org/articles/1438.html

Moerman, D., *Native American ethnobotany* (Oregon: Timber Press, 1998).

Mooney, James, 'The sacred formulas of the Cherokees', in *7th Annual report, Bureau of American Ethnology* (1891) pp. 302-397.

Plants For a Future at www.comp.leeds.ac.uk/cgi-bin/pfaf.

Schafer, E. H., *The golden peaches of Samarkand* (Berkeley: University of California Press, 1963).

Sino Herb King at www.sinoherbking.com.

Smith, Huron H., 'Ethnobotany of the Menomini Indians', in *Bulletin of the Public Museum of the City of Milwaukee* vol. 4 (1923) pp. 1-174 (*Panax quinquefolius*, p. 80).

Smith, Huron H., 'Ethnobotany of the Meskwaki Indians', in *Bulletin of the Public Museum of the City of Milwaukee* vol. 4 (1928) pp. 175-326 (*Panax quinquefolius*, p. 204).

Smith, Huron H., 'Ethnobotany of the Forest Potawatomi Indians', in *Bulletin of the Public Museum of the City of Milwaukee* vol. 7 (1933) pp. 1-230 (*Panax quinquefolius*, p. 41).

Speck, Frank G., 'A list of plant curatives obtained from the Houma Indians of Louisiana', in *Primitive man* vol. 14 (1941) pp. 49-75 (*Panax quinquefolius*, p. 61).

Speck, Frank G., 'Medicine practices of the northeastern Algonquians', in *Proceedings of the 19th International Congress of Americanists* (1917) pp. 303-321 (*Panax quinquefolius*, p. 310).

The Star Online at kuali.com.

Sturtevant, William, *The Mikasuki Seminole: medical beliefs and practices,* 1954.

Swanton, John R., 'Religious beliefs and medical practices of the Creek Indians', in *SI-BAE Annual report* no. 42 (1928) pp. 473-672 (*Panax quinquefolius*, p. 656).

Tantaquidgeon, Gladys, *Folk medicine of the Delaware and related Algonkian Indians* (Harrisburg: Pennsylvania Historical Commission, 1972) (*Panax quinquefolius*, p. 32).

Taylor, Linda Averill, *Plants used as curatives by certain Southeastern tribes* (Cambridge, Mass.: Botanical Museum of Harvard University, 1940) (*Panax quinquefolius, Panax trifolius*, p. 44).

Vestal, Paul A., 'The ethnobotany of the Ramah Navaho', in *Papers of the Peabody Museum of American Archaeology and Ethnology* vol. 40 no. 4 (1952) pp. 1-94 (*Talinum parviflorum*, p. 26).

Williams, L. O., 'Ginseng', in *Economic botany* vol. 11 (1957) pp. 344-348.

Yeung Him-Che, *Handbook of Chinese herbs and formulas* (Los Angeles: Institute of Chinese Medicine, 1985).

Walk on the Wild Side

Daphne Derven

In the *Odyssey*, the goddess Calypso lived in a cave 'trailing round the very mouth of the cavern a garden vine ran riot with great bunches of ripe grapes while from four separate but neighbouring springs four crystal rivulets were trained to run this way and that and in soft meadows on either side the iris and the parsley flourished...It was indeed a spot where even an immortal visitor must pause to gaze in wonder and delight.'

Long ago, our ancestors did the equivalent of strolling the aisles in a supermarket when they took a walk. Early humans are frequently referred to as foraging for their food; or as hunters and gatherers. Although we tend to envision this as perilously difficult, in reality the entire world was their garden. Some of the oldest legends we know of talk of lush and bountiful pieces of land, gardens of the gods, and paradise. Life was spent searching for nourishment by wandering from place to place. To truly live off the land requires vast knowledge of the environment. I would like to explore the archaeological evidence from that borderline between the tradition of foraging and the origins of cultivating. Some attribute this shift to our desire for more complex civilizations. By about 3500 years ago, all of today's major food crops, except sugar beets, were under cultivation in some part of the world. This means our species spent most of our existence as foragers, but today, those few remaining foraging peoples are truly endangered.

It has been a widely held belief that the boundaries between foraging and agriculture were fairly distinct. Domestication evolved, as did accompanying sedentary life in a direct and systematic way. In archaeology, recent applications of various scientific techniques have provided clearer and more detailed information from evidence that identifies, dates and traces early domesticated plants and animals, and these results are being applied to a wide range of long-term research projects on several continents. The deliberate cultivation of wild plants by seeding an area to ensure future harvests and feeding wild animals to encourage their presence are the foundations of husbandry and domestication.

The determination that a plant or animal is an early domesticate requires very detailed analyses of a myriad of characteristics. The results of this research are pushing the envelope worldwide. Ancestors to early domesticates have been specifically located for both einkorn wheat from Abu Hureyra, Syria and *Curcurbita pepo* from the Phillips site in Missouri.[1] Currently, the domestication of key crops in several parts of the world has been dated much earlier than previously: rye 11000 years BP in Syria, *Zea mays* (corn) in Central America 6000 years BP, rice in China at 8000 years BP, sheep and goats at 11–9000 years BP, Einkorn wheat 10000 BP bananas in New Guinea 7000 BP and *Curcurbita pepo* (squash and gourds) 10000 BP in Mexico.[2] But in every case, in would be thousands of years before domesticates dominated the plate. It is a winding road in which wild foods remained a significant part of the diet for millennia and for many generations. It has been argued that while most foraging societies exploit their environment, they stop short of exterminating specific food resources. Whether this is actually the case is the subject of much debate.[3]

There is little or no argument about the level of environmental knowledge and awareness evidenced by hunters and gatherers. It is also generally accepted that roles appear to be gender specific; gathering and small game hunting by women and children and men the hunters. Originally, we scavenged for our meat but with the advent of hunting, estimated at least 700,000 years ago, meat became a significant part of the diet in certain areas.[4] In a foraging society, meat acquisition, sharing and carcass division had both dietary and status implications. The successful hunter provides nourishment for others and is valued as a significant member of society.

But the smaller the animal, the lower the return in terms of both available food and status. Smaller animals have less fat. Energy yield estimates by Smil and others indicate that a single mammoth would equal 100 large deer, or one bison would equal 200 rabbits.[5] Therefore, hunters in many areas and on several different continents engaged in mass slaughter. They utilized fear, deception, traps and natural formations to kill as many animals as possible, indiscriminately, frequently during seasonal migrations. These activities are credited with demonstrating organizational and strategic skills as entire groups or tribes would be required to successfully slaughter, butcher and preserve the resulting quantities of meat. Evidence, primarily from faunal materials left behind indicates that certain parts were consumed on the spot, some say ritualistically, with the bulk of the kill prepared and transported. This meat would be divided and cached according to the priorities of the group.

The origins of husbandry have been attributed to many factors; failure of seasonal migrations, climate change that dispersed favoured populations of prey, extinction brought about by herd encompassing slaughters, or convenience. Husbandry is seen originally as a passive system which provided food and controlled water resources gradually leading to domestication of sheep, then goats, followed by cattle, pigs, horses, then camels and finally poultry. This is seen as a very slow process beginning 11000 years BP and continuing for thousands of years.[6] Alvard and Kuznar estimate herds of 100 domesticated animals could be amassed (when beginning with two individuals) in 24 years for goats, 40 for sheep and 72 years for cattle.[7] Most accept 30 years as the span of a human generation; therefore the switch from short-term food supply to a legacy-based system indicates an enormous alteration in perspective and lifestyle. The need to forgo culling a herd for meat when trying to build its numbers would argue the need for ongoing hunting of wild animals. Ötzi, also known as the Iceman, died about 5000 years ago. He was finally defrosted recently so that very specific samples could be taken to determine what foods he had eaten. Obviously, this is a whole other story so I will just say that the evidence recovered indicates a mixture of wild and domesticated foods: red deer, domestic goat, cereals of the wheat and rye family.[8]

Husbanding a herd so it reaches the point of sustainability requires a radical alteration in thinking about food. One would need to become a futurist and think about the animals as legacy. Herd size would only be stabilized for subsequent generations, arguably with no benefit to the current one. The newly domesticated animals would be used not for short-term food supply but 'banked'. Food acquisition had been a shared responsibility with food division benefiting the group as a whole. Some have argued that animals were domesticated for very specific reasons, but not regular consumption, rather feasting, a resource for barter, consumption in times of need and non-meat uses such as rituals, dairy and traction.[9]

In the case of plant domestication, various different studies have estimated the numbers of wild plants used for food by different foraging groups. These estimates frequently indicate a pantry of over 100 different wild plants with the variety declining markedly after domestication to fewer than 10.

Virtually all sources agree that plant and animal domestication is more labour intensive and possibly less secure than foraging. What would cause individuals who were experts in analyzing the natural world around them, to undertake a change of lifestyle that required social, cultural, environmental and most likely spiritual upheaval? Particularly stark is the shift from communal food supply to individually-held property. To domesticate plants would require a total alteration of their known landscape, their supermarket, and their way of apportioning food.

Why would anyone do this? There are really no answers, but several possibilities seem plausible. Catastrophe, immediate or imminent, being one. Extreme climate change, disease, population increase, or drought; these deplete the once reliable food supply causing dramatic shifts. Revelation is another possibility in which a visionary, divine or mortal, has an epiphany and realizes that food can be tamed. Another is the stock market approach, which makes food a commodity with short- and long-term gains. In many ways these possibilities mirror the methods of harvesting wild foods; uprooting, cutting and beating. It is indeed a puzzle given that wild food as diverse bounty with domestication a more restrictive alternative. This is the beginning of a project in which agriculture and foraging will be explored. Currently, there appear to be many questions and few answers.

Bibliography

Alvard, M. and L. Kuznar, 'Deferred Harvests: The Transition from Hunting to Animal Husbandry', *American Anthropologist*, vol.103 no. 2 (2001), pp. 295–311.

Brown, K., 'New Trips Through the Back Alleys of Agriculture', *Science*, vol. 292 no. 5517 (2001), pp. 631–33.

Crowe, I., *The Quest for Food: Its Role in Human Evolution and Migration*, (Gloucestershire: Tempus, 2000).

Denham, T., S. Haberle, et al, 'Origins of Agriculture at Kuk Swamp in the Highlands of New Guinea', *Science*, vol. 301 no. 5630 (2003), pp. 189–93.

Fritz, G. 'Gender and Early Cultivation of Gourds in Eastern North America', *American Antiquity*, vol. 64 no. 3 (1999), pp. 417–29.

Goren-Inbar, N., N. Alperson et al, 'Evidence of Hominid control of Fire at Gesher Benot Ya`aqov', *Science*, vol. 304 no. 5671 (2004), pp. 725–27.

Hayden, B., The Dynamics of Wealth and Poverty in Transegalitarian Societies of Southeast Asia, *Antiquity*, vol. 75 no. 289 (2001), pp. 571–81.

Moore, A., G. Hillman and A. Legge, *Village on the Euphrates: From Foraging to Farming at Abu Hureyra*, (England, Oxford University Press, 2000).

Pauketat, T., K. Kelly, G. Fritz, et al., 'The Residues of Feasting and Public Ritual at Early Cahokia', *American Antiquity* vol. 67 no. 2 (2002).

Piperno, D. and K. Flannery, 'The Earliest Archaeological Maize (Zea mays L.) from highland Mexico: New accelerator Mass Spectrometry Dates and Their Implications', *Proceedings of the National Academy of Sciences* (PNAS) vol. 98 no. 4 (2001), pp. 2101–03.

Pople, K., M. Pohl, et al, 'Origin and Environmental Setting of Ancient Agriculture in the Lowlands of Mesoamerica', *Science*, vol. 292 (2001), pp. 1370–3.

Pringle, H., 'The Slow Birth of Agriculture', *Science*, vol. 282 no. 5393 (1998), p. 1446.

Rollo, F., M. Ubaldi et al, 'Ötzi's Last Meals: DNA Analysis of the Intestinal Content of the Neolithic Glacier Mummy from the Alps', *PNAS*, vol. 99 no. 20 (2002), pp. 12594–99.

Smil, V., 'Eating Meat: Evolution, Patterns and Consequences', *Population and Development Review* vol. 28 (2002), pp. 599–639.

Smith, B., 'Enhanced: Between Foraging and Farming', *Science* vol. 279 no. 5357 (1998), pp. 1651–52.

Smith, B., 'Documenting Plant Domestication: the Consilience of Biological and Archaeological Approaches', *PNAS* vol. 98 no. 4 (2001), pp. 1324–26.

Notes

1. Smith (1998), p. 1651.
2. Smith (2001), p. 1324; Brown, p. 632; Piperno and Flannery, p. 2101; Pringle, p. 1446; Denham et al, p. 189.
3. Alcard and Kuznar, p. 297.
4. Smil, p. 603.
5. Smil, p. 603.
6. Moore, Hillman and Legge, p. 519.
7. Alvard and Kuznar, p. 301.
8. Rollo et al, p. 12598.
9. Hayden, p. 579.

Where the Wild Things Are: From Wild Olive to Present-Day Cultivars and a Tasting of New World Feral Olive Oils

Anne Dolamore

The true origin of the olive tree is unknown. It is among the oldest known cultivated trees in the world. It is said to have appeared back in the mists of prehistoric times and to have originated in southern Asia Minor, about 6000 years ago. It appears to have spread from Syria towards Greece by way of Anatolia. In his treatise *The Origin of Cultivated Plants* written in 1883, Alphonse de Candolle, the Swiss botanist, identifies Syria as the birthplace of the olive. Other botanists agree with this theory of its origin claiming it originated between the southern Caucasus Mountains and the high plateau of Iran and the Mediterranean coasts of Syria and Palestine, but suggest it then passed through to Egypt and, by way of Cyprus, over to Turkey.

There is speculation that the olive may have appeared first west of the Nile Delta and although its commerce is mentioned in Egyptian records and olives are depicted in tomb paintings, and sarcophagi have been found with crowns made out of olive branches, this only really proves that the olive was known by the Egyptians of that era.

Some theories claim it originated in the Mediterranean basin but consider Asia Minor to be the birthplace of the *cultivated* olive tree. However the claim that the olive tree originated in Europe could arise from the Greek myth about the contest between Pallas Athene and Poseidon for control of Athens. Some hypotheses even claim it originated in Ethiopia although, considering the climatic conditions of the country, this doesn't seem very likely. Coffee yes, olive trees, no.

The olive must have occurred naturally in Greece, however, because the Greeks gave it their own name – *elaia*. If it had come from Syria surely they would have adopted the Hebrew word *zayit* or *zeit*, as it became in the Arab countries of North Africa.

To support this some historians claim that archaeological discoveries prove that wild olive trees existed before civilization in Crete and that their cultivation began between 5000 and 3500 BC and that from Crete the trees spread to Egypt (2000 BC), and thereafter to the islands, Asia Minor, Palestine and mainland Greece (1800 BC). In fact inscribed earthenware tablets dating back to 2500 BC, from Crete at the time of King Minos are some of the oldest surviving references to olive oil.

From the 6th century onwards the Carthaginians spread the olive tree throughout the Mediterranean basin, reaching Tripoli and Tunis, the island of Sicily and from there to southern Italy. It is said that it may have arrived in Italy during the period of Lucius Tarquinius Priscus (616–578 BC), the fifth legendary King of Rome, although others claim that it arrived in Italy three centuries before the fall of Troy (at least 1200 BC). Once in Italy, it quickly spread from south to north, from Calabria to Liguria.

After the Punic Wars, the Romans reached Africa, and they found out that the Berbers were already cultivating the olive tree and that in the Carthaginian territories a true olive culture had existed since the 9th century BC.

In his book *Spain at the Dawn of History*, R. J. Harrison states that towards 3000 BC olives were harvested and eaten in Spain. Its cultivation, nevertheless, was introduced there by the Phoenicians, probably in the 8th and 7th centuries BC but did not develop until the arrival of Scipio (212 BC) and Roman rule (45 BC). After this olives spread towards the central and Mediterranean coastal areas of the Iberian Peninsula, including Portugal. The Arabs brought their varieties with them to the south of Spain and influenced the spread of cultivation so much that the Spanish words for olive *aceituna*, oil *aceite* and wild olive tree *acebuche* and the Portuguese words for olive, *azeitona* and for olive oil, *azeite*, have Arabic roots.

After the discovery of America the olive travelled to the New World. The first olive trees were carried from Seville to the West Indies. By 1560, olive groves were in production in Mexico, then later in Peru, Chile, and Argentina and by Spanish Jesuit missionaries to California, hence the name of the American varietal Mission.

More recently, it has continued to spread and is now grown in South Africa, Australia, New Zealand, Japan and China.

One can see from all these theories that the olive has a confused past: for alongside the cultivated olive exists the wild ancestor, the oleaster, from which the cultivated olive derives, as well as other forms of 'wild' olive, which are very similar in appearance to the oleaster but are in fact cultivated forms which have returned to a wild state.

Until now, scientists considered that true oleasters were a homogeneous group confined to the eastern part of the Mediterranean basin, and that all cultivated olives derived from a single oleaster tree. Domestication probably took place at around 3700 BC in the Middle East, whence olives spread to colonize the entire Mediterranean basin. According to this theory, the wild forms observed in western parts of the basin were not true oleasters, but the progeny of cultivated olive trees which had returned to the wild state. These feral types are difficult to distinguish from genuinely wild trees.

By studying three different types of genomic molecular markers, researchers have now definitely called this theory into question. These markers make it possible to measure the degree of genetic proximity between trees, to reveal migrations and thus to put forward hypotheses concerning the evolution of the olive. The genetic profile of the populations studied indicates that true oleasters have been present since the Ice Age, in both the west and east. Oleasters survived the last period of the Ice Age in at least four different regions (north-west Africa, the Iberian Peninsula, the Middle East and throughout Sicily and Corsica). It is possible that they diversified westwards (North Africa, Spain, France, and Sicily) before the Ice Age, and that only one type reached the east.

Domestication of the cultivated olive was achieved from the oleaster not only in the east but also, and probably at the same time, in the North Africa, Spain, France and in Corsica. To confirm this hypothesis, researchers are planning to study olive stones found during archaeological digs. Cultivated olives were obtained in different regions from the first olive trees domesticated in the east and from local oleasters, which therefore allowed rapid local adaptation. True oleasters in the west therefore constitute precious genetic resources for the olive.

Genuinely wild olive trees, though rare, can still be found in some forests around the Mediterranean Sea. In a survey, researchers used gene analysis to distinguish between cultivated and wild trees. Most genuinely wild olive trees were found in Morocco, Portugal, and Spain. Many olive trees that seem to grow wild on the hillsides of countries bordering the Mediterranean are, in fact, descendants of cultivated trees returned to the wild.

Roselyne Lumaret, of the Centre National de la Recherche Scientifique in Montpellier, France, and Noureddine Ouazzani, of the Ecole Nationale d'Agriculture in Meknès, Morocco, surveyed ten forests in seven Mediterranean countries to identify surviving genuinely wild olive trees. They scored the trees for genetic markers associated with characters unsuitable for domestication.

'These wild stocks are genetically distinct and more variable than either the crop strains or their derived feral forms,' the researchers wrote in *Nature*. They report that wild types still survive in the western part of the Mediterranean area, whereas none were identified in Egypt, Syria, Turkey, Crete, or Greece – areas where olive trees have been extensively cultivated for a longer period of time.

'The domesticated olive represents a sample of the genetic variation in genuinely wild olive populations that persist today,' the researchers write. This should encourage both conservationists and plant breeders alike to preserve these trees.

The olive is a member of the family Oleaceae, which comprises 30 species such as *Fraxinus* (Ash), *Syringa* (Lilac), *Ligustrum* (Privet) and *Jasminum* (Jasmine). *Olea Europaea* (the domesticated olive tree) is one species of about 20 evergreen trees and shrubs with opposite leathery leaves.

Today some 850 million olive trees are cultivated worldwide. There are 1000 inventoried varieties; 139 of which are included in the *World Catalogue of Olive Varieties* published last year by the International Olive Oil Council. These 139 varieties are from 23 countries and account for 85% of the olives grown (8.7 million hectares).

Today several dozen varieties are grown commercially around the world. Cultivated olive trees come in many different varieties, which usually originate in the region where they are best grown. In the Mediterranean, hundreds of olive tree cultivars have been selected over the centuries for their adaptation to various microclimates and soil types. Some cultivars are common only locally, while others are found in several countries.

There is a lot of confusion regarding the names of the different cultivars. The same name has been given to similar but clearly different selections, and different names may be used for identical cultivars.

In my first book, *The Essential Olive Oil Companion*, I stated – without fear of contradiction – that olives were only grown around the Mediterranean, along a band of southern Europe and North Africa. Since then, much has changed: olives are now cultivated throughout the New World, from South Africa to Latin America.

The most incredible statistic is that in Australia, one million trees are being planted every year. Most sadly are Italian cultivars which in my experience do not suit the Australian terrain or the climate but Australian oil didn't rate a mention when I was writing my book originally. Many of the Australian oils made from European olive varieties lack complexity, but the best-flavoured oils, according to grower Maggie Beer, (and I agree wholeheartedly from those I've tasted) come from wild, South Australian olives: 'Verdale gives a wonderfully flavoured oil, but in very small quantities. The intensity of flavour from the wild olives is the best.'

Dr Michael Burr, another Australian grower, claims it is government policy to support the wholesale eradication of roadside wild olives. These are feral species, dating back to the 1860s, that have run wild from colonial plantings. But Burr argues that, because these have been crossbreeding for up to a century, they could well be a genetic treasure trove, 'We're silly to go for overseas varieties before we've looked more carefully at our own.'

The big olive distinction is between the 'Colonial' and the 'Feral'. The Colonial refers to the olives from trees brought into the country and cultivated from around 1820. (Some were even brought over from California – the Redding Picholine and the ubiquitous Mission.) When neglected, the trees cross-pollinated, leading to the Feral, which still grows wild along the roads. It was despised for consuming water, littering and led to a state-wide 'adopt an olive tree program'. This neglect began around the late 1890s after a small olive oil boom did not survive cheap imports, disinterest and a cuisine based upon one-pot meat and vegetables.

However to the delight of the Mediterranean migrants arriving from the 1950s there were olives to be harvested from the neglected olive trees of South Australia, especially round Adelaide. They took their harvests to the few traditional presses remaining from the colonial olive boom.

Olive growing has also caught on in New Zealand. In the 1980s, there were only about two producers. Now the New Zealand Olive Association is 600-strong. And there is real quality to be found among some of these oils.

Every oil I have tasted that contained oil from feral trees had a much brighter taste sensation and, when comparing different harvests, stood up longer than the other varietals or blends. The two olive oils I hope we shall be tasting, if samples arrive, are Waiheke Wild from Waiheke Island, Auckland in New Zealand, where Jeryl and Howard Alldred have been pressing oil from Waiheke gardens. In 2000, their first harvest, they harvested 2 tonnes of fruit; hand washed it and pressed it in a small continuous press. The second is Fleurieu Feral made by Zannie Flannigan and George Konodis in South Australia from the Greek Koroneiki cultivar grafted onto feral root stock. This is a gold-medal-winning oil.

Sources

Brooker, Margaret, *New Zealand Food Lovers' Guide* (New Zealand: Tandem Press).

Dolamore, Anne, *The Essential Olive Oil Companion* (London: Grub Street, 1988).

Dolamore, Anne, *A Buyer's Guide to Olive Oil* (London: Grub Street, 2000).

Lumaret, R. and Ouazzani, N., 'Ancient Wild Olives in Mediterranean Forests', in *Nature*, October, 2001.

Reichelt, Karen and Burr, Michael, *Extra Virgin* (South Australia: Wakefield Press, 1997).

International Olive Oil Council.

Joint Research Unit for Cultivated Plant Diversity and Genome Plant Breeding and Genetics Department, Montpellier Research Centre.

113

Irish Seaweed Revisited

Elizabeth Field

Ireland has had a long and tangled relationship with seaweed. Rubbery, black-green ropes of kelp (*Laminaria hyperborea*), fan-shaped translucent sheets of red-brown dulse (*Palmaria palmata*), and purple bushes of gelatinous carrageen moss (*Chondrus crispus*) are just three of the 16 species used commercially for food and industry in Ireland, out of a whopping 501 species of marine algae found along its 3,000-kilo-metre coastline.[1]

Mesolithic people at the time of Newgrange (*c.* 2500 BC) ate seaweed, along with fish and shellfish; while St. Columba's monks in the 6th century foraged for dulse. Settlers for centuries ate thick soups, or pottages, made from wild herbs, nuts, seeds, berries, seaweeds, cereals, and the occasional bit of bird, fish, meat or game.[2] 'Duilesc', or dulse, was among the foods stipulated to be offered to callers to one's door, according to the 7th- to 8th-century law text, *Crith Gablach* ('Branched Purchase')[3] and the tradition of eating dulse and yellowman (*yallaman*), a handmade yellow toffee, which began at the annual Lammas Fair in Ballycastle, County Antrim in August, 1606, continues.[4]

Seaweed fed the fields and offered sustenance for impoverished coastal dwellers over hundreds of years, while at the same time providing a meagre income, in the form of a by-product, iodine, which was sold for medicine, soap and glass-making. Seaweed as a fertilizer continued until around 1950, when jobs became more available and incomes increased. But vestiges of the old seaweed culture remain in south and western coastal regions, and a small, €8.8 million commercial industry produces seaweed for food additives, cosmetics agricultural products, and biomedical use.[5]

While seaweed is gaining more recognition as a delicious and nutritious food, it is still an under-utilized, sufficiently sustainable, wild resource that's viewed rather sceptically by the public. You'd be hard-pressed to find sea vegetables on contemporary Irish restaurant menus. Fortunately, there are a few innovators nowadays who are making seaweed the culinary star it deserves to be.

Put simply, seaweeds fall under three major phyla or divisions, which are identified by colour: brown algae (*Phaeophyta*), red algae (*Rhodophyta*), and green algae (*Chlorophyta*).

The many different species under these divisions have been used for everything in Ireland from knife handles made from wracks,[6] to babies' soothers, in which infants were given the rubbery stalks of sea rods (kelp, or *Laminaria hyperborea*) to suck on, to the 19th-century equivalent of steroids – carrageen as a food supplement to fatten up cattle for market quickly.[7]

Bladderwrack (*Fucus vesiculosus*) was said to cure a man's nasty skin disease.[8] Sloke was good against boils and gout.[9] Some reedy sea grasses were woven into baskets.[10]

For food, intensely salty and tough dulse (also called dillisk) was either plucked from the rocks, and chewed *au naturel*, or dried and nibbled as a snack, a practice that continues today on the County Antrim coast in Northern Ireland, and on the west coast of the Republic. It is sometimes sold from carts or little stands by the side of the road; and was apparently (and maybe still is) sent in little parcels to relatives in New York or Boston who retained a craving for it.[11]

Dulse could also be a tasty addition to mashed potatoes (champ), or to soups and fish stews, or served between buttered bread as a tasty, nutritious sandwich. It could be stewed with a little milk and butter, salt and pepper, and served with hot buttered oatcakes. Or it could be enjoyed with poteen (home-brewed spirit), cockles and mussels on Easter Monday.[12] You never said you were 'eating seaweed,' though; you were 'eating dulse.'[13]

Sloke (the *Porphyra* species) was taken as a 'kitchen' (a tasty relish) with potatoes, or simply boiled and dressed with butter, cream and pepper, according to John Keogh's 1735 work, *Botanalogia Universalis Hibernica* [An Irish Herbal].[14] The short, ribbon-like strands are delicious with hot buttered oatcakes, fish, ham or roast lamb.

Carrageen (from the Irish *carraigin*, or 'little rock'), with its highly gelatinous quality, was traditionally used as a milk thickener for a popular bedtime drink, considered to be good for sleeplessness. It was also used in preparing blancmange *Amhlaoibh Ui Shuileabhain*; a schoolteacher and draper from Callan in County Kilkenny referred to it as a thickener for sweet puddings, or 'second courses'. In his diary entry for 25 June, 1830, he says: 'I see a plant like edible seaweed which they call carrageen moss. It is largely used by cooks as an ingredient for the second course, to give it substance.'[15] Carrageen was typically used in cough syrups, either combined with burdock root, broom and furze tops, and boiled with sugar, or boiled with water, honey and lemon juice. Regina Sexton suggests adding a generous dash of whiskey to accelerate the curing process![16] Carrageen (available in health-food stores) is used in Myrtle Allen's ethereal carrageen moss pudding from Ballymaloe House – a recipe appears at the end of this paper.

115

Michele Haugh, a culinary arts student from Kilkee, County Clare, describes a 'black seaweed stew' called something like 'schlock' and eaten by some of the older men in her town. She wasn't sure of its ingredients, but perhaps it is similar to the *crusach* (roughly translated as 'strength' or 'vigour'), a mixture of seaweeds boiled together with limpets, that Regina Sexton mentions as a speciality of Inishmurray, a small island off the coast of County Sligo.[17]

Other edible sea vegetables include the bright green marsh samphire and rock samphire, which may be either lightly boiled and served with butter, or pickled in a little salt and white wine vinegar.

In her highly readable book, *Two Months at Kilkee*, a young Quaker gentlewoman named Mary John Knott offers a compelling account of her visit to the coastal resort town of Kilkee, County Clare, about 30 miles from Limerick, during the summer of 1836. We get an accurate picture of Irish life as it was then: travelling by boat along the Shannon River she passes the regal demesnes of English and Anglo-Irish landlords like Stafford O'Brien, Earl Dunraven, Mountiford Westropp, Bolton Waller, and the Knights of Glin. On her arrival at Kilkee, expecting her dinner, she naively comments about a Clare lass peddling 'porcupines' (sea urchins) and 'dilisk' (*Focus pamatus*, a species of seaweed, which is dried and eaten in this county).[18] During her stay, while enchanted by the sea air, spectacular scenery, and other natural phenomena ('cavities in the rocks, like little grottoes, with the rarest sea-mosses, enlivened still more by coral of a pink shade, sea anemones, shells and stones of different colours … whilst the sea urchins in thousands have either embedded themselves in the rock or lie like pavement, throwing their dark shade into the picture'),[19] her eyes are gradually opened to the harsh realities of coastal peasant life.

The drowning of a newlywed couple while harvesting seaweed – a not uncommon event – and the continual sight of ragged men and women struggling under the weight of heavy creels of wet seaweed, or trying to clothe their half-naked families, prompts her to write her book, which, while personally exultant, ultimately condemns the awful conditions of coastal poverty.

'Uvvery creel of [seaweed] is a ridge of pweaties [potatoes], with the blessing of God upon it,' says the boatman of the canoe in which Mary's party is making an excursion one day.[20] That's the economic truth in a nutshell: for coastal tenant farmers during the 19th and first half of the 20th centuries, seaweed was as important to their survival as their pig and potato patch. It fed the earth, which grew the potatoes, which fed the people.

In conversation with Liam Mac Con Iomaire, a native Irish speaker and authority on coastal Irish history and culture, I learned that no matter how poor, every householder had a wooden rowing boat and/or a canvas canoe. He would be entitled to a patch of seaweed, too, although there are numerous accounts of neighbourly and landlord-tenant disputes.[21] In fact the Irish term *spite feamainne* meaning 'seaweed spite,' refers to encroachers on one's seaweed patch

The coastal year revolved around seaweed harvesting. According to Liam Mac Con Iomaire, in the winter months, storms would sweep 'driftweed', usually a combination of mayweed, oarweed, knotted wrack, sea thong and other varieties, onto the shore, or else two or three men would go out in a boat, and use a 16-foot-long *croisin* (wooden pole with a knife on the bottom) to remove seaweed from the rocks. It would be set aside on rocks to dry.

In early spring, people would continue to cut seaweed from offshore rocks, and tow it ashore on a seaweed raft. They would lay it on the fields in March, placing cow manure on top of the seaweed. They might not sow potatoes immediately. Some of it would be burned in round stone kilns to make 'kelp,' which originally referred to the ash of the brown seaweed. Subsequently, 'kelp' came to apply to the seaweed itself.

From April on, they would prepare their land and sow potatoes. They would go to the inland bogs to cut turf, which required good weather to dry out. To save their land for sowing, they would move their cattle up to the turf lands, which became grassy in summer.

In May, they would harvest oarweed with their *croisins*. Of course, there was a superstition against gathering seaweed on May Day or on Sundays or at Christmas. Stories of harsh penalties for offenders are plentiful in Irish folklore.[22]

During the summer into early autumn, there would be more harvesting of other kinds of seaweed, including carrageen, as well as more kelp-burning.

Again, a mother-lode of seaweed lore, songs, spells and taboos, informed an extremely rich culture of coastal Irish life. Much of the material was oral, but two excellent translations, *The Shores of Connemara* by Seamus Mac an Iomaire and *Seaweed Memories* compiled by Heinrich Becker, capture a dreamy oceanic realm that is both dangerous and beautiful.

'Poor people need never be hungry when you have the strand,' writes Bridget Guerin, of Ballyheighue, Co. Kerry, in Darina Allen's *Irish Traditional Cooking*.[23] Guerin recalls her childhood, when people picked *bairneachs* (limpets), winkles, and seaweeds, such as *dilisk, sliuhane*, and carrageen off the seashore and sold them. Enterprising and hardworking people all around the coast of Ireland collected what they could to feed themselves and to supplement what was often a meagre income.

Indeed, during the worst famine years many people, homeless and starving, wandered the coastline in search of cockles, winkles, birds' eggs, seaweed – anything to assuage their hunger pangs.[24] It was the collective memory of scavenging food from the seashore coupled with the fact that the eating of contaminated fish in bygone days had been a common cause of death, that persisted in folk memory and turned people against shellfish. It has taken over a century to change this prejudice, according to Brid Mahon.[25]

John Martin, an author of a National Seaweed Forum Report sponsored by the National University of Ireland, Galway, also suggests there are some negative attitudes toward kelp and other seaweeds precisely because of their association with the famine.[26]

Old wives' tales and superstitions aside, seaweed *is* a healthy food. It is high in protein, carbohydrate, B group vitamins, vitamins A and C, and minerals including iron, iodine, zinc, magnesium, sulphur, potassium and phosphorous. The vitamin B12 that is found in sea vegetables is not found in any land vegetables, and is hard to source outside of meat. Some scientists consider it an anti-oxidant against cancer. And who knows what else is in it? Mary Knott describes 'imperceptible saline particles' in Kilkee's sea air, which restore health,[27] while Padraig Murphy avers that the 'micro-ionized' marine algae, used in his wife's seaweed baths also in Kilkee (see below), is ideal for back problems and muscular pain.[28]

I visited Kilkee in County Clare in late July (2004) to see how much of the tradi-

117

tional seaweed culture remains. The town still resembles what Mary Knott described as 'a place where the invalid can, without fatigue or interruption, enjoy the exhilarating sea-breeze and surrounding scenery'.[29]

There is a main street, on which sits the Stella Maris hotel, a wooden Victorian building with a balcony and a corner window with a superb view to the sea, and several pubs and shops. On the way down to the strand are two more streets, filled with restaurants, bars and shops. There are B&Bs all over the place. Obviously the place is a popular resort town, still attracting families and weekend revellers from the Limerick area mainly, but also from other parts of Ireland, and Europe. The main street slopes downhill to a wide, white, curving, horseshoe-shaped sandy strand, where kids play and build sand castles, as older folks sit on park benches in the sun (sometimes eating sweet-salty tender winkles) just above them on a grass and concrete walkway.

At the top of the strand, on the walkway, is a painted wooden stand emblazoned: 'Kelly's Seafood Since 1900'. Frank Kelly, tanned, muscular with a black buzz-cut and a gold hoop earring, seemingly in his early 40s, presides over a large rectangular tin of winkles (they sell for €1.50 for a large bagful; you eat them with a pin extracted from a velvet pin cushion.) Next to the winkles is a container filled with bags of dried dulse. It looks like thin, purply lettuce. A trim, wiry, muscular man called Joe, aged 72, in a black leather jacket, alights from his motorcycle and grabs a handful of dulse, popping it into his mouth to chew. He tells me, with a big laugh, it's 'good for love.' He can't resist taking a few winkles, too; telling Frank how fine they are. 'Good protein,' he says. 'Look at him,' says Frank, admiring his friend's physique. 'That's what you get from eating seaweed.'[30]

I follow the same pursuits as Mary Knott did on her stay: taking a cliff walk, admiring the 'puffing holes' (offshore rock caves in which seawater becomes compressed, then spews out the top in a spray), the birds, and the 'pollock holes', or natural swimming pools formed in the shelf-like expanse of rocks that extends from the beach at low tide. I take a relaxing warm seaweed bath at the Kilkee Thalassotherapy Centre – seaweed baths in antique porcelain tubs with Titanic-era brass fittings are found at some turn-of-the-century bathhouses along Ireland's west coast – and now it's time to watch how Padraig Mulcahy gathers the seaweed for his wife Eileen's thalassotherapy spa.

It's a daily ritual: walking out on the slippery rocks at low tide, about 100 feet from shore, barefoot, and hauling up wet dripping armfuls of *Fucus serratus*, considered to be the best seaweed for body treatments, into heavy black plastic bags. The weed, also known as wrack-jaw or common wrack, is at the peak of its maturity now, and drips with gooey alginate in web-like filaments reminiscent of sugar syrup. With a slight blush, Padraig tells me that this substance is called 'semen'.

It's now about 7:30 p.m. and the light is gorgeous where we stand, facing west. The strong evening sunlight sheds a clarity on the water and rocks that I am not used to. Padraig tells me that if I like this, the light is even stronger in the Aran Islands, in Galway Bay. Further south-west, down Ireland's jutting coastline on the Dingle Peninsula in County Kerry, Olivier Beaujouan and Maja Binder are artisan food producers who have adapted some of the old techniques of seaweed foraging for more modern usage. The two, who 'met over a bed of seaweed,' are French and German, respectively. Perhaps their coming from more food-oriented cultures (and without the negative attitudes to seaweed of the Irish) has enabled them to work more freely with seaweed as an enhancer and prime ingredient, just the way a chef or home cook would readily gather wild blackberries for blackberry-apple pies, or morels to be sautéed in butter and cream.

Around five years ago, Olivier started collecting and drying dulse, sea spaghetti, marsh samphire, kelp (aka *kombu* in Japan), and other varieties of 'sea vegetables' on the beaches near their home. He experimented with pickling the seaweeds, some of which had to be boiled first, in ginger, garlic, and wine for different durations. He might then add olive oil, sunflower oil, gherkins, capers, tomatoes, and pickled onions. The pickles end up 'not tasting like seaweed; they taste like vegetables from the sea'.[31]

He has come up with a range of tapenades, sea vegetable pâtés and seafood rillettes under the *On the Wild Side* label (www.onthewildside.ie), which he sells at farmers' markets in south west Ireland. They are wonderful, prize-winning products, which go well with mashed potatoes, fresh or smoked fish, stir-fries, rice, sandwiches, crackers or as appetizers on their own. Innovatively, he uses carrageen as a thickener for his fish pâtés, replacing half the butter he would normally use. His partner, Maja, uses dark red, hand-harvested dulse to flavour her semi-hard, raw cows'-milk Beenoskee cheese, giving it a salty, smoky tang. It won the Irish Cheese Awards Silver Award in 2000.

119

All of which illustrate the range of exciting culinary possibilities surrounding seaweed. While admiring and valuing the wonderfully rich seaweed culture of traditional Ireland, let's encourage the new breed of seaweed pioneers to take advantage of an abundance of wild sea vegetables. Go out there and free the fronds!

Carrageen Moss Pudding (Serves 4–6)

From Darina Allen's *Ballymaloe Cookery Course* (Gill & Macmillan, 2001).

8g (¼ oz) cleaned, well-dried carrageen moss (1 semi-closed fistful), available
in health food stores
850 ml (28 fl oz) milk
1 tablespoon caster sugar
1 egg
½ teaspoon pure vanilla essence or a vanilla pod
Softly whipped cream
Soft brown (Barbados) sugar

Soak the carrageen in tepid water for 10 minutes. Strain off the water and put the carrageen into a saucepan with milk and vanilla pod, if used. Bring to the boil and simmer very gently with the lid on for 20 minutes.

At that point and not before, separate the egg, put the yolk into a bowl, add the sugar and vanilla essence, if used, and whisk together for a few seconds. Then pour the milk and carrageen moss through a strainer onto the egg yolk mixture, whisking all the time. The carrageen will now be swollen and exuding jelly. Rub all this jelly through the strainer and beat it into the liquid. Test for a set in a saucer Put it in the fridge – it should set in a couple of minutes. Rub a little more jelly through the strainer if necessary.

Whisk the egg white stiffly and fold it in gently. It will rise to make a fluffy top. Serve chilled with soft brown sugar and whipped cream, or with a fruit compote, say, poached rhubarb.

Bibliography

Abbott, Vivienne, *Irish Cooking* (Newbridge, Co. Kildare, Ireland: Goldsmith Press, 1993).

Allen, Darina, *Irish Traditional Cooking* (Dublin: Gill and Macmillan, 1995).

Allen, Myrtle, *The Ballymaloe Cookbook* (Dublin: Irish Books & Media, 1984).

Becker, Heinrich, *Seaweed Memories*, trans. by author (Dublin: Wolfhound Press: 2000).

Bord Bia, *Bord Bia Seaweed Suggestions*, Press release (Dublin: Bord Bia, 2004).

Bord Iascaigh Mhara, *The School of Fish* (Dun Laoghaire, Co. Dublin: Bord Iascaigh Mhara, Irish Sea Fisheries Board, 2003).

Breatnach, Cagilte. Kinvara, *A Seaport Town on Galway Bay* (Kinvara, Co. Galway, Ireland: Tir Eolas, 1997).

Caherty, Mary, *Real Irish Cookery* (London: Robert Hale Ltd., 1987).

Chapman, V.J. and Chapman, D.J., *Seaweeds and their Uses* (London: Chapman and Hall, 1980).

Connery, Clare, *Irish Food & Folklore* (London: Reed Consumer Books, 1997).

Cowan, Cathal and Sexton, Regina, *Ireland's Traditional Foods* (Dublin: National Food Centre, 1997).

Davidson, Alan, *Oxford Companion to Food* (New York: Oxford University Press, 1999).

FitzGibbon, Theodora, *A Taste of Ireland* (London: Pan Books, 1970).

FitzGibbon, Theodora, *Irish Traditional Food* (Dublin: Gill and Macmillan, 1983).

Knott, Mary John, *Two Months at Kilkee*, facsimile of 1836 edition (Ennis, Co. Clare, Ireland: Clasp Press, 1997).

Mac an Iomaire, Séamas, *The Shores of Connemara*, trans. Padraic de Bhaldraithe (Kinvara, Co. Galway, Ireland: Tir Eolas, 2000).

Mahon, Brid, *Land of Milk and Honey: Story of Traditional Irish Food & Drink* (Dublin: Poolbeg Press, 1991).

Morrissey, Stefan Kraan and Guiry, Michael D., *Guide to Commercially Important Seaweeds on the Irish Coast* (Dun Laoghaire, Co. Dublin: Bord Iascaigh Mhara/Irish Sea Fishers Board, 2001).

Sexton, Regina, *A Little History of Irish Food*, (Dublin: Gill and Macmillan, 1998).

Thomson, George L., *Traditional Irish Recipes* (Dublin: O'Brien Press, 1986).

Notes

1. Bord Iascaigh Mhara, p. 6.
2. Theodora FitzGibbon (1983), pp. 13, 47.
3. Regina Sexton, p. 105.
4. Ibid., p.119.
5. Bord Iascaigh Mhara (BIM), press release, 4/2004.
6. Seamus Mac an Iomaire, p. 25.
7. Doagh Famine Village, Doagh Island, Inishowen, Co. Donegal, lecture/tour 1/8/04.
8. Heinrich Becker, p. 148.
9. Cathal Cowan and Regina Sexton, p. 69.
10. Doagh Famine Village, Doagh Island, Inishowen, Co. Donegal, lecture/tour 1/8/04.
11. Darina Allen, p. 187.
12. Theodora FitzGibbon (1970), p. 103.
13. Liam Mac Con Iomaire, AI, 15/6/04.
14. Regina Sexton, p. 107.
15. Ibid., p. 109.
16. Ibid., p. 111.
17. Ibid., p. 107.
18. Mary John Knott, p. 34.
19. Ibid., pp. 69-70.
20. Ibid., p. 47.
21. Heinrich Becker, pp. 88, 92, 97 and Seamus Mac an Iomaire, p. 146.
22. Heinrich Becker, pp. 135 -142.
23. Darina Allen, p. 185.
24. Brid Mahon, p. 47.
25. Ibid.
26. John Martin, Lecture, Bord Iscaigh Mhara (BIM) and Bord Glas-sponsored trip for journalists to Galway, 13/6/02.
27. Mary John Knott, pp. 73-74.
28. Padraig Murphy, AI, 27/7/04.
29. Mary John Knott, pp. 36-37.
30. Frank Kelly and 'Joe', AI, 28/7/04.
31. Cork Free Choice Consumer Group, lecture, 27/5/04.

The Significance of Samuel Pepys'
Predilection for Venison Pasty

John Fletcher

Apologia

My fascination for the history of consumption of wild meat, and specifically venison, derives from a biological, even evolutionary, education as well as a practical back-ground in the esoteric field of deer husbandry. Inevitably I approach this subject from these perspectives rather than from those of the professional historian, nevertheless I humbly submit this discussion in the hope that cross-fertilization between disciplines may be useful.

Introduction

It is generally accepted that since the appearance of *Homo erectus* about two million years ago wild meat has been a vital part of the hominid diet. It is only in biological terms extremely recently, perhaps for Europeans a maximum of five thousand years ago, that we have been able to eat the fattier meat of domestic livestock that were all, with the exception of pigs, primarily bred to provide traction, milk, and for other purposes than meat. Nevertheless, selection for fatty carcasses, perhaps especially for tallow for candles, must also have begun at an early stage. It is highly probable there-fore that we are evolutionarily adapted to the lean meat of wild animals and that our inbred inability to assimilate meat from the modern carcasses of grain-fed animals, which are the products of that selection, together with dairy produce, is a factor in today's epidemic of cardio-vascular and obesity related disease.

It may therefore be entertaining to consider the attitudes of those who, like Samuel Pepys, were among the first regularly to have a choice of both wild and domestic meats. He lived at perhaps the last time in England when almost everyone must have had some first-hand experience of agriculture. In addition Pepys' whole life from 1633 to 1703, was lived to the accompaniment of abundant agricultural produce and urban prosperity. The corollary of this was that, despite the government's financial endeavours to encourage exports, farmers had to contend with a prolonged period of depressed prices. At such times, as Joan Thirsk (1997) has emphasized, farmers are bound to seek alternative sources of income and grow less mainstream crops. In mid-16th century England she lists a profusion of new agricultural products: potatoes, Jerusalem artichokes, pumpkins, fennel, cabbages, Roman beans, liquorice, saffron, French peas, mustard, teasels, madder, osiers, willow, French furze, hops, flax, musk melons, weld, coriander, aniseed, cumin, canary seed and asparagus, as well as timber, silkworm and honey bees. No wonder it has been called the 'Consumer Revolution'.

Pepys was born at a time when England's population was growing at an unprecedented rate. From 1541 when the population numbered around 2.7 million it had by 1656 reached an estimated 5.3 million. It was the beginning of the Augustan era in literature, while for scientists and the cream of the intelligentsia, the Royal Society was founded. In 1684 Pepys became its president. Within its ranks were his friend, another celebrated diarist, John Evelyn, as well as Dryden, Christopher Wren, Isaac Newton, Robert Hooke, and a whole galaxy of other thinkers from philosophers and mathematicians to anatomists, astronomers and instrument makers. Charles II was its patron and, if he did not often attend, he at least sent gifts of venison to its dinners.

A background to English venison eating

As the ice retreated from Britain around 14,000 years ago, reindeer, red deer and roe deer were early colonizers. Since then we have lost the reindeer but gained other species, notably the fallow introduced by the Normans. Throughout the Mesolithic, roe deer and especially red deer were the most common mammalian prey species found in most of Europe (Jarman, 1972). Steven Mithen (1994) has pointed out that,

> the hunting of large terrestrial mammals remained central to the Mesolithic for even if they were not the staple food supply in all areas they may have required the greatest time to exploit and they had considerable social significance.

123

Until recently it has been supposed that Europe, from the post-glacial period until the advent of agriculture, had been covered by a closed forest dominated by oak, elm, lime, ash, beech, hornbeam and hazel regenerating in areas where windblown trees created gaps in the canopy allowing light to enter (Watt, 1947). This theory has recently been succeeded by one in which the value of the large herbivores has been recognized as creators of 'a mosaic of large and small grasslands, scrub, solitary trees and groups of trees' (Vera, 2000). This is similar to what is now often called 'wood-pasture'. In contrast to the closed canopy such a habitat would have been perfect for both roe and red deer and could have supported very high population densities of both species: in the forests of medieval Britain deer habitat seems likely to have been optimal. Their only significant predator other than man would have been the wolf which was so heavily persecuted that it became extinct in England at the beginning of the 14th century and in Scotland by the mid-17th.

How much venison came out of those forests? It can only be the most approximate of comparisons, but our modern landscape may give us some idea. Much of today's habitat is obviously unavailable to deer but on the other hand fertilizer use and abundant cropping may have increased carrying capacity. Current estimates of the numbers of wild deer culled in England each year are, including all species, about 85,000 (Ward, 2003), yielding perhaps 1,500 tonnes of venison. This does not appear to be sufficient even to stabilize the numbers of deer, which are thought to be increasing steadily. If we assume conservatively that a similar number of deer inhabited medieval England with a human population of three million, then this would equate to only 0.5 kg of venison per annum for every man, woman and child. We don't know if medieval hunting pressure was sufficient to control the deer population but there must have been strong economic incentives to protect the crops apart from the value placed on the meat. Certainly, by the 17th and 18th centuries, enough deer were being hunted to push them close to extinction so that by the early 19th century hunters redirected their efforts towards the inedible fox.

Even in prehistory we know that so many red deer were being used for venison, with some evidence that they were being selectively culled, that some authors have even suggested a degree of husbandry of the wild deer (Jarman, 1972). How could this have been done? A clue comes from Simmons and Dimbleby (1974) who found curiously high pollen counts of ivy in mesolithic house sites and suggested that the inhabitants must have been gathering and storing ivy, perhaps as animal feed. Celia Fiennes' journal (1947 edition) describes how in the late 17th century she saw free-ranging deer in the New Forest which were regularly fed browse (twigs and shoots cut as fodder) and had become so habituated to it that they were, 'very fatt and very tame so as to come quite to eat out of your hand'. They would come into a railed enclosure to be fed when called by the keepers. It was therefore 'a great privilege and advantage to be a Cheefe Keeper of any of these Lodges, they have venison as much as they please and can easily shoote it when the troop comes up within the paile'. There is no reason why a similar system of culling might not have been practised thousands of years earlier in the Mesolithic.

So far I have not mentioned the deer parks. I have considered it appropriate to include park deer in this contribution to a symposium on wild foods because they contain deer which are still legally deemed wild, unlike the farmed deer of today, and have undergone little or no selection as livestock. Within the medieval forests the king, unless he had specifically granted the land to a noble, or except insofar as commoners could exercise their rights of pannage (grazing pigs), estover (collecting firewood) or common (grazing cattle and sheep), retained all rights including, of course, hunting. Rights to empark were granted by the king to permit someone to create a hunting reserve within which the forest laws were suspended.

Early English Anglo-Saxon deer parks were known as 'haies'. Vera (2000) discusses this word and it is generally accepted, for example by Rackham (1980) and Cantor (1982), that it denoted an impenetrable barrier through which deer could not pass but it also came to mean an enclosed area into which deer might be driven in order either to kill them or capture them for transport to stock a deer park, or even perhaps a closed deer park in which deer were permanently contained. The Domesday Survey lists more than 70 such 'haies' and 31 deer parks (Whitehead, 1950).

During the 12th and 13th centuries a plethora of grants to empark were made:

3000 in England according to Bazeley (1921), or 1,900 (Cantor, 1982), and a further 300 are mentioned by Gilbert (1979) as existing in Scotland. Not all of these were in existence at any one time of course but they nevertheless comprised a very significant land-use as has been emphasized by Jean Birrell (1992). Many parks were quite small and it is quite impossible to imagine any formal hunting on horseback and with hounds, *par force de chiens*, as described, for example, by Cummins (1988), within them. Anyone who has, like me, spent many happy hours in deer parks, gently approaching deer in a vehicle or on foot in order to catch them with a tranquillizer dart, will find the notion of hunting deer with horse and hound within any park of less than a couple of hundred acres absurd. This is even more the case when one considers that few park surrounds were of stone; most were merely a ditch with a wooden pale or hedge on top. After the mid-13th century, when the introduced fallow deer came to replace red deer, then this was even more true. Though fallow deer may be readily tamed by feeding, they are much more 'flighty' when chased and much more likely to leap the pale. Where hunting in parks was ever more than the simple assignment of a servant to go and shoot deer for the table then it must have been by what was called bow and stable hunting in which deer were drifted carefully to a pre-arranged ambush by bow-men and -women (Almond, 2003). In this way several deer could be killed in a day without unduly disturbing the entire herd and risking escapees. If any did jump out they would generally be easy to return to the park, perhaps using a deer leap, as any deer farmer will know.

Fallow deer were never the more esteemed 'beast of venery' but deemed less noble 'beasts of the chase' (*Boke of St Albans,* cited by Cummins, 1988), however they were considered better eating than the hart, 'The buckes flesshe is more savery than is that of the herte or of the Roo bucke. The venyson of hem is ryght good, and ykept and salted as that of the hert.'(*Master of Game,* cited by Cummins, 1988). Perhaps this was because the hart was hunted to bay by hounds while the fallow was more often cleanly shot.

Dyer (1983) has described the diet of the late Middle Ages. He points out the heavy dependence of the noble household on meat and fish: 2–3 pounds per day was normal. Deer parks could be relied upon to provide meat at most times of the year and the animals could easily be killed on demand by a crossbowman concealed in a tree or, rather more fancifully, in a stalking-horse or, as described above, by taming the deer with feed, or by a simple bow and stable hunt. It is not surprising then that there are few historical accounts of actual organized hunting *par force de chiens* in parks until one reaches the reign of Queen Elizabeth. By that time a number of very large parks had been created and in some cases the Queen hunted from one park to another *par force* or, more often, the deer were confined to a small paddock within the park where the Queen could shoot them with a crossbow or have them driven past her as in bow and stable.

If venison was not consumed within the owner's household it would be given as a gift, a strong tradition that lasted well into the 17th century; indeed, as the royal warrant, gifts of venison were made until the late 20th century. As Jean Birrell has pointed out, deer park owners would be unlikely to assist in creating a market, and so encouraging poaching: the 'production of deer for the market would have devalued an important aspect of the aristocratic way of life and privilege.' A similar philosophy still guides the prohibition of venison sales in many states in America, whilst many landowners in Britain remain reluctant to see venison prices rise too high in case it stimulates the poacher to action.

It is the majority of the population rather than the nobility whose venison intake may surprise us. Despite the evidence of numerous deer parks and of hunting in the chases and forests restricted to the nobility, Dyer suggests that relatively little venison was consumed by the nobility, who reserved this meat for feasts and important events. Amongst the lower orders, the only livestock kept entirely for meat production were pigs, whilst cattle and sheep could for the main part only be eaten once they had ceased to be productive. Dairy produce was more accessible. Dyer's analysis of seigneurial and court records reveal 'a good deal of poaching by peasants' whilst, for example, excavations of a deserted medieval village, Potter's Lyveden, Northants, found that deer bones represented 'between 6 and 23 per cent of those identified' (Steane and Bryant, 1975: cited by Dyer, 1983). Poaching in the forest and in parks seems to have been a popular medieval pastime. The Lord of Okeover lost by his own account 100 of the 125 deer in his park to poachers in 1441 (Birrell, 1992). Later, William Shakespeare is reputed to have poached deer from Charlecote Park, and the dowager-Countess of Oxford complained to Wolsey in 1524 of how 'by estimation' five hundred persons of which one hundred were bowmen, and 'every one of them their bows bent and an arrow in their bow', broke the pale and gate of her park and killed a large part of her deer.

There are few references to management of deer parks although Gilbert (1979) and Birrell (1992) provide some. Probably so commonplace as not often to create documentary evidence, was the feeding of browse. Jean Birrell describes the practice in Needwood Chase, where in 1417–18 four hundred cartloads were provided for the deer. It is easy to imagine that this would have made the deer quiet enough to allow culling as described by Celia Fiennes.

A larderer was employed at Tutbury for five weeks in 1370–1 to salt and place venison in barrels; he used three quarters of salt for twenty-four carcasses, presumably of fallow deer (Birrell, 1992). Cummins gives a figure of two bushels of salt per hart (a red deer stag, twice the size of a fallow buck) being used in France in the 14th century.

By the 1500s parks were being used for more than deer, with subdivisions for horses and cattle, yet in 1577 William Harrison (cited in Shirley, 1867) wrote that, 'the twentieth part of the realm is employed upon deer and conies already… the owners still desirous to enlarge those grounds do not let daily to take in more'. Only

25 years later Carew was able to write how a great many parks, 'within the memory of man have been disparked, the owners making their deer leap over the pale to give the bullocks place', and Morison in 1616 (cited in Shirley, 1867) wrote 'this prodigall age hath so forced Gentlemen to improve revenewes, as many of these grounds are by them disparked, and converted to feede Cattell.'

Deer parks don't benefit from wars and the Civil War was no exception whilst the republic following the execution of Charles I in 1649 did little to reinstate them – although it is interesting that Oliver Cromwell's signature graces the grant to empark Badminton (Whitehead, 1950). However, once the restoration of Charles had taken place in 1660, pomp and show was back with a vengeance and hunting became again a popular pastime. Deer were imported, the parks were restocked, trees planted, and the severity of the game laws was increased. Venison resumed its importance as a socially acceptable gift and with the increased number of parks much more venison was consumed. Yet at the same time beef also became, for the first time, available to a wider public. As Dyer has commented, 'the age of the European carnivore had begun'.

Famously the turnip, which had first been introduced into England in the 16th century by foreign immigrants as a vegetable for human consumption had eventually caught on. By the 1630s the use of this root to sustain cattle in the winter, as had been practised in the Low Countries for many years began to appear in East Anglia. This trend gathered momentum throughout the 17th century and turnips together with clover, lucerne, sainfoin, timothy grass and other more exotic forage species such as lupins, lentils, fenugreek, and millet permitted the fattening of cattle on arable systems and effectively brought them into an arable rotation (Thirsk, 1997).

127

Pepys and venison

The latest edition of the diary edited by Robert Latham and Will Matthews has a magnificent index produced by the former which carefully lists the 76 entries for venison and 40 for beef. It is a simple and pleasurable task to read them all but since we are only concerned with wild foods, I have restricted this light-hearted discussion to venison.

It seems likely that most if not all the venison Pepys ate was of fallow deer. Bucks and does are often cited which would refer to fallow and there is no mention of red deer or stags and hinds. We can suppose also that most of the deer were taken from parks or at least are unlikely to have been the subject of prolonged horseback chases (the produce of which would perhaps have been more likely to have been divided amongst the participants of the hunt). As described by Celia Fiennes only twenty or thirty years after Pepys' diary years, it is likely that some, perhaps most, of the deer might have been shot at close range by bow whether they were in or out of a park. This would have made for much better eating and afforded more chance of avoiding putrefaction in the summer heat.

Whether Pepys was eating a fair cross-section of venison dinners, which seems likely, or whether he actually had a predilection for venison pasty and sought them out, one cannot be clear, but it is obvious that most often venison was served as a pasty. On the 76 occasions he ate venison, only 26 were other than pasties, including 11 haunches, a shoulder, an umble pie, and on two other occasions umbles. The rest are unspecified.

Considering how our modern stalking seasons for red and fallow deer require most of the deer to be killed during the autumn and winter, Pepys writes on 25th November 1662, 'to the Dolphin to a venison pasty, very good and rare at this time of the year'. In fact, the seasonal distribution of his eating more or less bears this out. Between 1660 and 1669 he ate venison in one form or other as follows: in January on 3 occasions, in February 2, none in March and April, May 1, June 5, July 16, August 20, September 13, October 4, November 6, December 6.

The eating of venison pasties in the summer season seems to have been something of a feature reaching a climax on 6th September 1662 when Pepys comments: 'to the Trinity House where we had at dinner a couple of venison pasties of which I eat but little being almost cloyed having been at 5 pasties in 3 days: viz 2 at our own feast & 1 yesterday and 2 today.'

Our modern close seasons are designed to avoid killing females when they are either very heavily pregnant (early spring) or when lactating with calves at foot (spring and summer), and also males during the summer when they are growing their antlers 'in velvet'. In other words our close seasons are designed with the welfare of the deer in mind as well as the antler trophy. These are probably concepts that would have been totally alien to Pepys' contemporaries. Whilst the importance of avoiding disturbing deer in the forest during the 'fence month' was well recognized in the medieval literature and even in the forest laws, this may have been to avoid diminishing a valuable calf crop rather than concern over the welfare of the deer. According to the *Boke of St Albans* the red deer stag (hart) is in season from Midsummer Day (21st June) to Holy Roode Day (14th September) and Gaston Phoebus gives the season for hinds as from the 14th September until Lent; the fallow season is likely to have been similar (Cummins, 1988). The sex of Pepys' venison is mentioned on only three occasions: bucks on 9th September and 18th July and a doe on 11th November, which is in keeping with those traditional seasons. The concept of antler trophies, which discourages the killing of stags until the late summer, was completely foreign to medieval deer hunters and only entered the British consciousness in the 19th century, probably from Germany. Instead, the objective of the medieval hunter was to kill deer during the 'time of grease' when they were at their fattest. Pepys' seasonal eating pattern wholly confirms this with a clear peak in July, August and September. This comes as no surprise. From *Sir Gawaine and the Green Knight,* in which deer fat 'fully two finger-widths on even the leanest' is extolled, to Jane Austen, who, in *Pride and Prejudice,* talks approvingly of 'venison roasted to a turn; everyone said they had never seen so fat a haunch', it is clear that the fat was highly valued whether as a by-product for candles or for soap, or whether just as a very satisfying part of the diet. Clearly the hunter-gatherer's instinctive yearning for fat was as strong in Pepys' day as it is in ours.

Did Pepys show any preference for venison over beef? This is not easy to determine categorically, but it is certainly very clear that venison was treated as something special. Venison features as a gift 11 times in the diaries as well as the very many occasions when it was the basis for hospitality. Apart from the excess of pasties mentioned above, Pepys complains of 'a pasty that was palpable beef which was not handsome' on 6th Jan 1660, ' a poor venison pasty' on 27th August 1661, ' a venison pasty which proved a pasty of salted pork' on 17th October 1661 and famously on 1st August 1667: 'my wife and I dined at Sir W Penn's on a damned venison pasty that stunk like a devil however I did not know it till dinner was gone'. Four days later he returns to another pasty at Sir William's which he found very good, 'better than we expected the last stinking basely'. On another occasion on 6th July 1663 he writes: 'on our way eating some venison pasty in the barge I having neither eat nor drunk today which fills me full of wind,' but this does not really detract from the pasty. A year later, at Sir William's, he had a 'bad' pasty. Overwhelmingly though he is complimentary: 'all very well done'; 'very welcome'; 'venison pasty and other good plain and handsome dishes'; 'rare'; 'best venison pasty ever I eat of in my life'; 'a whole doe…a fine present'; 'an umble pie hot out of her oven extraordinary good'; 'a very great dinner and most excellent venison'; and countless venison pasties were pronounced 'good' or 'very good'.

The very fact of passing off beef and salted pork as venison proves beyond a doubt that venison was the preferred meat of the age and, of course, this is a common finding up to the 19th-century ersatz German venison haunch and hare recipes described by Ursula Heinzelmann in this symposium, and even to Elizabeth David's pork chops to taste like wild boar.

129

Conclusion
Venison was a very regular item on Pepys' and his friends' menus. It remained a treat, and, contrary to our notions perhaps inherited from the 19th century, it was especially a summer-season treat. Pepys certainly preferred it to other meats but whether this was due to an instinctive realization that it was healthier or, more likely, a genuine appreciation of its superiority, or perhaps even an innate snobbishness for a meat most available to the landed gentry, we shall probably never know.

References.

Almond, Richard, *Medieval Hunting* (Stroud, Gloucestershire: Sutton Publishing 2003).

Bazeley, M., 'The extent of the English forest in the Thirteenth Century', *Transactions of the Royal Historical Society*, 4th Series IV, pp. 140–72.

Birrell, Jean, 'Deer and Deer Farming in Medieval England', *Agricultural History Review* (1992) vol. 40, II, pp. 112–26.

Cantor, L., 'Forests, chases, parks and warrens', in *The English Medieval Landscape* (London: Croom Helm, 1982) pp. 56–85.

Carew, Richard (1602), *Survey of Cornwall*, ed. F E. Halliday (London: A. Melrose,1953).

Cummins, John, *The Hound and the Hawk – the art of medieval hunting* (London: Weidenfeld and Nicolson, 1988).

Dyer, C., 'English diet in the late Middle Ages', in *Social Relations and Ideas: Essays in Honour of R. H. Hilton*, ed. T. H. Aston, et al. (Cambridge University Press, 1983).

Fiennes, Celia, *The Journeys of Celia Fiennes*, ed. Christopher Morris (London: Cresset Press, 1947).

Gilbert, John M., *Hunting and Hunting Reserves in Medieval Scotland*. (Edinburgh: John Donald, 1979).

Jarman, M. R., 'European deer economies and the advent of the Neolithic', in Higgs, E. S. ed., *Papers in Economic Prehistory* (Cambridge University Press,1972). pp 125-49.

Mithen, Steven J., 'Mesolithic Age', in *The Oxford Illustrated History of Prehistoric Europe* ed. Barry Cunliffe. (Oxford University Press, 1994).

Pepys, Samuel, *The Diary of Samuel Pepys*, a new and complete transcription ed. Robert Latham and William Matthews (Cambridge University Press,1971).

Rackham, O., *Ancient Woodland. Its history, vegetation and uses in England* (London: Edward Arnold, 1980).

Shirley, E. P., *Some Account of English Deer Parks*. (London: John Murray, 1867).

Simmons, I. G. and Dimbleby, G. W., 'The possible role of ivy (*Hedera helix* L.) in the mesolithic economy of Western Europe', *Journal of Archaeological Science*, (1974) vol. 1, pp. 291-6.

Thirsk, Joan, *Alternative Agriculture – a history from the Black Death to the Present Day* (Oxford University Press, 1997).

Vera, F. W. M., *Grazing Ecology and Forest History* (Wallingford: CABI Publishing, 2000).

Ward, A. I., 'Increasing ranges of British deer 1972–2002'. Paper presented at the Mammal Society Easter Conference, 2003.

Watt, A. S., 'Pattern and process in the plant community', *Journal of Ecology* vol. 35, (1947) pp.1–22.

Whitehead, G. Kenneth, *Deer and their Management* (London: Country Life Ltd., 1950) .

Angelica: From Norwegian Mountains to the English Trifle

Ove Fosså

'What is that green stuff?' No one recognized the pieces of candied angelica on a cake I made earlier this year. When told that it was *kvann*, most got a puzzled look on their face. Angelica is not found in Norwegian kitchens today, candied angelica has never been much used here. You are more likely to bite into a piece of angelica if you are having trifle in England. Elizabeth David admitted to its being one of her favourite flavourings,[1] though Jane Grigson urged you to 'try and avoid the brassy effect of angelica and glacé cherries'.[2] So where did the green stuff come from? Some would say Niort, France, and not be entirely wrong, but that is only part of the story.

Angelica archangelica L. is a stout plant that starts out with a rosette of large (30–70 cm in length), compound leaves with a hollow, tubular leaf stalk. In its first year or two (occasionally more) it will accumulate nutrients in its thick taproot, then it will flower, set seeds, and die. The green, occasionally purplish, flower stem may grow to a height of 2 m or more. The small, greenish flowers are set in spherical umbels, 10–15 cm or more across. When bruised, the whole plant has a strong aromatic scent.

Its relative the wild angelica, *Angelica sylvestris* L., can be mistaken for the real thing. It is not the wild form of the cultivated angelica, but a different species. It can be distinguished by the flattened inflorescence. The central rays of its umbels are shorter than the lateral ones, whereas the umbel rays of true angelica are all more or less the same length. Wild angelica *A. sylvestris* has little scent.

True angelica is usually subdivided into the two subspecies, *A. archangelica* subsp. *archangelica* and *A. archangelica* subsp. *litoralis* (Fr.) Thell. To know one from the other is not easy, even the specialists do not fully agree. Subsp. *litoralis* is native along the seashores of Scandinavia. It has a harsher taste and is generally considered inedible. The best distinguishing feature is the seeds, smaller (5–6 mm) and with rounded ribs in subsp. *litoralis*, longer (7–8 mm) and with keeled ribs in subsp. *archangelica*.[3] All the forms of angelica discussed in this paper are generally recognized as belonging to subsp. *archangelica*. When necessary, I will use 'angelica in the wild' for *A. archangelica* subsp. *archangelica* growing in the wild, to avoid confusion with 'wild angelica' *A. sylvestris*.

A number of synonyms, no longer valid scientific names, have been used for the edible angelica. The most common of these are *Angelica officinalis* Moench, *A. sativa* Mill., *Archangelica officinalis* Hoffm., *Archangelica norvegica* Rupr.[4]

Angelica is native to Norway, Sweden, Iceland, Greenland, the Faeroes, Finland,

Russia, and eastern parts of continental Europe. It has become naturalized in countries to the south and west of its natural range. It grows in moist places up in the mountains and in mountain valleys and, towards the north of its range, also in the lowlands.[5]

The oldest written sources relating to the use of angelica are the Icelandic sagas, and Old Norse lawbooks. In the saga of the sworn brothers (*Fóstbræðra Saga*) we hear about Thorgeir and Thormod going up into the mountains to gather angelica. They found a grassy ledge, later to be known as Thorgeir's Ledge, with a number of large angelicas. Thormod carried the bundle up to the top, while Thorgeir remained behind. Suddenly Thorgeir lost his footing, but grabbed hold of an angelica stem, close to the ground, to avoid falling off the ledge onto the rocks far below. Thormod wondered what took him so long and called out to ask if he had found enough yet. 'I reckon', Thorgeir calmly replied, 'I'll have enough once I've uprooted this piece I'm holding.' Thormod then went down to the ledge again and saved Thorgeir.[6]

Two great angelicas with a small angelica (*hvannarkálfr*) between them is the solution to one of the riddles told by Odin to the king in the saga of king Heidrek.[7]

The saga of King Olav Tryggvasson contains the best-known piece of old angelica lore. One spring day as King Olav was walking in the streets, he met a man with a bundle of angelica stems, remarkably large for the season. The king took a large stem in his hand, and went back to the house. Queen Thyre was weeping as the king entered. He presented the stem to the queen, who rejected it, saying that she was used to finer gifts. The story, as told by Snorri Sturluson, is thought to show their loveless marriage, by Snorri's use of the fertility symbol angelica. It was recognized as a symbol of fertility, possibly due to the great power with which this massive plant appears early in the spring.[8] At Voss, wedding processions on horseback were common till around 1880. The riders at the front of the procession all carried angelicas, the largest one was in the hands of the bride.[9]

Some of the first sources of information about gardening in Norway can be found in the old laws, for example the Gulathing's law, written in the 11th century AD. The paragraphs on tenant farming (*landleiebolken*) defined the rights of a tenant farmer to take his angelica plants with him. The theft paragraphs (*tjuebolken*) set penalties for entering another man's garden, and stealing from it. If a man was caught with stolen angelica, he was deemed without legal rights, and could be punished as the owner of the garden saw fit. The oldest law texts knew only two kinds of gardens, namely angelica and leek[10] gardens. As the laws evolved, kale gardens were added to the law texts, then gardens for apples, turnips, peas and fava beans, until finally including 'all that can be enclosed by fences and walls'.[11]

Similar paragraphs on stealing from gardens do not appear in Swedish law till much later, and angelica is not mentioned.[12] The Icelandic lawbook *Grágás* does not mention angelica gardens; on the other hand it sets penalties for gathering angelica on another man's land.[13] Several 14th- to 16th-century Icelandic diplomata are easements giving rights to gather angelica on another man's land.[14]

In the Scandinavian languages,[15] angelica is known by a form of its Norse name: like *hvönn* in Icelandic, *hvonn* in Faeroese, *kvann* in Norwegian, *kvan* in Danish, *kvanne* in Swedish. Greenland Inuit is not a Scandinavian language, but got the name *kuannit* on loan along with the plant from Norse settlers. That name even came in handy when *kuanniusat* (rhubarb) appeared in Greenland many centuries later.

The name *angelica* is used both in English and Italian, *angélica* in Spanish, *angélique* in French, *Engelwurz* in German, *engelwortel* in Dutch, and *väinönputki* in Finnish.

The western Scandinavian languages have a number of words for angelica, or related to it, indicating that angelica and its use is, or at one time has been very important in the area. Old Norse has *hvönn* and *hvanne* for the plant, *hvannnjóli* for the flower stem, *hvannkalfr* (lit. angelica calf) is a small plant sprouting from the root of an older one, after-growth, and *hvannagarðr* is an angelica garden. *Hvannjólatrumbu* is a tubular piece of stem. Most of these words in a modernized form are used in Norwegian: *kvann, kvannjol, kvannkalv, kvanngard*. The name *kvann* in Norwegian does not include wild angelica (*A. sylvestris*), which is known as *sløke*.

In Icelandic, *hvönn* can mean any plant of the genus Angelica, including *ætihvönn* (lit. edible angelica), *erkihvönn* (both are *A. archangelica*), and *geithvönn* (*A. sylvestris*). *Hvannjóli* or *hvannastrokkur* is the flower stalk, and *rótarfjall* (lit. root mountain) is a mountain where angelica is growing.

Faeroese has a particularly rich range of words: *hvonn* is any plant of the genus Angelica, including *bakkahvonn* and *bjargahvonn* (*A. archangelica* in the wild), *heimahvonn* (cultivated *A. archangelica*), *sløkjuhvonn, trøllahvonn*, and *sløkja* (*A. sylvestris*). The flower stem is called *hvannjólur* or *hvannleggur*, the after-growth is *hvannkálvur*, and *hvanngarður* is a garden where *heimahvonn* is grown. Places where angelica grows profusely in the wild are known as *hvannabøli, hvannabøkkur, hvan-*

133

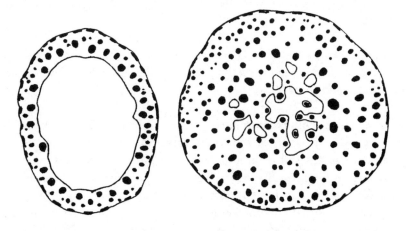

nakassi, *hvannaland*, or *hvannrók*. A *hvannatjóv* is someone who commits *hvannastuldur*, steals angelica. Someone who eats too much angelica risks getting *hvannakreppingar* or *hvannakrymp*, upset stomach or stomach pains. Another risk is *hvannsár*, an inflammation, usually of the lips or the area around the lips, caused by angelica sap and sunlight.[16] Even the best bits for eating have been named: the lower part of the leaf stalk is the 'sweet bite', *søtabiti*, *grand*, *skálkur*, or *goturstykki* The upper part of the leaf stalk, where it divides into three, is the 'best bite', *bestibiti*, or *mua*.

In Sami the young, vegetative plant is *fádnu*, the flowering plant is *boska*. *Boska* is also used in the meaning 'to gather angelica'. A loan word from Norse *gras*[17] is Sami *rássi*, more specifically *olbmorássi* (human grass), *borranrássi* (edible grass), and *olbmoborranrássi*.[18]

The ample selection of places and topographic features named after angelica are another indication of the importance of this plant in Scandinavia. Some examples from Iceland are: Hvannadalshnúkur (the highest mountain peak in Iceland at 2,119m above sea level), Hvanná, Hvannalindar, Hvanndalir, Hvanneyri, Hvannfell, Hvannavellir, Hvannavallagil, Hvannstøð, and Hvannstaðafjallgarður. In the Faeroes we have: Hvannadalsá, Hvannadalur, Hvannafelli, Hvannagjógv, Hvannasund, Hvannasundshagi, Hvannhagi, and Hvannhólmur. Some Norwegian examples are Kvannås, Kvannbekkli, Kvanndal, -dalen, Kvanndalsfjellet, -hornet, -nuten, -rabben, -sætra, -vold, Kvangarsnes, Kvannkjosen, Kvannlien, Kvanes, Kvannvik, Kvanna, Kvangrøvann, Kvangrøfjell, Joldalshorn, Jolgrøhorn, Jolgrøvann, Jolhorn, Kvannjolvann, and Kvannjolfjell.[19] These are far from all, one Norwegian atlas alone has over 50 names beginning with *kvann-*.

The first topographical descriptions of Norway do not go in great detail about a single plant or foodstuff. That the use of angelica is mentioned at all must indicate that it was important at the time. It was not one of those plants eaten only during famines, nor was it used primarily for medicine. In fact, many 16th-18th-century writers specifically said that it was eaten as a delicacy. Schønnebøl wrote that angelica was eaten in the summer for pleasure, raw,

> just like apples, pears and nuts are eaten in Denmark. It is their fruit. Apart from that, and what God gives the poor from the sea, here is nothing but the skies, water, and stone.[20]

Strøm described how peasants used to go up in the mountains on Midsummer Day, only to feast on angelica stems. He called this a disappearing tradition, but as late as 1928 it was still common in parts of Northern Norway.[21] According to Hiorthøy angelica was much sought-after by the peasants, and the stem was eaten 'like carrots', it was not as sharp in taste as the root.[22]

Some mentioned that the root was used for medicine, often describing it together with gentian.[23] Friis said that stems and root, both eaten raw, were used as a remedy against scurvy.[24] The poet Henrik Wergeland pointed out the medicinal properties of the root and recommended the stem as a healthy food.[25]

The dried root was chewed or smoked like tobacco, or used as an addition to real tobacco. Six pipes of forged iron, for smoking angelica root, are in the Heiberg Collections in Sogn, western Norway. The roots were also used in spirits.[26]

Linnaeus encountered the Sami use of angelica on his travels in Northern Sweden. He described meeting a Sami man with an armfull of angelica stems. The young stems, not yet in flower, were peeled, then eaten as a delicacy, 'like an apple'. On another occasion, he said 'like a turnip'. He added that it really tasted well, particularly the upper and softer parts of the stalk, which were the most sought-after.[27]

Leem wrote about the coastal and mountain Sami in Finnmark, Norway. According to him, angelica was among the foods the Sami ate not to satisfy hunger, but for pleasure, as they had no apples, nuts or other fruits. With great appetite they peeled the stems and ate them raw, occasionally cooked on embers, or boiled in milk. The Sami in Finnmark used to eat a lot of angelica stalks, usually raw. In some coastal districts the stalks were eaten with fish oil, this was considered a particular delicacy. The Sami also used the young inflorescences, still enclosed in the leaf sheaths, chopped them up and boiled them in reindeer milk to a porridge-like substance. This was stuffed in a reindeer stomach for winter supply. [28]

The account by Eggert Ólafsson and Bjarni Pálsson of their travels in Iceland in the years 1752–1757 contains much information on where angelica grew in Iceland, and how it was used. Angelica grew profusely and at times to such a size that a grown man could put his arm into its cut stem. Sauðlauksdal church had the right to gather as much angelica as could be cut by six men in one day, or by one man in six days. We learn that the stems were eaten raw, sliced, with butter, often as a vegetable or salad with fish. Some ate the roots as a vegetable with stockfish, with milk, cream, or butter. In the south, some had taken up the ancient practice of growing angelica gardens.[29]

According to Debes, angelica was frequently planted both in special gardens and in cemeteries in the Faeroes, but was also common in the wild, in fields and up in the mountains. Again, we learn that the peeled, hollow stems were eaten raw, as a delicacy, like people elsewhere ate fruits. In years of hardship, they even used the roots 'instead of food'. The tradition of communal trips into the mountains to gather angelica, as described in Norway, was also known in the Faeroes until early in the 20th century. Until the end of the 19th century, no household was deemed complete without a decent angelica garden, but even so, they also gathered angelica in the wild from nearby *hvannabøli*.[30]

We have heard that angelica was eaten as a delicacy, but what does it actually taste like? Clarke, travelling in Scandinavia in the summer of 1799, said they often ate the stalks of the plant: 'it reminded us of celery, but had a warmer flavour.'[31] Its aroma has been likened to that of musk, the taste sweetish, balsamic at first, followed by warmth and bitterness. Grieve compared the flavour of angelica to that of juniper berries.

It has variously been regarded as pleasantly fruity, strongly aromatic but somewhat acrid,[32] even as a happy mixture of gentian and mint. I tend to agree with Madame de Sévigné who described its taste as indescribable: 'Son bon goût ne rappelle en rien dont on se souvienne et il ne ressemble à aucun autre goût que le sien.'[33]

Since the old lawbooks, nothing was written about angelica gardens in Norway for hundreds of years. Early in the 20th century we learn the first details about the angelica garden and the cultivated plant. The angelica garden was a small enclosure, usually by the south wall of the house. A layer of ashes and charcoal was used to fertilize the plants and keep weeds away. Young plants with three leaves were *skjerd*, or ready to have the outermost (and largest) leaf harvested.

Grønlien pointed out that the cultivated angelica from Voss differed from the wild form. The wild plant is bitter, and has hollow, tubular leaf stalks. The other is sweeter, tastier, and has a fine aroma. Its stalks are almost solid, with a barely noticeable hollow.[34] The cultivated variety contains around 50% more sugar than its wild relative.[35] He also found differences in the size and lifespan of the plants, but those characters are more likely to be influenced by the place and method of cultivation, rather than being genetic variations.

The use was different, too. It was the flower stem that was cut from the wild plant and eaten. That is not very economical. You only get one stem from each plant, and the plant will then die without setting seed. Harvesting the leaves of the cultivated plants may actually prolong the life of the plants, as they will need more time to grow

Angelica. Såck fein beschreibung im Ersten Teyl diß es Contrafayten Kreuterbüchs/ am. CCC. vnb. fviiii. blatt.

Errengelica
Angelica archangelica

strong enough to flower and set seed.

Grønlien had found the cultivated variety in only one location and thought that it was doomed. Fægri was just as pessimistic about its future:

> Somewhere an old grandma potters about her angelica garden, soon she will be gone, and the angelica will die with her. That is a pity: not only does a very rare plant disappear, but with it a thousand years of Norwegian cultural history.[36]

Fægri named the cultivated angelica *Vossakvann* and described it as a botanical variety, based on a type specimen from Mestad.[37] It is now known as *Angelica archangelica* var. *maiorum* Fægri.

Remains of angelica gardens have been found only on a few farms on the outskirts of Voss.[38] Today there is only one of these, Mestad in Teigdalen, which still has a viable population of *Vossakvann*. The old Norse laws tell us that angelica must have been grown in other parts of the country as well, but not where. It must have gone out of use long time ago. From nearby Granvin, Modalen and Gudvangen, old people have remembered having seen angelica gardens, but nothing is left of these.[39] The cultivated plants known from other countries do not seem to have any of the characteristics of *Vossakvann*.

To maintain the qualities of the *Vossakvann*, an active selection will be necessary. The variety has been on the brink of extinction for most of the 20th century, but there is hope that it will survive.

137

Angelica was unknown to the Greeks and Romans and was not mentioned in any of the first herbals. Before the spread of angelica as a medical remedy throughout Europe, *archangelica*, *archangel*, and *herba angelica* were names for plants of the genus *Lamium* (dead-nettles) and some related genera (*Galeopsis, Stachys, Ballota*). Coelius Sedulius is said to have used the name angelica in the 5th century AD, while the first use of archangelica appears to have been in the Latin grammar of Aelfric *c.* AD 1000.[40]

Why angelica was unknown in continental Europe, and how it came into use is not known. The most likely theory seems to be that monks learned about the the plant in Scandinavia, and brought the knowledge south. We also know that angelica root used to be exported from Norway.[41]

Alexander Hispanus, in the 13th century, was probably the first to use the name angelica in its present sense, describing the medical virtues of angelica root.[42] Another early source is Matthaeus Silvaticus' *Pandectae medicinae* (*c.* 1300).[43]

The oldest reference to angelica in the *Oxford English Dictionary* is from 1578,[44] unless you happen to look under *jag*, or under *lungwort*, in which case the *OED* predates itself to 1568,[45] 1565 and 1552.[46] The first to use the name *Archangelica* for angelica seems to have been Matthias de l'Obel in 1576 in his *Plantarum seu stirpium historia*.[47]

The first edition (1530) of Otto Brunfels' *Herbarum vivae eicones* is known for its excellent and accurate wood engravings. In a 1537 edition published after Brunfels' death, the earliest known illustration of an angelica is added, unfortunately drawn from the artist's fantasy.[48]

Angelica eventually became known as a panacea; it has been used as a remedy for just about every imaginable ailment. Alexander Hispanus recommended that ground angelica root boiled with honey be put on the wound to help against the bite of a rabid dog.[49] Parkinson wrote that:

Angelica, the garden kinde, is so good an herbe, that there is no part thereof but is of much vse, and all cordiall and preseruatiue from infectious or contagious diseases, whether you will distill the water of the herbe, or preserue or candie the rootes or the greene stalkes, or vse the seede in pouder or in distillations, or decoctions with other things.[50]

Gerard said that:

The roote of garden Angelica is a singular remedie against poison and against the plague, and all infections taken by evill and corrup aire; if you do but take a peece of the roote and holde it in your mouth, it doth most certainly drive away the pestilentiall aire.[51]

If you believe in aphrodisiacs, you may like to try Curnonsky's recipe for *eau archiepiscopale*, with angelica root, in his book *La table et l'amour*.[52] If you don't, you may prefer to believe Parkinson: 'The dryed roote [...] will abate the rage of lust in young persons'.[53]

'The large and strong plant was known to boost both carnal desire and pugnacity' is the message spread across the page in bold lettering, when a health magazine writes about a new product made from angelica. Not surprisingly, there is no reference for this claim. An Icelandic company is now marketing a tincture from angelica seeds. They do claim, in much smaller letters, that they can document its effect in increasing energy, endurance and general well-being.[54]

Angelica was cultivated in English gardens prior to 1568, but considerable quantities were still being grown near London in the late 19th century, for candying.[55] Dorothy Hartley gave a recipe for candied angelica, explaining that it was 'mentioned specially as a home-made product up to 1860, as "it can seldom be bought in market".'[56]

Today, angelica is cultivated on a large scale in several countries, including Germany (30-50 ha.), Belgium (16 ha. in 1998), Holland, Poland, and France.[57] Its main uses are in herbal medicine, and in the production of various alcoholic beverages, like vermouth, Bénédictine, Chartreuse, and gin. In France, angelica is cultivated for use in confectionery in Niort, and apparently on a lesser scale in Clermont-Ferrand and Apt.[58] The green stuff with which we started, the candied angelica, may now seem like a mere trifle in the long history of angelica.

Bibliography

Baumann, Susanne, *Pflanzenabbildungen in alten Kräuterbüchern* (Stuttgart: Wissenschaftliche Verlagsgesellschaft, 1998).

Beyer, Absalon Pedersøn, 'Om Norgis Rige' (1567) in *Historisk-topografiske Skrifter om Norge og norske Landsdele*, ed. by Gustav Storm (Christiania: Brøgger, 1895), pp. 1-116.

Buche, Vincent, *L'angélique de Niort et du monde entier* (La Crèche: Geste éditions, 2003).

Clarke, Edward Daniel, *Travels in various countries of Europe, Asia and Africa.* (London: Cadell and Davies, 1824).

Curnonsky, *La table et l'amour. Nouveau traité des excitants modernes* (Paris: Clé d'Or, 1950).

Czygan, Franz-Christian, 'Engelwurz oder Angelikawurzel', in *Zeitschrift für Phytotherapie*, vol. 19 (1998), pp. 342-8.

David, Elizabeth, *Spices, salt and aromatics in the English kitchen* (London: Penguin, 1970; repr. Grub Street, 2000).

Debes, Lucas Jacobsøn, *Færoæ et Færoa Reserata* (København, 1673; repr. Thorshavn, 1903).

Eggert Ólafsson, *Vice-Lavmand Eggert Olafsens og Land-Physici Biarne Povelsens Reise igiennem Island* (Sorøe: Jonas Lindgrens Enke, 1772).

Fjellström, Phebe, 'Fjällkvannen (*Angelica archangelica*) i samisk tradition', in *Samisk etnobiologi*, ed. by Ingvar Svanberg and Håkan Tunón (Nora: Nya Doxa, 2000), pp. 241-52.

Francis, Frédéric, *Report from the state of Belgium forming part of the IENICA project* (Gembloux: Faculty of Agricultural Sciences, 2000).

Friis, Peder Claussøn, 'Norriges oc Omliggende Øers Beskriffuelse' (1632) in *Samlede Skrifter af Peder Claussøn Friis* (Kristiania: Brøgger, 1881).

Fröberg, Lars, Angelica, inedited manuscript for *Flora Nordica* vol. 6 (Lund: 2004).

Fægri, Knut, 'Kvanngard og gardakvann', in *Bergen Turlag Årbok* 1949 ([Bergen]: 1949), pp. 161-7.

— 'Kvanngarden, en parkhistorisk relikt' in *Lustgården* (1951), pp. 5-17.

Grieve, Maud, *A modern herbal.* (London, 1931; repr. Penguin, 1977).

Grigson, Jane, *Jane Grigson's English food* (London: 1974; rev. ed. Penguin, 1992).

Grønlien, Nils, 'Um kvann og kvannagardar' in *Vossabygdene*, vol. 18 (1928), pp. 46-9.

Hartley, Dorothy, *Food in England* (London: Macdonald, 1954; repr. 1973).

Hauberg, Poul, *Henrik Harpestræng* : Liber Herbarum (København: Hafnia, 1936).

Hegi, Gustav, *Illustrierte Flora von Mitteleuropa*, vol V part 2 (Berlin: Paul Parey, 1965).

Heiberg, Gert Falch, 'Kvanne og kvannrot-piper', in *Maal og Minne* (1933), pp. 77-80.

Hiorthøy, Hugo Frederik, *Physisk og ekonomisk beskrivelse over Gulbransdalens provstie* (Kiøbenhavn: Nicolaus Møller, 1785).

Hiroe, Minosuke, *Umbelliferae of world* [sic] (Tokyo: Ariake, 1979).

Holm, Ingar, 'Kvann – vikingenes egen medisin', in *Life-magasinet*, vol. 2004: 1, pp. 70-2.

Hunt, Tony, *Plant Names of Medieval England* (Cambridge: Brewer, 1989).

Høeg, Ove Arbo, *Planter og tradisjon* (Oslo: Universitetsforlaget, 1974).

Ingólfur Daví_sson, 'Ætihvönn' in *Náttúrufræ_ingurinn*, vol. 41: 2 (1971), pp. 106-12.

Jackson, John R., 'The Angelica' in *The Garden*, 23 Dec. 1882, p. 555.

Joensen, Hans Debes, 'Um hvonnina í Føroyum, serliga um nýtsluna til matna og um hvannsárið', in Varðin, vol. 29 (1951), pp. 129-54.

Keil, Gundolf, 'Alexander Hispanus' in Die Deutsche Literatur des Mittelalters : Verfasserlexikon, 2. ed. (Berlin: de Gruyter, 1983), vol. IV, pp. 53-8.

KLNM / Kulturhistorisk leksikon for nordisk middelalder, 22 vols (Oslo: Gyldendal, 1956-78).

Leem, Knud, Beskrivelse over Finmarkens Lapper (Kiøbenhavn: Salikath, 1767).

Lid, Johannes, Norsk og svensk flora (Oslo: Samlaget, 1979).

Lid, Nils, Joleband og vegetasjonsguddom (Oslo: Dybwad, 1928).

Linnaeus, Carolus, Lapplandsresa år 1732 (Stockholm: Wahlström & Widstrand, 1965).

Nedkvitne, Knut, 'Kvann' in Gamalt frå Voss, vol. 2 (1995), pp. 17-29.

Norges gamle Love indtil 1387, 5 vols (Kristiania: Grøndahl, 1846-95).

Olsson, Alfa, 'Färöiska kostvanor' in Rig, vol. 37: 3 (1954), pp. 79-91.

Parkinson, John, Paradisi in sole, paradisus terrestris (London: 1629; facs. edn. Amsterdam: Theatrum Orbis Terrarum, 1975).

Pontoppidan, Erik, Norges Naturlige Historie, 2 vols (Copenhagen, 1752-53; facs. edn., Rosenkilde og Bagger, 1977).

Qvigstad, Just, 'Lappiske plantenavne' in Nyt Magazin for Naturvidenskaberne, vol. 39: 4 (1901), pp. 303-26.

Ramus, Jonas, Norriges Beskrivelse (Kjøbenhavn: 1715).

Schønnebøl, Erik Hansen, 'Lofotens och Vestraalens Beskriffuelse' (1591) in Historisk-topografiske Skrifter om Norge og norske Landsdele, ed. by Gustav Storm (Christiania: Brøgger, 1895), pp. 177-218.

Schübeler, Frederik Christian, Viridarium Norvegicum, vol 2 (Christiania: Fabritius, 1888).

Skelly, Carole J., Dictionary of Herbs, Spices, Seasonings, and Natural Flavorings (New York: Garland, 1994).

Stein, Siegfried, Gemüse aus Großmutters Garten (München: BLV, 1989).

Strøm, Hans, Physisk og Oeconomisk Beskrivelse over Fogderiet Søndmør, 2 vols (Sorøe, 1762-66).

Sverrir Tómasson, 'Hvönnin í Ólafs sögum Tryggvasonar' in Gripla, vol. 6 (1984), pp. 202-17.

Thompson, Robert, The gardener's assistant, practical and scientific (London: Blackie & Son, 1878).

Viðar Hreinsson, ed., The Complete sagas of Icelanders (Reykjavík: Leifur Eiríksson, 1997).

Wergeland, Henrik, Den norske Bondes nyttige Kundskab ... (Christiania, 1831; repr. in Samlede Skrifter, vol IV:1, Oslo, 1923)

Wille, Hans Jacob, Beskrivelse over Sillejords Præstegield (Kiøbenhavn: Gyldendal, 1786).

Øvstedal, Dag Olav, Vossakvann-prosjektet ved Botanisk Hage, Universitetet i Bergen (Bergen: 1993).

References

1. David, p. 63.
2. Grigson, p. 261.
3. Lid (1979), p. 544; Fröberg.
4. Hiroe, p. 1347.
5. Hegi, pp. 1340-1.
6. Vi?ar Hreinsson (1997), vol II: pp. 360-1.
7. Hervarar saga og Hei?reks in Netútgáfan <http://www.snerpa.is/net/forn/hervar.htm> [accessed 20 June 2004].
8. Lid (1928), p. 208.
9. Grønlien, p. 47.
10. Possibly sand leek, Allium scorodoprasum L., Fægri (1951), p. 6.
11. Norges gamle Love: vol. I pp. 38, 241, 253, 326, 331; vol. II pp. 172, 272; vol. IV p. 335.
12. Fægri (1951), p. 5-7.

13. Schübeler, p. 228.
14. KLNM vol IX, p. 535.
15. The following dictionaries have been used here: *Íslensk or?abók* , ed. by Árni Bö?varsson, 2nd ed. (Reykjavík: Mál og menning, 1996); *Føroysk or?abók* (Tórshavn: Føroya Fró?skaparfelag, 1998); *Sámi-dáru sátnegirji* , ed. by Brita Kåven and others (Kárásjohka: Davvi Girji, 1995); *Ordbog over Det gamle norske Sprog*, ed. by Johan Fritzner, 2nd rev. ed. (Kristiania: 1886-96; repr. Oslo: 1954); *Ordbog over Det gamle norske Sprog. Rettelser og tillegg*, ed. by Finn Hødnebø (Oslo: 1972); OED / *The Oxford English Dictionary* on CD-ROM, 2. ed., Ver. 3.0 (OUP, 2002).
16. The sap increases the photosensitivity of the skin, thus the combined exposure to angelica and sun may lead to a severe case of phytophotodermatitis (Joensen).
17. English *grass*, not in the botanical sense, but in the wider, popular sense of herbage.
18. Fjellström, pp. 244, 251; Qvigstad; Lid (1928), p. 205.
19. Joensen, p. 134; Schübeler, p. 229; and other sources.
20. Schønnebøl, p. 199.
21. Strøm, vol 1 p. 71; vol 2 pp. 128, 500; Lid (1928), p. 206.
22. Hiorthøy, p. 41; Wille, p. 105.
23. Beyer, p. 63; Ramus, p. 19; Pontoppidan vol. 1, p. 185.
24. Friis, p. 393.
25. Wergeland, p. 103.
26. Pontoppidan vol 1, p. 185; Strøm, p. 71; Wille, p. 105; Heiberg; Wergeland, p. 103.
27. Linnaeus, pp. 80, 90.
28. Leem, p. 127; Schübeler, p. 225.
29. Eggert Ólafsson, pp. 158, 429, 431, 459, 943, 939.
30. Debes, pp. 108-9; Olsson, p. 89.
31. Clarke vol 10, p. 151.
32. Jackson; Grieve, p. 38; Stein, p. 63; Skelly, p. 12.
33. Buche, p. 31.
34. Grønlien, p. 48.
35. 39 % of dry matter, as opposed to 25 % in wild kvann, Fægri (1951), p. 12.
36. Fægri (1949), p. 167.
37. Fægri (1951), p. 17: '*Angelica archangelica* var. *maiorum* nov. var. Differt a forma typica [»*A. archangelica* var. *norvegica* (Rupr.) Rikli»] petiolis fere solidis. – In hortibus rusticis prope Voss culta. Typus ex Mestad Teigdaliae in Museo botanico Universitatis Bergensi.'
38. Grønlidi (Grønlien, p. 47), Mestad in Teigdalen, Markhusteigen in Langedalen/Vossestrand, Gjerald in Bordalen (Fægri 1951), Elje near Evanger, and Tveite in Holbygdi (Øvstedal; Nedkvitne).
39. Høeg, p. 205.
40. Hunt, p. 33; Hauberg, p. 159; OED, s.v. 'archangel'.
41. Czygan, p. 347; Beyer, p. 63.
42. 'Angelica est radix optima' etc. The book survives mainly in the Codex D 600. 8°, written c. 1490, now in the Uppsala University library. It was published by Hauberg in 1936 and attributed by him to Henrik Harpestræng (d. 1244). Keil (1983) has shown the author to be Alexander Hispanus.
43. Lid (1979), p. 739.
44. OED, s.v. 'angelica': 1578 Lyte Dodoens 297 The rootes of Angelica are contrarie to all poyson.
45. OED, s.v. 'jag': 1568 Turner Herbal iii. 5 Angelica hath leves [...] lyke lovage, but not so far iagged in.
46. OED, s.v. 'lungwort': 1552 Elyot Dict. s.v. *Angelica*, Of this herbe be two kindes, .. 1565 Cooper *Thesaurus*, Angelica, an hearbe whereof be two kindes, one of the garden called angelica ...
47. Lid (1979), p. 739.
48. Baumann, pp. 66, 115, 135.
49. Hauberg, p. 113; Keil, p. 58.

50. Parkinson, p. 470.
51. Jackson.
52. Curnonsky, p. 228.
53. Parkinson, p. 529.
54. Holm.
55. Jackson; Thompson, p. 145.
56. Hartley, p. 454.
57. Czygan, p. 343; Francis, p. 56.
58. Buche, pp. 32-3.

A Wild Herb Nursery in Alicante

Vicky Hayward

For over fifty years Pedro Pérèz Roque has been observing wild herbs near Alcoy in the mountains of inland central Alicante. He began studying them at the age of 11 and his hobby grew into a vocation. Exploring the sierras, he would collect and study samples, classify them by eye and aroma, and plant them on home ground at different altitudes and in different soils. In 1990 he took one step further: he started a nursery to preserve the species he had identified, to propagate and catalogue them. Financially independent and cooperatively owned, the nursery now houses a total of 800 aromatic or medicinal species and subspecies. In 2003 Pedro began to lay out a botanical garden within the nursery.

Pedro, aged 61, grew up in a small town, but when he was eleven, the family moved out of town. Pedro left school to begin to work on the land. His father, a sharecropper, grew cereals and also had almond trees, vines and olive trees. The work on the farm was hard. Grapes were trodden by foot and the land was ploughed with horses. Pedro had two sisters, but no friends of his age close to hand, so he played and spent most of his time with two older neighbours, Juanet and Kiko La Tiliana. They were the first people to teach Pedro about the herbs that were then in everyday use.

In the 1940s and 1950s these herbs were in everyday use, but they were more important medicinally than in cooking. At that time there was no welfare state, medicines were scarce and doctors were paid in wheat, potatoes or barley during the so-called 'Years of Hunger' that followed the Civil War. Carmen – Pedro's first cousin, who collects herbs to make infusions, cook and so on – remembers penicillin being brought specially from Valencia, over 130 kilometres (just over 80 miles) away, for serious cases in the 1950s. She also remembers her father-in-law selling a piece of land to be able to pay for his teenage son to see a specialist doctor in Madrid.

Herbal remedies, then, were of real importance for everyday complaints, usually taken as infusions – wild camomile for stomach aches and eye infections, thyme for digestive problems, mallow with honey for chest infections, 'herba de la sangre' (*Lithidora fruticosa*) for blood pressure, *sideritis* as an anti-inflammatory, sage as a blood cleanser and to treat diabetes, hot mustard poultices or even hot prickly pear leaf poultices for chest complaints. It is still traditional today to take a cup of dried linden-flowers and leaves round to somebody who is to be given bad news – for example, of death in the family – so they have a tranquilizing infusion to hand. Other herbs – thyme, again, but especially a local sub-species called *pebrella*, oregano, fennel and *albasana*, a mint – were used liberally in cooking.

By the age of 14 Pedro was beginning to collect these wild herbs and grow them for pleasure, observing the differences according to altitude and the soil where they grew.

'As time went by I became more interested in tracking down different sub-species of local herbs growing in the sierras.' Nearby, close to Alcoy, are the Sierra de Aitana and the Sierra de Mariola, both known for their native wild flowers and herbs. When he was not working on the land, he built up a small collection, which he planted out on two hectares of land rented cheaply from a neighbour.

Finally, in the 1980s, he turned his interest into a bigger project. 'The original idea was not to sell anything – it was to identify sub-species and preserve them.' For four to five years he spent as much time as he could prospecting throughout south-eastern Spain, especially in certain sierras: for example, the Sierra de Filabres in Almeria. He tracked down herbs with the help of local people who knew the mountains. 'Often they did not know if the plants were good or bad, but they knew where they were.' This prospecting work, which he still continues today, has also taken him along the coast and into natural parks, where permits are required to collect specimens.

'In this kind of dry Mediterranean climate, it's not just a question of the right moment,' he says, 'It's a question of the right year – many years there may not be enough rain for a herb to flower, for example.'

After a first rough on-the-spot identification, generally by growth habits and aroma, the specimens are taken back to Castalla where they are propagated from cuttings or reproduced from cell tissue, and are planted out in different plots within a total of 27 hectares of land. The plots are scattered at different altitudes and on different soils – with subspecies kept well apart to avoid natural hybridization. Some need to grow on slopes to avoid the roots being waterlogged. Others respond badly or well to being cut back. They are observed for at least two to three years to see how each species and sub-species develops, and then seeds of the most interesting types go into Pedro's seedbank, stored in jars in fridges at his home and at the nursery.

Fifteen years ago, after a visit from members of the Valencian cooperative movement, Pedro turned the project into a cooperative, called Proagri, which was founded to cultivate the herbs for sale with the idea of ploughing the profits back into expanding the collection and researching it in full.

Today half of Pedro's business is supplying other nurseries on an informal basis. The other half is selling herbs – harvested and dried, with a price per kilo – to the companies which extract their essences for use in cosmetics, soaps, shampoos and alternative medicine. The nursery also supplies aromatic and medicinal plants to the local authorities for environmentally friendly planting along motorways and around roundabouts. The fields remain scattered and are largely organic. Iron sulphate is used against snails and some crops are irrigated – lavender and lemon verbena, for example. Others, like rosemary, are not. Weeding is by hand.

As a business, Pedro's problem is not finding a market. He hired a stand once at Iberflora in 1992 and in the first morning he received so many orders – a total of

97,000 plants – that he knew he could not supply any more customers. The main problem today is finding sufficiently large areas of land with an adequate water supply for drip irrigation at critical moments to produce quantities of the herbs at an accessible price and on a large enough scale to give profits to reinvest in research.

A second problem is the funding of detailed laboratory analysis. 'Herbs are like cars from the point of view of their medicinal or other properties,' says Pedro. 'One can be a Rolls Royce and another can be a baby Seat.' The components of the essential oils used in perfumes, for herbal treatments or for flavour in culinary herbs can vary hugely from one sub-species to another. In thyme, for example, there are some 38 traceable chemical components, in particular thymol, which may make up 14-56% of the essential oils, depending on the sub-species. This is a little researched area, but one that Proagri is beginning to explore in endemic indigenous sub-species little known elsewhere, usually in collaboration with different university departments. But the research to establish those levels using chromatography is expensive – around 700 euros a plant – and the growing trials to see how these essences vary with altitude and soil are also lengthy.

How far Pedro will be able to develop this research depends on the profits he can reinvest: the applications that currently interest him are non-toxic colourings, natural fungicides and plant pesticides.

Meanwhile, the local wild herb culture still flourishes – in a fashion. Most local restaurants serve thyme infusion rather than coffee to follow the local speciality, *gazpachos* – a kind of game stew served with flatbread. Carmen, my neighbour, now in her seventies, makes up her own infusion of linden flower, thyme and wild camomile for drinking after meals every day. On the other hand, other herbs, like Valeriana, are bought in pill form from the pharmacy. The spit-roast chickens sold by travelling vans at food markets are invariably stuffed with a big bunch of dried thyme. Rosemary is routinely added to paella to replace the flavour of wild rabbit – which is now usually farmed – and fennel is added to snails. In cooking the most important herb remains *pebrella*, or native thyme: it is added to *gazpachos*, to jars of preserved olives and to *morcillas de cebolla* – soft blood sausages with onion.

On another level, from an outsider's point of view, the local herb culture seems to be undervalued. Local politicians have never valued or encouraged its development, despite its economic potential to the community and would rather make money from property development. Some local people also see herbal medicines as one element of a rural past they would rather leave behind.

Meanwhile, Pedro presses on. One of his latest projects has been a small botanical garden within the nursery. It is laid out in terraces with different topsoils, with samples of different sub-species planted together, in the same beds, designed to provoke natural hybridizetion. He is also planning a new nursery, with much larger growing fields, grouped together in an upland area without roads or houses, to start registered organic growing. Ideally, in the long term, he would like to install a small laboratory and workshop for extracting the essences himself. Pedro makes his work sound simple. He focuses laconically on details – the date for harvesting thyme, the perfume of a local lavender and the planting pattern in a new field, for example – but he glides over big issues. One day, talking in the shade of a huge pine tree in his nursery, I asked him how he plotted the direction of his work. He laughed and quoted Antonio Machado, the poet, '*Al andar, se hace el camino*'. (Walking, you make the path.)

But that begs another question. Why has Pedro chosen to make such a particularly long, tricky path? Pressing deeper, it turns out that complex ethical issues shape his work. In the early years, he twinned his interest in recording and preserving wild herbs' diversity with the slower trial-and-error process of learning how to grow them. Today, as the uncontrolled harvesting of wild herbs threatens certain species, that provides us with a key model. More recently, his focus has shifted towards the need for research into herbs' potential – still largely uncharted territory – but with the proviso that the results, like local traditional herbal wisdom, should remain in local people's hands. That, he believes, will mean treading the next stretch of the path very carefully, very slowly.

One day, we drive up to see the windblown fields of newly planted organically grown herbs. I asked Pedro when he hoped this new project would come to fruition. Again, he laughed, 'It's a thousand year project'.

At the time I thought it was a throwaway line. Now, looking back, I have a hunch he has done his maths.

146

Bibliography

Usos Tradicionales de las Plantas en la Provincia de Alicante, textos José Benito Ruiz Limiñana, Exma. Diputación Provincial de Alicante, Área de Medio Ambiente, 2001

Gastronomía de la Provincia de Alicante, Francisco G.Seijo Alonso, Editorial Villa, Alicante, 1977

Wild about the UAE

Philip Iddison

The Emirati diet was substantially dependent on wild food resources in the past and there is still evidence of this in contemporary consumption. From prehistoric times to the present, fish has been a mainstay of the diet, the main protein supply and equivalent in importance to dates, cereal and dairy products which provided the bulk of sustenance.

Other wild resources had high cultural values and while some are no longer available and therefore only have a folklore influence, others are subject to ongoing exploitation. In specific instances this exploitation has been transferred to other countries. It is now illegal to hunt game in the Emirates, yet falconry is an expensive and revered pursuit for nationals. Wild honey is still collected and is an expensive commodity. This has encouraged thriving commercial apiculture to meet demand. By comparison the use of wild plants is low key but was extensive and still has a minor role in the food culture.

The physical culture of the Emiratis was simple yet sophisticated. It was essentially close to nature. The simplicity was imposed by the relative lack and limited range of resources, harsh conditions and the sparse population.

The sophistication arose in part from a finely detailed knowledge of many aspects of the natural environment. This knowledge was propagated through a strong oral tradition. This was part of a rich social culture that was robust to meet the demands of a harsh life. The landscape, weather and natural resources were dominant and determined peoples lives to an extent difficult to imagine in our cossetted technological world. As an example, a distant rainstorm in the desert would be noted and committed to memory so that flocks could be taken to the area to graze on the fresh vegetation that would appear a week or so after the storm. This knowledge could be crucial for wellbeing or even survival.

Function of Wild Foods
Wild foods have had and continue to have a number of functions in the Emirati diet and food culture:

As principal food resources, for example fish;
As cultural status markers, for instance hunting with falcons, hounds and guns;
Adding diversity to a diet that was dominated by staple foods;
Providing the only fungi in the traditional diet;
Through associations with specific festival food;
Through an interface with traditional medicines.

There is archaeological evidence for thriving groups of hunter-gatherers in past millennia. Along the coast there are many large shell middens, built up over extended periods, which testify to consumption of a large selection of gastropods and bivalves collected from the shoreline. Coastal settlements also consumed a large selection of fish from the fifth millennium BC.[1] Emirati sustenance in the immediate historic period has been derived from pastoral, fishing and agricultural activities augmented by wild food resources.

Foraging

The Emirates have diverse landscapes from sand dune deserts, through rock and gravel deserts to mountainscapes and also a long coastline with many features such as creeks, rock and sand shorelines. The flora and fauna are more diverse than might be expected in an arid environment.

All these provided direct or indirect foraging opportunities for man. In the past these were exploited in a number of ways. Nomadic tribes followed the vegetation available in the desert, often travelling considerable distances in a yearly cycle.

Transhumance was an important survival option. Families moved from the date gardens on the coastal plain to the mountains with their flocks to find forage in the peak summer months. Other groups travelled from desert oases to the shoreline for fishing and pearling opportunities.

Much of the harvesting from wild resources was seasonal; the opportunism of locating fresh grazing from erratic rainfall is an example, as is the occasional early spring harvest of dessert truffles.

Fauna

In the culinary culture of the Emirates, the most reliable source of wild food was the sea. Fishing was a highly developed and skilled occupation for a substantial part of the population. The resulting food provided fresh and preserved ingredients for the local cuisine. Nine hundred and thirty fish species have been recorded from the UAE and northern Omani waters and a high proportion are edible and of high culinary quality.

Inter-leaved with pearl fishing and trading efforts, the fisheries provided an economic base for the coastal communities and enabled these communities to exist year round in very harsh terrain.

Hunting birds, reptiles and mammals probably never produced significant dietary inputs as the early and ready availability of domestic animals ensured a meat supply and more importantly a range of versatile dairy products, all from reliable managed resources.

Key species such as houbara bustard and stone curlew; oryx, tahr,[2] sand and mountain gazelle were the prey for organized hunts with falcons, salukis and mounted hunters. These hunts carried substantial cultural cachet and in some cases was the exclusive preserve of ruling families.

Game hunting is now illegal in the UAE and one result has been the transfer of the activity to other countries. Hunting expeditions to Pakistan and other countries supporting the same or similar wildlife are the preserve of the wealthy and are usually regular annual events. These involve large entourages and the shipping of a supply of brand new four-wheel-drive vehicles to the hunting location. Through these activities the prestige and culture associated with hunting is preserved. It is thus an aspiration of many, as witnessed by the popularity of falconry, despite the reality that this may involve only the training of a falcon and the hunting of feral pigeons.

Cape hare and other small mammals, such as jerboa and *jird* were the subjects of more casual and opportunistic hunting by travellers and herdsmen in the past. This did not always require weapons. Thesiger's companion on his Rub al Khali journey was able to run down a Cape hare, *Lepus capensis*. The animal's defence was to stay absolutely still until the last minute when it was unable to escape the fleet foot of his companion. He also records one companion pulling hares from their shallow burrows where they were hiding from eagles, which were quartering the area.[3]

Reptiles such as the spiney tailed lizard, *dhub* (*Euromastyx aegypticus microlepis*) and skinks, *halaj*, were also consumed. The tail of the spiney tailed lizard is frequently mentioned as food and it's popularity led to its protection.[4] The Dhaheri tribe was locally noted for its consumption of the skink population. Thesiger recorded that Bin Kabina, his companion, was sickened by a meal that included a stew made from skinks

Locusts are the only insect recorded in the Emirati diet in the past. They are now effectively extinguished from the local fauna. Their massive swarms provided a glut resource, some of which was cooked and stored in jars. They were a famine food, an opportunity to exact revenge on the potential contributors to the famine.

Apart from marine products wild fauna does not appear at all in the local markets these days.

149

Flora

The flora of the UAE is remarkably diverse taking into account the aridity and high temperatures. There are a significant number of plants and fruit that have been foraged for food in the past.

The recent publication of the first comprehensive flora of the United Arab Emirates has enabled an analysis to be carried out of the food potential of this resource. A total of 580 plants have been recorded in the UAE and the immediately adjacent provinces of Oman comprising the whole of the north-eastern section of the Arabian Peninsula. Of these plants over 50 are recorded as having food uses. A similar number are recorded as fodder plants. There is also substantial use as medicine, for craft work and as fuel. This speaks of a deep knowledge of the natural environment established over many centuries of use and maintained by the strong oral tradition of the region.

Various parts of the plants are utilized for food; some of which are not immediately obvious and indicate some bold experimentation in the past. Many are identified as emergency foods for famine conditions. Some are relished and are very actively sought, the premier example being *fugaa*, the desert truffle, *Tirmanea nivea* [5].

A small amount of wild plant food does appear in the markets. *Fugaa* is extremely rare but there are short seasons for small amounts of ham'd, *Rumex acetosa*, eaten as a sour salad green; *Caralluma* spp. succulents relished for their thirst quenching properties; *nabak*, the astringent fruit of the very common jujube tree, *Ziziphus spina-christi*; and the young stems of *Leptadenia pyrotechnica* appear for use in *eid* festival celebratory dishes.

Wild Honey

Wild honey, the product of the efforts of *Apis florea*, the dwarf honeybee, is considered to be the aphrodisiac par excellence amongst the Emirati male population. The bees produce a relatively small comb which is usually wrapped around a small tree branch. The brood comb hangs below the honey storage section of the comb and can be detached by clamping between two sticks and cutting between the brood and honeycomb. The sticks are then secured back in the tree to enable the bees to rebuild the storage comb.

Tree blossom is the main source of nectar and pollen for the bees, *sidr* (*Ziziphus spina-christi*) and *samr* (*Acacia tortillis*) trees are the two main sources and produce appreciably different honey. The trees flower at different times and in great profusion resulting in single blossom honeys. The difference in taste is much appreciated by the local people.

150

The output of the wild honeybees is limited and the cost of the honey is suitably elevated. The asking price for a re-cycled Vimto bottle of wild honey can exceed £60. To meet market demand the Western hive bee, *Apis mellifera*, is now extensively farmed with hives being positioned to target the same tree blossom sources.

At a promotion in a major supermarket in Dubai a local commercial honey producer, Emirates Honey, had a range of local honey on sale. Four different types were sampled. The first three were from nectar collected from the *sidr* tree and were quality and source graded. The most expensive sample was claimed to be a dwarf bee honey and had the most intense aroma and flowery flavour of the three [6].

The fourth sample was *samr* honey and was £15/Kg. It had a medium red-brown colour with a light haze and medium viscosity. It had a considerable depth of flowery aroma and taste and was also claimed to be produced by *Apis florea*.

Custodianship

The concept of ownership of wild resources is changing in many cultures. In the past ownership was fragmented and frequently without formal record. Modern societies have aggregated and formalized this ownership largely driven by social, economic and political forces.

In the pre-development era in the Emirates there was a low population density and the pressure on resources was correspondingly low. The population had few immigrants and skills and duties were maintained by strong traditions. The wild resources were also of a limited nature with little opportunity for development. Some were ephemeral, only appearing under specific circumstances and many were strictly limited, either in quantity or geography. Marine resources were the most abundant and reliable and although apparently accessible to all were subject to a licensing system under the local sheikh's control.

Studies in the Emirates have shown that practically all long-term wild resources had a custodian. More ephemeral resources such as the plant growth after infrequent rain were usually held under wider tribal control. In both cases the custodianship embraced rights to use, responsibility for maintenance and preservation against misuse. In the case of a water well these rights and duties are readily understood in any culture. Applied to a tree which can provide shade; wood for kindling and construction; foliage for animal browse; pollen and nectar for wild bees, and fruit for animal or human consumption, they present a complex resource control requirement. This management includes maintenance, protection, harvest and product disbursement.

In the case of the exploitation of flora this custodianship was closely linked to the territorial control of a person, family or tribe. Work on the ethnography of the tribes of Ras al Khaimah[7] has identified that practically every individual element of the landscape including trees and vegetation was identified with a name and under the control of an individual or group of people. This reinforced the stewardship of these resources based on a detailed knowledge of and longstanding interest in the qualities, quantities and preservation of the resource.

The population movements that occurred during the development era significantly weakened this custodial role as people moved away from their traditional communities. The government role in collective land ownership was established during this era. This is now being challenged by individuals in Ras al Khaimah who are returning to traditional lands to assert their inherited rights to homes, fields and grazing rights.

There is an interaction between resource custodianship and the hospitality traditions of the nationals. There was a special attitude to travellers and the sharing of resources with people passing through an individual or group's sphere of resource control. For instance travellers were entitled to utilize the milk from milch camels that they found unattended in the desert without seeking permission. This is a form of collection from the wild.

Commercial Impact

Financial investment has become the driving force behind many food supplies and the matching of commercial collecting and processing systems against natural resources cannot cope with the fluctuations in those resources and their finite nature. This is particularly detrimental when improvements in technique and capacity are

151

unconstrained leading to over exploitation of the resources.

The UAE fisheries are an example of this developing mismatch. Traditional fishing was based on a wide variety of techniques, using fixed and moveable traps and various types of net. Wind and muscle power were used in combination with a range of wooden fishing boats. The fisheries were artisanal, seasonal and dependent on substantial depth of knowledge and skills. Their scope was constrained by the resources available. There was no distribution system for fresh fish other than the division of the catch on the beach between the fishermen and their families. There were some methods for processing excess catches to preserve their value for the future. There was also a tradition of free distribution of food to the community at large and in particular to those in need. The resources were in the hands of national fishermen who had the opportunity to exercise custodianship over them.

The situation, which has developed over recent decades, presents a very different picture. Significant investment in fishing equipment, modern materials and fishing techniques combined with a ready supply of skilled immigrant labour have boosted the capacity and haul of the fishing industry. Initially this fed demand from the significant increase in population arising from the rapid development of the Emirates. Development has however continued to supply a growing fish processing and export industry.

In parallel the involvement of national men in the workforce has been diluted particularly through lack of recruitment of young nationals. This has weakened the custodianship of the fisheries. There have been incidents of excess catches, which would not bring a good market price, being dumped at sea and coming to public attention by subsequently being washed ashore. The use of wire mesh fish traps has also been indiscriminate; many are abandoned on the seabed turning them into fish mortuaries as they continue to trap fish that are not collected by the fishermen.

Another stress applied to marine resources is the marketing of almost all the edible fish caught. In the past the Emirati diet concentrated on specific desirable fish. Now the population is cosmopolitan with a broad range of tastes in fish and as a result most edible species are now marketable.[8] Fish that might have been discarded at sea to live or become food for other fish are now sold for human consumption, further reducing the stocks. If they are not sold they are trashed.

The resulting depletion of resources has meant that the size of key species of fish on sale in the market has been reducing and many juvenile fish are seen, which have not had the chance to breed and replenish stocks. Action has been taken at government level but has yet to have quantifiable effects. Assessment of fish stocks has only just commenced so that the data to assess variation in fish stocks is not yet available. Government controls have to cope with market demand and the desire for commercial activity in an industry that is notoriously difficult to regulate.

A different example of resource depletion is the exploitation of the desert truffle or *fugaa*. The winter of 1996–7 provided ideal conditions for a *fugaa* crop with heavy early winter rain. This is a trigger for the development of the fruit bodies of the fungi. The timing and quantity of the rain appears to be crucial for any crop to develop. That winter the rain was widespread and also in areas where *Helianthemum lippii*, a member of the rock rose family grows in quantity. *Fugaa* have a symbiotic relationship with this plant which is very common along the coastal plains of the gulf littoral. Due to their rare appearance and valued organoleptic qualities, they command a high price, typically 15 times the price of any other vegetable. That winter many immigrant workers searched the plains around Dubai and were seen selling plastic carrier bags full of the truffles by the side of the main road from Abu Dhabi to Dubai. There was a heavy demand for a free product on sale in an excellent free market position and all for a substantial return. The impact on the wild stock cannot be assessed but must have reduced the chances of a good crop after the next winter rains.

The financial viability of collection from the wild for sale in the market is questionable these days. The items, which do appear, are limited in scope and form only a minor component of market trade. As such they cannot be used to assess the current general use of wild foods. In the market it is noticeable that the wild foods which are present are often for sale in quantities well below anything which would produce an economic rate of return. Traders are often elderly, many are national women and the wild foods are on sale amidst a plethora of small household goods. Traders spend a significant time in social contact with market visitors rather than making a hard sales pitch. The inevitable conclusion is that the trade is an excuse for attending the market for social reasons and perhaps to perpetuate traditions. There is also comfort to be gained from the familiar for both vendor and purchaser. Purchases are occasionally made and the knowledge of the properties and use of wild products is still common.

153

The Energy Balance

One major factor in wild food consumption is the energy balance. On one hand the food which can be foraged by chance as part of other essential activities such as travelling or herding a flock have a positive energy balance contribution.

On the other hand the physical energy required finding, harvesting and process the food may be in excess of the calorie value of the food ultimately consumed. This is unsustainable in purely nutritional terms in any marginal or subsistence diet and would not warrant harvest from the wild. Whilst calorie values of foods are a function of modern food knowledge, an appreciation of the nutritive value of foods can be inferred from past patterns of food consumption in societies. This is particularly evident in those with a constrained culinary repertoire, as was the case in the Emirates that was substantially self-sufficient in the pre-development era. In these societies the food resource types remain constant over an extended period allowing a substantial body of knowledge to be accumulated. If the range of foods were limited then knowledge about the individual characteristics would be expected to increase with continued use. This would include valuation of taste, nutritional value, medicinal effects and effect on the digestion system.

Foods that are cultural icons can transcend the negative aspects of the energy equation. Hunting falls into this category in the UAE. Large quantities of energy can be expended on hunting for very little culinary gain, particularly when compared to the raising of domestic animals. The energy may not be human. For instance horse, hound, camel and avian power were used for terrestrial hunting. However maintaining these assistants also requires continuous human effort if only to herd the camels or grow fodder for the horses.

The cultural transcendency of the hunt for *houbara* (McQueen's bustard) and *rim* (sand gazelle) are therefore very strong markers of the privilege which is attached to these activities. Viewed from a different angle the right to carry out such activities despite the meagre energy returns was a good indicator of power and privilege.

Miscellany

Wild resources contribute to the human food experience through secondary benefits. The meat and milk from animals grazing on wild food resources are still appreciated above those foods derived from managed grazing or artificial feeds. The essence of wild food is therefore available through the food chain at second hand. Doughty noted on his travels that the milk produced after grazing on the fresh vegetation after winter rains was eagerly anticipated for its exceptional flavour [9].

Collection from public 'wild' sources in the city of Al Ain is still permitted. There are many thousands of date palms along the streets of Al Ain and other UAE cities accessible to anyone. Consumption is limited to the person's immediate needs and collection for storage or on behalf of other people is precluded [10].

Two further wild resources related to food might be mentioned. Salt was collected both on the coast and at inland locations. As would be expected solar evaporation was the production process and the product was used particularly to salt fish for preservation. A small salt works on the coast was still active in Umm al Qawain in 2001 but the majority of the product was sold to bakers for use in raising the temperature of their ovens. Inland salt pans on the edge of the Rub al Khali were also exploited.

Finally water was a wild resource until it was tamed into pipes and taps. Water was available in the Emirates from springs, *falaj*[11] fed by permanent groundwater sources, seasonal streams fed by those springs and run-off, rainwater collection into cisterns and wells. These were the only sources until the development era when piped water supplies were one of the highest priorities.

Conclusion

In the past the Emiratis' knowledge of wild food was far more widespread and detailed, as it was a major input to their survival and also their general physical culture. Appreciation of one's natural environment is a fading skill under the onslaught of the built and controlled environment to which many now seem to aspire.

Like many communities the young population of the Emirates has only limited interest in the details of domestic existence in the past. This is particularly marked amongst young men. Practically the sole interest that remains is hunting and it has had a devastating effect on the fauna involved. This general indifference will inevitably lead to a lack of continuity in the detailed knowledge of past domestic culture.

The flora and particularly the fauna are heavily stressed by the increasing population and continuing development that is taking place and which looks set to continue. There is a continuing loss of all natural habitats. Perversely the overall lack of interest in these wild resources may assist somewhat in their preservation but the overall prognosis for any continuing viable use of wild foods is not good.

Bibliography
Beech, Mark, *In the Land of the Ichthyophagi*, Archaeopress, Oxford, 2004.

Doughty, Charles M., *Wanderings in Arabia*, Duckworth, London, 1926.

Iddison, Philip, 'Desert Truffles', in *Petit Propos Culinaires* 55, Prospect Books, London, 1997.

Jongbloed, Marijcke, *The Comprehensive Guide to the Wild Flowers of the United Arab Emirates*, Environmental Research and Wildlife Development Agency, Abu Dhabi, 2003.

Lancaster, William and Fidelity, Draft Commentary and Archive compiled for the National Museum of Ras Al Khaimah, unpublished manuscript held in the RAK National Museum, Ras Al Khaimah, UAE, compiled 1997–2000.

Osbourne, Patrick E. (editor), *Desert Ecology of Abu Dhabi*, Pisces Publications, Newbury, 1996.

Randall, John E., *Coastal Fishes of Oman*, Crawford House Publishing Pty Ltd, Bathurst NSW, 1995.

Thesiger, Wilfred, *Arabian Sands*, Penguin, Harmondsworth, 1964.

Notes
1. Mark Beech has collated data on the archaeological evidence of fish consumption from the fifth millennium BC to the late Islamic period in the Arabian Gulf and the Gulf of Oman.
2. The Arabian *tahr*, *Hemitragus jayakari*, is similar to a cross between wild goats and sheep and is now extremely rare, a specimen was camera-trapped on Jebel Hafeet in 2004.
3. Thesiger, *Arabian Sands*.
4. The spiney tailed lizard has been protected by law since 1983 as a result of over-exploitation.
5. Iddison.
6. My capacity to describe honey flavours is extremely limited and I am not aware of any lexicon of words to describe honey in a manner similar to the oenophile's vocabulary.
7. Lancaster in manuscripts held by the National Museum, Ras al Khaimah.
8. In his books on seafood, Alan Davidson noted several times that a fish which was esteemed in one locality was rejected by a nearby community or culture, thus with many cultures present in the population the spread of demand is more encompassing.
9. Recorded by Doughty.
10. Incidentally the remaining dates from these trees, some of which are sub-standard for human consumption, are collected by municipal workers and made available as animal feed, particularly for camels.
11. *Falaj* are irrigation systems with a combination of open and underground channels which can convey springwater many kilometres from source to date plantations and fields in the Arabian peninsula.

The Taming of the 'Shroom

Cathy Kaufman

Act IV, scene iii of Shakespeare's *Taming of the Shrew* opens with Petruchio's servant Grumio teasing the hungry and volatile Katharine with dishes of calves' foot, tripe, or beef with mustard. Grumio quickly withdraws the tantalizing offers as unwholesome for Katharine: her hot temper would have been stoked by these foods, which buttressed choleric humours. Shakespeare's audiences understood that such hot and dry qualities were more appropriate to men and that woman, humorally speaking, should be cooler and moister. Grumio could have offered Katharine a dish of mushrooms, categorized as cold and moist since antiquity, if he had wanted to correct her temperament through food.

In addition to their more feminine humoral balance, mushrooms had many different associations with women. Considered aphrodisiac, mushrooms were sought after by sybaritic gourmets to enhance love's pleasures and condemned by prissy clergy who saw Eve's temptations in a plate of pickled mushrooms. Mushrooms were largely women's work: until about 1600, mushrooms for the dinner table were exclusively harvested by gathering, a humble, traditionally feminine chore. Mushrooms also were linked to witches who lived in forests, a place where deadly mushrooms lurked for the unwary. Adding to the witchy superstitions, 17th-century Anglophones called any poisonous mushroom a 'toadstool', possibly derived from the German homophone *tode*, meaning death. Toads were part of witches' black magic: their touch was thought to poison otherwise safe mushrooms. With no reliable guides to differentiate between poisonous 'toadstools' and edible fungi, the English especially tended to eat mushrooms sparingly. Early American colonists inherited England's culinary indifference.

All this changed in the later 19th century when gathering and growing mushrooms in America suddenly was catapulted from women's work to a respected pastime or vocation for men. Changing American tastes demanded a reliable, year-round mushroom supply that outpaced the seasonal foraged crops. The United States Department of Agriculture and a few innovative farmers and botanists flooded the willing reader with different techniques for cultivating the common button and field mushrooms, *Agaricus bisporus* and *A. campestris*. Market forces, however, are not the complete story, for the traditionally feared wild mushrooms also became part of the dining scene with unprecedented enthusiasm. Americans optimistically believed that science had solved the treacherous problem of wild mushroom identification. Mycologists attached Linnaean Latin binomials to illustrations of wild mushrooms, substituting scientific precision for a tangle of folk names, and used the popular press to spread the new gospel. Foragers created local mycological societies starting in the 1890s to swap information and sallied forth with new confidence. These triumphs of science, the domain of 19th-century men, allowed mushrooms to become a valued source of wild, gourmet food as well as a cultivated cash crop in America. Mushrooms were no longer feminine; the wild and domestic species developed distinctly masculine associations.[1]

To put the dramatically changing American attitudes to mushrooms in context requires a brief historical survey of European, and especially English, attitudes towards mushrooms, starting with the classical world. The ancients appreciated that one unguarded indulgence could mean a premature rendezvous with the Grim Reaper. The emperor Claudius notoriously met his end through a plate of *Amanita caesara* kissed with the juice of its deadly cousin, *A. phalloides*. Reports had it that his evil wife Agrippina was behind the assassination, aided by the mistress of poisoning, Locusta. Greek and Roman physicians offered antidotes, often in the form of vile emetics, for those who ate what Nicander called 'the evil ferment of the earth' that caused 'swellings in the belly or strictures on his throat'.[2] Celsus's *De Medicina* advised anyone who had eaten poisonous mushrooms to consume 'draughts of salt and vinegar,'[3] somewhat more pleasant alternatives to the dung purgatives.

Even if one did not fear poisoning, most physicians discouraged eating mushrooms in much the way contemporary cardiologists discourage eating saturated fats: Galen thought mushrooms of little nourishment and productive of cold and clammy humours; he considered it 'far safer to have nothing to do with them.'[4] A few mushrooms had their defenders, as Dioscorides attributed medicinal value in certain mushrooms. Eating mushrooms also communicated one's social and economic status and philosophical beliefs: as a free, foraged food, inferior mushrooms were the stuff of subsistence peasants and luxury-shunning Stoics, while rare, choice species were gathered for market and landed on the tables of wealthy connoisseurs, prepared according to a handful of recipes in Apicius' *De re coquinaria*.

Mushrooms' ambiguous status carried forward into the cookbooks, religious literature, and great herbals of the English Renaissance. John Gerard cribbed directly from Galen, concluding that mushrooms exacerbated phlegmatic humours or worse, were venomous and profoundly hazardous to one's health.[5] The Reverend Jeremy Taylor exploited conventional wisdom on the dangers of too-liberal consumption of mushrooms to inhibit libertine behaviour. He cautioned against,

> private society with strange women, …amorous gestures, garish and wanton dress, feasts and liberty… some of these being prologues to lust, and the most innocent of them being like condited and pickled mushrooms, which, if carefully corrected and seldom tasted, may be harmless, but never can do any good.[6]

Ironically, mushroom recipes, with their focus on capturing heady aromas, would exude an almost pornographic sensuality in late-Victorian America.

157

Exactly how and why mushrooms started to come into favour may relate to chang-ing dietary theories, which required new foods, methods of preparation, and flavour balances.[7] Keeping in mind the adage that kitchen practice precedes kitchen print, mushrooms probably emerged as a marker of classic French cuisine in the 16th cen-tury. Although a handful of mushroom recipes appeared earlier, by the publication of Pierre de La Varenne's *Le cuisinier françois* (1651), mushrooms were being used copiously in French kitchens and their imitators. La Varenne introduced *duxelles* as a pantry staple along side of his other novelty, roux; both were liaisons to bind sauces, used freely in the cook's discretion. Mushrooms garnished, stuffed, and starred in modern foods.

It was also in the 16th century that the French first successfully cultivated mush-rooms. Olivier de Serres' *Théâtre d'agriculture et mésnage des champs* (1600) presaged the future marriage of practical science with mushrooms. Serres praised man's great curiosity, which unravelled the puzzle of how to grow *mousserons* (believed to be an agaric with a white top and pale wine-coloured underside, probably *A. campestris*). Rather than awaiting mushrooms' mysterious and uncontrollable appearance, Serres created beds of manure mixed with earth, two to three *pieds* deep, and doused them with water in which *mousserons* had been boiled, to grow mushrooms in control-led locations.[8] One hundred years later, Joseph Pitton de Tournefort's *Mémoires de l'académie des Sciences, année 1707*, refined the methodology for an overtly scientific audience. Mushrooms became a cash crop in 18th-century France, when the dank limestone caves and quarries outside of Paris, with their relatively consistent tempera-tures, became a year-round source for white agarics.

The French interest in cultivating mushrooms did not initially catch on in England or America, at least among gentlemen farmers. As late as 1699, John Evelyn reiterated much of the ancient world's fear of mushrooms, calling them 'excrescences' and 'malignant and noxious'. He claimed that he would have declined to address them in his treatise devoted to sallets but for the fact that so many others esteemed them. He noted varieties that could be foraged in England, preferring 'such as rise in rich, airy, and dry pasture-grounds,' and rued England's expensive imports from France. Although he offered some advice for growing various salad herbs, he was less interested in exploring mushroom cultivation. He dismissed the Neapolitan technique of raising mushrooms on compacted soil in wine cellars and the French technique of impregnating manure, probably because of his disdain for the use of poorly composted dung.[9]

Soon thereafter, both gourmet and scientific passions for mushrooms invaded England's agricultural writers. Richard Bradley opined that those who had 'been accustomed to eat *Mushrooms*, will certainly allow them to be one of the greatest Dainties the Earth affords.' He lauded the wild morels found in English forests and the cultivated French *champignons*, sharing the secrets of raising the latter from his observations in France and claiming that every English gentleman now grew mushrooms using his advice. On a pure intellectual level, he marvelled over tiny mush-rooms visible in microscopes.[10]

This passion did not carry over to America, where I have found no evidence of serious interest in mushroom science and cultivation prior to the 19th century. J. B. Bordley's *Essays and Notes on Husbandry and Rural Affairs* (1799), omitted any discussion of mushrooms, even though it contained suggestions for cultivating wild crops such as brambles. Thomas Jefferson's extensive, meticulous gardening and farming notebooks merely note when mushrooms appeared in the Washington, D.C. market.[11] Curiously, it seems that this lover of French food and avid agriculturalist never tried to grow them. Instead, mushrooms appear as women's work. Imported editions of Hannah Glasse's *Art of Cookery* (1747) mentioned growing mushrooms in hot beds in April, presuming that the reader knew how to create the compost. The first American edition in 1805 added an unusual entry entitled 'to raise mushrooms'. Addressed to the cook who needed mushrooms for her kitchen, the recipe prescribes 'fine garden mould' covered with 'three or four inches thick with moldy long muck, of a horse muck-kill, or old rotten stubble,' infused with some past prime mushrooms boiled in a bit of water, and thrown over the bed, to await the emergence of pristine and delicate caps from the dark earth.[12]

Mushrooms appeared relatively infrequently in colonial and early federal America. Some foraging undoubtedly took place, with mother teaching daughter the ways to identify proper mushrooms. There are scattered market references and limited mushroom recipes in manuscripts and early American cookbooks. But Americans, whose cooking still bore the heavy imprint of traditional English fare, relegated mush-rooms to the ubiquitous ketchups and pickles, bolstered by an occasional sauce or stewed dish, or recipe for drying mushrooms into a seasoning or thickening powder. Mushroom ketchups and pickles in particular may have been popular because, in addition to preserving a seasonal crop, these preparations took the ancient remedies of salt and vinegar and used them in the recipes to neutralize poisonous mushrooms. For those eating fresh mushrooms, the time-tested prescription lingered as late as 1888, when Juliet Corson advised the cook who mistakenly tasted a bitter, and presumably toxic, mushroom to 'instantly' swallow a spoonful of salt 'for the purpose of neutral-izing any possibly poisonous effect.'[13]

With the growth of the American cookbook industry, many authors, removed from their reader's elbow, felt the need to guide the naïve, foraging housewife in identifying wholesome mushrooms. Among the earliest advice published in America dates to the 1820s and comes from Englishwoman Maria Rundell:

> The cook should be perfectly acquainted with the different sorts of things called by this name [mushrooms] by ignorant people, as the death of many persons has be occasioned by carelessly using the poisonous. The eatable mushrooms first appear very small, and of a round form, on a little stalk. They grow very

159

fast, and the upper part and stalk are white. As the size increases, the under part gradually opens, and shows a fringed fur of a very fine salmon-colour . . .[14]

Her warning and description would be repeated, oft-times verbatim, by many prominent American cookery writers of the next generation. Its shortcoming, of course, is that it offers little reliable guidance for mushrooms other than *A. campestris*, the meadow or field mushroom.

Cooks needed foolproof tests to gauge edibility, as no reliable guides yet catalogued the cornucopia of mushroom varieties that could be found in the nation's different habitats.[15] Some of the most popular tests were in Eliza Leslie's *Directions for Cookery* (1837). Perhaps sensing that these tests were nothing better than old wives' tales, Leslie couched them in the language of hearsay and possibilities:

> It is said that if you boil an onion among mushrooms the onion will turn a bluish black when there is a bad one among them . . .. If in stirring mushrooms, the colour of the silver spoon is changed, it is also most prudent to destroy them all.[16]

She urged distinguishing edible from poisonous by knowing the physical characteristics of the varieties: colour, season of harvest, habitat, and changes after harvesting. Although the advice sounds scientific, there were no books to consult, the best Leslie could offer was that,

> Mushrooms of the proper sort generally appear in August and September, after a heavy dew or a misty night. They may be known by their being of pale pink or salmon colour on the gills or under side, while the top is of a dull pearl-coloured white; and by their growing only in open places….The poisonous or false mushrooms are of various colours, sometimes of a bright yellow or scarlet all over; sometimes of a chalky white stalk, top, and gills.

Like any good real estate agent, Leslie emphasized location as the key to successful mushrooming: 'Good mushrooms are found only in clear open fields where the air is pure and unconfined. Those that grow in low, damp ground, or in shady places, are always poisonous.'[17] Lurking beneath her words is the old-fashioned rejection of the dark forest, home to witches and toads. She further warned never to, 'give mushrooms to children. Even in their best state they are not wholesome. The taste for mushrooms is an acquired one, and it is best not to acquire it.'[18]

Cooks feared of mushrooms. Lettice Bryan's pickled mushroom recipe in *The Kentucky Housewife* (1839) warned the cook to select the 'esculent' varieties, as some mushrooms were 'very poisonous'. Even though Sarah Josepha Hale's early work, *The Good Housekeeper* (6th ed., 1841), encouraged economical home manufacture of many comestibles, she recommended store-bought mushroom ketchup because of 'the difficulty in our country of obtaining the right kind of plant, (some are poisonous) renders a receipt of little consequence.'[19] Her more mature works paraphrase Rundell's and Leslie's warnings and add a gold ring test, reminiscent of the talisman of a unicorn's horn to assay poisons: 'Rub the upper skin with a gold ring or any piece of gold; the part rubbed will turn yellow if it is a *poisonous fungus*.' More constructively, Hale republished Glasse's horticultural advice, promising an 'easy method of producing mushrooms' by pouring a mushroom infusion or placing broken bits of mushrooms on an old bed.[20]

The popular attention paid to mushrooms surged in the generation following the American Civil War as French food and fancy restaurants became major influences on the American dining scene. The trend-setting *Harper's Weekly* had berated Americans for their prejudice against mushrooms as late as 1871,[21] but soon *Harper's* and other national press began publishing lengthy essays on mushrooms, some seeking to demystify their peculiar biology and others reporting on the burgeoning acceptance of mushrooms as a food for all. Even so, 1870s writers called fungi 'repulsive in form and colour; in not a few the smell is intolerably offensive.' That same article praised toadstools for their 'fermentive and putrefactive energies [by which] they decompose the hardest vegetable substances, and this provide an inexhaustible supply of vegetable mould for succeeding generations, besides destroying these substances which, having served their end, need to be removed, but are kept under some other form, waiting for the plastic touch of the Almighty to transform them into some of His endlessly diversified cosmical arrangements.'[22]

No matter how bizarre mushrooms might seem, they were moving from witches' brew to part of God's divine plan. And, as part of the Divine plan, mushrooms needed to be studied, categorized and understood.

Professional and amateur mycologists took to field and forest hunting for mushrooms, possibly for food, but just as often for the joy of scientific inquiry. Both public and private sectors participated in this mushroom mania. As early as 1876, the United States Department of Agriculture published materials on edible fungi, prompting curious letters from folks who had shied away from exotic-looking mushrooms through ignorance. One Nebraska farmer wrote about large puff-balls, reassuringly identified by the government as *Lycoperdon giganteum*, that were 'quite abundant on the prairies in the summer, and if edible would offer a large amount of food.' In 1885, the USDA published an illustrated guide to twelve edible American mushrooms in its annual report. The guide included recipes and a favourable nutritional analysis of mushrooms as good sources of 'nitrogenous nutriment,' i.e. protein, and lobbied to dispel the

prejudice [that] has grown up concerning [mushrooms] in this country which it will take some time to eradicate. Notwithstanding the occurrence of occa-

161

sional fatal accidents through the inadvertent eating of poisonous species, fungi are largely consumed both by savage and civilized man in all parts of the world, and while they contribute so considerable a portion of the food product of the world we may be sure their value will not be permanently overlooked in the United States, especially when we consider our large accessions of populations from countries in which the mushroom is a familiar and much prized edible.[23]

The manual was reprinted annually into the 1890s.

Domestic economy and the trickle-up effect of Chinese and Italian foodways brought by new immigrants all worked together to make mushrooms familiar comestibles, aided by books and articles in popular outlets such as *American Naturalist, Popular Science Monthly, Harper's Monthly* and the aptly-named *Garden and Forest.* Some were replete with Audubon-like engravings, so that the mycologist William Hamilton Gibson boasted that 'the element of danger is practically eliminated, so far as the identification of the above [illustrated] species is concerned...'[24]

Practically, but not completely. Rumours of deaths from foraged mushrooms continued, and in 1897, the Department of Agriculture published a pamphlet on mushroom poisoning, cautioning that foraged mushrooms should not be eaten unless approved by an expert. As amateur mycological societies were sprouting like toadstools (the first was founded in Boston, Massachusetts in 1895, with others following soon thereafter), expertise was readily available. Government mycologists were happy to defer to old-fashioned folk wisdom, and in particular respected the expertise of women foragers who brought wild mushrooms to market:

> the judgment of the colored market women in Washington that a particular species is edible I consider as safe a guide as the decision of the highest botanical authority, not because their knowledge of mushrooms is extensive but because they are thoroughly familiar with the two or three edible species they handle and know them as certainly from poisonous kinds as they know persimmons from crab apples or opossums from rabbits.[25]

While mycologists were hearing the call of the wild, American horticulturalists were experimenting with methods for growing button mushrooms, *Agaricus bisporus*, in cellars and greenhouses, and for improving yields of *Agaricus campestris*, the pink-gilled field mushroom. *Harper's Weekly* described the impact that these newly learned techniques were having on the dining habits of New Yorkers, whose markets were now 'profusely' supplied with button and field mushrooms.[26] New York's William Falconer enthusiastically recommended mushroom cultivation for fun and profit. A farmer from Long Island, a region that still acts as a source of truck farms for Manhattan's voracious appetite, Falconer urged combining mushroom cultivation with other farm products by constructing mushroom houses that would permit the simultaneous growing of two crops in the same floor space. White 'French' mushrooms, which required no or limited sunlight, could be cultivated in beds set beneath vines, tomatoes, lettuces, and even roses. Further cutting costs, Falconer suggested that farmers buy manure from city stables after selling their produce in the city, utilizing the return trip to transport cheaply acquired fertilizer. Falconer recommended that farmers sell directly to restaurants, hotels, and fancy food shops, as the fragile mushrooms could be damaged through clumsy wholesalers. He included a chapter of mushroom recipes (devoted solely to agarics) in his 1891 *Mushrooms: How to Grow Them. A Practical Treatise on Mushroom Culture for Profit and Pleasure.*

Falconer's timing was impeccable. Although the perfection of canning had allowed for the import of significant quantities of French mushrooms since the 1850s,[27] fresh mushrooms could not be successfully imported. Limited and seasonal local foraging made fresh mushrooms disproportionately expensive. Falconer's techniques were incorporated into Department of Agriculture circulars in the 1890s, further disseminating the growing practices.

The most visually striking contribution to America's fungus frenzy was George Francis Atkinson's *Mushrooms: Edible, Poisonous, Etc.* Originally published in 1900, the volume is the first of which I am aware that has photographs, rather than drawings, of American mushrooms. With over 250 extraordinary, life-size photographs, Atkinson hoped that

163

> By careful observation of the plant, and comparison with the illustrations and text, one will be able to add many species to the list of edible ones, where now is collected 'only the one which is pink underneath.'[28]

In addition to his encyclopedic knowledge of wild varieties, Atkinson had strong opinions on mushroom cultivation and disputed Falconer's belief in the economy of mushroom houses: between construction costs and the heating the houses in winter and cooling in summer, Atkinson saw financial disappointment unless the houses were at least partially subterranean. His solution was to follow the French model and cultivate mushrooms in tunnels, caves, or abandoned mines for large-scale production, which he illustrated with surreal photographs of mushroom mines in New York State. For smaller crops and personal consumption, he suggested devoting an unused part of the cellar, provided that the manure was thoroughly cured and rid of noxious odours before bringing it into the dwelling. Although the experts disagreed on technique, by the dawn of the 20th century, the American mushroom industry was launched.

Botany relentlessly invaded the kitchen, where cooks were taught to revere mushrooms. Starting with Juliet Corson's *Family Living on $500 A Year* (1888) and Mary Ronald's *Century Cook Book* (1896), cookbooks might devote a chapter to mushrooms, highlighting edibility tests (folklore of questionable reliability still appeared) and the economy to be gained by foraging for elite treats. The *Century Cook Book* was the first to use the Latin binomials to identify different mushrooms for the cook: recipes were given for *Marasmius oreade*; three different members of the *agaricus* genus; two different members of the *coprinus* genus; *boleti*; *morchellae esculentae*; *hydnum caput medusae*, and *clavaria*. The reassuringly scientific nomenclature was adopted by Kate Sargeant in the first full-length American cookbook devoted exclusively to mushrooms, *One Hundred Mushroom Receipts* (1899), and in Sarah Tyson Rorer's chapter of mushroom recipes that formed part of Atkinson's study. How could one be poisoned if one could label a wild mushroom with scientific precision? With this new language, Sargeant makes 'no attempt to describe the edible, nor to warn against the emetic and poisonous kinds. To do so would require too much space, and besides, such knowledge is to be presumed.'[29] Her work is divided into chapters by culinary function (sauces, stews, salads, etc.), with recipes for such delights as *Coprinus comatus* soup, *Agaricus campester* stew, *Lepiota procera* sauce, and *Lycoperdon giganteum* with tomatoes.

Rorer's home economics training is apparent in her approach: rather than merely offer recipes using the scientific name for the chosen mushroom, Rorer bunches recipes for each genus of mushrooms, explaining that because,

> varieties of mushrooms differ in analysis, texture and density of flesh, different methods of cooking give best results. For instance, the *Coprinus micaceus*, being very delicate, is easily destroyed by over-cooking; a dry, quick pan of the 'mushroom bells' retains the best flavor; while the more dense *Agaricus campestris* requires long, slow cooking to bring out the flavor, and to be tender and digestible. Simplicity of seasoning, however, must be observed, or the mushroom flavor will be destroyed.[30]

This was science tempered by sensuality: preserving and enhancing the flavour of the mushroom was the cook's goal, not masking them with spices and vinegars.

Among the most sybaritic mushroom recipes of the late 19th century were mushrooms under glass. The following recipe, from Falconer but by no means unique, used either *A. campestris* or *A. bisporus*:

> Mushrooms à la Casse, Tout, are cooked under glass: Cut a round of bread one-half inch thick, and toast it nicely; butter both sides and place it in a clean baking sheet or tin; cleanse the mushrooms ... and place them on the toast, head downwards, lightly pepper and salt them, and place a piece of butter the size of a nut on each mushroom; cover them with a finger glass and let them cook close to the fire for ten or twelve minutes. Slip the toast into a hot dish, but do not remove the glass cover until they are on the table. All the aroma

and flavor of the mushrooms are preserved by this method. The name of this excellent recipe need not deter the careful housekeeper from trying it. With moderate care the glass cover will not crack. In winter it should be rinsed in warm water before using.[31]

Rorer gave a similar recipe a decade later, explaining that,

> The object in covering with the bell is to retain every particle of the flavor. The bell is then lifted at the table, that the eater may get the full aroma and flavor from the mushrooms.[32]

Although cookbooks continued to warn of the dangers of poisonous mushrooms, there was no turning back from American's new-found love for mushrooms on the table once they had been stripped of mystery and tamed by science. If any additional proof was needed that the mushroom had its wild, exotic mystique in late 19th-century America, consider Sargeant's recipe for *Polyporus sulphureus* soup: what could be blander than her reassurance to the reader that 'this mushroom tastes and smells, when cooking, like chicken'?[33]

Bibliography

Atkinson, George Francis, *Mushrooms: Edible, Poisonous, Etc. with Recipes for Cooking Mushrooms* by Mrs. Sarah Tyson Rorer [1st ed. 1900], 2nd ed. (New York: Hafner Reprint, 1961).

Chandra, Aindrila, *Elsevier's Dictionary of Edible Mushrooms* (Amsterdam: Elsevier, 1989).

Collins, Edmund, 'The Mushroom Harvest,' in *Harper's Weekly*, Oct. 3, 1891, p. 758.

Falconer, William, *Mushrooms: How to Grow Them. A Practical Treatise on Mushroom Culture for Profit and Pleasure* (New York: Orange Judd, 1891).

Findlay, W.P.K., *Fungi: Folklore, Fiction, & Fact* (Richmond, Surrey: Richmond Publishing, 1982).

Fine, Gary Allen, *Morel Tales: The Culture of Mushrooming*, (Cambridge, MA: Harvard University Press, 1998).

Houghton, William. 'Notices of Fungi in Greek and Latin Authors', *Annals and Magazine of Natural History*, ser. V, vol. 15, 22-49, Jan. 1885.

March, Andrew L. and Kathryn G. March, *The Mushroom Basket* (Bailey, CO: Meridian Hill, 1982).

Peterson, T. Sarah, *Acquired Taste: The French Origins of Modern Cooking* (Ithaca and London: Cornell University, 1994).

Sargeant, Kate, *One Hundred Mushroom Receipts* (Cleveland, OH: C. Orr, 1899).

Senyah, J. K., 'Mushrooms and Truffles', in *Encyclopedia of Food Science, Food Technology and Nutrition*, vol. 5 (San Diego, CA: Academic Press, 1993).

Wasson, Valentina Pavlovna and R. Gordon Wasson, *Mushrooms, Russia and History* (New York: Pantheon, 1957).

Notes

1. A parallel argument, that science masculinized certain food production, could be advanced for the chicken in America. Relegated to women's and children's work as a modest household supplement through the mid-late 19th century, once 'hen fever' and the science of breeding spectacularly-plumed game birds swept American gentlemen-breeders in the 1850s, the first efforts to create a domestic poultry industry followed within a generation.

2. Houghton, William, 'Notices of Fungi in Greek and Latin Authors' in *Annals and Magazine of Natural History*, ser. V, vol. 15 (Jan. 1885), 22-49, p.24.

3. Celsus, Aulus Cornelius, *De Medicina*, trans. W.G. Spencer, (Cambridge, Mass: Harvard, Loeb Classical Library, 1989), Bk. V.27.12C.

4. Houghton, p. 38.

5. John Gerard, *Herball* (1597), quoted in Wasson, p. 20.

6. Jeremy Taylor, *Holy Living and Dying* (*ca.* 1650), quoted in Wasson, p. 21.

7. Laudan, Rachel, 'A Kind of Chemistry', in *Petits Propos Culinaires*, vol. 62 (Aug. 1999), pp. 8-22.

8. These casual instructions seem to have met only with intermittent success, as an early 19th century annotated edition of Serres' seminal work admits that it is impossible to have complete faith in these instructions and gave much more detail as to the proper preparation of the manure in advance of creating mushroom beds, whose dimensions are measured more precisely in centimetres. *Le Théâtre d'agriculture et des mesnage des champs d'Olivier de Serres . . . Nouvelle edition con forme au texte, augmentée de notes et d'un vocabulaire*, (Paris: Société d'agriculture), t. II, pp. 279-80; 467-9. In these 19th-century notes to Serres, the only mushroom under cultivation is the so-called *Agaricus esculentus de Linné*. Serres, p. 469.

9. Evelyn, John, *Acetaria, A Discourse of Sallets* (1699), ed. Christopher Driver and intro. Tom Jaine (Totnes: Prospect Books, 1996), pp. 31; 33; 69.

10. Bradley, Richard, *New Improvements of Planting and Gardening, both Philosophical and Practical*, 5th ed (London: W. Mears, 1726), pp. 264-8; 582-6.

11. Jefferson, Thomas, *Thomas Jefferson's Garden Book*, 1766-1824, anno. Edwin Morris Betts, (Philadelphia: American Philosophical Society, 1944), p. 639.

12. Glasse, Hannah, *The Art of Cookery Made Plain and Easy* [Alexandria 1805], intro. Karen Hess, (Bedford, MA: Applewood Books, 1997), p. 279.

13. Corson, Juliet, *Family Living on $500 A Year: A Daily Reference-Book for Young and Inexperienced Housewives*, (New York: Harper, 1888), p. 124.

14. Rundell, Maria, *American Domestic Cookery, formed on Principles of Economy, for the Use of Private Families, by an Experienced Housekeeper*, (New York: Evert Duyckinck, 1823), p. 194.

15. A remarkable 1831 article devoted to American fungi came from the Moravian clergyman, Lewis David de Schweinitz, whose 'Synopsis fungorum in America boreali media degentium' in *Trans. Am. Phil. Soc.*, vol. 4:141-318 (Philadelphia, 1834) identified 3098 species of North American fungi, more than one-third of which were previously unknown. The text and mushroom characteristics were written in Latin and while of interest to scientists, had little impact on the habits of the public.

16. Leslie, Eliza. *Directions for Cookery; Being a System of the Art in its Various Branches*, (Philadelphia: E.L. Carey & A. Hart, 1837), p. 201.

17. Leslie, *Directions for Cookery*, p. 201. These sentiments can also be found in N.K.M. Lee's *The Cook's Own Book, being a Complete Culinary Encyclopedia* [Boston: Munroe & Frances, 1832] (New York: Arno Reprint, 1972), p. 117.

18. Leslie, Eliza, *Miss Leslie's New Cookery Book* (Philadelphia: T.B. Peterson, 1857), p. 322.

19. Hale, Sarah Josepha, *The Good Housekeeper* [6th ed 1841], intro. Jan Longone (Mineola, NY: Dover, 1996), p. 71.

20. Hale, Sarah Josepha, *The New Household Receipt-Book: Containing Maxims, Directions, and Specifics for Promoting Health, Comfort, and Improvement of the Homes of the People* (New York: H. Long, 1853), pp. 193; 296.

21. 'The Food of Besieged Paris', in *Harper's Weekly*, March 4, 1871, p. 207.

22. 'Fungi', in *Harper's Weekly*, Sept. 7, 1878, p. 724.

23. Taylor, Thomas, M.D., *Twelve Edible Mushrooms of the United States, Illustrated with Twelve Colored Types, How to Select and Prepare for the Table* (Washington: Government Printing Office, 1885), pp. 5-6; 14.

24. Gibson, W. Hamilton, 'A Few Edible Toadstools and Mushrooms', in vol. 89, *Harper's New Monthly Magazine* (Aug. 1894), pp. 390-403; at 403.

25. Colville, Frederick V., *Observations of Recent Cases of Mushroom Poisoning in the District of Columbia*, United States Department of Agriculture, Division of Botany, Circular No. 13 (Washington, D.C., 1897), pp. 2-3.

26. 'Gardening for New York', in *Harper's Weekly*, August 25 1883, p. 541.

27. Hooker, Richard J., *Food and Drink in America: A History* (Indianapolis and New York: Bobbs-Merrill, 1981), pp. 229-30.

28. Atkinson, p. 3.

29. Sargeant, unnumbered preface.

30. Rorer, in Atkinson, p. 277.

31. Falconer, pp. 156-7.

32. Rorer, in Atkinson, p. 279.

33. Sargeant, p. 11.

The Water Tiger: The Pike in English Cooking

Sam Kilgour

Once considered a dish fit for a king and a king amongst freshwater fish, the decline in consumption of the pike reflects the changing social and economic climate in England over the years. Wild coarse fish adorned the dinner tables of the rich and poor for centuries and until very recently freshwater species were a common source of food.

In medieval times the pike was considered of great value. Its price was double that of salmon and more than ten times that of turbot.[1] It was also considered greatly medicinal, with each part of the pike assigned healing properties. But by the Victorian era, pike was diminishing in popularity and today it is rarely eaten at the table and difficult to obtain.

This paper will explore the history of catching, cooking and eating pike in England.

The pike found in the rivers and lakes of England belong to the species *Esox lucius*, also known as the northern pike, and have perhaps the most interesting reputation of all the freshwater fish. Renowned for his greedy habits (he is an allegedly indiscriminate gastronome), terrific exploits (eating whole ducks, frogs, rats and occasionally biting unsuspecting humans) and fearsome appearance the pike is well known but not always well loved. However, pike is the most delicious of all England's freshwater fish and for many centuries was a staple in its kitchens. Although pike has all but disappeared from the English diet it was once a sought-after delicacy. From the earliest medieval banquets through to Escoffier's kitchens, pike has been found alongside the most luxurious and expensive foods.

The pike is a fish of unusual and distinctive appearance. Long and almost uniform in size from the head to the dorsal fin, the body then narrows towards the tail. The fins are rearward placed which gives the pike great speed and agility, and he has an unmistakable dappled skin. The head is pointed, with a snout that is fearsome in appearance. The teeth are particularly alarming and extremely sharp, quite essential given that the diet of the pike is entirely carnivorous. Ducks, geese, poultry, mice, rats and frogs have all been consumed by the hungry pike. Large pike have even been known to attempt to consume each other, with the unfortunate result of becoming stuck and incurring the demise of both fish. Although a pike will take and eat any creature which will fit into its gaping mouth, in reality the majority of the pike's diet consists of other fish. Pike lie in wait for their prey, carefully concealed in banks of weeds or other places providing cover. Izaak Walton, author of *The Compleat Angler* (1653), comments that the pike is 'a solitary, melancholy, and a bold fish … because he fears not a shadow'.[2] Known variously as the water tiger, the water wolf and the tyrant of the rivers, the pike has a 'bold, greedy, devouring disposition, which is so keen.'[3]

The pike is now a common fish in England although this has not always been the case: pike were once rare due to their excellent texture and flavour and their high value. Numerous attempts to farm this species appear to have failed, apparently due to the pike's preference for solitude, a refusal to accept artificial food and of course, its legendary gastronomic excesses.

Early angling literature places a great emphasis on fish as food. The cooking and eating of the catch is of much interest, even if not quite as fascinating to the authors as the angling itself. Unlike modern coarse fishing, where the fish are returned to the water in all but exceptional cases, early coarse fishing, like fly fishing, had the acquisition of food as its raison d'être. In 1496 the author of the *Treatyse of Fysshynge wyth an Angle* commented that the angler had 'the fragrant smell of the meadow flowers to make him hungry,'[4] whilst he awaited his catch.

In medieval times the reputation of the pike was at its peak. Pike were frequently found at the tables of the rich during this era. At a royal banquet given in 1397 pike was served alongside venison, boar's heads, swan, capon, peacock and heron.[5] Clearly then, pike was a luxury food which rated inclusion in a feast of such proportions. In addition to fish as part of a banquet, substantial feasts consisting almost entirely of fish were common in the Middle Ages. A royal banquet in the reign of Henry IV consisted of three courses and over thirty dishes, which, with the exception of the sweets and the subtleties, were made up of fish.[6]

In the general prologue to *The Canterbury Tales*, Chaucer writes that the Franklin was 'Epicurus owene sone,'[7] (an Epicurean) and that 'Ful many a fat partrich had he in muwe/And many a breem and many a luce in stuwe.'[8] A 'stuwe' here is a fishpond, stocked with bream and pike for the enrichment of the Franklin's diet. Believed to have been written in the 1390s, the inclusion of pike in the list of earthly comforts enjoyed by the Franklin again places pike as a sought-after and important food in the 14th century.

The popularity of pike owed perhaps as much to social reasons as gastronomic ones. For many centuries, the strict religious rules on the consumption of meat had an overall effect on how much fish was consumed. In 1629 the unfortunate Claude Guillon was beheaded in Burgundy for eating 'a morsel of Horseflesh on a Fish-day'.[9] The popularity of pike would therefore have owed much to the prevailing religious dietary constraints as well as its flavour and supposed medicinal qualities. The difficulty of transporting fresh food meant that sea fish was not usually available far inland unless preserved or salted in some way; therefore freshwater fish of all varieties were widely consumed, as is still the case in much of Europe. With fast days making up almost half the days of the year, fish would have provided a valuable source of protein and nutrients for those who could afford it or catch it.

However, since the beginning of the 20th century, pike has been eaten in England by only a very few people. Anglers continue to enjoy the fruits of their labours but otherwise pike is difficult to obtain.

Fishing literature offers as many theories on how to catch a pike as there are fishermen and fishing writers. The 15th-century manuscript transcribed in *Stere Htt Well* offers this intriguing method: 'To take a pike in the water – Take a raw chicken and clean it and fill it with black soap and sew together both ends and prick it full of holes and lay it in the river and as soon as the pike has eaten it he will come to land.'[10] How extraordinary that someone should dream of using a whole chicken to land a pike, not to mention the supposed pike-attracting quality of black soap. Pike must indeed have been a rare luxury if a whole chicken might be sacrificed in the hope of gaining one. One can only assume that poorer fishermen managed well-enough without the chicken.

Catching pike is not a simple affair. Perhaps because of the dubious reputation of this fish, anglers have built up a great number of myths and legends about both the pike itself and the best means of procuring one. In *The Compleat Angler*, Izaak Walton gives detailed instructions on not only how to catch pike, but also on choosing the best for eating:

> but that it be observed, that the old or very great pikes have in them more of state than goodness; the smaller or middle-sized pikes being, by the most and choicest palates, observed to be the best meat[11]

The Treatyse of Fysshynge with an Angle offers the following advice for catching a pike which is still current amongst anglers to this day.

> Take a codling hook, and take a roach or a fresh herring…and draw the hook into the cheek of the fresh herring…cast it in a pit where the pike useth and this is the best and most surest craft of taking the pike[12]

It would appear that the manner of catching pike is individual to each fisherman. There is much debate as to the superiority of deadbait over livebait, coarse fishing over fly fishing, but ultimately success appears to relate more to luck than judgement, and every angler will have his or her own theory on how best to proceed. Interestingly, fly-fishing for pike is not uncommon. Although usually used for catching salmon and trout, fly-fishing is an apparently effective way to land a pike of adequate size for the dinner table.

It is taken as given that to successfully catch pike it is useful to understand what they eat, how they capture and consume their victims and where they like to hunt. Because of his occasional foray into eating small mammals and frogs the pike's reputation has been cast as an indiscriminate gourmet. In spite of this reputation pike apparently require less food than many other fish per pound of body weight. Pike use minimum effort to locate food and generally lurk until prey fish swim into their hunting zone. Once sighted by a pike prey fish are usually dinner. The pike is extremely fast and powerful and capable of snatching its victims before they have a chance to escape.

From the river bank, to kitchen, to banquet, the journey from rod to table is an important one. Once you have caught your pike, how you choose to cook him is a matter of personal taste.

Throughout the ages there have been many ways of enjoying this magnificent fish. Apicius, writing in the late 4th century AD. gives an excellent recipe for pike fillets in cumin sauce which is not dissimilar to many medieval English recipes for pike with spiced sauces. Popular recipes include Izaak Walton's classic stuffed baked pike, pike in galentyne, gefilte fish, pike in cinnamon and the intriguing medieval luce wafers. Escoffier gives a recipe for quenelles of pike with instructions for serving with slices of truffle, and Mrs Beeton's *Book of Household Management* (1861) contains a recipe for pike although consumption of pike was already in decline at the time.

Once caught the pike must be cleaned, gutted and scaled, then either filleted or prepared for baking whole. Quenelles have long been a favoured way of serving pike in order to avoid the notorious bones. If not cooking pike whole, Butterworth recommends in *Now cook me the fish* that 'the best portions of pike are those over the ribs, which have, in addition to superiority in flavour, the advantage of being freer from those forked bones with which the other parts of the fish are plentifully supplied and which prove exceedingly troublesome'. [13]

In 1927 E.G. Boulenger commented that 'the pike, which is still eaten on the Continent, was at one time the most popular and expensive fish in England.'[14] Yet pike was eaten and enjoyed not only for its flavour, but also for its supposed health-giving properties.

The component parts of the pike were said to cure a vast array of ailments. In the *Angler's Sure Guide* of 1706, Robert Howlett describes the extraordinary medicinal qualities of this king of fish:

> The Croslike bone in his Head is given against the Falling-Sickness; and his Flesh is so harmless and excellent, that it may be given to a sick Person. His Spawn and Row provoke both to Vomit and Stool, and are used for that Purpose; the Jaws calcin'd helps the Stone, cleanses and dries up Ulcers, old Sores, and Haemorrhoids; the Teeth in Powder gives ease in the Pleurisie; the Grease takes away Coughs in Children, by anointing the Feet therewith; the Gall taken inwardly, cures Agues; outwardly helps Spots and Dimness of the Eyes; the Heart eaten cures Fevers. [15]

With a pike in the house who would require any other form of medical treatment?

171

To read this description one would think that an almost universal panacea had been found in one creature. It is no wonder that with these ascribed curative powers the pike was in such high demand. The 15th-century manuscript transcribed in *Stere Htt Well* gives this recipe to cure the 'flux':

> Take the chokes off a pikes head so that the teeth stick in and burn them on a tiled stone and make powder thereof and drink it with stale ale or eat it in your pottage.[16]

Adding burnt and powdered pike's teeth to one's breakfast seems more likely to induce indigestion than to cure other ailments but it would appear that some at least had faith in this remedy.

Since the turn of the 20th century consumption of pike has continued its decline in popularity. Although still widely enjoyed in other European countries, here in England freshwater fish in general is spurned in favour of sea fish.

So what did cause the downfall of this once great delicacy? With the dawn of the industrial revolution, many changes were wrought upon the fish-eating habits of the nation. The advent of reliable and speedy transport, in the form of railways and the motor vehicle, meant that fresh sea fish became widely available. The old practices of eating freshwater fish or preserved sea fish were no longer necessary. Later still, fish farming ensured a cheap and easily obtainable supply of popular fish such as salmon, which were once the preserve of the rich (or of poachers). In addition, pollution from the factories and mills built during the industrial revolution threatened the health of many English rivers and streams, destroying or rendering inedible the stocks of fish which once thrived in them.

New angling regulations also forced change. As early as 1878, anglers collaborated to provide protection for coarse fish stocks. The law already protected both the salmon and the trout, which were now reserved for the wealthiest of anglers. However, other coarse fish could be taken and killed at any time, including the spawning season, a practice which threatened further the essential restocking of rivers and lakes. After much debate a closed season was declared by angling clubs to last from March 15 to June 15 each year.[17] Following on from this, the 1878 Freshwater Fisheries Act brought all anglers and poachers under the arm of the law. Local size limits were introduced across the country which meant that undersized or young fish were returned to the water to continue growing and enable natural repopulation of the rivers. Slowly but surely, fewer coarse fish were taken for the table, a reversal of the earlier norm where fish were only taken for food. Anglers now returned their catch to the water after weighing.

During the First World War the government and the National Federation of Anglers, looked at the possibility of once gain using coarse fish stocks as a food supply to bolster and supplement dwindling resources.[18] In 1915 a revision of Thames byelaws was suggested, but never acted upon, 'that pike no longer…be afforded the same protection as other fish'. There were even recommendations from the Thames Angling Preservation Society that all pike should be removed from the Thames. Neither of these recommendations was acted upon and the pike remained at large.[19]

Arthur Ransome once wrote:

> There are fashions in fish. It is possible in angling literature to watch, for example, the decline and fall of the pike from the eminence he once enjoyed… with the pike the other coarse fish have lost their kitchen reputations…Yet once upon a time a pike would be the chief dish at a banquet.[20]

The pike has adorned the tables of the rich and poor for many centuries but now very few in England have the opportunity to enjoy eating pike. Yet with the dwindling stocks of sea fish, caused by both over-fishing and the disproportionate popularity of a few species, perhaps it is time for pike to return to its previous place at table: as a king of fish.

Appendix

The classic recipe given by Izaak Walton is lengthy, and apparently 'somewhat the better for not being common':[21]

> First, open your Pike at the gills, and if need be, cut also a little slit towards his belly; out of these take his guts, and keep his liver, which you are to shred very small with thyme, sweet-marjoram and a little winter-savory; to these put some pickled oysters, and some anchovies two or three, both these last whole; for the anchovies will melt, and the oysters should not; to these you must add also a pound of sweet butter, which you are to mix with the herbs that are shred, and let them all be well salted: if the Pike be more than a yard long, then you may put into these herbs more than a pound, or if he be less, then less butter will suffice: these being thus mixt with a blade or two of mace, must be put into the pike's belly, and then his belly sewed up, and so sewed up, as to keep all the butter in his belly if it be possible, if not, then as much of it as you possibly can, but take not off the scales; then you are to thrust the spit through his mouth out at his tail, and then with four, or five, or six split sticks, or very thin laths, and a convenient quantity of tape or filleting, these laths are to be tyed round about the pike's body from his head to his tail, and the tape tied somewhat thick to prevent his breaking or falling off from the spit: let him be roasted very leisurely, and often basted with claret wine, and anchovies, and butter mixed together, and also with what moisture falls from him into the

pan: when you have roasted him sufficiently you are to hold under him, when you unwind or cut the tape that ties him, such a dish as you purpose to eat him out of; and let him fall into it with the sauce that is roasted in his belly, and by this means the pike will be kept unbroken and complete: then to the sauce, which was within, and also in the pan, you are to add a fit quantity of the best butter, and to squeeze the juice of three or four oranges: lastly, you may either put into the pike with the oysters, two cloves of garlick, and take it whole out, when the pike is cut off the spit; or to give the sauce a haut-gout, let the dish into which you let the Pike fall, be rubbed with it: the using or not using of this garlick is left to your discretion.[22]

Mrs Beeton's Boiled Pike: Ingredients. – ¼ lb. of salt to each gallon of water; a little vinegar. Mode. – Scale and clean the pike, and fasten the tail in its mouth by means of a skewer. Lay it in cold water, and when it boils, throw in the salt and vinegar. The time for boiling depends, of course, on the size of the fish; but a middling-sized pike will take about ½ an hour. Serve with Dutch or anchovy sauce, and plain melted butter. Time. – According to size, ½ to 1 hour. – Average cost. Seldom bought. Seasonable from September to March.[23]

Original recipe for pike in galentyne: Take a pike and seth him ynowe in gode sauce; And then couche him in a vessell, that he may be y-caried yn, if thou wilt And what tyme he is colde, take brede, and stepe hit in wyne and vinegre, and cast there-to canell, and drawe hit thorgh a streynour, And do hit in a potte, And caste there-to pouder peper; And take smale oynons, and myce hem, And fry hem in oyle, and cast there-to a few saundres, and lete boyle awhile; And cast all this hote vppon the pike, and carry him forth.[24]

Notes

1. Yarrell, William, *A History of British Fishes* (London: J. Van Voorst, 1836), ed. Sir John Richardson, accessed July 2004 <http://home.planet.nl/~zoete004/pike.htm>.
2. Walton, p. 143.
3. Walton, p. 140.
4. Berners, Dame Juliana, *A Treatysse on Fysshynge wyth an Angle*, accessed July 2004, <http://www.flyfishinghistory.com/treatise_prologue.htm>.
5. *Curye on Inglysch: English Culinary Manuscripts of the Fourteenth Century*, edited by Constance B. Hieatt and Sharon Butler, Early English Text Society (Oxford University Press: London, 1985), p. 39.
6. Mead, William E., p. 154.
7. Chaucer, Geoffrey, *The Riverside Chaucer*, edited by Larry Benson and F. N Robinson, (Oxford: Houghton Mifflin, 1987), p. 28.

8. ibid, p. 29.
9. Daniel, Rev. W. B, *Rural Sports* (1801), p. 127.
10. *Stere htt well : a book of medieval refinements, recipes and remedies* (London: Cornmarket Press, 1972) trans. G.A.J. Hodgett, p. 13.
11. Walton, p. 140.
12. Berners, Dame Juliana, *A Treatysse on Fysshynge wyth an Angle*, accessed July 2004, <http://www.flyfishinghistory.com/treatyse_fish_2.htm>.
13. Butterworth p. 54.
14. Boulenger, E. G., *A naturalist at the dinner table* (London: Duckworth,1927), p. 6.
15. Howlett, Robert, *The Angler's Sure Guide* (London: G Conyers, 1706).
16. *Stere htt well*, p. 36.
17. Phillipps, Ernest, *Fishing* (Watmoaghs: Bradford, 1936), p. 29.
18. Waterhouse, T. A., *History of the NFA* (London: 1936), p. 48.
19. Calcutt, W. G., *The History of the London Angler's Association* (London: 1924), p. 126.
20. Ransome, Arthur, *Rod and Line* (Oxford: Oxford University Press, 1980), p. 79.
21. Walton, p. 151.
22. Walton, p. 150.
23. Beeton, Isabella, *Book of Household Management* (1861), accessed July 2004 <http://etext.library.adelaide.edu.au/b/beeton/household/household.html>.
24. Austin, Thomas, *Two Fifteenth-Century Cookery-Books. Harleian MS. 279 & Harl. MS. 4016, with extracts from Ashmole MS. 1429, Laud MS. 553, & Douce MS 55*, London: for The Early English Text Society by N. Trübner & Co., 1888.

Bibliography

Berners, Dame Juliana, *A Treatysse on Fysshynge wyth an Angle*, accessed July 2004, <http://www.flyfishinghistory.com/treatise_prologue.htm>.
Berriedale-Johnson, Michelle, *Festive Feasts* (London: British Museum Books, 2003).
Butterworth, Margaret, *Now cook me the fish, 146 fresh-water fish recipes collected by Margaret Butterworth* (London: Country Life, 1950).
Edwards, John, *The Roman Cookery of Apicius* (London: Random Century, 1998).
Escoffier, *The Complete Guide to Modern Cookery*, translated by H. L. Cracknell and R. J. Kaufmann (London: Heinemann, 1983).
Mead, William E., *The English Medieval Feast* (London: G. Allen & Unwin, 1931).
Spurling, Hilary, *Elinor Fettiplace's Receipt Book* (London: Penguin Books Ltd, 1987).
Walton, Izaak, *The Compleat Angler* (London: Oldhams Press, date unknown).
Wilson, C. Anne, *Food and Drink in Britain* (London: Constable, 1973).

Entomophagy

Bruce Kraig

'Do you know how good these are? Don't you know that this is the cleanest food you can eat, not like filthy pigs. They eat only natural grain, they are full of vitamins and proteins, and you know, they taste good.' A small, cheerful woman, wizened from the sun, the lecturer stood at her table heaped with mounds of lime-cured, red-black chapulines in several sizes. Seeing that we were impressed, she went on about how chapulines nourished 'our ancestors,' making it something of a patriotic obligation to feast upon them. Then, reaching up to a cord stretched on two poles, she pulled down a string of *gusanos de maguey* and said, 'These are really good.' And indeed they are, only unlike *chapulines*, they don't come with their own toothpicks.

We were in one of the Mexican state of Oaxaca's markets, this one near the street of the chocolate grinders. *Chapulines* are grasshoppers (*Tettigoniidae* or similar family) and *gusanos de maguey* are moth larvae that feed on agave plants. *Gusanos* are of two kinds and they are eaten seasonally: the white 'worm,' or *chicharra*, from the leaves of the plant, in the spring; and the *chinicuil*, smaller and reddish in colour, that appears in the fall. It happens that my colleagues and I had been videotaping grasshopper-catching and scenes of entomophagy for a couple of weeks. So much did we like the tastes that we were shopping for *gusanos* to snack on, and *sal de gusanos*, to go with Donahjis, like a Tequila Sunrise but made with local Oaxacan mezcal. Delicacies in Mexico and delicious, most North Americans offered caterpillars (or any insect) as food react with horror at the suggestion. Of course, that is exactly why we have taped and shown insect eating in programmes made largely for American audiences.

Insects are the ultimate wild foods, protein on the wing, leg, and belly. So, why not eat insects? In 1885 Vincent M. Holt published a now classic tract of the same title.[1] Mixing earnestness and wit, Holt set out almost all the arguments that proponents of insect ingestion have put forward ever since. From traditional western medicinal uses, to ethnographic examples, drawing on authorities (Erasmus Darwin, for example), social utility, and plain gustatory satisfaction, all are marshalled to put the question. Using Holt as a template, what follows are some comments on the subject.

Distaste

According to a 1921 article in *Natural History*, during World War I, food shortages were so acute that:

> the eminent entomologist, Dr. L. O. Howard, was asked to ascertain the food value of insects. Favorable as the results may have proved, one can well imag-

ine the storm of protest that would have resulted had the adoption of such a program by the general public been advocated. Yet to many it is surprising and can be attributed only to prejudice, that civilized man of today shows such a decided aversion to including any six-legged [or eight-legged to include the class Arachnida] creatures in his diet.[2]

Holt argued the same thing, only his prescription was meant for both the urban and rural poor:

what a pleasant change from the labourer's unvarying meal of bread, lard, and bacon, or bread and lard without bacon, or bread without lard or bacon, would be a good dish of fried cockchafers or grasshoppers. 'How the poor live!' Badly, I know; but they neglect wholesome foods, from a foolish prejudice which it should be the task of their betters, by their example, to overcome.

Grasshoppers and their ilk are not tref. Almost every commentator on the subject cites the touchstone of food taboos, the Bible:

Yet then may ye eat of all winged creeping things that go upon all fours, which have legs above their feet, to leap withal upon the earth; even these of them ye may eat; the locust after its kind, and the bald locust after its kind, and the cricket after its kind, and the grasshopper after its kind. (Leviticus, XI: 21–22)

177

As Holt and others have asked: If God says it is all right to eat certain kinds of insects, then why not us? In every one of my food history classes, I ask students about their reluctance to become insectivore (perhaps one out of every twenty will actually taste insect preparations that I bring to classes). The responses fall into familiar categories. One is gustatory, especially about larvae of any kind, and accompanied by the expression, 'Yuk!' or 'Yukkie!' Larvae resemble worms and worms are thought to be slimy because of a perceived epidermal sheen. That their intestines are visible through their skins only makes them more repellent (Note 1). Snakes seem to evoke the same responses. All other considerations aside, it is texture that brings forth disgust: the 'slimy,' quality. Asked if they eat jellied meats, or animal cartilage, the students shudder. When I hand out Gummie Worms, however, they disappear down gullets rapidly. Gelatinous is acceptable to Americans if it is sweet, but never savoury (Note 2).

Appearance is a second locus of distaste. Holt and many others point out a paradox:

The lobster, a creature consumed in incredible quantities at all the highest tables in the land, is such a foul feeder that, for its sure capture, the experienced fisherman will bait his lobster-pot with putrid flesh or fish which is too far gone even to attract a crab. And yet, if at one of those tables there appeared a well-cooked dish of clean-feeding slugs, the hardiest of the guests would shrink from tasting it. Again, the eel is universally eaten, fried, stewed, or in pies, though it is the very scavenger of the water – there being no filth it will not swallow – like its equally relished fellow-scavenger the pig, the 'unclean animal' of Scripture. There was once an equally strong objection to the pig, as there is at present against insects. What would the poor do without the bacon-pig now?

Well, what's wrong with grasshoppers? I ask my students. The reply is that they are ugly and 'filthy'. All those legs and buggy eyes are unappetizing. Crustaceans, from shrimp to crawdads, are delectable, multiple legs, hideous faces, and vile eating habits notwithstanding. Sowbugs, or woodlice (genera *Oniscus* and *Porcellio*) would never do, though they, too, are crustaceans. Perhaps that the desirable arthropods live in symbolically purifying water rather than crawling on or in the earth makes them edible. Asked to speculate, students rarely come up with suitable answers. Logic only works occasionally in the world of food taste and distaste.

People are schooled in modes of disgust. Insects are so alien as to give rise to fears. I confess to a certain arachnophobia, even knowing the sources of this irrationality. One is having seen as a young child a monstrous, blood-sucking spider in the classic movie fantasy, *The Thief of Baghdad*. Nightmares followed. The other was having awakened one morning in my boyhood home in rural New Jersey to find a black widow spider on my chest, its multiple eyes staring me in the face. I owe my later success as a sprinter on the school track team to that spider. Though I have eaten varieties of insects, the beautiful photograph of a young Cambodian woman munching on a fried tarantula on the cover of *Man Eating Bugs* sends a frisson through me and countless others with arachnophobia.[3] The vehicles of popular culture have made insects so alien as to evoke the same emotions, whether through personal experiences or not.

Yet a third reason for loathing insects as food is the modern obsession with germs. Since the discovery of disease carrying microbes in the late 19th century, most people have been afflicted with some form of microphobia, bacterophobia chief among them. People wash compulsively, antibacterial washing liquids are hyped by advertisers and sold in great numbers (even though they are no better than plain soap), and many more products are sold in the never ending struggle to gain total antisepsis. If the students are any example, insects are guilty whether or not an individual insect genus is a vector for human diseases. Holt would have found this attitude foolish, but might have appreciated its religious qualities.

Only when one points out that each person in North America unwittingly ingests, by estimate, half a kilogram of insects each year does it become clear that eating insects might not be unusual for western peoples. The United States Food and Drug Administration permits certain numbers of insects in processed foods. For example, ketchup can contain 30 fruit fly eggs per 100 grams, peanut butter, 30 insect fragments for each 100 grams, canned corn, 2 insect larvae per 100 grams, 2 maggots for each 100 blueberries, 100 insect fragments per 100 grams of curry powder, 1 per cent of wheat may be infested, 5 per cent of sesame seeds, 10 per cent of coffee beans, and horror of horrors, 60 insect fragments in each 100 grams of chocolate. Now we can appreciate the old sailors' joke about extra protein in their maggot-infested hardtack and apples.

A large majority of the world's people knowingly eat insects. But, until recently western attitudes toward this dietary supplement has been tinged with awe and pity:

> Nowadays the use of insects as a diet is practically restricted to wild or half-civilized peoples, but even so they form an important item in the food supply of mankind... It is, perhaps, among African negroes that insects are most extensively used a food – a practice undoubtedly due more to necessity than choice. Owing to peculiar climatic conditions and the ravages made by animal diseases, but few goats, sheep, and cattle are kept by the natives and these are too highly prized to enter very frequently into the diet, serving rather as signs of wealth; chickens and occasionally dogs are the only domestic animals freely eaten. The meat supply of the various tribes is, therefore, limited, necessarily consisting mainly of fish and game, the capture of which involves not a little trouble and is dependent on too many contingencies. To this scarcity is attributable the perpetual craving for animal food from which the black race has been suffering for centuries and which is undoubtedly to a large extent responsible for cannibalism[!!].[4]

Similar arguments have been made for Asia and Mexico, including cannibalism among Aztecs. Equating anthropophagy and entomophagy is an odd pairing, but provides maximum shock. That much is easily observed in the recent pop culture phenomenon, reality television. Set as contests, participants gobble down worms, spiders, leeches accompanied by squeals of terror from the diners and the viewing audience: *Grand Guignol* with bugs.

Traditional Entomophagy

Holt cites travellers ancient and modern who approvingly described entomophagy outside the western world. In this, he touched upon a voluminous literature past and present. A good sampling of this has been collected by Emeritus Professor Gene R. DeFoliart, a distinguished entomologist at the University of Wisconsin, Madison.[5] One of the best studied insect-devouring regions of the world is Mexico, past and present. As Raymond Sokolov observed Mexico offers a splendid opportunity to uncover the roots of a national cuisine (or cuisines), including the use of insects.[6] Sophie Coe's discussion of some, based on the observations of Sahagún and others is a good concise account.[7] There is good archaeological evidence for broad spectrum food gathering by the peoples of Mexico since deep in prehistory. Eating patterns developed over millennia had not changed by the Hispanic period – having no food aversions anything walking, swimming, flying or crawling was fair game. For the Aztecs, or Méxica, living on Lake Texcoco (and other peoples throughout the country) sustenance came from the water. Fish, frogs (tadpoles, too), young salamanders (*Axolotl*), and lots of insects were on the menu. As Clavigero, an Italian visitor, noted at the end of the 18th century: 'At all times the markets are full of a thousand species of vermin, raw, cooked, fried or toasted, sold especially for the sustainment of the poor.' Among these were members of the water boatman family (*Corixidae*) including *axayacatl* (nymphs and adults) and *ahuautli* (eggs), and backswimmers (*Notonectidae*). Adult forms were ground, wrapped in corn husks and cooked.

> The bug eggs were collected on loosely twined ropes flung into the lake. They could be made into tortillas, tamales, or wrapped in maize husks to be toasted. They were said to taste like fish, or like caviar. Izeahuitli were tiny worms netted on the lake. When cooked with salt and chili, they became blackish and had the consistency of crushed bread crumbs. They were made into tortillas to dry and keep, but they did not last very long.[8]

180

Having eaten these and other insects that follow, I can report that these do not have much flavour when mixed with flour and water and then fried into small cakes. When served up *au naturel* as 'caviar,' then indeed they taste like fish.

Water insects are but one of many insects in the Mexican food vocabulary. DeFoliart cites a report that 200 species are still consumed.[9] *Escamoles* are the eggs and larvae of a kind of black ant. Appearing in the spring and resembling tiny white eggs, they are usually sautéed and served with mildly spiced sauces. Their flavour, and texture, is very much that of fresh corn kernels, as if just shucked from the ear. They are really good when scooped up with a bit of fresh corn tortilla.

Like much of Mexico's food, taste in insects are regional. *Axayacatl* and like creatures are specialities of Mexico City, but in Taxco *Jumiles* are the local treat. Members of the 'stink bug' family (*Pentatomidae*, Order *Hemiptera*) are abundant in the spring. Small, green, and shield-shaped beetles, they feed on *encina* (an evergreen oak) leaves. When in season, families from Taxco swarm into the neighbouring mountains (Taxco is a charming mountain-top town) to collect them. *Jumiles* are usually mashed in a *molcajete* (grinding bowl), mixed with a fresh tomato-onion-chili sauce, and served with fresh corn tortillas. The crushed insects emit a distinctive odour, slightly cinnamon-like, but upon eating the flavour is like iodine because they are loaded with it. *Jumiles* are an acquired taste, especially when eaten raw as vendors and collectors will, and are perhaps the reason locals say that once you have tasted *jumiles* you'll never leave Taxco.

Other insects are national in character, though the preparations are local. Among them are the grasshoppers and *gusanos de maguey* mentioned above. They are the white larvae of the giant skipper moth (*Aegiale hesperiaris* and *Agathymus* spp.) and the pink larvae of carpenter moths (*Xyleutes redtenbacheri*). The former are the infamous 'worms' found in bottles of mezcal (Note 3). *Gusanos* are addictive, especially the *chicharra* or white ones, pickled in lime juice, dried, or fresh. Roasted and salted, they are tasty enough to be served regularly in the cafeteria of the huge food processor Herdez. The general manager says that the workers cannot get enough of them. In the countryside, traditional cookery calls for peeling the skin of the maguey plant, wrapping the caterpillars in a bag made from it, and then toasting the insects in hot wood ash. Called *mixiote* when made with meats, this is a glorious dish. The flavour of *gusanos* when cooked just so is very much like a very good smoked bacon.

Chapulines are the other most widely eaten insects, not just in Mexico, but worldwide. There are several kinds of *Orthoptera* eaten, but the 'long horn' is likely the most widely used. Grasshoppers swarm in the fall, just as large seeded grasses upon which they dote come to fruit. As the *chapulin* vendor said, they eat grain intended for us, so we eat them. Precisely the same point Holt made about several 'verminous' species which devour good English gardens. In the morning, before the creatures really stir themselves, people armed with long-poled nets set out along the roads and in fields to capture their prey. Once caught, the grasshoppers are placed in large clay pots with leaves in order to 'purge' their guts. They are then plunged into boiling water for a few minutes, after which the heads, wings and some legs can be removed. Drained and dried they are ready for cooking or drying and curing. Rarely, if ever, are they ground as in some African countries. *Chapulines'* flavour varies with the ingredients with which they are cooked or preserved. Lime, for instance, imparts a delicious limey flavour. Normally, they are sautéed and served plain with lime and salt, or with a sauce; *chile pasilla* is usual but *chile guajillo* is also good.

Why Not Eat Insects?

For a variety of reasons such delectables as *gusanos*, *chapulines*, and *escamoles* have become desirable items in upscale restaurants. Not only is this so in Mexico, but in North America, as well. Tastes for food insects has been growing through entomophagic organisations and the usual organs of publicity. The summer of 2004 saw the emergence of 17-year cicadas, called Brood X. Television and newspapers were filled with stories about the hordes that descended upon the East Coast, many accompanied by recipes. Cooking contests were held and chefs tried their hands at fancy preparations (it's best to roast them). Amusing though these stories are, there are other good reasons to consume insects.

Again, Holt anticipated modern arguments. In his day the poor were always short of protein, so why not use a source ready at hand. Compared to food of ordinary food animals, insects are remarkably efficient protein and mineral delivery devices. The following table gives some idea of nutritional values.

Insect	Protein (g)	Fat (g)	Carbohydrate(mg)	Calcium (mg)	Iron (mg)
Giant Water Beetle	19.8	8.3	2.1	43.5	13.6
Red Ant	13.9	3.5	2.9	47.8	5.7
Silk Worm Pupae	9.6	5.6	2.3	41.7	1.8
Dung Beetle	17.2	4.3	0.2	30.9	7.7
Cricket	12.9	5.5	5.1	75.8	9.5
Small Grasshopper	20.6	6.1	3.9	35.2	5.0
Large Grasshopper	14.3	3.3	2.2	27.5	3.0
June Beetle	13.4	1.4	2.9	22.6	6.0
Caterpillar	6.7	N/A	N/A	N/A	13.1
Termite	14.2	N/A	N/A	N/A	35.5
Weevil	6.7	N/A	N/A	N/A	13.1
Beef (Lean Ground)	27.4	N/A	N/A	N/A	3.5
Fish (Broiled Cod)	28.5	N/A	N/A	N/A	1.0 10

Crude protein per body weight amounts to 30–70% of body weight and, based on studies of tryptophan, lysine and other elements, insect protein is of good to middling quality. As DeFoliart says:

> We don't know how much it would cost to cultivate insects as food; however, we believe that because of their high protein content, high digestibility, variety in food diets, high conversion efficiency, and great reproductive potential associated with a short life cycle, the useful biomass obtained would be significant when compared to other products which are used to obtain protein. That is why insects should be taken into consideration as a food alternative for a world in which human nutrition has been a huge problem.[11]

Besides, prepared well, insects taste good, as in Holt's pungent phrase, talking about cockchafers:

> What a godsend to housekeepers to discover a new entrée to vary the monotony of the present round! Why should invention, which makes such gigantic strides in other directions, stand still in cookery? Here then, mistresses, who thirst to place new and dainty dishes before your guests, what better could you have than 'Curried Maychafers'– or, if you want a more mysterious title, 'Larvae Melolonthae à la Grungru?

And now that 'bugs' of all sorts are becoming familiar, cute and anthropomorphised, through movies (see both versions of *Men in Black*, *It's a Bug's Life*, and *Joe's Apartment*, the latter with sentient, talking cockroaches) it won't be long before formerly disgusting creatures grace the everyday table. Simply consider *Babe*.

Bibliography

1. Vincent M. Holt, *Why Not Eat Insects?* (repr. with intro. by Laurence Mound, London: British Museum, 1988 [1885]).
2. J. Bequaert, 'Insects as Food: How They Have Augmented the Food Supply of Mankind in Early and Recent Times', *Natural History*, March-April 1921.
3. Peter Menzel and Faith D'Aluisio, *Man Eating Bugs, The Art and Science of Eating Insects* (A Material World Book: Napa, CA, 1998). Note also the rather good horror movie, *Arachnophobia*.
4. Bequaert.
5. <www.food-insects.com/book>. DeFoliart gives a lengthy bibliography including classic studies such as F.S. Bodenheimer, *Insects as Human Food* (The Hague, W. Junk, 1951).
6. Raymond Sokolov, 'Before the Conquest' (*A Matter of Taste*, August, 1989). Two other columns on entomophagy followed, including 'Insects, Worms, and Other Tidbits' in September, 1989, with recipes, one of them for *Jumiles*.
7. Sophie D. Coe, 'Aztec Cuisine', *Petits Propos Culinaires*, 19, 20, 21 (London, 1985) and Sophie D. Coe, *America's First Cuisines* (Austin, TX: University of Texas Press, 1994).
8. Coe, p. 99.
9. Gene R. DeFoliart, cited in *Food Insect News*, 1991.
10. Data collected from *The Food Insects Newsletter*, July 1996 (Vol. 9, No. 2, ed. by Florence V. Dunkel, Montana State University) and *Bugs In the System*, by May Berenbaum (Iowa State University Entomology Department, February 25, 2000 by John VanDyk).
11. DeFoliart, Chapter 3, 'The Use of Insects as Food in Mexico,' <www.food-insects.com/book>

Notes

1. Worm repulsion, equated with rejection, is commemorated in this version of a children's folk song: 'Nobody loves me, everybody hates me/Think I'll go and eat worms. Long ones, short ones, fat ones, thin ones/See how they wriggle and squirm/I bite off the heads, and suck out the juice/And throw the skins away/Nobody knows how fat I grow/On worms three times a day/ Ohh...nobody loves me.' (<http://www.niehs.nih.gov/kids/lyrics/worms.htm>)

2. This particular taste preference is relatively new since jellied meats were common into the 20th century, especially among German-Americans. Newly arrived Americans often retain their old tastes for gelatinous meats: *Carnitas* among Mexicans is an example, but they also consume insects. The next generation tends not to.

3. Menzel and D'Aluisio (p. 116) give an interesting explanation for the worm in the bottle. Real tequila and mezcal are made from agave which give home to the caterpillars. The true beverages are double distilled and must be at least 110° proof, but the animals' bodies can only be preserved at 140° proof or above. Therefore the worm at the bottom of the bottle shows authenticity and percentage of alcohol.

See also:
F. S. Bodenheimer, *Insects as Human Food* (The Hague: W. Junk, 1951).
Charles Curran, *Insects in Your Life* (New York, Sheridan House, 1951 [1937]).

Tracking the Wild in 'Wild' Foods

Steven Kramer

Glancing through a recent edition of *Food &Wine* magazine I came across an article extolling the virtues of the cuisine at a somewhat earthy guest ranch in the mountains of Colorado.[1] Along with a list of locally grown organic produce the author made special note of the 'magnificent' elk and pheasant that were a staple offering at the ranch. On a cursory look, this sounds much like the cuisine served at my table. As an avid hunter, my diet is dominated by a steady stream of game meat. However, on closer inspection there are some important distinctions between the elk and pheasant served at this ranch and that which currently resides in my freezer. The elk on the guests' menu, it turns out, is purchased from a local 'elk ranch' while the 'free-range pheasants' are not shot in the field but come from a nearby farm. The real distinction here is that these farm-raised animals are distinctly different from the wild ones that I pursue. But what exactly are we invoking when we apply the predicate 'wild'? Is it a quality of the animal itself? Is it a quality of our subjective experience? Is it some kind of reference to the environment things live in? Does it refer to its life history? Is it something about their relationship to human beings? Is it a reference to the danger-ous or mysterious quality of something? My aim in this paper is to track down the nature of this elusive property. In so doing I will show that an adequate understand-ing of wildness only comes about when we place it as one of a trio of properties of environmental concern.

Before going any further, let me briefly make a few comments about some issues that I will not be exploring in this paper, though they are very worthy projects in their own right. The first is the difference in the methods of procurement – buying food versus hunting or gathering it oneself. While this difference does raise impor-tant concerns about the kind of contact we have with wild things, this does not seem to get us any closer to understanding the property of wildness itself. After all, a wild king salmon from Alaska is no less wild because it is shipped halfway across the United States to my Midwestern supermarket. Though I obviously will not have had the chance to experience this wildness for myself, it is still a very different fish from the farm-raised salmon lying next to it on the fish counter. Another important set of issues involves the commercial exploitation of wild foods. While this certainly raises concerns about sustainability and the preservation of biodiversity, hunting and gathering by individuals and groups is not altogether free from these concerns. If we are going to address the issue of sustainability, however, we first have to get clear on what it is that we are trying to sustain. To say that it is biodiversity is not an adequate answer as biodiversity might be sustained in gene banks, zoos, or game farms full of exotic species – hardly the ideal of those of us concerned with the preservation of wild things.[2] The last issue that I am going to set aside involves the difference in taste that might be found between wild foods and their farm-raised or domesticated cousins. While I could extol at length the exquisite taste of various wild foods, I find that it is not taste alone that draws me to them. Here I am in much agreement with Henry David Thoreau when he wrote:

> The bitter-sweet of a white-oak acorn which you nibble in a bleak November walk over the tawny earth is more to me than a slice of imported pine-apple.[3]

There is something beyond the taste that draws the lover of wild foods. It is the wildness of the thing itself. Let us now turn to the question of exactly what that is.

One of the obvious places to turn for help in this matter is the vast array of American environmental literature. It is hard to pick up a book in this area without finding some reference to wildness and a concern for its preservation. Aldo Leopold, for instance, opens his seminal text in American environmental thought, *A Sand County Almanac*, by stating:

> There are some who can live without wild things and some who cannot. These essays are the delights and dilemmas of one who cannot.[4]

And it was Henry David Thoreau who gave us the famous dictum, 'In wildness is the preservation of the world.'[5] This claim is echoed by the environmental philosopher J. Baird Callicott who flatly states that the distinction between wild and domesticated animals is one of the 'two distinctions fundamental to an ecological ethic.'[6] However, exactly what Leopold, Thoreau, Callicott and others mean by wildness is not altogether apparent. Many authors simply use the word as if its meaning is self-evident. When authors do attempt to flesh out the concept of wildness their discussion is often couched in fairly vague terms. For instance, in his discussion of the appeal to wildness in nature writing Don Scheese states:

185

> all nature writers, no matter where they live … are able to find and celebrate wildness: the existence of nonhuman elements – whether they be geographical, botanical, or zoological – in spite of the forces of modernity.[7]

What exactly is included under the rubric of 'nonhuman elements' is not at all clear. Strictly speaking the dog that lies beside me as I write this paper is nonhuman, even if he sometimes does not seem to think so. He is, though, a far cry from being wild. Much the same can be said for the carrots growing in my garden. Perhaps then the appeal to nonhuman elements is meant to include all of those things that have been shaped or impacted by human activities. Since my dog and carrots are the result of a long history of selective development by humans they would not count as being wild. At its extreme it is this sense of wildness which is invoked when people talk of 'going off to the wilds of Alaska' or some such place. What they seem to mean is somewhere removed from all signs of human activity. This understanding however raises the significant question of whether any such place or thing actually exists, given the extensive impacts that humans have had on this planet.[8] If we back off from this extreme and allow some impacts of human activity the question remains open as to just what those are.

Further confusion is raised by the fact that another term prominent in environmental literature, namely naturalness, is defined in much the same manner. This has led many authors to use these terms interchangeably. For instance, in his book *Faking Nature*, Robert Elliot gives one of the most detailed philosophical accounts of the property of naturalness to date. Elliot argues that however skilled we become at restoring damaged environments, there is one thing that we can never restore, that is the area's naturalness. This is because, as Elliot puts it,

> what is natural is best thought of as what has not been modified as a result of people exercising their rational capacities.[9]

Naturalness is thus a historical property. It refers to a causal history dominated by the non-intentional, ateleological forces of nature. Restored nature simply lacks this historical continuity because of the involvement of humans in creating it. However, just a few pages after defining naturalness in this manner Elliot states:

> What is significant about wild nature is its causal continuity with the past, its relationship with an evolving series of states that are the products of natural forces.[10]

Naturalness and wildness thus appear to be the same thing for Elliott and he is certainly not alone in committing this equivocation.

A different concern arises when we note that none of these previous articulations of wildness seems to fit with what Thoreau or Leopold had in mind. Thoreau quite clearly applies wildness to humans and non-humans alike when he states: 'Give me for my friends and neighbors wild men, not tame ones.'[11] Along a similar vein, Leopold did not see wildness and human activity as being incompatible. After all, *A Sand County Almanac* revolves around his effort to restore a run-down Wisconsin farm. He often described these efforts in familiar agricultural terminology as 'husbanding the wild'.[12] This was, for him, a recreational pursuit that he was modelling so that other landowners could see the rewards it offers and follow suit. While I think that Leopold would agree with Elliot that his efforts could not restore the naturalness of his farm, he nevertheless thought he could work to restore its wildness.[13]

This raises a very interesting question for the participants in this symposium. If Leopold could husband wildness on his farm, is it possible that we could somehow husband wild foods as well? If so, how might this be done? The answer to these questions rests

186

on a more precise understanding not only of wildness, but also of the sort of husbandry we are talking about. Nevertheless, I think that we have made some significant progress in our understanding of wildness by teasing it apart from the property of naturalness. Focusing our attention now on the specific class of wild foods will help us toward our ultimate goal and avoid some important pitfalls along the way.

I readily admit that at this point in the discussion most readers will find the concept of husbanding wild foods troubling, if not downright oxymoronic. This is because husbandry is usually a term associated with agriculture involving the raising of domesticated plants and animals. This association is reinforced by the inherent appeal to domesticity involved in any reference to the term 'husband'. If there is anything more starkly contrary to wildness it is domestication. While I am very much in agreement with this latter point I think that understanding wildness in this manner can be as confusing as it is helpful. This is because domestication, as it is commonly understood, is a complex concept that invokes several properties of concern here. In order to show this clearly I want to analyze another definition of wildness offered by Hettinger and Throop. In an insightful article they propose grounding an ecologically based ethic on the central value of wildness. By wildness they mean that 'something is wild in a certain respect to the extent that it is not humanized in that respect. An entity is humanized in the degree to which it is influenced, altered or controlled by humans.'[14]

While this definition is closely related to Scheese's that was discussed earlier, its fuller articulation allows us to see that some very different things are being conflated here. It is one thing to influence or alter something but it is quite another to control it. Thinking about wild foods reminds us of this fact. While I certainly alter things to some extent when I go out on my yearly forage for wild plums, this seems something more akin to interaction than control. Similarly, while I certainly influence the behaviour of game when I startle it in an unsuccessful stalk, its very flight away from me is a reminder that I am not in control of things here. Even a high degree of influence and alteration does not necessarily equate with control, though the two are often associated with one another. Domesticated animals, for instance have certainly been influenced and altered in significant ways to make them produce leaner meat, larger breasts, faster growth, etc. This all has gone hand in hand with exerting an ever increasing amount of control over them. However, this close association does not necessarily have to be the case. Think, for instance of artifacts that escape our control. Such entities are standard fair for a vast array of literature from *Frankenstein* to modern science fiction. In fact it is just such a scenario in the realm of genetically modified organisms created for food production that causes some to refer to them as 'Frankenfoods'.

What is needed here is a recognition of the distinction between the properties of naturalness and wildness. The former focuses our attention on the history of how something came to be what it is. The greater the influence or alteration that humans exert in that historical process, the less natural the thing becomes. Wildness, on the other hand, seems to focus our concern on the amount of control that humans exert over the thing in question.

While we still have further work to do on clarifying the concept of wildness, the value of the rough distinction outlined above is quickly apparent in the realm of wild foods when we look at cases concerning introduced exotics and feral organisms. Though feral can simply mean untamed, it is generally used to refer to an organism that was once domesticated but has now returned to a wild or untamed state. A good example might be the feral hogs that are expanding their range in a number of places in the United States. There is no doubt that they provide excellent table fare, as well as a challenging hunting experience. They also seem to be every bit as wild as the wild elk mentioned at the beginning of this paper. They are, however, lacking one important quality of concern and that is naturalness. The long history of selective breeding in the process of domestication has essentially made them into an artifact, a biotic artifact but an artifact nonetheless. Thus I find the elk I hunt to be a more valuable wild food than a wild hog because of its additional property of naturalness. A similar judgment can be made in comparing the elk with a pheasant. While I enjoy hunting and eating pheasants as much as anyone I still find them to be of less value and therefore of a much lesser concern when it comes to managing their populations in a sustainable manner. This is because pheasants, along with a number of other game birds are Eurasian imports, brought into the United States for the specific purpose of providing hunters a sporting bird to hunt. Drastic habitat modification throughout the Great Plains has allowed these birds to virtually supplant native game birds such as the greater and lesser prairie chicken. Once again, however wild the pheasant might be, it still exhibits a much lesser degree of naturalness than wild elk do. Given the dramatic reduction of naturalness on this planet, I would argue that there is a very strong *prima facie* case for valuing natural, wild food over food that is merely wild.

Separating wildness and naturalness not only provides possible help in setting environmental policy, it seems to put us on the right track towards understanding exactly what it is that makes a wild food wild. Holmes Rolston has pointed out that the essential quality of wildness is 'a process outside the control of humans.'[15] Jack Turner echoes this claim when he states, 'to take wildness seriously is to take the issue of control seriously.'[16] However, this issue of control is in need of further refinement because it not only raises a variety of issues, there are also many different ways we might exert control over something. Once again, keeping focused on examples of wild foods will be of help in gaining clarity here.

One issue that immediately comes to mind when we think about control and a lack thereof is the issue of safety. There is certainly a long association in the history of western thought equating wildness with a sense of being out of control and therefore dangerous. It is this association, in fact, that fuelled the imperative to dominate and subdue the wild, therefore rendering it safe.[17] Traces of this association between wildness and danger can still be found today in the way that naturalness and wildness are portrayed in films, and pictures. While the naturalness of nature is often invoked through scenes of natural beauty and grandeur, wildness is invoked by the fierce, terrifying or threatening aspects of nature. Thus it is often the image of a predator, the torrent of a river rapid, or the power of a mountain storm that is called upon to represent wildness. While these things do indeed exhibit wildness, there is no necessary connection between wildness and danger. In fact, the subject of wild foods points us in the opposite direction towards that part of nature that nurtures and sustains us. A wild strawberry is, after all, every bit as wild as a female grizzly bear protecting her cub. Developing and promoting an appreciation for wild foods can help us to see this and may go some way towards challenging the often unquestioned call to continue in our path towards the complete domination of nature.

While danger is not the real issue of concern in keeping wild foods wild, there is a related concept that gets us closer to the mark, namely the quality of being tamed. This is certainly one of the important qualities that helps to distinguish wild and domesticated foods. I believe that it is this contrast between wild and tame that helps to point us towards the type of control that Thoreau and Leopold had in mind. Certainly one way to control an organism is to impose some kind of physical restriction on it. Domesticated organisms are often controlled in this manner. We fence in cows, cage chickens and tie up tomato plants in the act of producing our food. We can, and often do attempt to control wild organisms in the same way, such as trapping fish in a net to make them easier to catch and trimming the pesky blackberry bush that keeps overrunning the garden. Taming something though points us toward another way of controlling an entity. Taming involves the imposition of a kind of control that is internalized in a way that the previously mentioned external forms of control are not. Or, to put it another way, to fence an animal in or tie a plant up limits what it can do, but taming it limits what it strives to do. It is this later form of control which is central to understanding the concept of wildness.

189

Thoreau's understanding of wildness thus draws us close to the concepts of autonomy and authenticity. Recognizing this allows us to see why the preservation of wildness was a concern that bridged the human and nonhuman realm for him. I think Jack Turner gets about as close to capturing Thoreau's sense of wildness as anyone has when he points out that it invokes

> places where the land, the flora and fauna, the people, their culture, their language and arts were still ordered by energies and interests still fundamentally their own, not by the homogenization and normalization of modern life.[18]

Thoreau's main foil here is not the control exercised by human beings *per se*, but the overwhelming power exerted by civil society to impose its norms and expectations to mould the behaviour of those things that stand apart from it.

Whether or not one agrees with the ascription of wildness to humans, I think this sense of wildness accurately captures what is so fundamentally different about wild and domesticated organisms, apart from their different causal origins. The crucial point is not that they have been altered or affected by humans, but that somehow the drive to be predictable, to meet culturally prescribed expectations and fit societal norms has become internalized, either mentally or physically. Tame animals strive to grow and behave in ways that we dictate. They lay eggs, develop muscle tissue and acquiesce to our handling in order to fulfil our expectations, and they have adopted this mode of behaviour as their own. Domesticated plants no longer strive to grow, bloom and produce to their own rhythms but to our rhythms, meeting our commercial, aesthetic or nutritional desires.

With this understanding of wildness in mind, we are now in a better position to understand Thoreau's claim that 'all good things are wild and free'. While wildness and freedom are both concerned with the kind of control exerted upon something, they point towards very different types of control. While wildness invokes the capacity for authentic self-expression, freedom points us toward a concern over having a full range of opportunity for such expression. We need the latter as well as the former. Put in terms of the topic of this conference, it is not enough to simply protect isolated pockets where wild foods may continue to exist, or to try and cultivate them in some sort of specialized farm or ranch so they remain in existence. We have to allow them space to continue to live and flourish on their own.

There are two final points that I should make about the distinctions I have sketched above. The first is that all of the properties discussed above should not be thought of as delineating either/or categories. Instead, each of them should be seen as existing along a continuum with a contrasting set of properties – natural and artifactual, wild and civil, and, free and bounded. Each of these properties thus admits of degrees. A food isn't either wild or not, but can be seen as being more or less so. Recognizing this does not entail that there isn't a real distinction to be found on the opposite ends of the continuum, but it does mean that there is a rather gray area in the middle where one property slides into another. This just seems to me to be an accurate reflection of what we actually find instantiated in the world around us. The issue of concern for lovers of wild foods, like myself, is that the world is increasingly being tipped towards the opposite extreme. The second point is that while I have gone to some lengths to show that these properties are indeed distinct, they nevertheless generally interact with one another. For example, a diminution of freedom is likely to lead to eventually lead to a loss of wildness as well. Similarly an increase in artifactuality is often a trigger for a diminishment of wildness. What all of this adds up to is that a narrow focus on the wildness of wild foods is not only unlikely to help us in understanding this property, it is also an unsatisfactory from both a practical and moral perspective.

In this paper I have offered an analysis of the property of wildness by situating it in a matrix of three distinct properties – naturalness, wildness and freedom. I believe that these are the three properties of fundamental concern in preserving what David Abram has so aptly termed 'the more-than-human world'. The enjoyment and celebration of wild foods is one of the most intimate ways we come into contact with this world. It is through this contact that we come to recognize that the more-than-human aspect of this world has been seriously diminished. It is for this reason that I cannot join the author referenced at the beginning of this paper who heaped accolades on the farm-raised elk and pheasants served at the guest ranch. In fact, I feel the need to decry the further diminution of naturalness, wildness and freedom that the commercialized farming of game animals entails. This is not to say that all forms of domestication involving the reduction of these properties is necessarily a bad thing. It is merely to point out that at this point in history, the world is in much more need of strident voices singing the praises of these qualities and protecting them where they continue to exist than it is of apologists for the alternatives.

Notes

1. Bone, pp. 112–16.
2. This, of course, depends upon what one packs into the notion of biodiversity. For a detailed discussion of this see Takacs (1996)..
3. Thoreau (2000), p. 3.
4. Leopold, p. vii.
5. Thoreau (1862), p. 61.
6. Callicott, p. 151.
7. Scheese, p. 8.
8. This concern was clearly voiced in Bill McKibben's book, *The End of Nature*. In it McKibben claims that the buildup of greenhouse gasses and the advent of global warming will mean that humans have so thoroughly impacted the planet as to eliminate all vestiges of wildness.
9. Elliot, p. 123.
10. Elliot, p. 125.
11. Thoreau (1862), p. 66..
12. Leopold, p. 175.
13. For a more thorough development of this interpretation of *A Sand County Almanac* see Kramer (2003)..
14. Hettinger and Throop, p. 12.
15. Rolston, p. 102.
16. Turner (1994), p. 179.
17. Excellent resources in this area can be found in Nash's *Wilderness and the American Mind*, Oelschlaeger's *The Idea of Wilderness*, and Glacken's *Traces on the Rhodian Shore*.
18. Turner (1996), p. 12

191

Bibliography

Abram, David, *The Spell of the Sensuous: Perception and Value in a More-Than-Human World* (New York: Pantheon Books, 1996).

Bone, Eugenia, 'A Girl's Guide to Hunting & Fishing,' *Food & Wine* (August 2004): pp. 122–16.

Callicott, J. Baird, 'Comment: On Naess versus French,' in *Philosophical Dialogues: Arne Naess and the Progress of Ecophilosophy*, Nina Wiutoszek and Andrew Brennan, eds. (Lanham, MD: Rowman & Littlefield Publishers, 1991).

Elliot, Robert, *Faking Nature: The Ethics of Environmental Restoration* (New York: Routledge, 1997).

Glacken, Clarence J., *Traces on the Rhodian shore: Nature and Culture in Western Thought from Ancient Times to the End of the Eighteenth Century* (Berkeley: University of California Press, 1967).

Hettinger, Ned and William Throop, 'Refocusing Ecocentrism: Deemphasizing Stability and Defending Wildness', *Environmental Ethics* 21 (1999) pp. 3–21.

Kramer, Jon Steven, 'Natural, Wild and Free: A Discourse on Environmental Value,' Ph. D. diss., University of Colorado at Boulder (2003)

Leopold, Aldo, *A Sand County Almanac and Sketches Here and There* (New York: Oxford University Press, 1987).

McKibben, Bill, *The End of Nature* (New York, Random House, 1989).

Nash, Roderick, *Wilderness and the American Mind*, 3rd ed. (New Haven, CN: Yale University Press, 1982).

Oelschlaeger, Max, *The Idea of Wilderness* (New Haven, CN: Yale University Press, 1991).

Rolston, Homes III, *Conserving Natural Value* (New York: Columbia University Press, 1994).

Scheese, Don, *Nature Writing: The Pastoral Impulse in America* (New York: Twayne, 1996).

Takacs, David, *The Idea of Biodiversity: Philosophies of Paradise* (Baltimore, MY: Johns Hopkins University Press, 1996).

Thoreau, Henry David, 'Walking,' (1862), reprinted in *Civil Disobedience and Other Essays* (Mineola, NY: Dover Publications, 1993).

Thoreau, Henry David, *Wild Fruits*, ed. Bradley P. Dean (New York: W. W. Norton & Company, 2000).

Turner, Jack, 'The Quality of Wildness: Preservation, Control and Freedom,' in *Place of the Wild*, David Clark Burks ed. (Washington, D. C.: Island Press, 1994).

Turner, Jack, *The Abstract Wild* (Tucson: University of Arizona Press, 1996).

Cuitlacoche: Pest or Prize?

Jane Levi

Cuitlacoche is a culinary curiosity. A fungus belonging to the Basidiomycetes group, which also includes the common mushroom, the chanterelles, and the wood-rotting, jelly and rust fungi, *Ustilago maydis* or corn smut infects maize ears, causing them to deform into swollen fungal kernels, deep black inside and covered in a greyish-white skin.[1] In a family of more than 5,000 rusts and smuts, *U. maydis* is the only one that is commonly considered to be edible. Its taste is unique: as dark and rich as a kind of mushroomy squid ink, with just a hint of sweet corn; often the odd kernel will still be part of the chopped mixture. Although its flavour is highly distinctive, it tends to be used in the kinds of recipes that would commonly be used for other mushrooms. The name *ustilago* comes from the latin *ustus*, *ustulatos*, meaning burned or scorched, referring to the blackened interior and possibly the silvery, ashen appearance of the exterior.[2] It is quite soft (becoming softer and slimy as it ages), and like most mushrooms it exudes liquid – in this case a deep black – as it cooks. Although it can infect most cultivated strains of corn and teosinte, and hence may strike any maize crop across the world, only the Mexicans appear to have adopted this substance as an edible wild food. Others, put off by its appearance, and possibly fearing toxicity, dispose of the blighted crop, considering corn smut to be 'one of the most offensive diseases ever to attack a vegetable'.[3] But in Mexico, farmers receive a premium price for the infected crop, and it has apparently been prized since ancient times. This paper considers why this might have come about, and considers the distinct position this wild pest has now attained in the Mexican national cuisine.

'*Ustilago maydis* infects two plants only, maize (*Zea mays*) and teosinte (*Zea mexicana*), the putative progenitor of maize.'[4] Infected plants develop tumours or galls on their leaves, stems, tassels and ears, and the growth of the plant may be stunted. In the ears, where the edible form develops, 'the fungus completely replaces the kernel with masses of black spores', and so has a devastating effect on seed yield. It takes three forms during its lifecycle. First, the sporidium, or single cell, single nucleus form, which can grow by budding on non-living matter, lurking in the soil awaiting the next planting; second the dikatyotic filamentous form, a parasitic and pathogenic form which needs the plant for its growth and which induces disease in it; and finally the teliospore which is formed in the tumours as the disease develops within the plant, and which is eaten.[5]

From a culinary point of view, the best yield of cuitlacoche is achieved if the plant is infected about 6-8 days after the mid-silk growth stage, and the best quality cuitlacoche may be harvested 16-18 days later, once the teliospores are mature.[6]

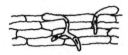

Figure 1: Basidiospores

Figure 2: Germination

One of the challenges in researching and discussing *U. maydis* as a food is to decide what to call it, and how to spell it. In Mexico, the dominant spelling is cuitlacoche, which is consistently used in the literature, and boldly printed on the cans which line grocery shelves. American chefs (for example Rick Bayless) have adopted the spelling huitlacoche, which was also initially used by Diana Kennedy. Kennedy switched to cuiclacoche in 2000, finally settling on cuitlacoche in 2003. Other than this, most references by non-Mexicans adopt the US's preferred initial letter h. Mexican chefs, such as Patricia Quintana, whether writing in Spanish or English, usually use the initial letter c. I will refer to it in this essay as cuitlacoche.

The origins of the word explain the tendency to stay close to the original language. According to Pilcher, cuitlacoche translates as 'excrement of the gods'.[7] More precisely, it derives from the náhuatl words *cuítlatl*, meaning excrement and *cochtli* meaning sleep. Apparently,

> Although today it seems to us an extraordinary name for a food, for the ancient Mexicans excrement was not waste, but a distillation of foods, and for the most part was considered to be a precious material. In fact, the root of the word derives from of one of the Aztec emperors, Cuitláhuac, referring to the dried excrement of the ancient priesthood, from which they made the floor of the temples at the summit of the teocallis.[8]

An alternative explanation is that the name simply alludes to its texture and grey or black colour.[9]

Understandably, English translations of cuitlacoche in recipe books and on menus steer well clear of any reference to excrement, godly or not. The precise terms chosen to describe it vary, depending on the perspective of the writer and, quite probably, the price of the restaurant dish. What premium might we be willing to pay for expensive-sounding 'caviar Azteca'; exotic 'Mexican truffles' and 'corn truffle'; or romantic 'inky corn mushroom'? Conversely, might we not think twice about ordering the slightly challenging 'corn fungus', or the downright off-putting 'corn smut'?[10] A more serious question is why the Mexicans, distinct from any other nationality, did decide to eat it, despite its name, and how long ago the love affair began.

Figure 3: Centéotl, god of maize (*Codice Vaticano*).

In considering the importance of cuitlacoche, it is wise to remember that it grows on maize, and it is well known that maize had a special, sacred status amongst the native peoples of Mexico.[11] The lowland Maya taxonomy of plants highlights maize as *jun-teek*, literally 'one plant', distinct from all other plants which are categorized according to their stem habit (whether trees, shrubs, vines or grasses).[12] The Maya epic, the *Popol Vuh*, describes how man was created from yellow and white maize dough or masa, previous experiments with clay, wood and flesh all having failed.[13] The Maya worshipped *Yum Kax* as master of the fields, agriculture and corn: the only other plant which merited its own deity was cacao, and it was considered – to the Spaniards' amazement – to be more precious than gold.[14] The Toltec goddess of food, Chicomecoatl, is depicted flanked by ears of corn.[15]

195

Besides Centéotl, their god or goddess of maize, the Aztecs worshipped several deities of corn, representing its various states: Xilonen, the goddess of the tender corncob (*jilote*); and Ilametecuhtli, the goddess of dried maize. There was even a god to watch over the sowing of the maize, Xipe-Totec. Maize was also an important component in the worship of other Aztec gods, the first ears of the harvest being offered to Tláloc, god of rain.[16] The fact that mushrooms were considered by the Indians to take on the life of the vegetation they grew upon suggests that cuitlacoche would retain a strong identification with its host, maize, for those who consumed it.[17] Given maize's place at the heart of both the spiritual and physical life of Mexican cultures, it is perhaps hardly surprising that the people would have decided to eat cuitlacoche when it appeared on their crop: anything associated with this staple gift of the gods should be considered a heaven-sent blessing rather than a curse, until proved otherwise. In this instance it seems that the Neolithic propensity to experiment with foods coincided with a religious imperative.[18] This, combined with a Mexican habit of consuming fungi, led to a delicious discovery for the cook and her audience. Cuitlacoche's eventual place in the everyday is emphasized by the folk tale of 'Corn Soot Woman', collected from the Conchiti (a Native American Pueblo tribe in New Mexico). Corn

Soot Woman weeps at being separated from the good ears of corn, saying that she is not rotten, and promises that if they keep the sooted corn, the new ears will grow fat, just like her. The women of the corn-grinding society agree, and give the soot a ceremonial name, Wesa, from then on singing songs to her as they grind the corn.[19]

Although fungi were foraged for and eaten throughout the ancient world (for example in Greece, Rome and China), they only appear to have formed a significant component of the ancient American diet in Mexico. In a study of the diet of the Inca, Muisca and Aztec peoples, only the Aztec diet includes any edible fungi.[20] This may go some way towards explaining why it is only in Mexico that cuitlacoche has long been known as a food. Garcia Rivas includes a recipe for a huitlacoche dish in the mushroom chapter of his study of *Prehispanic Mexican Cookery* (simultaneously providing a rare example of a Mexican using the leading h). The dish is a stuffing for tortillas made from green chiles, epazote, spring onions and huitlacoche, served with a salsa of poblano chiles, epazote and poultry broth.[21] Although it is well known that there was no onion in the pre-Hispanic larder (onion was introduced to the Americas by the Spanish) a small, native onion, *xonácatl*, is described by Bernadino de Sahagún in his *General History of the Things of New Spain*, and it is presumably this that would have been used orignally.[22] Bernardino de Sahagún also wrote lengthy descriptions of the mushrooms eaten by the indigenous population, recording the nuahatl names for many of them.[23] However, he does not draw particular attention to cuitlacoche; it is simply another mushroom.

Most contemporary writers choose to imbue cuitlacoche with a whiff of ancient-historical romance, describing it as a special Mexican ingredient 'treasured since pre-Columbian times' that has been 'used in ceremonial tamales and dark mole sauces for centuries'.[24] It is likely to be true that it has been known and consumed since the earliest domestication of maize, after the first crops had succumbed to infection by *U. maydis*, but very little evidence of its original discovery and incorporation into the diet survives.[25] Cuitlacoche is only available at certain times of the year (in the rainy season, from July to November); its appearance is somewhat unpredictable and mysteriously open to chance; and it has an unusual and desirable flavour – but these qualities are no different to other edible mushrooms. Apart from its connection to the revered maize, it is not clear that it was any more or less valued than other fungi which were all seen as good, seasonal wild foods. The similarity between traditional recipes

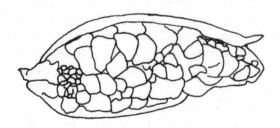

Figure 4: Maize ear infected with cuitlacoche.

for cuitlacoche and other mushrooms bears this out: in most cases, they are inter-changeable.[26] Indeed, the descriptions by de Sahagún, Bernal Diaz and other early conquistadors all include references to daily diet, foods for feasts, and ritual foods: but cuitlacoche does not appear to be highlighted by any of them as a particular delicacy, curiosity or ceremonial food.[27] An *atole* (thin gruel) with cuitlacoche, *Tsinari*, is said to have been drunk by the *mara'akame*, or singers to the gods, to replenish energy lost in the night and give them strength to sing, but presumably this was simply a seasonal variation on the traditional breakfast.[28] So why is cuitlacoche now singled out as one of the more important pre-colonial Mexican cultural symbols, and when did this start?

The tendency to romanticize the history of cuitlacoche as an ingredient is a rela-tively recent phenomenon, and represents a broader shift in Mexican national and cultural attitudes. Cuisine is, along with art, language and landscape 'among the things most evocative of the national identity'.[29] In the case of Mexico, prior to the revolution in 1910, the social and political elite had defined the national cuisine as essentially European, excluding native ingredients and dishes, especially corn, from 'respectable dinner tables.'[30] If corn itself was discouraged, what fate would lie in store for its pathogen and obligate parasite? The *Nuevo Cocinero Mexicano en forma de Diccionario* published in Paris in 1888 makes no reference whatever to cuitlacoche, even in its general maize and mushroom entries, implying that at this stage it was not viewed as an acceptable food for the middle-class readership of that publication. It was too indigenous; too wild.

197

Fortunately, corn survived the attempts to replace it with the more European wheat, and as the new Mexican nation asserted itself through a deliberate programme of nation-alism and rapid economic development, all kinds of 'peasant' foodstuffs became national symbols for all classes. Prominent cookbook authors began to seek out and popular-ize Indian regional dishes. Josefina Velázquez de Léon, Mexico's 'foremost advocate of culinary nationalism' in the early to mid-20th century, wrote more than 150 cookbooks 'revealing the mysterious nuances of regional cuisines and exalting lower class dishes such as enchiladas as symbols of national identity.'[31]

Cuitlacoche, however, was one of the last ingredients to become acceptable to the middle and upper classes who, as late as the 1940s, 'considered eating this spore to be a disgusting Indian habit': it had, of course, remained a key component of the common seasonal diet throughout.[32] It was initially made acceptable by associating it with French cuisine: a crêpe of cuitlacoche covered in béchamel sauce became the signature dish of Jaime Saldívar in Mexico City.[33] In the later 20th century, formal governmental and other institutional dinners (such as those given by the National Bank of Mexico) gradually began to feature cuitlacoche in their menus, until eventually 'Mexicans considered it one of their nation's great contributions to international haute cuisine, a sort of Mesoamerican noble rot.'[34] Today cuitlacoche is viewed as a desirable, high class ingredient; a flag-wav-ing representative of 'nuevo cocina Mexicana'. Smart restaurants from Mexico City to

Oaxaca feature cuitlacoche tarts, quiches, ravioles, risottos and soups on their menus, and it appears as the star ingredient in stuffings for chiles, squid, fish and chicken.[35] In these contemporary guises it has been reinterpreted as an acceptable component of the middle and upper class diet. Its image is that of a distinctive wild food tamed, retaining an exotic edge, and imbued with national pride.

It also retains its popular appeal, continuing to be available across the country as street food, prepared in the traditional style. The National Museum of Popular Culture published a cookbook in the late 1970s which recognized 605 distinct traditional ways of cooking corn, 11 of which are recipes for cuitlacoche. For example, *Quesadillas de cuitlacoche* are attributed to Tlaxcala, whereas Mexico City takes ownership of *Cuitlacoche con elote y calabacitas* (cuitlacoche with sweetcorn and squash).[36] In the course of two weeks early in the 2004 rainy season I sampled *tlacoyos de cuitlacoche* in Mexico City's Colonia Roma; and numerous *quesadillas de cuitlacoche* in Mexico City and Oaxaca, the most delicious of which were the deep-fried version at the Comedor in Coyoacan.[37] These simple dishes remain an inexpensive but delicious component of the local diet in the Distrito Federal (Mexico City), Hidalgo, Michoacán, Tlaxcala, Puebla and most of the central regions. Particular regional specialities include a drink called *esmoloc* from Chiapas, and the Tlaxcalan *mole prieto* (black *mole*), made with dried cuitlacoche.[38]

The price of cuitlacoche varies according to the season and the quality of the product, but even though some have complained that it used to be the cheapest of foods and is now relatively expensive, it remains affordable.[39] At the Mercado de la Merced in Mexico City in July 2004, prices were in the range of 15-17 pesos per kilo (€1-€1.20; $1.30-$1.50), for black piles of ready-chopped cuitlacoche taken from cobs infected to the core. In the more refined San Juan market, packaged whole cobs, still recognizable as corn, and with a more attractive growth of cuitlacoche cloaking some remaining kernels, retailed at 70 pesos per kilo (€5, $6.10). In both markets, the cuitlacoche is sold alongside the wild mushrooms that share its season, but is less expensive than most of them.

Major Mexican food manufacturers such as Herdez and La Costeña have been producing canned cuitlacoche since about the 1980s, and this is now generally accepted as an acceptable substitute if you can't obtain the fresh product.[40] Outside Mexico, cuitlacoche has become increasingly popular in the USA as the Mexican population has grown, and some farmers in Florida and Pennsylvania have begun to cultivate it in order to provide local supplies to upscale, mainly Mexican, restaurants. Nonetheless, Anglo-Saxon prejudices run deep, and stories of exploding threshing machines at harvest time (the spores of smut creating a black cloud 'which was more explosive than coal dust'), and ill-founded concerns about toxicity, no doubt continue to deter farmers from encouraging the proliferation of cuitlacoche on their crop.[41] Even though losses as a result of infection by *U. maydis* are 'usually less than 2% annually over large areas', and cuitlacoche attracts a premium price compared to corn, research into resistant strains of maize and protective means of cultivation continues.[42] At the same time, some more enlightened researchers, perhaps sniffing a market, have begun to acknowledge that the techniques developed whilst researching the elimination of the fungus could in fact be used to develop cultivation methods for a more consistent product.[43] For the most part, however, beyond its culinary home in Mexico, cuitlacoche remains a dark, inky taste of the wild.

Notes

1. Banuett, p. 181; Hererra & Ulloa, p. 295.
2. Ulloa & Herrera, p. 188.
3. Sommer (2001), p. 16.
4. Banuett, p. 181.
5. Banuett, pp. 182-183.
6. Grogan, p. 1.
7. Pilcher (1998), p. 131.
8. Zurita, p. 217: 'Aunque hoy parezca extraño nombrara así a un alimanto, para los antiguos mexicanos el excremento no era un desecho, sino un destilado de los alimentos, y por lo tanto podia considererse materia preciosa. De hecho, la raíz forma parte de uno de los emperadores aztecas, Cuitláhuac, que significa el excremento seco de los sacerdotes ancianos con que se hacía el piso de los adoratorios que se entontraban en la cima de los *teocallis*.' (My translation.)
9. Herrera & Ulloa, p. 295.
10. Weigner; Bayless, p. 159; Kennedy (1972), p. 123.
11. Fernández-Armesto, pp. 34-35.
12. Atran & Ucan Ek', p. 50.
13. Coe (1999), p. 41.
14. Covo T, pp. 52-53, 59.
15. A carved stone relief of Chicomecoatl in the Museo Rufino Tamayo in Oaxaca shows corn cobs to the right and left of the goddess' face.
16. *El Maíz, Fundamento de la Cultura Popular Mexicana*, pp. 39-40.
17. Atran & Ucan Ek', p. 50: 'All informants agree that mushrooms (*xikin-che'* lit. 'tree ear') have no *pusik'al* (lit. heart) and are not plants but take life away from the trees that host them'.
18. Bober, p. 16.
19. Benedict, p. 15.
20. Rojas de Perdomo, pp. 28-31.
21. García Rivas, p. 132.
22. Barros & Buenrostro, pp. 8, 21.
23. Rojas de Perdomo, p. 47.
24. Bayless, p. 159; Quintana, p. 274.
25. In 1949 Paul C. Mangelsdorf discovered corncobs in a cave in New Mexico, which were carbon-dated to 5,600 B.C., demonstrating the long history of the domestication of maize. No ancient traces of *Ustilago maydis* were reported.
26. Kennedy (1984), pp. 144-145, 240; Kennedy (1975), pp. 65, 76.
27. This suggestion is not the result of exhaustive study of the codices, and it is possible that references may be found. I was not able to uncover any in my reading of English translations of those authors listed in the bibliography.
28. Barros & Buenrostro, p. 49.
29. Pilcher (1998), p. 143.
30. Pilcher (1998), p. 153.
31. Pilcher (2003), p. 200.
32. Pilcher (1998), p. 131.
33. Pilcher (1998), p. 137. According to Susana Palazuelos (p. 97) a dish of cuitlacoche crêpes with poblano sauce was first devised for the Emperor Maximilian and his wife Carlotta. This would place

its origins between the years 1864-67, but I have been unable to trace an original source for this. The fact that cuitlacoche is missing from the *Nuevo Cocinero Mexicano en forma de Diccionario* of 1888 casts doubt on the likelihood that such a dish was served in the colonial court.

34. Pilcher (1998), p. 131.
35. Luengas.
36. *El Maíz, Fundamento de la Cultura Popular Mexicana*, pp. 61-62.
37. A *tlacoyo de cuitlacoche* is a thick, oval corn tortilla (often blue corn) stuffed with yellow (*hava*) bean paste, topped with cuitlacoche, and served with salsa, coriander and chopped onion. A *quesadilla de cuitlacoche* is a normal corn tortilla stuffed with cuitlacoche, folded in half and either fried or cooked on a *comal* (clay cooking surface).
38. Zurita, p. 217.
39. Kennedy (1984), p. 144.
40. La Costena's marketing department confirmed that cuitlacoche is only a 'medium volume' product, so no free samples will be provided to accompany the presentation of this paper!
41. Sommer (1995), pp. 21-22.
42. Snetselaar, Carfioli & Cordisco, p. 1390.
43. Snetselaar, Carfioli & Cordisco, p. 1398. For example, through the use of sterile male varieties or removing tassels before pollination.

Select Bibliography

Atran, Scott, and Edilberto Ucan Ek', 'Classification of Useful Plants by the Northern Petén Maya (Itzaj)', in *Reconstructing Ancient Maya Diet*, ed. Christine D. White, (Salt Lake City: University of Utah Press, 1999).

Banuett, F., 'Genetics of *Ustilago maydis*, A Fungal Pathogen That Induces Tumors in Maize', in *Annu. Rev. Genetics* 1995, 29:179-208.

Barros, Cristina and Marco Buenrostro, 'Cocina Prehispánica: Recetario', *Arqueología Mexicana*, 12, November 2002 (Edición Especial).

Bayless, Rick, *Rick Bayless's Mexican Kitchen: Capturing the Vibrant Flavors of a World-Class Cuisine* (New York, Scribner, 1996).

Benedict, Ruth, 'Tales of the Cochiti Indians., in *Bureau of American Ethnology Bulletin* no. 98, 1932.

Bober, Phyllis Pray, *Art, Culture and Cuisine: Ancient and Medieval Gastronomy* (Chicago and London: University of Chicago Press, 1999).

Coe, Michael D, *The Maya*, sixth edition (London: Thames and Hudson, 1999).

Covo T, Javier, *The Mayas (On the Rocks)* (Merida, Yucatan: Producción Editorial Dante S.A., 1987).

Díaz, Bernal, *The Conquest of New Spain*, translated by J. M. Cohen (London: Penguin Books, 1963).

El Maíz, Fundamento de la Cultura Popular Mexicana (Mexico City: Museo Nacional de Culturas Populares, 1982).

Fernández-Armesto, Felipe, *Food: A History* (London: Macmillan, 2001).

García Rivas, Heriberto, *Cocina Prehispanico Mexicana: La Comida de los Antigos Mexicanos* (Mexico City: Panorama Editorial, 1996).

Grogan, Helen, 'IV Conference on Mushroom Biology and Mushroom Products Cuernavaca, Mexico: 20-23 February 2002', in *BSPP News* Summer 2002 – Online Edition, Number 42, Summer 2002.

Herrera, Téofilo, and Miguel Ulloa, *El Reino de los Hongos: Micología basica y aplicada*, 2nd edn. (Mexico City: Fondo de Cultura Económica, Insituto de Biología, Universidad Nacional Antónoma de México, 1998).

Kennedy, Diana, *The Cuisines of Mexico* (New York: Harper & Row, Publishers, 1972).

Kennedy, Diana, *The Tortilla Book* (New York: Harper & Row, Publishers, 1975).

Kennedy, Diana, *Mexican Regional Cooking* (New York: Harper & Row, Publishers, 1984).

Luengas, Arnulfo, *La Cocina del Banco Nacional de México* (Mexico City: Fomento Cultural Banamex, A.C., 2000).

Mangelsdorf, Paul C., *Corn: Its Origin, Evolution and Improvement* (Cambridge Massachusetts: The Belknap Press of Harvard University Press, 1974).

Nuevo Cocinero Mexicano en forma de Diccionario (reproducción facsimilar 1888, Mexico City: Miguel Angel Porrua Grupo Editorial, 1998).

Palazuelos, Susanna, *México, the Beautiful Cookbook* (New York: Harper Collins Publishers Inc, 1996).

Pilcher, Jeffrey M, *¡Que Vivan los Tamales! Food and the Making of Mexican Identity* (Albuquerque: University of New Mexico Press, 1998).

Pilcher, Jeffery M, 'Josefina Velázquez de León, Apostle of the Enchilada', in *The Human Tradition in Mexico*, ed. Jeffrey M. Pilcher, 199-209, (Wilmington, Delaware: Scholarly Resources, Inc., 2003).

Quintana, Patricia, *Cuisine of the Water Gods: the authentic seafood and vegetable cookery of Mexico* (New York: Simon and Schuster, 1994).

Rojas de Perdomo, Lucía, *Cocina Prehispánica. Comentarios a la cocina de las altas cultruras prehispanicas: Azteca, Inca y Muisca* (Santafé de Bogotá D.C., Colombia: Editorial Voluntad S.A., 1994).

Sommer, Robert, 'Why I Will Continue to Eat Corn Smut', in *Natural History* 1/95, 18-22.

Sommer, Robert, 'Corn Smut Goes Upscale', in *Horticulture*, 2001, 16.

Snetselaar, Karen, Margaret A. Carafoli, and Kelly M. Cordisco, 'Pollination can protect maize ovaries from infection by *Ustilago maydis*, the corn smut fungus', in *Canadian Journal of Botany*, Vol. 79, 2001. 1390-1399.

Ulloa, Miguel, and Téofilo Herrera, *Etimología e Iconografía de Géneros de Hongos* (Mexico City: Universidad Nacional Antónoma de México, 1994).

Wiegner, Kathleen, 'One Man's Problem is Another's Delicacy', *Los Angeles Times*, July 12, D5 1995.

Zurita, Ricardo Muñoz, *Diccionario Enciclopédico de Gastronomía Mexicana* (Mexico City: Editorial Clío, 2000).

201

Acknowledgements

It would not have been possible to find much of my research material without the generosity of the librarians at the Biblioteca Jardin Etnobotanico de Oaxaca, Centro Cultural Santo Domingo.

I owe a debt of gratitude to Alex Veness, who not only tolerated my visits to the Oaxaca library whilst we were supposed to be on holiday, but who also introduced me to cuitlacoche in the first place, and then translated for me (and sampled with me) across the many markets and foodstalls of central and southern Mexico.

Thanks are also due to Dr John Levi, who patiently answered numerous calls to validate yeast and fungus-related facts during the writing of this paper.

Some Like It Raw: Buffalo Cookery and Foodways in America

Walter Levy

Buffalo entered the North American imagination and foodways early on. The Native American's method of preserving meat by cutting it into thin strips and then air dry-ing or smoking them was a preservation method familiar to the Europeans. Jerked buffalo was a staple for explorers and trappers on the Great Plains, but it is as tough as it is durable, and it did not make it to the genteel kitchens in the East. Without adequate means for transporting buffalo meat, it was eaten in situ, except for smoked tongues, and there was little interest in it by those not on the frontier.

The earliest comments on buffalo foodways come from the Spanish explorer Alvar Núñez Cabeza de Vaca, whose *Relación de Alvar Nunez Cabeza de Vaca* (written 1537, published 1555) includes a description of wild cattle, dubbed *vacas* (no pun intended). Cabeza de Vaca claims that the meat is better than cattle in Spain, but he does not provide any details as to how the beef was prepared, cooked, or served.[1] Father Louis Hennepin, a French missionary and explorer, had first-hand experience

with the beast that he called *buffle*, French for buffalo. In July 1680, Hennepin and a companion were so hungry that when they killed a buffalo and cooked its 'fat meat' in an earthen pot, they gorged themselves. Hennepin says that it took two days to overcome their indigestion.[2]

Buffalo sightings by English caused little gustatory interest in the early days of colonization and exploration. *The Relations of Maryland* (1635)[3] acknowledges hunt-ing 'Bufeloe' but gives no mention of its foodways. Exploring western Virginia, *circa* 1705, Robert Beverley reported 'Elks, Buffaloes, Deer and greater Game' so tame that they 'would suffer them to come almost within reach of their hands.'[4] The beast must have been killed and eaten, but Beverley does not consider foodways; likewise Daniel Boone who hunted buffalo in Kentucky in the 1760s.

Neither hunter nor explorer, Amelia Simmons, author of *American Cookery* (1796), America's first 'authentic' cookbook, was disinclined towards large wild game. Missing among the 130 recipes for small game, game birds, some local fresh water fish, is a recipe for buffalo. My guess is that for Simmons, the buffalo would have been an oddity, and unworthy of a genteel table. But Simmons omits even such familiar large game as deer, moose, and bear.[5]

Less finicky were Meriwether Lewis and William Clark, who ate buffalo on the range. They saw their first buffaloes during their trek through South Dakota in September 1804 – and cooked them soon after. Over the long, cold winter of

1804, Lewis and Clark's party dined on buffalo jerky provided by the local Native Americans. But in the spring, when hunting improved, Lewis recorded the first recipe for cooking buffalo meat. On Thursday, 9 May 1805, Lewis described how the party's chef Toussaint Charbonneau, a French trapper and husband of Sacajuwea, prepared *boudin blanc* or 'white pudding'. Not renowned for his palate, Lewis claims that he 'esteemed' the pudding as 'one of the greatest delicacies of the forest'. For those interested, Charbonneau's recipe calls for cutting a six-foot section of intestine and filling it with a mixture of chopped muscle from the shoulder, slices of beef , kidney suet, salt, pepper, flour, and a large quantity of fat. After a cursory washing , the sausage is parboiled and then fried in buffalo fat until brown. Lewis found it tasty: the 'boudin blanc,' he said, 'is ready to esswage the pangs of a keen appetite or such as travelers in the wilderness are seldom at a loss for.' William Clark, a pragmatic and laconic man, noted: 'Capt Lewis also killed one with verry good meat.'[6]

Charbonneau's *boudin blanc* never got East, and it was not commented upon even after Lewis and Clark's journals were published in 1814. Only Lydia Marie Child provides a buffalo recipe in *The Frugal Housewife, Dedicated to Those Who Are Not Ashamed of Economy* (1829). Child's instructions call for soaking 'a day and a night' and then boiling it for 'as much as six hours'. Since buffalo meat is lean, and the tongue is a tough muscle, long cooking was practical, but one wonders what boiled tongue might taste like after six hours in the pot: perhaps it just fell apart on the fork; perhaps not.[7] Since no other American 19th-century cookbook provides a recipe for buffalo, it may be conjectured that Child included this recipe on a whim or because she read James Fennimore Cooper's *The Prairie* (1827), a novel that serves up America's first fictional buffalo dinner.

Though Cooper's buffalo cookout has a ring of authenticity, he had no direct knowledge of the beast and cribbed his account from Lewis and Clark's journals and the travelogue of the western plains expedition of Major Stephen H. Long.[8] Cooper, a self-styled American aristocrat, preferred the pleasures of the dining-room table, but his hero, Natty Bumppo, prefers *al fresco* dining. In *The Prairie*, discussion of cookery alternates between standard diction of the narrator, i.e. Cooper, and the colourful 'unlarned' diction of the hunter. For example, Cooper prefers to use the taxonomically correct name bison, while Bumppo prefers buffalo. Bumppo cooks in the Indian fashion by roasting the meat (still covered with hair) in a 'subterraneous oven'. Cooper's narrator suggests that the 'savoury bison's hump' is 'the culinary glory of the prairies. So far as richness, delicacy, and wildness of flavour, and substantial nourishment were concerned, the viand might well have claimed a decided superiority over the meretricious cookery and laboured compounds of the most renowned artist; though the service of the dainty was certainly achieved in a manner far from artificial.' Bumppo suggests that the flavour of buffalo is strong: 'Ay, ay, well you may call it strong!' but 'strong it is, and strong it makes him who eats it!'[9]

A decade after *The Prairie* appeared, Alfred Jacob Miller, a painter, travelled to the

203

West as part of the hunting expedition of Captain William Drummond Lawrence, a Scottish adventurer. Miller's first-hand observations and watercolours give a fairly accurate description of buffalo hunting and cookery *circa* 1837. Miller's depiction of the breakfast and Cooper's dinner by campfire, are examples of good humour, camaraderie, and modest decorum among the participants. But there are other incidents in the lore of buffalo foodways that are matter-of-fact descriptions of the brutality of hunting and bouts of gormandizing and gluttony.

In his notes for the painting *Camp Providers* (1837), Miller rhapsodizes on the buffalo hump: 'When that incomparable piece, the hump rib, is brought to camp, Jean, our Chef, takes charge of it, and the manner in which he prepares it for the table, although simple enough, is perfection. He skewers it lengthwise, with a stick sharpened at one end, leaving sufficient room at the other end to plant it in the ground near the fire, inclining inward at the top. When done, it exceeds in flavour, richness, and juiciness, any beef we have ever tasted, and this judgment will be confirmed by all who have ever partaken of the glorious "hump ribs"' (1837).[10] Miller's words provide context for his painting *Breakfast at Sunrise* (1837), which illustrates the hunters' usual mess at which everyone sat on a waterproof India-rubber cloth and ate from tin plates. Forks are not used, and the meat is cut with a bowie-knife. Miller indicates that the Euro-Americans ate first, and Native Americans ate at the second sitting.

Ironically, the indecorous taste in the realms of buffalo cookery has been recounted by Washington Irving, one of the most sophisticated and international of American authors. In three of his works, *A Tour on the Prairie* (1835), *Astoria* (1836) and *The Adventures of Captain Bonneville, U.S.A.* (1837), Irving provides a mixture of first- and second-hand observations of buffalo foodways illustrating a descending order of gustatory sophistication. In *A Tour on the Prairie*, a travelogue of his own travels in Oklahoma and Kansas for several months during 1832, Irving fondly remembers the expedition's cook, Tonish (Antoine) whose signature dish is buffalo soup. As Irving recalls, 'Tonish served up to us his promised regale of buffalo soup and buffalo beef. The soup was peppered most horribly, and the roast beef proved the bull to have been one of the patriarchs of the prairies; never did I have to deal with a tougher morsel.' It was Irving's first taste of buffalo, so he 'ate it with a lively faith.' Tonish exhorted everyone to declare its excellence, and Irving agreed, though it was so heavily peppered that it burned his throat.[11]

A more crude instance of buffalo cookery appears in *Astoria* (1836, revised 1849), written at the behest of John Jacob Astor. Here, Irving tells the anecdote of how groups of starving hunters travelling in a wintry landscape chase 'an old run-down bull' which they kill and immediately butcher. 'So ravenous was their hunger,' Irving narrates, 'that they devoured some of the flesh raw. The residue they carried to a brook near by, where they encamped, lit a fire, and began to cook.' Later they made soup and spent the rest of the night 'cooking and cramming'.[12]

Irving brings buffalo foodways and dining to its crudest in *The Adventures of*

Captain Bonneville, U.S.A. (1837). Irving's excuse for this bit of crudity is that his source is the travel journal of Captain Benjamin L. E. Bonneville, an army officer turned explorer on the western plains. But Irving seems to take great pleasure in contrasting his own gentility with the action at hand, especially a buffalo bacchanal hosted by Bonneville: 'The captain now set to work with his men, to prepare a suitable entertainment for his guests.' Irving's narrator writes, ' It was a time of plenty in the camp; of prime hunters' dainties; of buffalo humps, and buffalo tongues; and roasted ribs, and broiled marrow-bones: all these were cooked in hunters' style; served up with a profusion known only on a plentiful hunting ground, and discussed with an appetite that would astonish the puny gourmands of the cities.'[13]

The cramming and gorging of this meal pales beside the story of Stanfield which Irving almost gleefully serves up. It goes like this: even though it was summer, game was scarce, and so 'when famished hunters after three days without food shot a buffalo, Stanfield sprang upon him, plunged his knife into his throat, and allayed his raging hunger by drinking his blood: A fire was instantly kindled beside the carcass, when the two hunters cooked, and ate again and again, until, perfectly gorged, they sank to sleep before their hunting fire. On the following morning they rose early, made another hearty meal, then loading themselves with buffalo meat, set out on their return to the camp, to report the fruitlessness of their mission.'[14] Why Stanfield might want to lay claim to drinking buffalo blood says something about a hunter's mentality; perhaps the enactment of an animal fetish. I wonder if Stanfield had read Cooper's *The Prairie* and recalled Natty Bumppo's admonition that 'strong it is, and strong it makes him who eats it!' It's pretty certain that Irving read Cooper, a fellow New Yorker, though they were not close.

Not be outdone, Francis Parkman, the historian, then twenty-one and newly graduated from Harvard College, made buffalo hunting a central event in *The Oregon Trail* (1847), a best-seller about his adventures on the Great Plains. On the one hand, Parkman is cautionary about the dwindling herds of buffalo; on the other, he revels in the gory glory of killing buffalos. 'In a moment I was in the midst of the cloud, half suffocated by the dust and stunned by the trampling of the flying herd,' Parkman exclaims, 'but I was drunk with the chase and cared for nothing but the buffalo.' After completing the kill, this scion of an élite Boston family, the victorious hunter, looks down at his victim and, 'No longer wondering at his fierceness,' he opens the beast's throat, cuts out the tongue and ties it on the back of his saddle.[15] Parkman apologizes because he's killed a tough old bull instead of a tender cow, but the prize probably was still dispatched to the commissary. How it was cooked and served up is unknown. Perhaps the cook had handy a copy of Lydia Child's buffalo tongue recipe.

Frederick Ruxton, who lived among the buffalo gourmands, portrays men eating like ravenous animals of prey, who went without forks and plates: 'Whether it is that the meat itself (which, by the way, is certainly the most delicious of flesh) is most easy of digestion,' he writes, 'or whether the digestive organs of hunters are "ostrichified" by the severity of exercise, and the bracing, wholesome climate of the mountains and plains, it is a fact that most prodigious quantities of "fat cow" may be swallowed with the greatest impunity, and not the slightest inconvenience ever follows the mammoth feasts of the gourmands of the far west.' Though Ruxton's *Life in the Far West*, sometimes called *Wild Life in the Rocky Mountains* (1848), achieved status as a cult travelogue, his recipe for cramming greasy intestines has not caught on.[16]

More ordinary buffalo cookery is recalled by Isabella L. Bird, an English adventuress whose *A Lady's Life in the Rocky Mountains* (1873) has this brief description: 'Yesterday morning the mercury had disappeared, so it was 20 degrees below zero at least. I lay awake from cold all night, but such is the wonderful effect of the climate, that when I got up at half-past five to waken the household for my early start, I felt quite refreshed. We breakfasted on buffalo beef, and I left at eight to ride forty-five miles before night.'[17] An intrepid traveller, Bird was inclined not to be a Victorian dilettante: her writing is descriptive and muscular and, by design, it scants the genteel nuances of foodways which she might have associated with femininity. Obviously, she had not read her Irving or Ruxton.

William F. Cody, who earned the nickname Buffalo Bill by remorselessly hunting buffalo, remembered a hunt dinner on the Kansas plains in 1871. Cody, then a scout for the U.S. Army, was volunteered by his commanding officer General Philip Sheridan as master of the hunt for an expedition of wealthy and prominent businessmen from New York and Chicago. In ten days, with Cody's help, the hunters amassed staggering kill rates, 600 buffalo and 200 elk, some of which found their way to the dining table. Twenty years after, Cody, by then a sophisticated world traveller, was still impressed that diners sat in large tents with carpeted floors and that meals were 'served every evening by waiters in evening dress and prepared by cooks brought from New York. The linen, china, glass, and porcelain had been provided with equal care, and a big wood fire lent cheerfulness to the dining-tent.'[18] The menu, by the way, printed in full by General Henry E. Davies, one of Sheridan's staff officers and a member of the hunt, in *Ten Days on the Plains* (1871), included: buffalo tail soup, buffalo filet au champignons, and buffalo-calf steaks along with: salami of prairie dog, broiled cisco (trout), fried dace, elk, antelope, black-tailed deer, wild turkey, teal, and mallard.[19] If Cody was weak on food, he seems to have remembered the champagne, wines, beers and liqueurs the empties of which, he quipped, were recognized for years after as sites where the hunting party camped and dined.

By the early 1930s, buffalo barbecues had become a tradition in the American heartland and, at the modern buffalo barbecue, families don't devour boudin blanc or drink blood from a dying animal.[20] Decorum and familiar gender roles prevail: men cook and women serve. 'The meat is always tough,' we are told, 'and despite the greatest care, has a flavor of smoke, but the sharp yet mellow sauce, combined with open-air appetites, makes second and third helpings inevitable.' Since it is well known that buffalo meat is low-fat and dry, why these Nebraska 'chefs' slow-cook meat to the consistency of shoe leather is a mystery. The meal is served on tables 'made of boards placed across trestles and is set up near the pit.' There were the usual baskets piled high with buns, pickles and, though we are not told, coleslaw, potato salad, and more. The beverage of choice is coffee, brewed in big pots, served with sugar and cream. The barbecue diners sit wherever they find the room; it's all very casual, and ritualized at the same time.

In our time, the buffalo barbecue has entered the realm of genteel urban and sub-urban foodways. Because most buffalo are now raised for market, about four hundred thousand of them, the meat is in plentiful supply. To be sure, there are still traditional hunts, but there are probably more buffalo hunters on the internet, who get their steaks, roasts, and sausages delivered frozen to their doorstep. For today's food-conscious consumer, buffalo meat is prized because it is lean. For a recent Thanksgiving, we purchased our buffalo via the internet: the man of our house grilled a sirloin in the backyard. The meat was marinated for two days, cooked rare, and served by the woman of the house. On the advice of our purveyor, we grilled the buffalo meat with some hickory smoked bacon strips for flavour. 'A bit of fat adds taste,' he said.

Notes

1. Cabeza de Vaca got the story of the wild cattle second hand. Vaca, Alvar Nuñez Cabeza de, 'The Story of Figueroa Recounted from Esquivel,' chapter 18 in *Relation That Alvar Nunez Cabeza De Vaca Gave of What Befell the Armament in the Indies Whither Panfilo De Narvaez Went for Governor from the Year 1527 to the Year 1536 When with Three Comrades He Returned and Came to Sevilla* (1555), ed. Frederick Webb Hodge, (New York: Barnes & Noble, 1946, 1953. Also, http://www.library.txstate.edu/swwc/cdv/about/index.html. Dan Flores, 'The Environmental History of De Vaca's Wondrous Journey.'

2. Hennepin, Louis, *A Description of Louisiana*, trans. and ed. by John Gilmary Shea, (New York: John G. Shea, 1880). Reprint, Ann Arbor, University Microfilms, Inc. 1966, 246-247.

3. .Hawley, Jerome and John Lewger, *A Relation of Maryland* (1635) reprinted in Clayton Coleman Hall, *Narratives of Early Maryland, 1633-1684* (NY: Charles Scribner's Sons, 1910), 63-112. Also see:http://www.mdarchives.state.md.us/megafile/msa/speccol/sc2900/sc2908/000001/000657/html/am657-3.html.

4. Beverley, Robert, *The History and Present State of Virginia* (1706, enlarged 1722), Vol. II. The Natural Productions and Conveniences of the Country, Suited to Trade and Improvement (Richmond, Va: J. W. Randolph, 1855) p. 59.

5. Simmons, Amelia, *American Cookery, or the Art of Dressing Viands, Fish, Poultry and Vegetables, and the Best Modes of Making Pastes, Puff, Pies, Tarts, Puddings, Custards and Preserves and All Kinds of Cakes from Imperial Plum to Plain Cake Adapted to This Country and All Grades of Life* (Hartford, CN: Hudson & Goodwin, 1796).

6. Lewis, Meriwether, and William Clark, *The Journal of the Lewis and Clark Expedition*. Edited by Gary E. Moulton. University of Nebraska: http://lewisandclarkjournals.unl.edu/index.html. Also Hallock, Thomas, 'Literary Recipes from the Lewis and Clark Journals: The Epic Design and Wilderness Tastes of Early National Nature Writing', *American Studies* 38, no. 3 (1997) pp. 43-66.

7. Child, Lydia Maria, *The Frugal Housewife, Dedicated to Those Who Are Not Ashamed of Economy* (Boston: Carter, Hendee, and Babcock, 1831). The cookbook was first published in 1829.

8. Erwin James, ed., *An Account of an Expedition from Pittsburgh to the Rocky Mountains; Undertaken in the*

Years 1819 and 1820. . . Under the Command of Major S[tephen]. H. Long (Philadelphia: Carey and Lea, 1823, 2 vols.); Muszynska-Wallace, E. Soteris, 'The Sources of the Prairie', *American Literature* 21, no. 2 (May) (1949) pp. 191-200.

9. Cooper, James Fenimore, chapters IX-X in *The Prairie*, edited by James P. Elliott, pp. 96-117, (Albany, NY: State University of New York Press, 1827. Reprint, 1985); McWilliams, Mark, 'Distant Tables: Food and the Novel in Early America', in *Early American Literature* 38, no. 3 (2003) pp. 365-93.

10. Tyler, Ron, Alfred Jacob Miller, *Artist on the Oregon Trail* (Fort Worth, Texas: Amon Carter Museum, 1982).

11. Irving, Washington, Chapter XXII, 'The Alarm Camp', in *A Tour on the Prairies*, in Washington Irving, *Three Western Narratives: A Tour on the Prairies, Astoria, and the Adventures of Captain Bonneville*, James P. Ronda ed. (New York: The Library of America, 2004), p. 99.

12 Irving, Washington, Chapter XLVII, 'Astoria', in *Three Western Narratives*, above, p. 516.

13. Irving, Washington, Chapter XLII, 'The Adventures of Captain Bonneville', in *Three Western Narratives*, above, p. 911.

14. Irving, Washington, Chapter X, 'The Adventures of Captain Bonneville', in *Three Western Narratives*, p. 699.

15. Parkman, Francis, Chapter XXIV, 'The Chase', in *The Oregon Trail*, illustrated by Thomas Hart Benton (Garden City, NY: Doubleday & Company, Inc., 1849, reprint 1946), pp. 287, 289.

16. Ruxton, George Augustus Frederick, Chapter X, 'The Passing of the Buffalo', in *Wild Life in the Rocky Mountains*, Horace Kephart ed. (New York: The Macmillan Company, 1847, reprint, 1916), see: http://www.xmission.com/~drudy/mtman/html/ruxton.html

17. Bird, Isabella L., Letter XVI, December 4, in *A Lady's Life in the Rocky Mountains*, intro. Ann Ronald, (Reno, Nevada: University of Nevada, 1873, reprint 1987).

18. Cody, William F., 'Famous Hunting Parties of the Plains', *Cosmopolitan* 17, no. 2 (1894) 137-40.

19. Davies, Henry E., *Ten Days on the Plains*, ed. Paul Andrew Hutton (Dallas, Texas: Southern Methodist University Press, 1871, reprint, 1985), pp. 111-112; Campbell, SueEllen, 'Feasting in the Wilderness: The Language of Food in American Wilderness Narratives', in *American Literary History* 6, no. 1, Spring (1994): 1-23.

20. Algren, Nelson. 'Nebraska Buffalo Barbeque', in *America Eats*, edited with preface by Louis I. Szathmáry, foreword by David E. Schoonover, pp. 46-47 (Iowa City: University of Iowa Press, 1992). In an unfortunate mix-up, the 'Nebraska Buffalo Barbecue' in *America Eats* is wrongly attributed to the novelist Nelson Algren. According to Anne Mendelson, Algren did not write this book, which is actually a series of essays written by various authors at the request of Elizabeth Kellock of the WPA and the Federal Writers' Project in the late 1930s. Algren was one of the participants. According to Mendelson, Louis Szathmáry wrongly concluded that Algren wrote the manuscript, and David Schoonmaker accepted the attribution without questioning its authenticity. Mendelson reached her conclusion after reading the manuscripts that now reside the Library of Congress. Based on Mendelson's reading, the 'Nebraska Buffalo Barbecue' episode was written by a local writer named McCandless, (Nebraska folder box A 831).

Bamboo for Life

Pia Lim-Castillo

Nang maliit ay gulay	(When small it is a vegetable)
Nang lumaki'y pambuhay	(When big it is an aid to life)
Buhat sa puno, hanggang dulo	(From bottom to top)
Puro kwarto	(It is full of chambers)
	Filipino riddles

Introduction

Bamboo has exerted a profound influence on the lives and cultures of three billion Asians. Known as the timber of the poor in third world countries, it is a plant of ancient and increasing importance for humanity because it is found almost everywhere. The uses of bamboo in Asia, from the earliest records, run the gamut from junks for seafaring people, scaffolding for building skyscrapers, bamboo needles for acupuncture to bamboo shoots as food.

Bamboo thrives in most places even in adverse conditions. It can adjust to seasonal changes, whether extremely dry or waterlogged. The firm stalk and yielding leaves help the plant survive the rays of the sun and the weight of the snow; in fact, bamboo only grows stronger as it adapts to environmental changes. In most Asian cultures, bamboo is a symbol of enlightenment, strength, adaptability and resilience in adversity. Bamboo is part of culture and folklore, it has its songs and seasons. It figures in literature, legends, songs and folklore and is used as subjects in paintings as well. In Philippine folklore, it is said that the first man and woman came out of a bamboo stalk that was split by lightning and they were named Malakas (Strong) and Maganda (Beautiful). The Philippine national dance Tinikling uses bamboo poles that are clacked rhythmically while dancers avoid being caught in between them. This dance mimics the way a bird called *tikling* avoids getting caught by the baits used during the rice harvest season.

Bamboo belongs to the grass family like common crops such as wheat, corn, rice, barley, sorghum, millet, oats, and sugar cane. It is the fastest growing plant in the world. It grows three times faster than the fastest growing tree. Bamboo matures in three to five years and can be harvested by that time. Bamboo plantations and thickets grow in tropical, subtropical and temperate regions of all continents, from lowlands up to 4000 metres in altitude, except in Europe or Western Asia. In South East Asia, bamboo groves are found in habitats that are dry or humid, on wastelands, swamps, or on dry or regularly flooded river banks. Bamboo, 'under optimum conditions, can provide 2–6 times as much cellulose per acre as pine. Forests in general increase 2–5%

yearly in total bulk or biomass, groves of bamboo increase 10–30%' (Farrelly, p. 3).

Bamboos are perhaps the most primitive subfamily of grasses. The rooting system are the rhizomes, they are an important aspect of the bamboo plant as there is no central trunk as in trees. The rhizomes are the foundations of the plant. The shoot is a new growth from the rhizome. It grows slowly at first, elongating rapidly, forming a new culm. Bamboos are broadly divided into sympodial and monopodial species based on their rhizome configuration.

Sympodial bamboos are clumping, frost sensitive tropical species, some enduring temperatures slightly below freezing. In sympodial bamboos, shooting or the growth of the culms occurs typically from summer to autumn or at the onset of the rainy season. It is controlled by moisture level and in warm regions with frequent rainfall throughout the year, the growth of sympodial bamboos may be virtually continuous.

Monopodial, free-standing bamboos are hardy to a few degrees below 0°C and thrive in climates with pronounced but not severe winters. The onset of shooting in spring is controlled by temperature. Most Japanese bamboos are monopodial.

A bamboo culm is separated by horizontal partitions or nodes into joints or internodes:.

> The growth of the bamboo culm, the most spectacular of the plant's visible behaviors, varies greatly depending on species, soil, age of stand and climate. Larger species may average between three to sixteen inches in a day. Night growth may be two to three times the growth by day in some species, in others the reverse is true. Sympodial bamboos complete their growth in 80–120 days. Monopodial species reach 93% of their total height within one month, then taper off with the second, slower period of roughly equal duration. After this the culm hardens and matures, but does not increase in height or diameter. (Farrelly, p. 141).

Most culms have cylindrical and hollow internodes and this, together with the dense, hard, thick or thin walls and nodes, gives the culm great mechanical strength. The diameter of the culm depends on the species and the environment varying between 0.5–20 cm. The diameter of a mature culm is already determined by the diameter of the young shoot (PROSEA, p. 29).

The leaves are therapeutic because they pump oxygen. This airy green filter and a dense underground life renowned for erosion control combine to make bamboo a healing force for the soil as well as the soul (Farrelly, p. 7). Leaves are also used as food wrappers in Asian cuisine.

Bamboo performs best on well-drained, rich soils; on poor soils, culms are shorter and have a much smaller diameter. Traditionally, people never apply commercial fertilizer to their bamboo groves as the leaf fall is enough for natural composting.

However, tests show that fertilizer application increases the production of shoots and culms (Quimio, p. 3).

Bamboo is harvested in accordance with the part to be used (culm or shoot), the age and the season. For pole production, harvesting is carried out during the dry season or is started at the beginning of the dry season, to prevent culms from being attacked by borers. Moreover, during the dry season the starch content is at its lowest. Shoots are harvested during the monsoon season and preferably cut off before they emerge above the soil when they are still fresh and tender. Everywhere it is available, bamboo is harnessed for a variety of purposes because of its characteristic mechanical properties, supply, price, and its diversified uses.

Bamboo in the Philippine context

The Philippines are composed of 7,100 islands and many communities depend on the sea for food and as a source of livelihood. Bamboo has long been used in fishing communities for its buoyancy and is said to increase in strength when subjected to salt water. Fishermen fashion the *salambaw*, a floating raft used for catching small fish, with graceful, arcing bamboo poles floating nets in shallow water. Fish cages called *bobo panmaligto* and traps are made from whittled bamboo. They are also used in making pens in both lakes and seas to raise fish, molluscs and other crustaceans. Aside from cages, bamboo stalks are cut into half-inch widths and lashed together creating spaces in between for slatted tables where fish are dried under the sun.

In farming communities, bamboo is planted to prevent erosion. They also plant bamboo to mark boundaries or to stake out fields. They prop up fruit heavy trees like mango and banana trees with bamboo cut to height. They make *paragos*, sleds to hitch to their *carabaos* for carrying sacks of seeds or fertilizers to their farm. They balance long bamboo poles between coconut treetops, walking these pathways in the sky when tapping the trees for *tuba* (coconut toddy), a favourite drink. When the rice fields are almost ready for harvest, bamboo becomes the skeleton for scarecrows to shoo birds away with their motion in the wind. Rice grains or *palay* are dried on bamboo mats laid out on the ground, called *amakan*. To carry produce, woven bamboo baskets are strapped astride workhorses or water buffalos.

Ethnic minorities still use blowguns for hunting making use of the straightest bamboo they can find. Blowpipes are handy hunting tools because they are light to carry, and made of material that is locally abundant. Bamboo is also whittled down and used as bait to trap wild chickens, lizards and other animals roaming the forest. It can also be used as a spear to catch river fish.

In jungle survival, green bamboo thickets are an excellent source of fresh water. Water from green bamboo is clear and odourless. To get water, a green bamboo stalk is bent from the top, tied down, and the top cut off. The water will drip freely during the night. The moisture content of culms increases from bottom to top. Moisture content is highest from 1–3 years and decreases in culms older than 3 years. It is much higher in the rainy season than in the dry season. Old, cracked bamboo may contain water but this isn't as potable as water from fresh bamboo. Dried bamboo, on the other hand, can be used to start a fire while fresh bamboo can be used as a cooking vessel.

The structure of the bamboo makes it an excellent cooking vessel. A long piece of bamboo is cut between culms to hold a leak free culm in the bottom and an internode to hold the food to be cooked, like rice, vegetables and meats. The top part is usually covered with banana leaves or other edible leaves found in forests.

In the Visayas, *binacol* is a dish which makes use of the internode of a freshly cut bamboo as a pot. Inside the internode, native chicken, tomatoes, onion and salt are put in together with leaves from a vine called *alumpilan* which climb on the bamboo stalk. These leaves impart a sour flavour to the dish. Once the culm is filled with the ingredients, the top is covered with lemongrass stalks which serve as a cover and a flavouring agent to the dish. It is cooked over coals until the outer layer of the bamboo is completely charred. The resulting dish comes out rather soupy imparting an earthy, woody and robust flavour released from the moisture in the walls of the internode. In certain dishes, wide bamboo leaves are used as wrappers the way coconut and banana leaves are used.

Tinubong is a snack in Luzon, where sticky rice is mixed with coconut milk and sugar and placed in young bamboo stalks that are cut between culms. These are pegged into the sand and cooked around a bonfire and turned until the bamboo is brown and dry on the outside. The size of bamboo used for this snack is much smaller than what is used to make *binacol*. Plain boiled rice can also be cooked in a bamboo and cooked the same way. To eat, just hit it against something hard to crack it open and remove the contents. It is also a food container with preservative qualities so that sticky rice cooked in bamboo will keep for many days – good for hiking in the mountains.

In areas by mouths of rivers like in Bulacan, fishermen cook their food inside the bamboo and bury these in mud for about three hours while they go out fishing. A hole is dug in the mangrove and the mud set aside. A piece of semi dried bamboo is cut open ensuring that one end has a node and it is filled with rice, fish from the river and some vegetables. The cut cover is returned once the bamboo has been filled and the whole piece is encased in mud. Charcoal embers are put into the hole covered with *nipa* fronds. The mud encased bamboo is put on top then topped off with the rest of the dug up mud. After fishing, the fishermen come back to dig the bamboo and wash the mud off with water from the river and it is split open to be eaten. The final dish is moist, steamy and full of mixed flavours of seafood, rice and nuances of bamboo.

Another dish called *puto bungbong* is extremely popular all over the Philippines especially during the Christmas season. Purple glutinous rice is inserted into smaller bamboo pieces and placed on a steamer where the bamboo serves as the cover to the air vent. The condensation from the steam seeps through the rice and cooks it inside the bamboo. Once cooked, the bamboo is tapped to release the cooked rice and it is served hot with butter, freshly grated coconut and muscovado sugar.

All local species of bamboo can be used for the above ways of cooking but the *buho* (*Schizostachyum lumampao*) is the preferred vessel. Other commonly used varieties are *kawayan-tinik* (*Bambusa blumeana*), *kawayan-kiling* (*Bambusa vulgaris*), *bolo* (*Gigantochloa levis*), *kayali* (*G. atter*), *patong* (*Dendrocalamus asper*), *bayog* (*B. merrilliana*), and *laak* (*B. philippinensis*).

Some non-food uses of bamboo in the Philippines are:

- For pedestrian bridges;
- carrying poles – loads of equal weight are fastened at both ends so as to keep the balance; carriers get into a swing and can take advantage of the recoil of the pole to make their load lighter as they step forward;
- posts and lintels and matting called *sawali* for the traditional Filipino home, called *bahay kubo;*
- trellises;
- fire starters and firewood;
- ladders;
- netting needles for fish nets;
- net Floats – bamboo's natural buoyancy makes it a natural net float;
- boat balances – *Katig;*
- rafts;
- furniture;
- musical instruments like flutes and our famous bamboo organ;
- leaves as hay and fodder for cattle and horses;
- erosion control – a flood tamer, soil builder and saver, windbreak and earthquake refuge.

213

In all the above uses, bamboo has served Filipinos and will continue to do so without wreaking havoc on the environment. Bamboo is a sustainable resource which self-generates quickly (within a season). Even if these are used only once, they are completely biodegradable. Second, cutting a full stalk for one's use does not kill the bamboo plant. More shoots will come out of the bamboo thicket once the rainy season sets in. In fact, one of the most difficult grasses to kill is the bamboo.

Bamboo as food
Bamboo leaves are used as fodder for cattle and horses. They are also used as wrappers particularly the varieties that have large leaves. These impart a specific flavour redolent of freshly cut bamboo stalks but are not edible.

The edible part of the bamboo is the shoot. Called *labong* in the Philippines, these are the tender young growths which sprout in abundance during the monsoon season. Shoots are harvested before they reach 30 centimetres in height, generally before they are two weeks old. The young shoots are crisp and tender like asparagus, with a flavour reminiscent of corn, and are widely used in Asian cooking. Canned bamboo shoots are commonly available, though fresh bamboo shoots are far superior in taste and texture.

Cultivation for shoot alone requires a different set of practices from its use as timber. Shoot cultivation requires better soil, water and light conditions, and more intensive management because shoots consume more mineral nutrients from the soil (Oberoi, www.tifac.org.in/nmba/fact_shoot.htm).

Bamboo shoots are easy to prepare and could be a better alternative and practical food since they are readily available. Shoots of most bamboo species can be consumed but quality shoots are those of *kawayan-tinik (Bambusa blumeana)*, *kawayan-kiling (B. vulgaris)*, *bolo (Gigantochloa levis)*, *kayali (G. atter)*, *patong (Dendrocalamus asper)*, *bayog (B. merrilliana)*, and *laak (B. philippinensis)* (Leila C. America, PCARRD S&T Media Services)

Shoots of certain types of bamboo contain cyanogens and may be toxic to cattle, but cooking destroys these substances and renders the shoots edible and tasty. A shoot that is fairly stout, light yellow or light brown, purple on the root buds, and white at the basal cut will be tender, fragrant, and tasty. On the other hand, a slender shoot with purple black skin, reddish root buds, and a dark coloured cut base will be tough and have little fragrance. Shoots that have grown above ground are very poor in quality.

To prepare bamboo shoots, peel off the outer layers which are tough. Once the inner layers are soft enough, hold the tip of the shoot and start slicing the bamboo shoot crosswise as thinly as possible starting at the base and moving upwards towards the tip. To avoid discoloration of the cut shoots, drop the slices in water. Stop slicing once you notice a black ring towards the top. This is the bitter portion. Boil freshly cut shoots once to remove the bitter flavour then drain. Bamboo shoots that are still bitter after a first boil can be given a second cooking in fresh water for approximately 5 minutes longer. After this step, you can now cook the shoots as part of a dish.

In the Philippines, bamboo shoots have been part of traditional dishes. For regional cooking, bamboo shoots are prepared differently depending on what are locally available in terms of vegetables, herbs and spices. There is *dinengdeng nga labong* (mixed vegetable sautéed with fish paste) for the Ilocanos, *paklay* (plain boiled vegetables with shrimps) for the Visayans, *atsara* or pickled labong for the Tagalogs, *bulanglang na labong* for the Batangueños, and *guinataang labong* (bamboo shoots with coconut milk) for the Bicolanos.

Bamboo shoots are never produced in large quantities either as big business or as a cooperative venture in the Philippines. Shoots are mainly gathered from the backyards, neighbourhood bamboo grove, or from the market. They are however an export industry in China, Taiwan and Thailand. The price of bamboo shoots depends upon the supply and the locality. Generally, prices are lower during the rainy season.

> To preserve bamboo shoots, they can be dried, desiccated, canned, vacuum-packed or bottled. Bamboo shoots are dried by removing the sheath and oven-dried to a moisture content of 14 percent. Bamboo shoots are desiccated by cleaning and chopping evenly, then oven- or sun-dried until the right drying conditions are met. They are vacuum-packed by using a vacuum sealer and high-density polyethylene plastics. Bamboo shoots can also be pickled and bottled in glass containers. Sensory evaluations on the shoots revealed no significant difference in terms of aroma, after-taste, flavor and texture but revealed significant difference in color. Bamboo shoots with light or cream color (*kawayan-tinik* and *kayali*) are more preferred than light orange (*kayali*). (Leila C. America, PCARRD S&T Media Services)

Considered as health food for the new millennium, fresh bamboo shoots are recommended for heart patients because of their high dietary fibre and low fat content. Bamboo shoots are low in calories and fat, containing only 14 calories and 0.5 g fat per half-cup serving. The same size serving also provides 2.5 g fibre, about one-tenth of the recommended daily amount. The fresh shoots are a good source of thiamin, vitamin B6 and other trace minerals. They are also rich in potassium: one cup contains 640 mg of potassium (18% of the recommended daily amount). This plays an important role in maintaining normal blood pressure and heart rate. Canned shoots, however, are stripped of most of their vitamins and minerals.

215

Bamboo shoots have also been found to be effective in cancer prevention particularly colon cancer, increasing the appetite, decreasing blood pressure and cholesterol levels in the human body. Bamboo shoot can be labelled as a heart protective vegetable and its component phytosterols may be suitable as nutraceuticals.

The good news about bamboo shoots as food is that they are low in saturated fat, and very low in cholesterol. They are also a good source of protein, thiamin, niacin, iron and phosphorus, and a very good source of dietary fibre, riboflavin, vitamin B6, potassium, zinc and copper. The bad news is they are high in sodium. Despite the high sodium content, bamboo shoots continue to be part of the seasonal Philippine diet, not only for their availability and flavour but also because of their health benefits.

Bamboo as Regreening Agent
Bamboo is one of the best examples of a sustainable natural resource in the tropics. Due to its adaptability to almost any kind of soil, rapid growth, availability, easy handling and other desirable properties, it is part of the daily life of local communities. The most significant uses are for building material, making baskets and as a vegetable.

The strength of the culms, their straightness, smoothness, lightness combined with hardness and hollowness; the facility and regularity with which they can be split; the different sizes, various lengths and thicknesses of their joints make them suitable for numerous purposes where other materials would require more labour and preparation.

Traditionally, bamboo is grown organically. Most people do not apply fertilizers to their bamboo groves. The grove will continue to produce shoots and bamboo poles without need for fertilization or replanting. Those that grow bamboo for its shoots do fertilize as the use of fertilizers increases the production of shoots and culms (PROSEA, p. 42).

Though soil moisture is an important factor in the bamboo's growth, it requires very little care and does not need watering as it gets enough water once the monsoon season sets in. However, restriction of water supply decreases carbon dioxide and so a plant with limited water supply is smaller than one with unlimited supply of water (Quimio, p. 3). Thus, bamboo grown in areas such as river banks, creeks and areas with high moisture content in the soil, grow not only faster but taller and bigger as well.

216

Due to the diminishing supply of wood, bamboo is now in high demand as raw material sources for furniture, handicraft and for many other products. The methods of using bamboo within the format of modern industry are multiplying. Instead of cutting up virgin trees which take a long time to grow, bamboo is being used in pulp and paper making, chopstick and toothpick production. Quality newsprint and kraft paper are being produced from bamboo fibres and these are comparable to those made from softwoods and Philippine hardwoods. In recent years, bamboo has also entered the tile and plywood arena in construction. The Department of Science and Technology's (DOST) Forest Products Research and Development Institute (FPRDI) of the Philippines has found a way to make veneers out of the base of the bamboo stem, producing tiles that can be used for floors, table tops and panels. These projects make use of the cheap and workable resource that thrives in the countryside, helping create jobs or additional sources of income in bamboo growing communities.

Lastly, bamboo is now used in agroforestry in Asia particularly for reforestation and reclamation of degraded land. It is the fastest growing canopy for the re-green-ing of degraded lands and releases 35% more oxygen than equivalent timber stands. Bamboo forests prevent landslides and protect river banks. The roaming mass of roots and interlocking rhizomes in the critical top foot of earth hold firm even in earth-quakes. Living, the bamboo leaves form a leaky umbrella that shields the ground from pounding rain. Dead, a 4-inch annual leaf fall equal in weight to the new growth of culms in some species, clogs the small ditches where erosion starts. The 2–4 inch mulch that bamboo leaves create makes it easier for the earth to hold water while increasing its organic content – the depletion of which is a major cause of man made erosion. Finally, the harvesting of bamboo does not disturb the soil surface.

With a burgeoning population and a diminishing food supply, bamboo can be harnessed to replace or indirectly decrease the consumption of three resources that are critically getting scarce in our planet – wood, metal and oil and at the same time feed man. It is a God-given renewable resource which multiplies at a pace rivalling the growth of other wood. Not only does the bamboo hold visual charm, it is also extraordinary in its physical vitality and is good to eat.

In spite of its many desirable growing characteristics and uses, bamboo has not been developed to its optimum potential in either its productive or protective functions. Among the issues in declining production are the lack of technical knowledge of bamboo production, harvesting and processing, a lack of managerial and entrepreneurial skills in growing and marketing of bamboo products, and the low prices of local bamboo products as compared to those made with hard woods.

Yet, despite the problems mentioned above, the prospects for the bamboo industry are bright. There is an increasing demand for traditional bamboo products, like furniture and decorative articles, both in local and export markets. Consumers now prefer products that are manufactured from renewable resources and environmentally friendly materials. Aggressive efforts should also be made to embark on the manufacture of industrial products made of bamboo to replace plywood and other construction materials since wood is becoming scarce. With the cooperation of both the private and public sector in realizing the value of bamboo and how it can be a big aid to the Philippines, it is hoped that the hectarage planted to bamboo will increase. As food, bamboo will continue to feed the peoples of Asia and the rest of the world who have learned to enjoy bamboo shoots.

217

Bamboo is a centuries-old material that has been and continues to be used by over half the world's population. Bamboo offers vital economic and ecological benefits for the lives of billions of people worldwide; providing food, fuel, housing, furniture, artisan products; food, soil and water conservation. These applications make bamboo a vital non-timber, non-petroleum resource. With a tensile strength superior to steel, it is one of the most versatile and durable natural resource of the world. It is truly the plant for the next millennium.

References

America, Leila, *Bamboo Shoots: Food for all season* (Internet posting: PCARRD S&T Media Services, 2003).

Blethen, Caitlin, Carol Miles and Gayle P. Alleman, *Bamboo Shoots* (Washington State University Cooperative Extension and American Bamboo Society, 2001).

Farrelly, David, *The Book of Bamboo* (San Francisco: Sierra Club Books, 1984).

Gonzales, Lucas L., Umali, Paulino A. Jr., Piñol, Agustin A., 'The Pilot Plantation in Pampanga' (Los Baños: *Canopy International*, March-April 1990).

Oberoi, V.S., *National Mission on Bamboo Applications* (New Delhi: www.tifac.org.in/nmba/fact_shoot. htm).

Paterno-Locsin, Ma. Elena, *Bamboo* (Manila: Centro Escolar University Centennial Collection, 2000).

PROSEA (Plant resources of South East Asia), *Bamboos*, 1995.

Quimio, Marcos J. Jr., 'Commercial fertilizer: Its effects on the shoot development of four bamboo species' (Los Baños: *Canopy International*, November-December 1999).

Tamolang, Francisco N., Felipe R. Lopez, Jose A. Semana, Ricardo F, Casin, and Zenita B. Espiloy, *Bamboo Research in Asia: Proceedings of a Workshop in Singapore* (Ottawa: IDRC, 1980).

Virtucio, Felizardo D., 'Growth Performance of eight bamboo species in pilot plantation sites in the Philippines' (Los Baños: *Canopy International*, November-December 1996).

www.ctl.com.au, *A Guide to growing bamboo for food production* (Yass: The Australian Bamboo Network, 2003).

www.nutritiondata.com/facts-001-02s02g.html.

218

A History of Seafood in Irish Cuisine and Culture

Máirtín Mac Con Iomaire

'One of the many paradoxes which bloom as freely as the shamrock in its native land is this; that the coasts of the emerald isle are rich in seafood, but that the Irish people have on the whole been shy of consuming it. One has only to imagine what would happen on these coasts, if the people of, say, Singapore were suddenly transplanted thither, to realise the extent of this shyness.'[1]

Introduction

Fish is one of the most abundant wild foods available to a small island nation. Certain species of seafood have moved from being 'poor man's food' to 'luxury food' over time. It may be said that the Irish do not behave as island people since we have little or no history of exploiting the sea compared to our European partners. Ireland was late developing its fishing industry and now suffers reduced EU fish quotas, the unfortunate but necessary result of decades of over-fishing on European waters. This paper investigates the historical role seafood has played in Irish cuisine and culture – past and present. The paper aims to dispel the myth that the Irish have no maritime food tradition and highlights that absence of evidence is not evidence of absence. Comparisons will be made between the consumption of seafood in Ireland and in other European countries. The paper identifies the factors (political, economic, cultural and religious) that have influenced Irish consumers in their purchase and consumption of fish, and discovers what food the Irish prefer to fish.

Mythology

The wild Irish salmon features strongly in Irish mythology and until the introduction of the Euro graced some of the nation's coinage. The salmon also appears in topography particularly in the County Kildare town of Leixlip (Léim an Bhradáin) meaning literally 'Salmon's Leap'. Leixlip derives from the Norse for salmon *lax*. A tale from the Fenian cycle of Irish mythology states that the River Boyne was home to a magical salmon that ate nuts from a hazel tree and was known as the Salmon of Knowledge. A druid had foretold that whoever first ate of the flesh of that magical salmon would have knowledge of all things. Demne's father was Cumhail Mac Art, a warrior killed before his child was born. Fearing for her son's safety at the hands of her husband's killers, Demne's mother sent him away to be raised by a woman warrior and druidess. Unable to avoid pursuit by his father's enemies, Demne decided to become a poet. A poet's high status in Celtic society would shield him from harm. He studied with a poet named Finnéagas who lived near the River Boyne. Having watched the salmon for many years, Finnéagas finally caught it and told his apprentice Demne to cook the fish. While the salmon was cooking, Demne burnt his thumb. To ease the pain, he licked the burn thereby tasting the magic fish. Demne told Finnéagas what had happened and his mentor decreed that the young Demne was the one intended to eat the salmon and changed his name to 'Fionn'. Henceforth known as Fionn Mac Cumhail, he received three gifts that would make him a great poet: magic, great insight, and the power of words.

History

Ireland's long and indented coastline extends to an impressive 7,000 kilometres, yet no place in the whole country is more that 100km from the coast. About 7,000 years ago the first inhabitants, who arrived by sea, set up home in the northeast of the island. From here they travelled the coastline from the northeast to the very southwest. Coastal areas supported many early settlers, as the interior parts of the country were heavily forested and inaccessible. The archaeological record shows that middens, huge heaps of shells and discarded bones, the remains of their fishing and hunting, mark the sites of their foraging.[2] It is believed that many of these sites were used seasonally.[3] The Mount Sandel site in County Derry was probably used during the summer to catch salmon, and eels during the autumn.[4] At Dunloughan Bay, near Ballyconneely in County Galway, shell middens, dating from the early Bronze Age to the 10th century AD, are being exposed by erosion and over-grazing. These sites give a wonderful snapshot of history and contain rich deposits of oysters, cockles, limpets, winkles, dog whelks and razorfish interspersed with burnt stones and wickerwork reduced to charcoal. Oysters seem to dominate the earlier Bronze Age sites, winkles and limpets the later ones.[5]

Christianity arrived in Ireland in the 5th century with Saint Patrick and established a foothold quickly, embracing many of the old customs and rituals of druidism. Monasteries became centres of learning and many of the larger archaeological remains of fish traps and complex wattle fences and woven baskets used for catching salmon and eels have been found at monastic sites, particularly in the Shannon Estuary.[6] It is suggested that Ireland saved western civilization after the Visigoths sacked Rome and Europe was plunged into the Dark Ages.[7] Irish monks preserved and copied many of the Greek and Roman texts and Ireland's Monasteries became safe havens and intellectual centres for Europe's learned classes. Along with Christianity came the custom of abstaining from meat on Fridays, on fast days and during Lent. Although abstinence from meat did not automatically mean the consumption of fish, as eggs were also a common source of protein, there was a clear correlation between the increased consumption of fish and days of fast and abstinence. For many inland areas these were the only times when fish was available. 'Cadgers' or salesmen travelled through the district in horse drawn carts, selling fish to locals, travelling many miles until their load was sold.[8]

The salmon was regarded as the 'king of fish'. Gaelic chiefs saved the prized posi-tion at their feasts for the salmon, which they roasted whole over an open spit and basted with wine, honey and herbs. There is evidence of an export trade in salmon. Indeed, between 1400–1416 almost thirty licences were issued to Bristol merchants who were permitted to import old wine, salt and cloth and afterwards return home with salmon and Irish goods. By 1540 Irish ship-owners were credited with having very up-to-date ships and Irish seamen were quick to take advantage of the great North Atlantic fisheries that were then opened. The Tudor conquest from the 16th century severely restricted the further development of native-owned shipping. Hugh O' Neill saw the importance of Irish commercial and fishing fleets and considered the possibility of an Irish navy, but his military failure after the Battle of Kinsale (1601) led to centuries where the Irish plied their seafaring skills in foreign navies.[9] During the 18th century large quantities of salted salmon were exported to Italy and France. Foreign trawlers fishing in Irish waters are not a new phenomenon either. French fishing fleets, particularly off the south-western coast, fished Irish mackerel shoals intensively. In 1757, a Cork City newspaper reported the presence of fifty French mackerel fishing vessels fishing near Bantry Bay in County Cork 'without interrup-tion from revenue cutters'.[10]

Fish was one of the principal elements of the modest diet of 18th-century Dublin, and was consumed in large quantities.[11] This was both because of its relative cheap-ness and on account of the religious observances of the majority of the population. The variety of seafood and freshwater fish available was remarkable and included, as well as staples such as herring and oysters, hake, haddock, whiting, turbot, trout, eel and salmon. It is interesting to note that city folk seemed to favour bi-valve molluscs like oysters and mussels while country folk favoured gastropods like winkles. The more prosperous members of society, who ate seafood from choice rather than neces-sity, consumed other shellfish such as crab, shrimp, lobster and scallops. The strand at Irishtown was renowned for the large quantities of shrimps caught there until the great frost of 1740 destroyed them and the shrimp fishery never recovered.[12] Isolated food items do not make an ethnic diet; the Irish have a long history of dairy products or 'white meats' as they were called, not to mention both the humble pig and the potato. The painter, Hugh Douglas Hamilton captured itinerant hawkers and sellers during the late 18th century in his 'Cries of Dublin'[13]. These illustrations include, along with many food peddlers, vendors in the fish and shellfish trade, particularly oyster and herring sellers. Oysters were transported to Dublin from Carlingford Lough, some 70km away, and were sold throughout the city, mostly for immediate consumption. There was such a large demand for oysters that artificial oyster beds were located north of the city near Clontarf, Howth and Malahide to ensure a steady supply.[14]

Herrings were an important part of the Irish diet as they could be eaten fresh or preserved for the winter months. They featured strongly on fast days, so much so that

221

following Lent, butchers led 'Herring Funerals' to celebrate their customers' return to meat, where a herring was beaten through the town on Easter Day, thrown into the water and a quarter of lamb dressed with ribbons was hung up in its place.[15] During great runs of herring the fish was sold cheaply, and many housewives preserved their own in barrels. Jonathan Swift, ever opinionated, maintained that the finest herrings came from Malahide. His fictional cry reads;

> Be not caring, Leave of swearing.
> Buy my herrings, Fresh from Malahide,
> Better never was tried.
> Come, eat them with pure fresh butter and mustard,
> Their bellies are soft, and as white as custard.
> Come, sixpence a dozen, to get me some bread,
> Or, like my own herrings, I shall soon be dead.[16]

The Dublin Fishery Company was established in 1818 to supply the Dublin Fish market with a better supply of fresh fish. Trawling was unknown or practically non-existent before this time and when the company purchased eight trawlers, English captains and seamen were brought over to operate them out of Ringsend.[17] Severe competition drove the price of fish down to one penny a pound in 1820. The company was wound up in 1830 but achieved a lot in its time including the discovery of new fishing grounds in the Irish Sea. One of the skippers stepped in and purchased the fleet and, to quote Brabazon Walloh, 'Thus the speculation that failed when ill managed under the amateur fishermen made this man's fortune.' The introduction of the technique of 'trawling' from Brixham, Devon to Ringsend led to the introduction of sole and turbot from the deep waters to the Dublin Market in large numbers.[18]

Bia Bocht (Poor Man's Food)

Whereas finfish need to be caught by hook, net or trap, certain shellfish can literally be picked up at low tide. Up until the 19th century it was mainly the poor who gathered shellfish. Such fare, called 'cnuasach mara' (sea pickings) was known as 'bia bocht' or poor man's food. For this reason shellfish failed to appear in the written accounts of commerce (and Taxation!) leading some commentators to conclude that they were not eaten here at all.[19] Thereby arose the myth that the Irish have no maritime food tradition. Things that are common or ordinary tend to be overlooked by 'History' and the gathering of simple seafood seems to leave no foothold on 'History's' pages. But we know that absence of evidence is not evidence of absence and what information we do have from archaeological digs, ancient writings and travellers' accounts, confirms that good use was made of shellfish in Ireland particularly in times of hardship.[20] The common or blue mussel (an diúilicín in Irish) is one of the most abundant and versatile of the Irish shellfish. Often called the poor man's oyster, it was used as bait in long-line fishing, used for food, and it was also spread on fields as fertilizer. Certain seafood were considered 'poor man's food' which is reflected in the 17th-century poet Aogán Ó Rathaille's lament for the days of his youth before the Battle of the Boyne in 1690, after which his Jacobite patron's lands were confiscated and the poet and his family found themselves dispossessed.

Is Fada Liom Oíche Fhírfhliuch

Is fada liom oíche fhírfhliuch gan suan, gan srann,
gan ceathra, gan maoin caoire ná buaibh na mbeann;
anfa ar toinn taoibh liom do bhuair mo cheann,
's nár chleachtas im naíon fíogaigh ná ruacain abhann

The drenching night drags on: no sleep or snore,
no stock, no wealth of sheep, no horned cows.
This storm on the waves nearby has harrowed my head
– I who ate no winkles or dogfish in my youth! [21]

This notion of equating shellfish with poor man's food may have been further enhanced by the evidence of the movement of starving people to the coast in search of food during the potato famine of the 1840s.

Salted ling, often known as 'battleboard', was in widespread use for centuries, either as Friday food in inland areas and as a winter staple in southern and western coastal areas. Indeed Florence Irwin[22] includes a one-pot recipe for salted ling and potatoes in her publication. Stockfish (dried fish) kept up to ten years if properly dried, but was understandably often unpleasant to eat.

223

Ireland since 1922

There were 4,321 craft of all sizes involved in sea fishing in Ireland in 1916 with 15, 789 men and boys employed as crew.[23] However, many of these were vessels of smaller tonnage, principally involved in small-scale fishing within a few miles offshore. The Congested District Board (1890–1923) established by Arthur Balfour to alleviate poverty in the western seaboard counties, many of which also happened to be the areas in which the Irish language was still widely spoken, did much to encourage fishing by building boat slips and fishing piers. In 1922, when independence was achieved, Arthur Griffith was the only one of the Irish Free State's founders to declare that for real prosperity, Ireland must have a strong maritime economy. His successors during the 20th century ignored this important observation; they and the great majority of the Irish intelligentsia have turned their backs on the sea and its huge possibilities.[24] Based on reports from 1910–1928, 'the number of steam trawlers on which reliance can be placed for the maintenance of regular supplies of white fish – engaged in land-

A Fishers Boy

ings in the Saorstát (Irish Free State) is seven only, an insignificant number having regard to the existing demand for this type of fish'.[25]

The report also highlights the dichotomy of an island nation, whose surrounding seas are full of a varied stock of fish, being dependent for its supplies of fish largely on external sources. The Department of Lands and Fisheries was re-constituted in 1928, following the report of a Commission appointed to advise on the measures necessary for the preservation of and for the economic betterment of the Gaeltacht (Irish-language speaking regions) along the western seaboard. Many of the factors that led to the improvement of marine resources were tied up with the Irish language, and were the result of inspired individuals rather than government policy. By 1932, fish consumption per capita was estimated at approximately 4.5 lbs, compared with 32 lbs per head in Great Britain at the same time.[26] Independence was followed by a bitter civil war, an economic war with England and the Second World War. It was not until 1952, with the establishment of Bord Iascaigh Mhara (BIM), the Irish state agency responsible for developing the Irish sea fishing and aquaculture industries, that progress began. Alan Davidson[27] describes Bord Iascaigh Mhara as a fertile and inventive organization, whose work in the field of fish cookery is unsurpassed by that of any sister organizations in larger countries. Other organizations involved in developing marine resources were Gael Linn (a charitable trust dedicated to promoting the Irish language), The National Science Council (NSC) and University College, Galway. The love for the Irish language of key individuals in each organization led to a rare cooperation between agencies.[28] Such cooperation was uncommon, as J.J. Lee[29] illustrates: 'In the promising field of fish farming, for instance, the industry must liaise with no fewer than fifteen official bodies presumably reflecting the massive duplication of effort...between the many state agencies in agriculture and food.'

In the 1950s and 1960s a Breton family, based in west Cork, dominated the shellfish trade. Knowledge of the biology, population structure and composition of the Irish shellfish stocks was poor at the time. Fishermen were glad to have any buyers at all for their catch and there was no really strong indigenous seafood company in the west of Ireland with good connections to the continental markets.[30] The real catalyst for the rapid modern development was the entry of Ireland into the EU – then the Common Market – in 1972. That event was also to trigger the explosive exploitation of the wild shellfish stocks that occurred in the ensuing decade.

Commercialization and exploitation

Transportation and refrigeration were key factors in the commercialization of seafood. The Railways opened up inland markets for fresh fish, and it is argued that live shellfish exports only became economically viable with the advent of the roll on / roll off ferries. Until then live periwinkles were transported on open decks with instructions for the ship's captain to have them doused with seawater at regular intervals. Before refrigeration the most common method of preservation was salting and smoking.

The exploitation of all marine resources can be categorized as moving through stages: The first is the gathering / harvesting stage where the animals are gathered for personal use within a family or among neighbours. This method usually makes little demand on existing stocks. Once any species becomes a traded commodity it moves into the exploitation stage. Professional fishermen enter the fishery and control effectively passes to market forces. Without the vital stage of resource management, the inevitable outcome of exploitation is over-fishing, resulting in the eventual depletion of natural wild stocks. The logical commercial stage that follows over-exploitation is (artificial) cultivation or fish farming, a practice used for oysters by the Romans over two thousand years ago.

225

Oysters.

Oysters

A staggering amount of oysters was consumed once they became fashionable among city-dwellers. They were the first real 'fast food' for the masses of the industrial revolution. An estimated one and half billion oysters were consumed each year in England in the 1860s.[31] Rule's Oysteria, founded in 1798 by Thomas Rule, has a strong claim to be London's first restaurant.[32] Two of Dublin's most famous restaurants Jammet's and The Red Bank shared the oyster theme. In 1901 they were named Burlington Restaurant and Oyster Saloons and the Red Bank Oyster Hotel respectively.[33] The shell middens offer archaeological evidence of extensive oyster consumption from the later Mesolithic period and written reports from the late 17th century illustrates their abundance and particularly the size of the native Irish oyster (*Ostrea edulis*). Throughout the 19th century the Irish oyster beds were continuously over-fished. The Government Oyster Commission reporting in 1870 recommended the utmost caution with respect to all attempts at artificial cultivation but, in 1903, the short-lived Ardfry Experimental Oyster Cultivation Station was opened in County Galway.[34] To remedy the decline in oyster production, the Pacific oyster *Crassostrea gigas* was introduced into Europe on a large scale in the late 1960s and into Ireland in the early '70s; the reason being that it was easier and faster to cultivate than the native oyster and it was not prone to the disease *Bonamia ostrea*.[35] The native oyster (*Ostrea edulis*) is seasonal, as it spawns during the summer months hence is only available when there's an 'R' in the month. The Pacific (*gigas*) oyster doesn't spawn in the cold waters around Ireland so is available all year round.

One possible reason suggested for the lack of seafood consumption in Ireland is that Catholics associated fish with penance.[36] This argument seems to ignore fish consumption patterns in other European Catholic countries. It is fair to suggest that in inland counties, where the supply of fish was poor in both quality and quantity, a more negative opinion of fish prevailed than in the coastal counties where fresh seafood was more readily available. Smoked salmon is mentioned in the diary of Amhlaoibh Ó Súilleabháin from Callan in the inland County of Kilkenny. On St Patrick's Day (17th March) 1829 he records: 'we had for dinner… salt ling softened by steeping, smoke dried salmon and fresh trout'. He also expresses the following sentiment in his diary entry on 2nd April 1832: 'I do not like salt fish and fresh fish was not to be had, except too dear and seldom'.[37] When railways became operational in Ireland in the mid-19th century, they were used to transport large quantities of fish each year from coastal ports to inland areas. In 1911 alone, 25,590 tonnes of fish were conveyed inland from Irish ports.[38] Steam train drivers had a novel way of cooking herrings, by placing them on the coal shovel then held in the firebox for two minutes – Irish railwayman's breakfast.

After Vatican II in the late 1960s, Catholics were no longer forbidden to eat meat on a Friday. Oral evidence from Johnny Opperman[39], a retired chef/entrepreneur now in his eighties, evokes an earlier era:

> Fish! God when you come to think of it! Jesus! you would commit bloody murder rather that eat a piece of meat on Friday,… when you come to think of it, the changes…

He goes on to describe his memories of Fridays whilst serving his apprenticeship in the Shelbourne Hotel in Dublin during the mid-1930s:

> Only one thing I remember about Fridays, if you were on garde on Friday there

was a certain priest used to come in, always in the afternoon, and he'd have a bloody big steak, and the steak was to be made so it looked like a piece of grilled turbot…(laughter)

Seafood Festivals and Restaurants

In the 1950s, with the foundation of Bord Fáilte, the Irish Tourist Board, there was a concerted growth in tourism. Hospitality has been synonymous with Irish culture and was enshrined in ancient times in the Brehon Laws. Festivals were seen as excellent ways to increase tourism and generate much needed revenue for local communities. The most famous of the seafood festivals is the Clarinbridge Oyster Festival that has been part of Galway's social calendar since 1954. Other festivals include the Bundoran Lobster Festival, the Foyle Oyster Festival in Inishowen, the Waterford estuary Mussel Festival at Cheekpoint and the more recent Bantry Mussel Fair that was inaugurated in the late 1980s. Wexford also has a famous Mussel Festival and hosts a local Cockle Festival at Duncannon. One of Dublin's famous seafood restaurants Restaurant na Mara originated from a seafood festival in Dun Laoghaire in 1971. The King Sitric restaurant was also opened in 1971 in Howth and has specialized in seafood ever since. Two other Dublin seafood restaurants, the Lord Edward and the Lobster Pot have not only preserved the classical fish dishes like sole bonne femme, but are also the last bastions of the classical table arts in Dublin.

Much of today's consumption of fish is linked with fish and chip shops. Leo Burdock's opened in 1911, Eduardo Di Mascio, a carpenter from Valveri, Italy, arrived

at the height of the Civil War in 1922 and opened his first fish and chip shop in Dublin's Marlborough Street. Also in 1922, Ivan Beshoff, a mutineer from the famous Russian battleship Potemkin, opened his first fish and chip shop in Usher's Island.[40] There are regional differences in the culinary terminology associated with fish. Lennox's is the name synonymous with chip shops in Cork City, where fish and chips are sometimes known as 'a bag of blocks and a swimmer'. In Dublin the vernacular describes fish and chips as a 'One and One', 'Blossom' is the term for black Pollock, and 'Rock Salmon' is dogfish fried in batter. Dogfish has recently been re-branded as 'cape shark'. Ray and particularly long ray is very popular in Dublin, so much so

Fresh & pickled Herrings

that Ringsend, a south city suburb, is commonly known as 'Raytown'. The term 'pissy ray' refers to the strong ammonia smell that can emanate from these cartilaginous fish if they are not absolutely fresh. One of Dublin's most famous chippers is Leo Burdock's and as a sign of the times we live in, they now have hoki fish from New Zealand on the menu as an alternative to the endangered cod.

Changing Consumption Patterns

Alan Davidson[41] attributes the preservation of Ireland from the invasion of foreign dishes and restaurants to a streak of conservatism running through the Irish character. Today's Ireland is the destination of not only New Zealand's hoki fish but many of her young population. Ireland has recently become a truly multi-cultural country and the new ethnic mix is creating demands for food provision to reflect increasingly pluralist cultural values. The consumption of fish has become fashionable particularly due to the associated nutritional benefits. Fish was once a cheap source of food, but many species now are equally or more expensive than prime cuts of meat.

Particular species of fish have gone through cycles of being in vogue at specific times in history. The eel is amongst the oldest of Ireland's traditional foodstuffs yet the consumption of eels declined steadily in the post famine (1850s onwards) period. Today eels are mostly exported, and those that are consumed are mostly in smoked form as part of seafood platters. Monkfish, although popular today, was once used to bait lobster pots. I remember P.J. Dunne, a lecturer of mine at Catering College, recalling how he, as larder chef in Jammet's restaurant, coped with shortages during the 'Emergency' (WW2), and how he became an alchemist, transforming monkfish, not a popular fish at the time, into collops of lobster, scallops and scampi. One satisfied customer summed up the fabulous fare in Jammet's during the years of the Second World War as 'the finest French cooking between the fall of France and the Liberation of Paris'.[42] Scallops were clearly common enough in the 1930s according to the story of a County Limerick housewife who was apologizing profusely to a German engineer working on the Ard na Crusha power station that all she had for his dinner were scallops! Whelks are fished mainly in Counties Wicklow and Wexford and are seldom sold in Ireland but exported mostly to the lucrative Asian market. A speciality of Connemara and the Aran Islands is *Ballach Buí*, a salted ballan wrasse, but its popularity has been waning over the last two decades. Tuna fish, once only known in its tinned variety, is now on restaurant menus as carpaccio, ceviche or char-grilled. Irish fishermen are now hunting deep-water species, which are not affected by quotas. They include grenadier, orange roughey, rabbit fish, mora-mora (deepwater cod) and red fish. This raises ethical issues since some of these fish take up to 70 years to mature and replenish. Wild Irish salmon to this day is highly prized although stocks are rapidly being depleted. Farmed salmon is now so widely available that it has become one of the cheapest fish on sale today.

The Portuguese are Europe's highest consumers of fish averaging 58.5 kg per capita in 1999 compared with Ireland's 20.1 kg. Ireland, incidentally, was slightly ahead of England at 20 kg, Germany at 15.6 kg, and the Netherlands at 14.5kg.[43] On the other hand, the Irish consumed a total of 96.8 kg of meat per capita in the year 2000, most of which was pig meat (38 kg) and poultry (32.4 kg) respectively. Over half of all seafood eaten in Ireland is consumed in food service outlets rather than in domestic settings. This contrasts with European countries like France, Italy, Spain and Greece where 75% of all seafood is consumed in the home.[44]

Analysis

Ireland's geographical location, on the edge of the continental shelf, surrounded by the Atlantic Ocean and Irish Sea, favours us with a vast array of seafood. The island's numerous lakes, rivers and streams and canals are an angler's paradise. Yet in spite of this Ireland lags behind most of Europe in terms of seafood consumption. Irish coastal waters appear to be sufficiently favoured by fish to make it worthwhile for foreign fishermen to come here. J.J. Lee argues that if Irish fishermen cannot compete with them, it is not because the fish have chosen to boycott them.[45] This belies the real politic; there is no such thing today as Irish fish, only EU fish in Irish waters. Countries like the UK, France, Belgium and Holland had established a tradition of fishing near our coasts for years before the Irish fishing industry became properly organized, and on this basis received quotas for certain species which are multiples of those allocated to Irish fishermen.[46] Tim Pat Coogan recalls an interview he conducted in 1965 with Brian Lenihan, who was at the time the junior minister responsible for fisheries, about the governments plans to develop the fishing industry (Ireland having probably the richest fishing grounds in western Europe at the time). The answer took the form of two questions relating to the number of both farmers and fishermen in the country. The number of fishermen at that time (approx 8,000), according to Lenihan, 'wouldn't elect one Fianna Fáil TD on the first count in a five-seat constituency'.[47] In the political calculations of the day, the farmers' numbers, not the long-term potential of the fertile sea, was the prime concern. Fishing rights were bartered away to other EEC members in return for concessions to the powerful farm lobby.[48]

The total value of the Irish seafood industry in 2003 was €665 million, with nearly 60% of that coming from exports. Within the EU, France (€91 million) remains the premier market for Irish seafood followed by Spain (€58 million) and Great Britain (€54 million) and the most important markets outside the EU were Japan (€19 million) and South Korea (€14 million).[49] From a culinarians point of view the biggest disappointment concerning fish in Ireland is that the best of the Irish catch never sees the Irish table.

The lack of exploitation of the sea by the Irish, compared to their European neighbours, may be understood if one studies the geographic location and the nature of the coastline. In Ireland such was the abundance of the shore and inland waters that the early Irish had no reason or need to seek sustenance or resource from the deep

ocean. To sail out into the Atlantic was not something that would be undertaken lightly. The Atlantic was so dangerous that the great maritime expansion to the West did not take place until the 15th century. There are always exceptions. Ireland's Saint Brendan the navigator is purported to have reached America in the 6th century and, according to Mark Kurlansky,[50] the Basques were supplying a vast international market in cod by the year 1000, based on their fishing fleet's surreptitious voyages across the Atlantic to North America's fishing banks.

The abundance of other foodstuffs clearly had a bearing on Ireland's historically low level of seafood consumption when compared to some of her European neighbours. The key as to what was not consumed may lie in what was. Masons employed on Christ Church Cathedral in 1565 were fed 2lbs of salted meat, 2lbs of wheaten bread and eight pints of largely oaten ale daily. In 1577 the diet of an English soldier in Dublin on fish days was 8 oz butter or 1 lb of cheese, or eight herrings. The Franciscan community of Cork city in the 1760s and 1770s, whose per capita income would have been half the wages of an artisan in regular employment, consumed an average of 38 lbs meat, 10–20 lbs butter and an estimated 24 lbs fish per annum, in addition to bread and potatoes.[51] Although pigs were always popular in Ireland, the emergence of the potato resulted in increasing both human and pig populations. The Irish were the first Europeans to seriously consider the potato as a staple food. By 1663 it was widely accepted in Ireland as an important food plant and by 1770 it was known as the Irish Potato.[52] The Potato transformed Ireland from an under populated island of 1 million in the 1590s to 8.2 million in 1840, making it the most densely populated country in Europe.[53]

Conclusions

Modern Ireland has a vibrant fishing industry, although fishing rights conceded during early membership of the European Union leave our fishermen with restricted quotas. More than half of the landed catch is exported and much of the fish consumed today is farmed. Over half the fish consumed today is in foodservice outlets, as the Irish seem less confident than their European neighbours in handling fish in a domestic setting. BIM are actively campaigning to promote seafood consumption both domestically, by marketing fish as a convenience product for the cash rich/time poor generation, and also in the food service sector through schemes such as the 'seafood circle' and féile bia' programmes promoting the use of indigenous foods. We have seen how

Irish dietary patterns have changed over time and today, fish and fasting on Fridays is a distant memory among the Celtic Tiger's young cubs. Most inland counties would have rarely seen fresh fish and interestingly, smoked fish sales are greater even today in the midlands than in the coastal parts of Ireland.[54] Once considered *bia bocht* or poor man's food, fresh wild seafood is now a luxury whose market share within Irish food consumption is challenged by numerous cheaper alternatives. Irish society has been radically transformed over the last twenty years from a land of emigrants to one of rising immigration. The growing Asian community now keeps in business Dublin's famous Moore Street fishmongers, whose best customers used to be the denizens of 'Raytown'. Perhaps Alan Davidson's reflections were indeed prophetic.

Bibliography

B.I.M. (2000), *Realising the Market Potential for Irish Seafood, B.I.M's Marketing Strategy 2001-2006.* (Dublin, Bord Iascaigh Mhara).

B.I.M. (2004), *Fall-off in Seafood Exports but Investment at Record Levels* (B.I.M. Press Release), (Dublin, Bord Iascaigh Mhara, www.bim.ie).

Bennett, D. (1991), *Encyclopedia of Dublin* (Dublin, Gill and Macmillan).

Bowden, G. H. (1975), *British Gastronomy: The Rise of Great Restaurants* (London, Chatto and Windus).

Cahill, T (1995), *How the Irish Saved Civilisation* (London, Hodder and Stoughton).

Clarkson, L. A. and E. M. Crawford (2001), *Feast and Famine, Food and Nutrition in Ireland 1500-1900* (Oxford, Oxford University Press).

Coogan, T. P. (2003), *Ireland in the Twentieth Century* (London, Hutchinson).

Cooke, J. (2000), *The Rise and Fall of Ringsend Oyster Beds. A Maritime History of Ringsend* (Dublin, Sandymount Community Services: 59-61).

Corr, F. (2004), 'Conservation And Politics Spur Seafood Prices.' *Hotel & Catering Review* (February 2004): 31-33.

Cowan, C. and R. Sexton (1997), *Ireland's Traditional Foods : An Exploration of Irish Local & Typical Foods and Drinks* (Dublin, Teagasc, The National Food Centre).

Cullen, L. M. (1992), 'Comparative aspects of Irish diet, 1550-1850' in *European Food History: A Research Review,* H. J. Teuteberg (Leicester, Leicester University Press).

Davidson, A. (2003), *North Atlantic Seafood* (Totnes, Devon, Prospect Books).

de Courcy Ireland, J. (2003), *Maritime History. The Encyclopaedia of Ireland.* B. Lawlor (Dublin, Gill & Macmillan).

Doyle, R. (2003), 'Fresh fish 'n chips and no bones about it', *The Irish Times* (Dublin: Commercial Property 9-10).

Harbison, P. (1994), *Pre-Christian Ireland* (London, Thames and Hudson).

Irwin, F. (1937), *Irish Country Recipes* (Belfast, The Northern Whig Ltd).

Kurlansky, M. (1997), *Cod:A Biography of the Fish That Changed the World* (New York, Walker and Co).

Laffan, W., Ed. (2003), *The Cries of Dublin* (Dublin, Irish Georgian Society).

Lee, J. J. (1989), *Ireland 1912-1985: Politics & Society* (Cambridge, Cambridge University Press).

Mac Con Iomaire, M. (2003), 'The Pig in Irish Cuisine past and present', *The Fat of the Land: Proceedings of the Oxford Symposium on Food and Cookery 2002,* H. Walker (Bristol, Footwork).

Mac Con Iomaire, M. (2004), *Dublin Restaurants 1922-2002: an oral history,* School of Culinary Arts and Food Technology (Dublin, Dublin Institute of Technology, Unpublished Progress Report for Doctoral Thesis).

Mannix, I. (2004), *Seafood in Irish Cuisine and Culture, Past, Present and Future,* School of Culinary Arts and Food Technology (Dublin, Dublin Institute of Technology, Unpublished undergraduate thesis).

Mc Gowan, J. (2001), *Echoes of a Savage Land* (Dublin, Mercier Press).

Mc Grath, M., Ed. (1989), *Cinnlae Amhlaoibh Uí Shúilleabháin ; The Diary of Humphrey O' Sullivan,* Parts 1-4 (London).

O' Kelly, M. (1995), *Early Ireland – An Intoduction to Irish Prehistory* (Cambridge, Cambridge University Press).

O' Sullivan, A. (2001), *Foragers, Farmers and Fishers – An intertidal archaelogical survey of the Shannon Estuary* (Dublin, Royal Irish Academy).

Ó Tuama, S. and T. Kinsella, Eds. (1981), *An Duanaire: An Irish Anthology: 1600-1900: Poems of the Dispossessed* (Philadelphia, University of Pennsylvania Press).

Phillips, R. and M. Rix (1995), *The Potato in Irish History* (Dublin, Macmillan Press).

Ryan, J. (1987), 'There'll never be another Jammet's', *The Irish Times,* Dublin: Weekend 3, 11 April 1987.

Thom's-Directory (1901), *Thom's Official Directory of the United Kingdom of Great Britain and Ireland 1901,* pp. 1958 (Dublin, Alex Thom & Co. Limited).

Thom's-Directory (1919), *Thom's Official Directory of the United Kingdom of Great Britain and Ireland 1919* (Dublin, Alex Thom & Co. Limited).

Uí Chomáin, M. (2004), *Oyster Cuisine* (Dublin, A&A Farmer).

Wilkens, N. P. (2004), *Alive Alive O : The Shellfish and Shellfisheries of Ireland* (Kinvara Co. Galway, Tir Eolas).

Notes

1. Alan Davidson (2003), p. 468.
2. Nöel P. Wilkens (2004), p. 8.
3. M. O Kelly (1995), p. 27.
4. P. Harbison (1994), p. 22.
5. Wilkens (2004) p. 8.
6. A. O' Sullivan (2001), p. 143.
7. Thomas Cahill (1995).
8. J. Mc Gowan (2001), p. 94.
9. John de Courcy Ireland (2003) p. 694-695.
10. Cathal Cowan and Regina Sexton (1997), p. 54.
11. L.A. Clarkson and E.M. Crawford (2001), p. 45.
12. Jim Cooke (2000), p. 61.
13. William Laffan (2003).
14. Cooke (2000), p. 60; Laffan (2003), p. 62; J. Rutty (1772), Vol.1, pp. 376-7.
15. Cathal Cowan and Regina Sexton (1997),p. 47.
16. William Laffan (2003), p. 94.
17. D. Bennett, (1991) p. 61.
18. extracts from Brabazon Walloh, *The Deep Sea and Coast Fisheries of Ireland* (1848) quoted in A Maritime History of Ringsend, p. 83.
19. Wilkens (2004), p. 16.
20. Wilkens (2001), p. 16.
21. S. Ó Tuama and T. Kinsella (1981).
22. Florence Irwin (1937).

23. Alex Thom (1919), p. 696.
24. de Courcy Ireland (2003) p. 694-695.
25. A. Ó Brolacháin (1932), p. 129.
26. ibid, p. 128.
27. Davidson (2003), p. 468.
28. Wilkens (2004), p. 139.
29. J.J. Lee (1989), p. 635.
30. Wilkens (2004), p. 138.
31. Ibid, p. 100.
32. G.H. Bowden (1975), p. 19.
33. Alex Thom (1901), p. 1958; M. Mac Con Iomaire (2004), p. 39.
34. Wilkens (2004), p. 102.
35. M. Uí Chomáin (2004),
36. Davidson (2003), p. 468.
37. M. Mc Grath (1989).
38. Thom (1919), p. 696.
39. Interviewed by the author at his home in Wicklow on 28 April 2004.
40. R. Doyle (2003), p. 9-10.
41. Davidson (2003), p. 468.
42. John Ryan (1987), p. 3 weekend section.
43. Bord Iascaigh Mhara (2000) p. 24.
44. Ian Mannix (2004), p. 63.
45. Lee (1989), p. 523.
46. Frank Corr (2004), pp. 31-33.
47. Tim Pat Coogan (2003), pp. 455-456.
48. Ibid, p. 456.
49. B.I.M. (2004), www.bim.ie.
50. Mark Kurlansky (1997),p. 22.
51. L.M. Cullen (1992), p. 50.
52. Máirtín Mac Con Iomaire (2003), p. 209.
53. R. Phillips and M. Rix (1995).
54. Mannix (2004), p. 10.

Acknowledgement
The drawings reproduced on pages 224, 225 and 227 were made in 1760 by the artist Hugh Douglas Hamilton and have been published in *The Cries of Dublin* edited by William Laffan (The Irish Georgian Society, 2003). The originals are in a private collection.

Contemporary Novelists on GM Foods and Industrial Farming

Kathy Mathys

In *Frankenstein* (1818) Mary Shelley speculates about the possibilities and hazards of modern technology. Doctor Victor Frankenstein, the creator of the novel's doomed monster, expresses his wish to 'pioneer a new way, explore unknown powers and unfold to the world the deepest mysteries of creation.' His ambitions are not very different from the ones that drive today's scientists, working on genetically modified organisms (GMOs). If we are to believe newspaper headlines, GMOs or transgenic foods as they are also called, are nothing less than 'Frankenstein foods' or 'mutant grub'. This paper discusses the way in which novelists reflect on the latest developments in industrial agriculture and biotechnology. Although, at first sight, this may seem far removed from the 'Wild Food' theme of this symposium, the debate on GMOs entails issues as different as the loss of biodiversity and the contamination of wild plant species. To appease anxious customers, some companies even claim that the development of GMOs is just the next logical step in man's evolution from hunter-gatherers to rational farmers.

The blight of monocultures

American writer Barbara Kingsolver was trained as a biologist before she started writing novels, some of which deal with environmental issues, *Animal Dreams* (1990) and *Prodigal Summer* (2000), for instance. In her essay 'A Fist in the Eye of God', from the collection *Small Wonder* (2002), she emphasizes how different genetic engineering is from traditional plant growing techniques:

> I've heard … people comfort themselves on the issue of genetic engineering by recalling that humans have been pushing genes around for centuries, through selective breeding of livestock and crops. I even heard one howler of a quote that began, 'Ever since Mendel spliced those first genes…'

Kingsolver refers to the Austrian monk Gregor Mendel (1822–84), who was crossing and backcrossing different pea types in his monastery garden. As Kingsolver rightly remarks, 'he simply watched peas to learn how their natural system of genetic recombination worked'. Bioengineers, on the other hand, select a gene for one specific characteristic and they insert it into a plant of a different species. Kingsolver believes that the American school-system is to blame for people's ignorance of science in general and food safety in particular. Some American states have even banned the teaching of evolution from their curriculum because it does not quite match the Bible's version of creation. A catastrophe, according to Kingsolver, because Darwin's theory is at the root of everything. Darwin understood how biodiversity, 'in domestic populations as well as wild ones, is nature's sole insurance policy'. If a sudden climatic change destroys a crop, there will always be another variant to fall back on. Genetic engineers, however, work with a limited number of varieties, which give large yields. Their tendency towards monocultures might turn out baleful in the long run. As a scientist, Kingsolver is fascinated by bioengineering, but as an organic gardener she is very apprehensive about its possibilities. Life-science companies tend to simplify the way genetic engineering works, as if the insertion of one particular gene in a new organism invariably leads to one particular result. As the publication of the Human Genome Project in 2001 illustrated, this is not quite the case:

> Instead of the 100,000 or more genes that had been expected … we have only about 30,000 – about the same number as a mustard plant. This evidence undermined … the assumption of a clear-cut chain of processes leading from a single gene to the appearance of the trait it controls. Instead, the mechanism of gene expression appears vastly more complicated than had been assumed since Watson and Crick discovered the structure of DNA in 1953.

The idea that genetic engineering involves a certain gamble is also expressed by one of the characters in Ruth Ozeki's novel *All Over Creation* (2003). Geek, member of the environmental activists the Seeds of Resistance, claims that

> [genetic engineers are trying to] force alien words into the plant's poem, but we've got a problem. We barely know the root language. Genetic grammar's a mystery and our engineers are just one click up the evolutionary ladder from a roomful of monkeys, typing random sonnets on a bank of typewriters.

American author Ruth Ozeki's previous novel *My Year of Meat* (1998) dealt with the workings of today's beef industry. *All over Creation* is set in Idaho, home of the Russet Burbank potato. The novel's hero is retired farmer Lloyd Fuller, who has grown the Burbanks all his life. Lloyd and his Japanese wife Momoko still operate Fuller Seeds, a small business which specializes in European heirloom varieties and oriental seeds. In his business newsletters Lloyd rages about the scheming and manoeuvring of agribusiness and about the dangers of genetic engineering. Lloyd is approached by the Seeds of Resistance, who think he is 'an icon! Totally salt of the earth'. Lloyd and his new activist friends plan to organize a teach-in about worm composting and gene splicing. Meanwhile Lloyd's neighbour Will Quinn has decided to plant Nulife Potatoes, a variety which has been genetically engineered with a natural pesticide.

NuLife's manufacturer, Cynaco, promises that the beetles feasting on the potato leaves will die instantly. To complicate matters even further, Lloyd and Momoko's long-lost daughter Yummy returns to the family fold with her three kids. Yummy does not know that her latest lover, Elliot Rhodes, works as a spin-doctor for Cynaco. Ozeki swipes at this corporate public relations man, who will stop at nothing to improve Cynaco's public image:

> He[Rhodes]'d been pressing Cynaco to support InterTribal Agricultural Councils. Maybe he could even get a Shoshone spokesperson to endorse the NuLife – fewer pesticides mean clean water for our people, that sort of thing. Wisdom. Heritage. Indians always made for positive imaging.

The author does not attempt to hide the fact that her fictional company Cynaco refers to real-life biotech giant Monsanto. The NuLife Potatoes have the same attributes as Monsanto's NewLeaf Potatoes. Like Monsanto, Cynaco used to be a chemical plant, which reinvented invented itself as a life-science company after it had produced all the pesticides and herbicides it possibly could. Also like its real-life counterpart, Cynaco developed Agent Orange, the herbicide that was sprayed in Vietnam to destroy the foliage and thus expose the enemy. Will wants to give the NuLifes a try but his decision is a half-hearted one:

> In Vietnam, the government said spray and we sprayed. Never gave it another thought. Now I got this numbness in my arms that the doc says may be Agent Orange, only he can't tell for sure because of the exposure factor on the farm. It bugs me. Cynaco made Agent Orange for the army. They made GroundUp and now the NuLifes, too.

Lloyd shows some understanding towards his neighbour, who operates on tight margins. He realizes that, with the prices deflated, it is hard to make a profit. Yet, as an Irishman, Will should know how monocultures can amount to disaster. Between 1845 and 1848 Ireland was struck by four consecutive potato crop failures. For the Irish the potato was the only staple food at the time; the great potato famine cut Ireland's population by over 40 per cent.

Ozeki draws a vivid portrait of the Idaho farmers' fatalism, the workings of agribusiness and the protests of ecological activists. At the heart of her novel lies a fervent plea for biodiversity. Fuller Seeds is a colourful business, offering varieties such as the Chinese Bitter Lemon and the Red Silk Cotton Tree. To those who speculate that non-native plants will harm inland varieties, Lloyd replies that none of today's food crops in the U.S. were native to the continent in the first place. With her rich cast of characters, Ozeki equally seems to subscribe to her creed of biodiversity and multiculturalism. As a child Yummy felt out of place in Idaho because she was like 'a random fruit in a field of genetically identical potatoes.' Returning to her native country as a grown-up half-Japanese, Yummy brings along three kids from three different fathers. Like the Seeds of Resistance, Yummy and her children provide potato-country Idaho with an exotic touch. In her acknowledgements, Ozeki expresses her indebtedness to Michael Pollan, writer of *The Botany of Desire – A Plant's-eye View of the World* (2001), a blend of botanical history and memoir. Central to Pollan's book is the idea that in the course of history human beings and domesticated plants have formed a reciprocal relationship from which both parties have largely benefited. Genetic engineering has changed this delicate balance:

> While the other plants coevolved in a kind of conversational give-and-take with people, the NewLeaf potato has really only taken, only listened. It may or may not profit from the gift of its new genes; we can't yet say.

Wake Up (2002) by the English writer Tim Pears also features potatoes in a leading role, but it is set in the West Midlands. The novel's narrator John Staples has turned his father's small fruit and vegetable stall into a corporate business, called Sputnik. He has rationalized the production process and has done away with all vegetables but potatoes. John believes that the Age of Enlightenment has officially come to an end and that everybody should just grab as much money as they can. He finds himself only hindered by 'public opinion, a cautious, slow-moving animal, to be dragged along in the wake of brave pioneers'. John has lively discussions about his life ethics with his wife Lily, who has an organic garden, cooks ethnic meals and distrusts big corporations. Despite his obvious cynicism, John is plagued by sleeplessness and hypochondria, both of which are the result of his inner unease. It so happens that John has recently ventured into the business of edible plant vaccines. Sputnik has joined forces with AlphaGen, a pharmaceutical company which is trying to grow vaccines in plants by genetically engineering them. During a secret trial in the Venezuelan jungle with adult volunteers, two people die after having eaten transgenic potatoes into which Norwalk Virus-copy proteins had been inserted. The Norwalk virus causes severe diarrhoea and is an important cause of infant mortality. AlphaGen and Sputnik are hoping to grow the vaccine in bananas, a cheap staple food in many developing countries. Although the death of two volunteers upsets him, John still has high hopes for the future:

237

> At the moment you take your child to the clinic for a vaccine for measles, mumps, rubella, the nice cruel nurse administers a jab in your little one's thigh, making him or her cry, leaving a lump under the skin. The defilement. No longer. Have a spoonful of mashed potato. Here, child, eat a chip.

John intends to cover up the deaths of what he calls 'two aboriginal villagers who were possibly ill already'. In the finale of this satirical novel, John has to pay for his irresponsible behaviour. Lily organizes a big garden party but one guest after the other turns severely ill. It turns out that they have all tried the strawberries, which were not organic as Lily had requested. Because the supplier had no organic produce left, John had tried to pass on a non-organic variety for the real thing. Once people start vomiting in his backyard, he realizes that 'arsenic, as an illegal preservative, is still sprayed, in some parts of the world by unscrupulous bandit growers.'

From eco-disaster to bio-terrorism
Anthony J. Trewavas, professor at the Institute of Cell and Molecular Biology at the University of Edinburgh, is an outspoken proponent of transgenic foods. According to Trewavas, organic farming is not an option on a global scale. Ploughing up more forests to feed an exploding world population might lead to ecological mayhem:

> Global warming is the problem that requires the UK to develop GM technology. … Many think global warming will simply lead to a wetter climate and be benign. I do not. Excess rainfall in northern seas has been predicted to halt the Gulf Stream. … Even if the climate is only wetter and warmer new crop pests and rampant disease will be the consequence. GM technology can enable new crops to be constructed in months and to be in the fields within a few years. … In 535 AD a volcano near the present Krakatoa exploded with the force of 200 million Hiroshima A bombs. The dense cloud of dust so reduced the intensity of the sun that for at least two years thereafter, summer turned to winter …. Only those with agricultural technology sufficiently advanced would have a chance at survival. Colliding asteroids are another problem that requires us to be forward-looking, accepting that technological advance may be the only buffer between us and annihilation.

Trewavas' gloomy observations sound like the perfect scenario to a Hollywood disaster movie. With scientists speculating about jumping genes and ecological contamination, it is hardly surprising that thriller writers have turned to the muddy waters of biotechnology. The eco-thriller *Genesis II* (2001) by English writer Paul Adam is set in and around Cambridge. Adam combines a story line about a bird flu epidemic with one about hazardous GM potatoes.

Organic farmer Jeff Harrison and his daughter Sandy get infected by a violent flu virus, which virologist Karl Housman has never encountered before. As more victims find their way to the hospital, Housman starts to suspect that somehow they have caught the virus from pigs or hens. The novel's hypothetical scenario might be discarded as unsound by scientists, but as Housman remarks: 'If you play around with genes, theory goes out of the window and anything is possible.' In Adam's disaster scenario, a cauliflower mosaic virus used to genetically engineer potatoes has joined forces with a flu virus to form a new lethal strain. The human victims, all of whom live on or near farms, catch the deadly virus from pigs, which in turn caught it from hens. Near the end of the novel Housman discovers the dead hens had been stung by bees, notable collectors of pollen from potato flowers. Somehow the cauliflower mosaic virus, used to genetically engineer potatoes, had inserted itself into the potatoes' genetic make-up. When the bees collect the dangerous pollen and sting a hen, they pass on the cauliflower virus, which re-assorts with an avian flu virus to create a new hybrid. After having discovered this, Housman begins to fear that the virus will somehow find a way to pass from human to human, which ultimately ensues.

Adam's novel gives flesh to two issues central to the GMO debate: the dangers of 'vectors' and the risk of environmental contamination by GMOs. When a gene is transferred to a new organism, it is part of a package of genes, called a vector. This vector includes DNA promoters which control where and when the new gene is switched on, stop signals which switch the new gene off, and marker genes which show the scientist whether or not the package has been transmitted. One of the most efficient DNA promoters is the cauliflower mosaic virus, which has been repeatedly under attack because of its alleged instability. The tragic fate of the novel's organic farmer shows the consequences of gene flow from GMOs to non-engineered varieties. Although bioengineers tend to minimize the ecological risks of biotechnical agriculture, the pollen of GMOs is likely to contaminate wild or organic plant varieties. At the end of the novel the reader learns that a biotech company has been secretly growing transgenic crops, in agreement with the English government. Adams cleverly describes the revolving-door relationship between the Ministry of Agriculture and the agrochemical industries. In *Genesis II*, the government acts on behalf of industry, rather than protecting the health of the population. With BSE and foot-and-mouth disease still fresh on his mind, Housman has, perhaps understandably, little confidence in the government's policies.

In *Genesis II*, the biotech company and the government did not intend for the epidemic to break out. American writer Peter Clement's *Mutant* (2001) deals with a deliberate act of bio-terrorism. In *Safe Food: Bacteria, Biotechnology and Bio-terrorism* (2003), author Marion Nestle argues that the centralization of the food supply leaves our water and food vulnerable to 'malevolent tampering'. Dr. Donald Henderson, an expert on infectious diseases, smallpox eradication and bio-terrorism, believes that biological weapons are to be greatly feared. He is particularly concerned about the role biotechnology might play in the development of biological weapons:

At least 10 countries are now engaged in developing and producing biological weapons. What with the growing power of biotechnology, one has to anticipate that this technology, like all others before it, will eventually be misused.

This is exactly what happens in *Mutant*. Steve Patton, CEO of environmental

239

group Blue Planet Society, wants to expose the dangers of bioengineering through an act of terrorism. He calls in a group of Afghan terrorists to execute his gruesome plan. Patton's real concern is of course not so much the protection of the environment, but the increase of his own political power. After his orchestrated eco-disaster, the world would hang on to every single word he said, because the Blue Planet Society had been warning them all along. Kathleen Sullivan, a famous geneticist in the book, worries about the dangers of naked DNA vectors. Conventional wisdom in the industry holds that DNA vectors, used to insert an alien gene into a new organism, cannot escape into the environment after fulfilling their part. It outrages Sullivan that no one is running tests to assess the possible dangers of these vectors. Although Sullivan is very concerned, she could never have anticipated the horrible scenario that Patton has in mind. He intends to release naked vectors with Ebola virus into the American heartland. Flying by helicopter over the targeted corn fields, a technician explains the process:

> The naked vectors carrying the viral genes, delivered in a spray of lipid particles to keep them intact, will soon penetrate the tiny holes that the previous bombardment had produced in the cell walls of the corn seedlings. … By morning fragments of the vectors and their special cargo will be inside the nuclei of cells in the plant, ready to enter their host's genetic machinery. Here they will be read, copied and passed on to newly formed cells. … it will become feed not just to farm animals, but to scavengers as well – rodents, birds, even insects. We're betting that in at least one of these creatures our passenger will find what it needs to survive, establishing itself in an American host where it will replicate – just as it once found a living haven in Africa.

The second part of Patton's plan involves the spraying of liquid DNA vectors with Ebola virus onto the spectators of the 4th of July fireworks in New York. Eerily enough, *Mutant* was published prior to the terrorist attacks of 11 September 2001 (first edition, July 2001). According to Marion Nestle, the anonymous letters with anthrax spores, sent to civic and media leaders in the aftermath of 9/11, have altered the meaning of the notion 'food safety', which now also refers to the protection of the food supply against terrorists. Although the biotechnological applications in *Mutant* could only be delivered by high-tech facilities, not all biological weapons are as difficult to develop. Because of the vast number of channels available for supplying them, they are hard to track down. In 2002, the Bush administration authorized $1.1 billion for bio-terrorism control. Nestle worries that the government's scaremongering will only divert the public from the real issues at stake. She champions the setting-up of a single food agency, because at the moment nearly four-dozen federal agencies protect the U.S. against possible acts of bio-terrorism. Furthermore, she believes that food safety is not so much a military issue, but a public health one:

The focus on 'homeland security' … diverted attention and resources away from basic public health needs. International actions also focused on matters other than public health, even when providing food aid. No responses to the crisis – domestic or international – were addressing 'root causes' – the underlying social, cultural, economic, or environmental factors that might encourage terrorist activities. From the perspective of public health, bio-terrorism may never entirely disappear, but it seems less likely to be used as a political weapon by people who have access to education, health care, and food, and who trust their government to help improve their lot in life.

ChickieNobs Nubbins at the Watson-Crick Institute

Genesis II and *Mutant* deal with impending catastrophes that can be prevented at the very last instant. *Oryx and Crake* (2003) by Canadian writer Margaret Atwood, however, opens three months after an apocalypse has wiped nearly all of humanity off the face of the earth. Except for the novel's narrator, Jimmy, and the Crakers, cloned human beings created by Jimmy's best friend Crake, the world seems deserted. Atwood describes the Crakers as 'each one naked, each one perfect, each one a different skin colour – chocolate, rose, tea, butter, cream, honey – but each with green eyes. Crake's aesthetic.' Sitting on the beach watching the Crakers play, Jimmy starts reflecting on how things managed to go so horribly wrong. Like his friend Crake, Jimmy grew up in the Compounds, the tightly secured units where biotechnological companies were housed. Outside the Compounds, there was only chaos, places Jimmy only knew from television:

241

> [There were] endless billboards and neon signs and stretches of buildings, tall and short; endless dingy-looking streets, countless vehicles of all kinds, some of them with clouds of smoke coming out the back; thousands of people, hurrying, cheering, rioting.

For OrganInc Farms, Jimmy's father worked on the pigoon project, the goal of which was to grow human-tissue organs in a transgenic pig host. A rapid-maturity gene made the organs grow faster, with some animals even growing five or six kidneys at the same time. The pigoons were just one example of the bioengineering projects running at the time. Geneticists were having a field day, creating rakunks, an odour-free animal derived from raccoons and skunks, and wolvogs, a vicious blend of wolf and dog. By the time Jimmy went to high school, his father had moved on to HelthWyzer, where they used animals to develop skin-related biotechnologies. HelthWyzer did not merely clone animals, it also provided its own schools and even its own food, as the following description of life at HelthWyzer High illustrates:

> … fruit-flavoured punch, with or without alcohol, and Happicuppa coffee,

and little plastic tubs of SoYummie Ice Cream, a HelthWyzer Own Brand, in chocolate soy, mango soy, and roasted-dandelion green-tea soy.

After high school, Crake went to the Watson-Crick Institute, where all geneticists and future bioengineers got educated. On a visit to the institute Jimmy felt repulsed by one of the projects, aimed at the cloning of animals for fast food industry meat.

'Those are chickens,' said Crake. 'Chicken parts. Just a breast, on this one. They've got ones that specialize in drumsticks too, twelve to a growth unit.'
'But there aren't any heads,' said Jimmy. ...
'That's the head in the middle,' said the woman. 'There's a mouth open-ing at the top, they dump the nutrients in there. No eyes or beak or anything, they don't need those.'
'This is horrible,' said Jimmy. The thing was a nightmare. It was like an animal-protein tuber....
'No need for added growth hormones,' said the woman, 'the high growth rate's built in. You get chicken breasts in two weeks – that's a three-week improvement on the most efficient low-light, high-density chicken farming operation so far devised. And the animal-welfare freaks won't be able to say a word, because this thing feels no pain.'

242

A few months later the ChickieNobs Nubbins were commercialized and Atwood describes them as of a 'bland, tofulike consistency'. Crake preferred the kanga-lamb, 'a new Australian splice that combined the placid character and high-protein yield of sheep with the kangaroo's resistance to disease and absence of methane-producing, ozone-destroying flatulence'.

Underneath Atwood's playful and vividly rendered universe hides a clear warning for the future. According to Atwood, who has repeatedly declared that she is not anti-science, *Oryx and Crake* is speculative fiction:

It invents nothing we haven't already invented or started to invent. Every novel begins with a what-if? and then sets forth its axioms. The what-if? of *Oryx and Crake* is simply, What if we continue down the road we're already on? How slippery is the slope?

Apart from criticizing scientists playing God, Atwood warns us about the symbio-sis between the industry and universities. One of the most famous critics of the food industry is the Indian physicist and philosopher of science, Vandana Shiva:

In any case, in the corporate-controlled food system, the same company may perform the research, sell the seeds, and provide the data about its products. Thus, the patient, diagnostician, and physician are rolled into one, and there is no objective basis of assessment of yield performance or ecological impact.

Biotechnological research is so expensive that few scientists can conduct independent research. Furthermore, biotech companies have patents on the products they develop, which hampers independent research even more. Biotech companies do not limit themselves to patenting their own inventions, they also send bio-prospectors to tropical forests to collect genetic material. Developing nations fear that biotech companies might eventually be able to engineer crops that grow in northern climates to produce tropical foods:

> Coffee was another developing world commodity under siege, at least in theory. The center of origin of coffee is the highland region of Ethiopia, but in North America, caffeine genes have been inserted into soybeans. As the Harvard evolutionary biologist Richard Lewontin asked provocatively, 'Why not Nescafé from Minnesota?'

In *Oryx and Crake* this theoretical risk has turned into a reality. The launch of a new type of the Happicuppa bean, developed by HelthWyzer, leads to the onset of the gen-mod coffee wars. Until then individual coffee beans on each bush had ripened at different times, but the Happicuppa coffee bush was designed so that its beans would turn ripe at the same time. The beans could then be harvested with machines, driving small growers into bankruptcy.

World on Fire (2002) by American writer Michael Brownstein is not a novel, but it handles issues that are similar to the ones in Atwood's novel. It is a mixture of treatise, poem and political pamphlet about the effects of globalization. The writer/narrator testifies about a post-apocalyptic society, in which food has become scarce, trees are burning, buildings are collapsing and the air is too thick to breathe in. Although Brownstein does not give any details as to the how and why of his Armageddon, we know that the year 2012 has come and gone. The image of colonization is a recurring one in *World on Fire*. First the West colonized foreign nations, then it started colonizing all human life forms:

> Terra nullis – colonization's doctrine that the land is empty, underutilized by the savages who inhabit it.
> Giving us the excuse to move in and take over.
> As now we're taking over bodies, cells, genes.
> Bio-colonialism without accountability or liability.
> Biological samples collected and stored in gene banks without consent.

Despite the pessimism of *World on Fire*, Brownstein does not leave the reader totally disheartened. He ends by stimulating us to make a small change to our lives:

> Teach your children biodiversity.
> End your reliance on pharmaceuticals.

Stop filling your face with dead food.
Reject the cattle culture and its myriad depredations.

Conclusion

The latest developments in the food industry and in the realm of biotechnology have inspired some of today's fictional authors. As Margaret Atwood has rightly remarked, science and literature sometimes deal with similar questions, albeit in a very different manner. Novelists are not expected to produce real science, so they have the freedom to speculate and to prophesy. Whether in the shape of a dystopian novel like *Oryx and Crake* or in the form of a dark satire like *Wake Up*, writers have been asking prominent questions about the ethical, political, ecological and health issues brought about by bioengineering. Although novels present fictional worlds, the authors discussed in this paper, have laced their writing with important technical, scientific and ethical arguments.

Bibliography

Adam, Paul, *Genesis II* (London: Time Warner Books, 2001).

Aris, Ben, 'Secret German GM Crop Trials Revealed', *Guardian*, 7 May 2004 <http://www.guardian.co.uk/gmdebate/Story/0,2763,1211329,00.html> [Accessed 25 June 2004].

Atwood, Margaret, *Oryx and Crake* (London: Virago Press, 2004).

Brownstein, Michael, *World on Fire* (New York: Open City Books, 2002).

Clement, Peter, *Mutant* (New York: Ballantine Books, 2001).

Conlogue, William, *Working the Garden: American Writers and the Industrialization of Agriculture* (Chapel Hill: The University of North Carolina Press, 2001).

Goldenberg, Suzanne, 'Cloned Meat a Step nearer US Menus', *Guardian*, 1 November 2003 <http://www.guardian.co.uk/gmdebate/Story/0,2763,1075570,00.html> [Accessed 7 June 2004].

Griffiths, Sean and, Jennifer Wallace, eds, *Consuming Passions: Food in the Age of Anxiety* (Manchester: Mandolin, 1998).

Hubbell, Sue, *Shrinking the cat: genetic engineering before we knew about genes* (New York: Houghton Mifflin Company, 2001).

Kingsolver, Barbara, 'A Fist in the Eye of God', in *Small Wonder*, by Barbara Kingsolver (London: Faber and Faber Limited, 2003), pp. 93–108.

Klein, Naomi, *Fences and Windows* (London: Flamingo, 2002).

Lambrecht, Bill, *Dinner at the New Gene Café: how genetic engineering is changing what we eat, how we live, and the global politics of food* (New York: Thomas Dunne Books, 2001).

Meacher, Michael, 'GM Food is heading for your Fridge', *Guardian*, 25 June 2004 <http://www.guardian.co.uk/gmdebate/Story/0,2763,1247034,00.html> [Accessed 26 June 2004].

Myerson, George, *Donna Haraway and GM Foods* (Cambridge: Icon Books, 2000).

Nestle, Marion, *Food Politics: how the industry influences nutrition and health* (Berkeley: University of California Press, 2002).

Nestle, Marion, *Safe Food: Bacteria, Biotechnology and Bioterrorism* (Berkeley: University of California Press, 2003).

Ozeki, Ruth, *All Over Creation* (New York: Penguin Books, 2004).

Ozeki, Ruth, *My Year of Meat* (London: Pan Books, 1998).

Pence, Gregory, *Designer Food: Mutant Harvest or Breadbasket of the World?* (Lanham: Rowman & Littlefield Publishers, 2002a).

Pence, Gregory, ed, *The Ethics of Food: A Reader for the 21st Century* (Lanham: Rowman & Littlefield Publishers, 2002b).

Pears, Tim, *Wake Up* (London: Bloomsbury Publishing, 2003).

Pinstrup-Andersen, Per, *Seeds of Contention: World Hunger and the Global Controversy over GM Crops* (London: The Johns Hopkins University Press, 2000).

Pollan, Michael, *The Botany of Desire: A Plant's-eye View of the World* (London: Bloomsbury Publishing, 2002).

Pringle, Peter, Food, Inc.: *Mendel to Monsanto – The Promises and Perils of the Biotech Harvest* (New York: Simon & Schuster, 2003).

Proulx, Annie, *That Old Ace in the Hole* (London: Harper Perennial, 2002).

Shelley, Mary, *Frankenstein or, the Modern Prometheus* (London: Penguin Books, 1985).

Vandana Shiva, *Stolen Harvest: The Hijacking of the Global Food Supply* (Cambridge, Mass.: South End Press, 2000).

Some Thoughts on Wild Fruits

Robert Palter

The longest and most circumstantial – certainly the most passionate – account of wild fruits I know is by Henry David Thoreau (1817–62) in an unfinished manuscript now in the New York Public Library and first published in its entirety in 2000. Thoreau composed the manuscript during the years 1859–61 (more than a decade after his Walden period – Thoreau was living at the time with his parents and sister in a house in Concord, Massachusetts) but the work was based on field observations in the environs of Concord, going back for at least a decade. One section of the manuscript is a self-contained essay on wild apples, delivered as a lecture by Thoreau in 1861 and published posthumously in the *Atlantic Monthly Magazine* for November 1862; it has since been reprinted many times. As to the general character of the manuscript, I quote the editor of its recent publication, Bradley P. Dean of the Thoreau Institute in Lincoln, Massachusetts, who describes it as a 'sacramental vision of nature – a vision compelling in part because it grew out of an approach to the natural world at once scientific and mystical.'[1]

Thoreau does not bother to characterize 'wildness' at the beginning of his wild fruits manuscript; rather, he seems to take for granted the distinction between wild and cultivated, as when, in one of his opening paragraphs, he contrasts oranges in the marketplace and checkerberries in the pasture.[2] (Checkerberries, by the way, are the fruit of the wintergreen, a low herbaceous, evergreen plant common in Thoreau's time in eastern North America.[3]) But in the wild apples section of his manuscript he does at least refer to the discussion of wildness by two ancient writers: the Greek Theophrastus (4th century BCE) and the Roman Pliny the Elder (1st century CE). Pliny, Thoreau tells us, adopts the distinction of Theophrastus between trees which are 'altogether wild' (Pliny's term is *sylvestris*) and those which are 'more civilized' (Pliny's term is *urbanius*).[4] Unfortunately, Thoreau does not tell us the basis for the distinction in either author. Theophrastus' discussion is, in fact, as befits Aristotle's associate and successor, probing and subtle. 'As with animals which do not submit to domestication.' Theophrastus suggests, 'so a plant which does not submit to cultivation [*agrios*] may be called wild [*hemeros*] in its essential character.'[5] To the objection that every plant exists in both cultivated and wild forms and hence that the terms signify only which plants happen to have been cultivated and which have not, Theophrastus responds by drawing a distinction: it is true that any cultivated plant can revert to wildness by neglect, but not every wild plant, in his words, 'may be improved by attention'; hence, he concludes, 'we must make our distinction and call some things wild, others cultivated – the latter class corresponding to those animals which live with man and can be tamed.'[6]

Even today, however, with the accumulated experience of several thousand years of plant cultivation at our disposal, the distinction between wild and cultivated fruit may often be difficult to apply in practice. Consider the case of the so-called Kokee plum on the island of Kauai, in Hawaii. Here is how the American author, Kathryn Hulme (1900–81), begins her delightful little piece, 'Plum Crazy', in the periodical *Honolulu* for November 1969: 'Every summer, up in the cloudlands of Kokee State Park on Kauai, there comes an event for which the whole island waits – the opening of plum season when everyone can go into the woods and pick his quota of the red plums which grow wild in the mountains.'[7] The plum in question, known to horticulturists as the 'Methley', is of Japanese, as opposed to European or American, origin; the fruit is from 1½ to 2 inches in diameter and, when ripe, is dark red with sweet, red flesh. If we ask how this variety of plum reached Hawaii, the answer is that it was brought to the Big Island from Natal, South Africa, in the spring of 1926, in the form of a single tree. Four years later cuttings from the tree were sent to two other islands, Maui and Kauai. On the latter island, the cuttings failed to root and were tossed aside onto a rubbish heap. Discovered by a forester named A. J. MacDonald, the twenty cuttings were replanted and this time took root. Eventually, some 18,000 trees were planted throughout Kokee State Park. And now I want to quote again from Hulme's account:

> it is the crowd at large that gives the real character to the Kokee plum harvest: The huge family groups whose members span three or more generations, with every head counting for one daily quota of plums [ten pounds per person].... The singing and laughing echoing through the forests. The great clan picnics spread over the green tables of the Park's camping sites, international menus on display – Chinese, Japanese, Hawaiian, Portuguese, American and Filipino foods set forth on paper plates, with occasional box lunches from the big hotels to prove, thank heaven, that not all tourists sit around the hotel grounds thinking they are seeing Kauai.[8]

247

Are the Kokee plums, then, wild or cultivated? The best answer, I believe, is that the plums can be designated consistently as both because the distinction in question is culturally – not biologically – mediated. So, for those visiting the park to pick plums, the trees may well appear wild – indeed, the pickers would probably prefer to think of them as wild; while anyone who knows the horticultural history of the plum trees in the park will probably consider them cultivated. And, to return to Thoreau, in his wild apples essay he fully recognizes this relativity of the wild/cultivated distinction, when he writes:

> Nevertheless, our wild apple is wild only like myself, perchance, who belong

not to the aboriginal race here, but have strayed into the woods from the cultivated stock. Wilder still, as I have said, there grows elsewhere in this country a native and aboriginal Crab-Apple.... It is found from Western New York to Minnesota, and southward.[9]

Thoreau saw his first crab-apple tree exactly one year before his death, on a visit to Minnesota.

Let us turn now to Thoreau's claim for the inimitable educational values of picking wild fruit, especially for children but certainly not limited to children (the particular fruit he has in mind in this passage is huckleberries but his discussion clearly applies to any species of wild fruit):

> I well remember with what a sense of freedom and spirit of adventure I used to take my way across the fields with my pail...toward some distant hill or swamp, when dismissed for all day, and I would not now exchange such an expansion of all my being for all the learning in the world. Liberation and enlargement – such is the fruit which all culture aims to secure. I suddenly knew more about my books than if I had never ceased studying them. I found myself in a schoolroom where I could not fail to see and hear things worth seeing and hearing, where I could not help getting my lesson, for my lesson came to me. Such experience, often repeated, was the chief encouragement to go to the Academy and study a book at last.[10]

It is worth emphasizing that Thoreau is not proposing anything so radical as to replace book learning completely with the experience of nature in the wild; rather, Thoreau's pedagogical goal is to place book-learning in a proper perspective by, in Bradley Dean's words, 'unlocking the miraculous in the commonplace'.[11] Discovering the miraculous in the commonplace is no easy task and it is clear that, for Thoreau, the very process of overcoming the difficulties in any particular case is an essential part of what is discovered. This is beautifully illustrated by Thoreau's description of his 'going a-graping' on 20 September 1858. The site of Thoreau's foray is some miles below Concord on the Sudbury River; he has rowed down with a friend, probably the poet William Ellery Channing, one of his neighbours in Concord. Here is a portion of Thoreau's account:

> Sometimes I crawl under low and thick bowers where they have run over the alder only four or five feet high and see the grapes hanging from a hollow hemisphere of leaves over my head. At other times I see them dark-purple or black against the silvery underside of the leaves, high above my head where they have run over birches or maples, and either climb or pull them down to pluck them.

Methinks the true grape trellis or arbor is a wild apple tree, its top wholly covered with vine, like a tree caught in a net, as that near the old lime-kiln. Though quite low it is difficult to break off the large bunches without some dropping off, and if I am climbing to them, I am disappointed to see the ripest rattle off and strew the ground before I reach their clusters; or, while I am standing on tiptoe and endeavoring gently to break the tough peduncle of some particularly fair cluster, the petiole of a leaf gets entangled in the bunch, and I am compelled to strip them all off loosely. The ripest drop off at the slightest touch, and if they fall into the water they are lost, going to the bottom.

I love to bring some home if only to scent my chamber with them, for they are more admirable for their fragrance than their flavor. But it is impossible to get them home in a basket with all their rich bloom on them, which no less than the form of the clusters makes their beauty.

What is a whole binful that have been plucked to that solitary cluster left dangling inaccessible from some birch far away over the stream in the September air, with all its bloom and freshness? [12]

Several things are worth dwelling on in this passage. First, there is the sheer physical exhilaration involved in the finding and picking of not readily accessible grapes. Next, there is Thoreau's discovery of a striking connection between wild grape vines and his beloved wild apple trees. Then, there is Thoreau's near disdain for eating his wild grapes, whose scent is prized far above their taste (though Thoreau does also report that six years earlier, in September of 1852, he discovered 'a particularly sweet red grape',[13] which he succeeded in cultivating in his garden). Finally, Thoreau turns out to prefer, above all, those wild grapes which, being totally inaccessible, must be left in place with their 'bloom and freshness' intact. And this last preference of Thoreau's – which may at first seem merely private and self-regarding – is eventually extrapolated into a public and community-minded recommendation in the last pages of his manuscript: 'I think.' he writes, 'that each town should have a park, or rather a primitive forest, of five hundred or a thousand acres, either in one body or several, where a stick should never be cut for fuel, nor for the navy, nor to make wagons, but stand and decay for higher uses – a common possession forever, for instruction and recreation.'[14]

249

Thoreau's anxiety about the disappearance of wild spaces reflects, of course, what was happening all around him. Almost a century earlier, travelling across the Carolinas, Georgia, Florida, Alabama, and Louisiana, in the years 1773–76, the American naturalist William Bartram (1739–1823) had no such anxiety; his anxiety was rather about money: how to pay off the creditors from his failed mercantile career and how to find financial support for a new career as a naturalist. When Bartram's father died in 1777, his younger brother John inherited the family house and gardens outside Philadelphia, where Bartram was to live and work for the rest of his life. It was not until 1791 that Bartram succeeded in getting his account of his travels published in Philadelphia (with advance subscriptions from President George Washington, Vice-President John Adams, and Secretary of State Thomas Jefferson!). A London edition of the *Travels* came out a year later, with a second edition in 1794. Coleridge and Wordsworth owned copies of this second edition, extracts from which Coleridge copied into his journal.

My concern here is with the wild strawberries Bartram encountered in May of 1775. Before vicariously savouring Bartram's intense experience of these strawberries, let us just glance at the remainder of his travels. On May 22, Bartram had reached a trading settlement named Cowee in the mountains of western North Carolina. Deciding not to proceed any further into Cherokee territory – he was, after all, travelling alone – he turned south and proceeded westward through Georgia with a large party of traders. Eventually, Bartram passed through Alabama and reached the Mississippi River in Louisiana. Reversing his route, he then returned to Philadelphia.

Here is how Bartram describes his initial encounter with the wild strawberries:

> Soon after entering on these charming, sequestered, prolific fields, we came to a fine little river, which crossing, and riding over fruitful strawberry beds and green lawns, on the side of a circular ridge of hills in front of us, and going round the bases of this promontory, came to a fine meadow on an arm of the vale, through which meandered a brook, its humid vapours bedewing the fragrant strawberries which hung in heavy red clusters over the grassy verge.[15]

250

But just how 'wild' were those berries? The sentence just prior to the one quoted tells us that, 'Here had formerly been a very flourishing settlement; but the Indians deserted it in search of fresh planting land, which they soon found in a rich vale but a few miles distance over a ridge of hills.'[16] It seems likely, therefore, that Cherokee cultivation of the fields in question – always preceded by clearing the land of native growth – somehow improved the conditions for strawberry cultivation, perhaps simply by destroying all competing plants. (But any such procedure amounts to what is usually called plant domestication.) In any case, Bartram blurs the line between 'nature' and 'culture' when he deliberately includes in the 'sylvan scene of primitive innocence' lying before him not only the 'vast expanse of green meadows and strawberry fields' but also the 'flocks of turkies', the 'herds of deer', and the 'companies of young, innocent Cherokee virgins'.[17] I might just add that Bartram was an ardent admirer of Cherokee government as 'the most simple, natural, and rational that can be imagined or desired'.[18]

In the summer of 1885, the eleven-year-old Robert Frost (1874–1963) helped his great-aunt and great-uncle gather blueberries to supplement the income from their New Hampshire farm. Memories of that summer would have contributed to Frost's composition, in 1912, of a poem called 'Blueberries' (included in his first book,

North of Boston, published in 1914) describing a family (the Lorens) whose entire life is centred around gathering wild berries (mostly blueberries but also cranberries and raspberries): they eat them, of course, but also exchange them for the other necessities of life. The unidentified narrator of the poem, while annoyed by the secretiveness of the Loren family, admires their way of life, in lines which occur exactly halfway through the 105 lines of rhymed couplets which constitute the poem:

> It's a nice way to live,
> Just taking what Nature is willing to give,
> Not forcing her hand with harrow and plow.[19]

Here, what grows wild with no obvious human intervention is privileged over the products of agricultural technique.[20]

Tolstoy was not so sanguine regarding the virtues of wild berries – or, at least, he was willing to employ them as a literary motif with highly negative connotations. In a late didactic short story called 'The Berries' (1905), the action takes place on a single day in June in and around a large villa not far from St. Petersburg. In his first four paragraphs, Tolstoy presents the setting. By contrast with Nicolai Semonich's 'magnificent villa, complete with tower, veranda, balcony, and galleries'[21] are the 'pretentious, ornate little houses'[22] of the vacationers. (I use a translation by Barbara Makanowitzky.) Among the peasants,

> The women were bringing sacks of cut grass out of the woods, the little girls and young maidens, trying to outdo each other, were crawling through the bushes of the felled wood, collecting berries to sell to the vacationers.[23]

Though we hear no more of the vacationers (presumably, they are affluent middle-class St. Petersburgers), Nicolai Semonich's guest for the day (also from the city, a 'St. Petersburg gentleman') is characterized in some detail – but only in terms of his political views; we do not even learn his name, though we do learn the (first) name of his coachman, Ivan. Both Nicolai Semonich and his guest favour 'constitutional principles' but the former is a Russian Orthodox Slavophile, while the latter is a liberal with European and socialist inclinations – two stereotypes familiar enough from late 19th-century Russian literature.

At the five-course dinner in the garden, there are some additional guests – a liberal doctor and the Semonich children's youthful, revolution-minded tutor (two more stereotypes, also unnamed) – and, in addition, of course, Nicolai's wife Mari and their three children. Owing to the heat, however, almost no food is consumed, so that

> the labors of the forty-ruble cook and his helpers, who had worked particularly hard for the guests, were almost wasted. They ate only a chilled herb soup with

fresh white fish from the Volga, and a varicolored ice cream in a pretty mold, decorated with spun sugar and biscuits.[24]

(Note that the readily available wild strawberries are apparently not served at all.) After dinner, the men discuss politics, including such pointless and futile questions as 'whether the elections should be held in one or two steps'.[25] The sheer fecklessness of the conversation is conveyed by such observations as this: 'The guest felt he had become mixed up and not said quite what he meant, but in the heat of the argument, he could not quite remember what he had meant to say.'[26] Finally, the conversation is interrupted by the appearance of a servant, who reports that the youngest child, Goga, is ill (as it turns out, from eating unripe strawberries, which some peasant boys had sold to Nicolai in his wife's absence). The doctor attends Goga, 'examin[es] the contents of a chamber pot by the light of a dripping candle',[27] and, announcing that the boy is in no danger, prescribes a dose of bismuth for his diarrhoea. But Mari is still furious with her husband as they go to bed.

The remaining half of the story is devoted mostly to the peasants, who are treated by Tolstoy, not surprisingly, with much more sympathy (for one thing, they all have names). Returning early in the morning from night pasture, the twelve-year-old Taraska Rezunov wakes his sisters Olgushka and Grushka to go out berrying: 'They had gotten pots and a pint measure ready the day before, and without eating breakfast or taking along any bread, had crossed themselves twice in front of the icons and run out in the street.'[28] The children, of course, know exactly where to find the strawberries:

> The berry patch was in a cleared woods. The girls went into last year's clearing first. The saplings had just sprouted, and among the young green bushes was a place with short grass in which berries were hidden, some still rosy white, others red.[29]

While gathering, the girls at the same time gorge themselves with berries – to no ill effect, of course, since they obviously know which berries are ripe. By now quite hungry, the children go home to eat. Later, attempting to sell their strawberries at the villa, they are turned away by Mari but waylaid by the oldest son Valya, who manages to buy the berries, out of his mother's sight, with money furnished by his nurse. And the story ends on an ironic note of harmony:

> Everything was now as usual in the family of Nicolai Semonich. Everything was in order. A three-course breakfast was ready, which the flies had eaten long ago; no one had come because no one felt like eating.
>
> Nicolai Semonich was satisfied with the rectitude of his judgment which was confirmed by what he was now reading in the newspapers. Mari was calm

because Goga was getting well. The doctor was satisfied that the remedy he proposed had brought results. Valya was satisfied because he had eaten a whole plateful of strawberries.[30]

Tolstoy was no Marxist, of course, but the crude quasi-commodification of wild strawberries which he depicts can surely be taken as a deliberate allusion to the deeply dysfunctional Russian rural society of his time.

Wishing to avoid any suggestion that wild fruits always have positive connotations for American writers, I want to consider now the wild-strawberry episode in Mary McCarthy's short novel, *The Oasis*, which was first published in London as the February 1949 issue of Cyril Connolly's *Horizon*. The story is about a group of some fifty left-wing intellectuals, mostly from New York City, who, seeking a refuge from an imminent World War 3, start a utopian community on an isolated mountain top in Massachusetts. Each of the principal characters is a caricatured version of some literary or political figure in McCarthy's circle of friends and acquaintances of the 1940s; the most easily recognizable are the head of the so-called realist faction of the colony, Will Taub (in real life, Philip Rahv, editor of *Partisan Review*) and the head of the so-called purist faction, Macdougal Macdermott (in real life, Dwight Macdonald, editor of *Politics*). (There is also a motley collection of characters belonging to the so-called centrist faction.) The feeble plot is really just a device for presenting, in contrived dialectical interaction, a sequence of personified but actually quite abstract literary and political positions; in practice, the characters argue interminably (and, finally, tediously) about everything from domestic arrangements to Marxist politics. The only genuinely non-verbal action occurs in the strawberry episode with which the novel concludes. In this episode – constituting some twenty per cent of the novel – the writing style becomes notably less turgid and more relaxed.

253

Briefly, this is what happens in the strawberry episode. One of the children of the community has discovered a large patch of wild strawberries, and on the Fourth of July weekend, 'A strawberry picnic was planned for noon in the high meadow'.[31] The strawberries remind Taub of his childhood in the Carpathian Mountains (of Central Europe): 'The minuteness of the fruit and its rarity, together with memory of himself, small and uniquely valued by the guardian presence of his mother, had struck him with awe and reverence... and the fact, which he slowly ascertained after many surreptitious woodland strolls, that the colony not only had these wild strawberries, but had them in a greater plenitude than he had ever known in his homeland topped off nostalgic sentiment with the creamy self-satisfaction of the well-pleased entrepreneur.'[32] Taub's wife Cynthia remembers something quite different; 'during a summer at Fontainebleau as a young lady, she would eat *fraises des bois* on a Sunday in an upper dining room of Lapérouse and dream of the career ahead of her in the great world of fashion.'[33] By chance, on the morning of the picnic, the Taubs stumble upon a family of strangers speaking with a foreign accent, who arrive in an old car, get out with their pails, and commence expertly picking strawberries. Reporting what they have seen to the others, the Taubs set off a passionate discussion by the colonists of how to deal with this unforeseen situation. One of the colonists goes to politely challenge the intruders, who respond rudely and continue picking. Two more of the colonists find a rifle and intimidate the intruders, who depart when they hear the gun shots. (It turns out that the rifle is loaded only with blanks – noisy, effectual against a minor menace, but at bottom, not to be taken seriously – just like the colonists?) Eventually, everyone 'openly acknowledged that the picnic has been spoiled',[34] and the novel ends in an orgy of mutual accusation and self-accusation, with the ultimate fate of the colony in doubt. As in Tolstoy's story, none of the adults seems to enjoy eating the wild strawberries and the very activity of picking them serves only to reveal the strains and contradictions of the colonists' utopian ideals, as they argue about private property, violence, and middle-class morality.

Notes

1. Thoreau, Henry David, *Wild Fruits*, ed. Bradley P. Dean (New York: W.W. Norton, 2000), p. ix.
2. Thoreau, *Wild Fruits*, p. 3.
3. For a detailed description of the checkerberry – also known as spring or creeping wintergreen, boxberry, and teaberry – see the classical account of wild fruits of the north-eastern United States by Maude Gridley Peterson (first published in 1905): *How to Know Wild Fruits* (New York: Dover Publications, 1973), pp. 114-116. According to Peterson, the checkerberry 'is dry and mealy, but has a delightful aromatic flavor' (p. 114). Both birds and deer seem to consume the berries during the winter.
4. Pliny, *Natural History*, Bk. 16, Chap. 32; tr. H. Rackham (London: William Heinemann, 1938), vol. 4, p. 439.
5. Theophrastus, *Enquiry Into Plants*, 3.2.2; tr. Arthur Hort (London: William Heinemann, 1916), vol. 1, p. 167.
6. Theophrastus, *Enquiry Into Plants*, 3.2.2; tr. Hort, vol. 1, p. 167.
7. Hulme, Kathryn, 'Plum Crazy', in *Of Chickens and Plums* (New Haven: Yale University Library, 1982), p. 26.
8. Hulme, 'Plum Crazy', p. 30.
9. Thoreau, *Wild Fruits*, p. 79.
10. Thoreau, *Wild Fruits*, p. 57.
11. Thoreau, *Wild Fruits*, p. xvi.
12. Thoreau, *Wild Fruits*, pp. 153-4.
13. Thoreau, *Wild Fruits*, p. 154.
14. Thoreau, *Wild Fruits*, p. 238.
15. Bartram, William, 'Travels Through North and South Carolina, Georgia, East and West Florida', Part 3, Chap. 3 in William Bartram, *Travels and Other Writings* (New York: The Library of America, 1996), p. 290.
16. Ibid., p. 290.
17. Ibid., p. 291.
18. Bartram, William, 'Observations on the Creek and Cherokee Indians', in William Bartram, *Travels and Other Writings*, p. 536.
19. Frost, Robert, 'Blueberries', *Robert Frost Collected Poems, Prose, & Plays* (New York: The Library of America, 1995), p. 64.
20. For a fuller discussion of Frost's poem, and a comparison with many other berry-picking poems, see

my *The Duchess of Malfi's Apricots, and Other Literary Fruits* (Columbia, South Carolina: University of South Carolina Press, 2002), pp. 710 ff.

21. Tolstoy, Leo, 'The Berries', *The Short Stories of Leo Tolstoy*, tr. Arthur Mendel and Barbara Makanowitzky (New York: Bantam Books, 1960), p. 498-99.

22. Ibid., p. 498.

23. Ibid., p. 498.

24. Ibid., p. 499.

25. Ibid., p. 500.

26. Ibid., p. 501.

27. Ibid., p. 503.

28. Ibid., p. 504.

29. Ibid., p. 505.

30. Ibid., pp. 508-509.

31. McCarthy, Mary, *The Oasis* (New York: Random House, 1949), p. 144.

32. Ibid., p. 145.

33. Ibid., p. 146.

34. Ibid., p. 167.

The Game of the Caliphs

Charles Perry

Medieval Baghdad had two cultural wellsprings: the Bedouin life of Arabia and the sophisticated court of the pre-Islamic Persian Empire. Both contributed to its use of game.

In 6th-century Persia, as in ancient Assyria, the royal hunt had been a ritual enactment of the king's power. A king was expected to fight lions on horseback, relying on the horse's superior speed to exhaust the cat until he could kill it with a spear. Kings also organized large-scale hunts with armies of beaters. When the game was cornered, the king could move in and pick off any animals he wanted or let his servants kill them for the royal table. All these traditions continued under the caliphs.[1]

The Bedouins of pre-Islamic Arabia had seen the hunt as a way of getting food, and in principle Islam permits it for that reason alone. But they clearly enjoyed it as a sport, and pre-Islamic poets included vivid hunting scenes in their odes. Al-Nabigha al-Dhubyani devoted half of his most famous poem to comparing the strength and courage of his camel to that of a wild bull cornered by a hunter and his hounds, fighting back ferociously, goring the lead dog as deftly as a fletcher splitting bamboo into arrow shafts. Surprisingly, the poet who established the hunt poem (tardiyya) as an independent genre, Abu Nuwas, was very far from being a Bedouin – he was the consummate urban aesthete of 9th-century Baghdad, as well known for his witty mockery of desert tradition as for his poems about wine and boys.

The Persian kings seem to have favoured the wild ass (*gor*), a byword for strength (Bahram V was nicknamed Gor). The Bedouin poets often mentioned wild cattle, but Abu Nuwas and later composers of *tardiyyāt* were typically after gazelles. In both Iran and Baghdad, all sorts of game birds were hunted with hawks and falcons, and hares were pursued with hounds.

In Europe, the nobility claimed game animals as their privilege, established game parks and meted out savage punishment to poachers. As a result, game had a certain aristocratic cachet for Europeans. The upwardly mobile yearned to display game on their menus, or failing that, imitation game: beef dressed as venison, loin of pork *en chevreuil* or *en sanglier*, and the like.

The situation was quite different in Baghdad, where there was no hereditary feudal aristocracy. Caliphs did not empark land for their subordinates, and if huntsmen damaged crops in the course of a hunt, they were expected to pay full compensation. The purpose of hunting seems to have been recreation, not the privilege of serving game meat. As evidence, game did not figure ostentatiously on the royal table; *Kitāb al-Tabīkh*, a collection of recherché recipes from 9th-century court circles,[2] calls for game in perhaps eight of its 287 meat recipes. Arab poets extolled the hunt but rarely mentioned game dishes.[3] Medieval Arab cookbooks do not give recipes for disguising domestic meat as game (what they are interested in counterfeiting is marrow, of which there was never enough to go around for all the guests).

Arab doctors considered game animals of somewhat dubious dietary value, though not as bad as camel.[4] All quadruped game was held to engender melancholic blood and increase black bile, even gazelle, the best of game meats and hare, the lightest. Among wild birds, francolin and pheasant were nutritionally similar to domestic fowl, *taihūj* partridge being lighter and *qabj* partridge coarser. Duck was the most powerful and most indigestible of fowl. Small birds were aphrodisiac, and sand grouse and all mountain fowl were strongly heating and productive of blood. The gizzards of the ostrich were more delicate and beneficial than its flesh. Crane was very muscular and needed to be hung, and its best part also was the gizzards.[5]

There exists a tale in Middle Persian[6] about an impoverished young aristocrat who asks for a position in the retinue of Khusrau I (531–79) on the ground that he has all the qualifications of a nobleman. To determine his suitability, the king quizzes him about the finest thing in 13 categories. The book was, in effect, a pocket guide to accepted gourmet opinions (9 of the 13 questions were about food), and it wielded wide influence. The tale's translator, Unvala, points out that a version of the text was translated into Arabic during the Islamic period.

We should not be surprised to find game in this list of Persian court favourites, but it does not appear where we might expect. In two cases, it is the fat of game that is valued; certainly a matter of conspicuous consumption, since wild animals tend to have less fat than domestic. The finest of nuts is hempseed fried in the fat of the mountain goat. The best sweetmeat, *charb angusht*, is made with gazelle fat. (The later Arabic translation describes a sweetmeat made from rice flour, sugar, milk and gazelle fat.)

257

According to the tale, the best red meats are domestic lamb and beef, and domestic fowl fattened on hempseed and olives is better than any game bird. Significantly, the only wild animals it mentions among the best dishes are those that have been rendered more tender and flavourful in captivity. The best meat to serve in aspic (*awsart*) is wild ass fattened on alfalfa and barley. The best meat to serve in *amich*[7] is female barren gazelle. Presumably the gazelle is barren because her womb has been surgically removed, as the Romans removed the wombs from sows.

This practice of raising or fattening game in captivity persisted in Baghdad. In *Kitāb al-Tabīkh*, a paragraph on the nutritional value of wild ass observes,

'That which is raised from the wild animal (sc. in captivity) has more praiseworthy meat than that (which grew up) in the wild (*mâ rubbiya min al-wahsh ahmad lahman min al-barri*), especially the young ass (*jahsh*)'. [8]

The book's only mention of cooking wildfowl occurs in the chapter on *mutajjanāt*, dishes of fattened fowl cooked with vinegar, soy sauce and pepper. *Mutajjanāt* are said to be made 'with birds such as chickens, pullets, small fowl, pheasants, *taihūj* partridge, *shafānīn*, larks and figpeckers'.[9]

The recipes[10] that specifically call for game fall into two categories. One was a dish called *bārida*, cold meat in some sort of dressing. For *bārida* of minced roast hare, the dressing was vinegar, oil, soy sauce, sugar and spices. Wild game and kid were boiled with raisins and pomegranate and then dressed with the cooking juices mixed with mustard, soy sauce, cinnamon and rue. Gazelle boiled in vinegar (optionally larded with almonds and pistachios) was merely sprinkled with celery, rue and mint leaves.[11]

The rest of the game dishes are all *mā'-wa-milh*. This name (literally, 'water-and-salt') appears to be a loan translation of the Persian *shorbā*, 'salty (viz. salted) stew'; it does not appear in later Arabic cookbooks, where *shorbā* replaces it. Three *mā'-wa-milh* recipes begin with an odd instruction not found elsewhere in the Arabic culinary literature: to boil the meat and then to throw the boiling water away. This was evidently a way of removing the scum of congealed blood that rises in boiling; Arab cooks more typically removed it by skimming. After this, the meat is boiled in fresh water mixed with salt and flavourings, typically onions, dill and sweet spices. One recipe calls for 'wild' meat (*lahm wahsh*), likely wild ass. Another calls for 'wild' meat or Busht mutton, a third calls for gazelle and a fourth does not specify a meat but is almost certainly for wild ass; it includes noodles and is preceded by an anecdote about how a Persian king invented noodles to vary a *mā'-wa-milh* of wild ass after a hunt.[12]

Other than that, game meat could be used for the same dishes as domestic meat. *Kitāb al-Tabīkh* mentions that wild ass could be served as *nārbāj* (a stew flavoured with pomegranate and raisins), *tabāhajāt* (fried sliced meat) or *sharā'ih mubazzarāt* (roasted sliced meat) as well as in *mā'-wa-milh*. Flesh of wild cattle could be served the same dishes except that *summāqiyya*, a stew flavoured with tart sumac berries, replaces *mā'-wa-milh* in the list.[13] Ostrich could be cooked in *fujliyya* (a cheap stew flavoured with radishes) and stews in which there was plenty of cheese, and its flesh was said to give an extraordinary flavour to *harīsa* (wheat porridge cooked with meat).[14]

But game could appear in other dishes as well, and one further game recipe is implied in *Kitāb al-Tabīkh*. It comes in a verse in which the poet Mahmud b. al-Hasan Kushajim invites a friend to a meal of cold kid and a *kushtābiyya* (stew of sliced meat) made from a gazelle. 'If we wish,' the poet adds, 'we may toast it with wine as soft as the cheek of a gazelle fawn, and as tawny as its flank.'[15]

Notes

1. For a description of the hunting techniques used (which included nets, traps, decoys and other devices as well as ordinary weapons of warfare), see M.M. Ahsan, *Social Life Under the Abbasids* (London and Beirut: Longman/Librairie du Liban, 1979), pp. 203-242.

2. Ibn Sayyar al-Warraq, *Kitāb al-Tabīkh*, Kai Öhrnberg and Sahban Mroueh, eds. (Helsinki: Studia Orientalia, 1987).

3. An exception appears in Ibn 'Abd Rabbihi, *Al-'Iqd al-Farīd* (Cairo: Lagnat al-Ta'līf wal-Targuma wal-Nashr, 1949); v. 6, p. 324. In describing an array of food, Musawir al-Warraq mentions '*masūs* of very good francolins and fully fledged birds (*nawāhid*), with which was brought roast meat'. *Masūs*, a dish of meat stewed with celery leaf and other herbs, was primarily a way of presenting kid.

4. *Al-'Iqd al-Farīd*, v. 6, p. 296.

5. *K. al-Tabīkh*, pp. 22-3.

6. *Husrau i kavātān u rētak ē, The Pahlavi text 'King Husrav and his boy,'* Unvala, Jamshedji Maneckji, trans. (Paris: P. Geuthner, 1921).

7. A dish of uncertain nature. The name seems related to the verb root *āmech-*, 'to mix'. Unvala translates it as 'seasoned meat in ragout'. In *A Concise Pahlavi Dictionary* (Oxford: Oxford University Press, 1971) D.N. MacKenzie renders *āmiz* (the later pronunciation) as 'side dish, vegetables'. In *Pahlaveren-Parsakeren-Hayeren-Rruseren-Angleren* Barraran (Yerevan: Mitk' Hratarakch'utiun, 1964), *amich* is translated as 'medicament' in English and adviyeh in modern Persian, but as both 'medicine' and 'spice' in Russian (*lekarstvo, prianost*) and Armenian (*degorayk, hamemunk'*), doubtless because of the dual meaning of adviyeh in Persian. A note declares that it also means 'condiment' in Armenian. In A. S. Piruzyan's modern Armenian cookbook *Armianaskaia Kulinariia* (Moscow: Ekonomika Press, Moscow 1971; p. 124), *amich* is roast turkey with a stuffing of raisins, nuts and dried fruits.

8. *K. al-Tabīkh*, p. 127.

9. Op. cit. p. 74. *Shafānīn* might be an Aramaic plural of the word that appears in Persian as *shafāna*, 'name of a large bird; a lark'.

10. With the possible exception of *mutajjana wāthiqiyya* (p. 106), which calls for *farrūj Kaskarī*: pullets, possibly of some variety of game bird, from Kaskar, an Iraqi town that had been of some importance under the Persian Empire.

11. *K. al-Tabīkh*, pp. 106-7: *bārida min arnab mashwī* (roast hare) *li-Yahyā b. Khālid, sifat bārida ukhrā tuttakhadh min luhūm al-wahsh wa-luhūm al-jidā* (wild meat and kid), *bārida ukhrā min lahm ghazāl lil-Wāthiq*.

12. pp. 129-30: *sifat mā'-wa-milh min lahm wahsh lil-Ma'mūn, sifat mā'-wa-milh Khorāsānī* (which says 'take if you want wild [meat] or *busht* sheep' – *al-ghanam al-busht* may represent Busht, a village of Khorasan in eastern Iran), *mā'-wa-milh min lahm ghazāl* (this is the recipe that does not throw away the first boiling water; it includes a garnish of walnuts, almonds, raisins, mustard and soy sauce). p. 200: *sifat al-mā'-wal-milh*, the dish with noodles (*lakhshā*), includes a garnish of walnuts, whey and garlic.

13. p. 127.

14. p. 23.

15. p. 129. 'Toast it': *sabahnā*, 'drink a morning draught to'.

The Edible, Incredible Cattail

Susan McLellan Plaisted

The cattail, *Typha angustifolia* (narrow-leaved cattail) or *Typha latifolia* (common cattail), is one of the most versatile wild food plants native to North America. The name *Typha* is derived from the Greek word for a cat's tail, but there is disagreement as to whether it is the seed stalk or the shape of the leaf when it emerges that it resembles a cat's tail. Described as a wild supermarket, it has a variety of food uses at different times of the year. Of the two main species, the *Typha latifolia* is more common inland, larger in size and bears more food than its counterpart *Typha angustifolia* noted as the more common species along the coast.[1]

A cattail stand is quite easily recognizable in the spring. Young green shoots, erect and sword-like, emerge from a thick maze of rhizomes underneath the mud of the shallow water of marshes, swamps, slow-moving streams, edges of ponds, or even drainage areas beside roadways. The young cattail shoots can be confused with non-poisonous calamus (*Acorus calamus*) or poisonous iris shoots and daffodil (*Amaryllidaceae*). Positive identification of the edible cattail is the furry, white seed-heads of last year's stalks that still stand in the spring.[2]

By late spring, the three- to nine-feet-high leaves camouflage the newly developing flower head until it matures. The flower head is very primitive in form with two distinct segments. The lower female segment is initially green with the smaller male segment directly above that produces the bright yellow pollen. Once the pollen is released, the male segment withers away and the compact cylindrical head of minute green flowers seed and turn to the familiar brown colour.[3] These brown seed heads, commonly referred to as 'cigars', candlewicks or ducktails, are actually thousands of tiny developing seeds. These seeds become white and furry over the winter and therefore a marker of the cattail stand after the leaves die.

The cattail is quite unique as a wild food source as almost every part of the plant can be harvested for food and is safe. Daniel Moerman in his *Native American Ethnobotany* lists the *Typha latifolia*, broadleaf cattail tenth in rank of plants with the greatest number of food uses by the Native American.[4] The Woodlands Cree stored dried cattail roots for winter storage, harvested stem bases and young shoots in July, and ate roots harvested just before the plant bloomed either raw or boiled in water. Similarly, the Objibwa boiled fresh green flower heads or dried them for food and utilized the pollen as flour.[5] The cattail was a vital food source for the Native American; it was in great supply and did not need cultivation. But it was not embraced by the European colonists who not only ignored the cattail as a food source but carelessly destroyed their habitats.

What most Europeans neglected was a year-round source of food, relatively easy to harvest, kind to the palate, and highly nutritious. In the spring before the flower forms, one can grasp the innermost leaves of the cattail, pull at the base of the plant, and slip the inner core from the root. The upper-most part of the leaves should be cut off and the tougher, outer layer of the stalk peeled away to reveal a tender white core that is excellent raw or can be boiled. The taste and texture raw is similar in nature to raw cucumbers. The white core can vary from just 2 to 3 inches in length to 18 inches. As soon as the immature flower sheaths emerge, the time for enjoying the white cores has passed. But the immature flower heads are another source of food that can be harvested over a six-week season. These green bloom spikes should be gathered when they appear ready to break through the papery sheath that encloses them but prior to any sign of the yellow pollen. The spikes are boiled and eaten similarly to corn on the cob. The sheaths are removed and the spikes held in the fingers while eating the cooked buds, like the kernels of corn, from the central inedible stalk.

Be certain not to harvest all of the green bloom spikes, as the bright yellow pollen is the next delicacy to harvest just before the summer solstice. The pollen season is quite short but calm, windless days are best to harvest this fine, talcum-powdered consistency pollen that is easily dispersed by the wind. A deep, rounded gourd or paper bag is recommended to collect the pollen by bending the flower heads and shaking the pollen off gently into the container. After sifting through a strainer, the golden flour, rich in protein and nutrients, is excellent mixed either half and half or with three times as much whole grain flour to use in preparing breads, pancakes etc. The pollen can be used raw as a topping sprinkled on yogurt or oatmeal. Pollen can be stored for future use but it must be thoroughly dried to prevent early spoilage.

In late summer, small horn-shaped sprouts, next year's cattails, will appear at the tips of the long rhizomes and remain all winter. These sprouts, with a sweet taste, can be harvested and eaten raw or boiled. In the very early spring, these same sprouts as they begin to grow but before they emerge through the surface of the mud, can be harvested, peeled, boiled and pickled. In the centre of these sprouts, at the base, there is a sizable, starchy lump similar to a potato that can be boiled and used in the same manner as the potato.

During fall, winter, and early spring, the shallowly buried rhizomes store food as starch. A square yard of cattail swamp will yield enough starch to make several pounds of nutritious white flour with a nutrition analysis similar to grain flour.[6] There are two methods to process this starch into flour. During World War I, a scientist from Cornell developed a method of making cattail flour by drying the peeled rhizomes, grinding them and sifting to remove the fibre.[7] A second method of flour preparation is to wash the rhizomes thoroughly, peel off the outer covering exposing the starchy core, and crush the core in a large bowl of water to separate the starch from the fibres. The fibres are then removed from the water, the starch allowed to settle to the bottom of the bowl and then the water poured off. The remaining flour can be used immediately in food preparation or dried to store for future use.

There is no plant, wild or domesticated, which exceeds the edible, incredible cattail in its diversity of food uses. More carbohydrates can be obtained from an acre of cattails than from an acre of potatoes, yet few people harvest cattails and their wetland environments are rapidly disappearing.[8]

References

1. Richard J. Medve and Mary Lee Medve, *Edible Wild Plants of Pennsylvania and Neighboring States* (University Park: The Pennsylvania State University Press, 1992), p. 150.
2. Steve Brill, *Identifying and Harvesting Edible and Medicinal Plants in Wild (and not so Wild) Places* (New York: Harper Collins, 1994), p. 69.
3. Medve, op. cit., p. 150.
4. Daniel E. Moerman, *Native American Ethnobotany* (Portland: Timber Press, 1998), p. 15.
5. Ibid. p. 574.
6. Euell Gibbons, *Stalking the Wild Asparagus* (Chambersburg: Alan C. Hood & Company, 1962), p. 57.
7. P. W. Claasen, 'A Possible New Source of Food Supply', *Scientific Monthly* August, 1919.
8. Medve, op. cit., p. 151.

262

Wild Plant Foods: Panacea or Just a Picnic?

Christopher Robbins

Introduction

The contemporary collection of wild plant foods (WPF) in industrialized societies such as Britain is a leisure pastime that enriches the Sunday stroll and the dinner table. WPF have had a more important role in diet and health, but the connection has been lost. The disconnection of present and atavistic practice is well illustrated by Richard Mabey in his introduction to the best-selling, *Food for Free*:

> though the morbid worries have long vanished, I still sometimes experience this sense of engaging in an eccentric and slightly hazardous activity whenever I gather or eat wild plants.[1]

Personal preferences vary, but a typical gatherer might be interested in one or at best a few seasonal delicacies. Sheep sorrel (*Rumex acetosella*) leaves collected on a summer meadow wander. Elder flower (*Sambucus nigra*) blooms in June for elder flower cordial or perhaps even 'champagne'. Elder berries in July make an impressive cassis substitute and, as a rob, provide a 'sweet meat' for the winter months. Autumnal mushroom collecting to bring that frisson of gambler's adrenaline and delicacies unprocurable from the best high-street delicatessen or supermarket. But WPF can reveal a greater intrigue and complexity in our plant choices, plus an understanding of the human dietary that could inform the future assessment of foods and diets.

Wild plant foods in history

In contemporary Britain, WPF are reduced to curiosities among the dominance of manufactured products and intensively farmed fruit and vegetables now gathered only from supermarket shelving and comprising the bulk of the modern diet. However within living memory WPF have had a more significant role in the British dietary. Mason and Brown list fourteen WPF among Britain's traditional foods.[2] Rose hips were collected and processed into Vitamin C syrup at UK government request during the Second World War. Traditional spring tonics made from nettles (*Urtica* spp), clivers (*Galium aparine*), and bistort (*Polygonum bistorta*) have been regular rural practice for centuries. As liver and general blood circulation stimulants they help the body recover from the relatively stodgy winter food of potatoes and lard, and offer relief from the rarity of winter green vegetables or fruits. Dandelion (*Taraxacum officinale*) and burdock (*Arctium lappa*) drinks have a similar healthy action and can still be found in a canned, carbonated form though most lack the original ingredients.

Acorns (*Quercus* spp) have long been a valued food for grazing pigs. Specific laws, or pannage, governed the grazing practices in forests. Human needs took preference in famine years. A passable flour was made from the acorns. Horse chestnut (*Aesculus hippocastenum*) fruit was often combined with the acorns or used alone.[3]

Wild plant foods as traditional foods in Britain, listed in Mason and Brown (1999).

> Bilberry
> Blackberry
> Hazlenut
> Alexanders
> Asparagus (wild)
> Bistort
> Nettles
> Dulse
> Good King Henry (*Chenopodium*)
> Laverbread
> Watercress
> Samphire
> Spearmints (and other *Mentha* spp)
> Sweet Cicely

264

Wandering both across cultures and back through time reveals that the gathering of WPF has specific contexts that carry great importance for daily life. Many countries have a rich legacy displayed in local food markets or in customary kitchen practice. Patience Gray's experience of being introduced to a great range of WPF on the Greek island of Naxos[4] is characteristic of the normality in southern Europe today of harvesting a wide variety of plants that are consumed in different ways and combinations. Such practice is the WPF version of filling a supermarket trolley from the vegetable aisles. Gray also records the same practice and diversity of plants used in Italy and Spain.

Most of the medicinal herbals allude to the food uses of their medicinal entries. Gerard gushes with typical pleonasm in the 1597 introduction to his *History of Plants* that:

> nothing can be confected, either delicate for the taste, delicate for the smell, pleasant for the sight, wholesome for body, conservative or restorative for health, but it borroweth the relish of an herb, the savour of a flour (sic), the colour of a leaf, the juice of a plant, or the decoction of a root.[5]

The ancient Greek herbalists had herbs that were gathered from the mountains by skilled collectors called rhizotomists.[6] Holiday-makers to Crete or the Greek islands can still find a modern version of these collectors offering fresh herbs for healing as well as for the kitchen. A common WFP is dittany, which was collected by the ancients to treat digestive disorders, is still brought down to the villages and street corners for sale. Dittany or dictamnus is *Origanum dictamnus*, a close relative of culinary oregano and marjoram.

Hippocrates, who rated diet highest among the paths to good health[7], included many traditional culinary spices along with burdock, mints, peony, saffron, violets, and willow in his *materia medica*.

Biblical references to WPF are legion. The general exhortation to go 'out into the fields to gather herbs'[8] in famine must have been wise advice from the beginnings of reliance on agriculture and decreased dependence on the unpredictability of gathering plant food. The identity of the best-known Biblical WPF, manna, remains speculative, but since the Hebrew translation for manna is 'what is it?', it is reasonable to assume that it wasn't a previously observed plant[9]. The Jews were on an expedition across unknown terrain so they may have encountered novel plants en route, including the exuding sap from a tamarisk (*Tamarix nilotica*), a desert shrub (*Hammanda salicornica*), or even a mixture of blue-green algae and lichens. WPF are specified in the Jewish Mishnah for eating with the Passover lamb. Depending on the geographical location of the reference between Egypt and the Promised Land, the named bitter herbs[10] include wild lettuce (*Lactuca sativa*), chicory (*Cichorium* spp.), eryngo (*Eryngium* spp.), horse-radish (*Armoracia* spp.), and sow thistle (*Sonchus* spp.). These 'bitter' plants symbolize the harsh and 'bitter' experience of expulsion from the homelands. Other Biblical WPF include purslane (*Portulaca oleracea*), bay (*Laurus nobilis*), fenugreek (*Trigonella foenum-graecum*), rue (*Ruta chalepensis* most likely and not R. *graveolens*) plus the probably-cultivated culinary *Umbelliferae* herbs, dill, coriander and cumin, as well as mints, mustard and linseed.

WPF: panacea or picnic?

Throughout the historical record, WPF are frequently associated with an explicit direct or symbolic medicinal purpose. A drug benefit of any food need not be a consideration in choosing to eat it. Nor need it be the only consideration in choice. How many chocolate eaters think about the stimulant alkaloids they consume alongside the sugar and fat? But the Hippocratic emphasis on food in health (not only in treating disease) or the Jewish requirement for bitter herbs with Passover lamb indicate how medicinal uses of any food can become established practice or symbolic gesture where the original context is either now lost or becomes irrelevant.

Food choice is complex. Whether selecting among menu items, or selecting a weekly shopping basket many factors come into play in complex interactions.[11] Apart from the more obvious income, culture, habitual taste and seasonality factors, there are intriguing factors like advertising and marketing, fashion, access to food outlets, the vintage effect, and of course the perception of health.

Contemporary interest in healthy eating in Britain has had a large impact on the marketing and consumption of food. Generally the interest is limited to crude nutritional factors: energy, fat (including fat fractions), carbohydrates, and vitamins. Two non-nutrient constituents, dietary fibre and water, are included in the 'A list' of factors. Interest in excluding agricultural and manufacturing contaminants and a wider group of environmental pollutants to protect health is fuelling the growth of organic food consumption.

However not only has the physical link with WPF been effectively severed, also lost is the understanding of the original, and now latent, benefits they confer on health and our understanding of dietary evolution and health. There is good evidence that many of the historic WPF choices had drug or pharmacological 'purpose'. That plants were selected during human evolution for their metabolic and therapeutic effects as well as any organoleptic effects or simple nutritional benefits offers an exciting additional consideration in analysing diets or individual foods. Hippocrates said:

> I am of the opinion that our present way of living and our present diet would not have come about if it had proved adequate for man to eat and drink the same things as an ox or a horse and all the other animals. In the beginning I believe that man lived on such food and the modern diet is the result of many years discovery.[12]

266

How could early humans have developed the discernment necessary to satisfy the Hippocratic theory?

Chimpanzee pharmacy

Among herbalists there is much speculation on the mechanisms that led the ancients to identify effective plant drugs. Trial and error is an easy speculation. It may explain how styptic plants were identified but it cannot so easily explain how the bone healing properties of comfrey (*Symphytum officinale*) or the cortisol-potentiating effects of liquorice (*Glycyrrhiza glabra*) were identified in different continents over 1000 years ago. Or how the Australian aboriginals knew the antiseptic properties of *Eucalyptus* spp around 60,000 years ago while the same use was known in South America around 5,000 years ago.

Studies of the way West African chimpanzees utilized *Aspilia* leaves is good evidence of some innate power of discernment.[13] The chimps were observed inserting into their mouth and folding up like a piano accordion, extremely bitter leaves that were not commonly included in grazing. The theory that these chimps were selecting specific antiparasitic WPF in *Aspilia* leaves was confirmed by careful recording of stool flora and fauna before and after the periodic ingestion of the leaves. After eating the leaves the stools were cleared of parasites. Interestingly the leaves were not broken down on passing through the gut. The chimps appear to have known they 'felt ill', selected the appropriate WPF drug, consumed it, then lay quietly under a shady tree as in a sick-bay, ending the procedure by the passage of stools cleared of a wide range of parasites.

The chimps' dramatic example of purposive self-medication with WPF is a clear example of pharmagastrology, the consumption of foods and diets with specific pharmacological benefits. The WPF legacy is a neglected dispensary.

Hidden drugs in the pantry

Many foods that are regular components of everyday eating in the British diet entered the diet as drugs. The original purpose of opening the Far Eastern spice routes by the Portuguese was not because spicy food was preferred but because the spices were drugs.[14] Every common culinary herb and spice (oregano, ginger, mace, nutmeg, cinnamon, pepper, and cardamom) started life in European diets as a drug.

The drug origin of these spices is evident in the original name of the apothecaries, Spicers and Pepperers. This title was changed to Apothecary in the mid-13th century. The task of importing the drugs and distributing from the wharves fell to the Spicers and Pepperers whereas the 'up-town' activity of bundling the drugs into packets of medicines for clients fell to the Apothecaries.

Plant drugs of long standing reputation were taken in the form of a gruel from Hippocratic times. It requires little imagination to see how, over time, the flavours of these drugs became both appreciated and habituated in their combination with food.

267

In some cases the traditional food uses had other benefits that may have favoured their retention. Strong aromatic flavours are associated with the cooking of meats in hot countries. Aromatic oils in spices like cinnamon, clove, ginger, coriander both mask the odours of decaying meat and aid the digestive disturbance precipitated by bacterial contamination of meat dishes. Hot chilli (*Capsicum* spp.) spices provided an additional antisepsis to protect the eater.

Cocoa, coffee, the coca leaf, and even the potato were originally drugs in South America before they were brought to Europe. The first three are well known central nervous system stimulants. Potato fruits (not the tubers) were used as an aphrodisiac and for impotence.[15]

Despite inevitable quality dilution through breeding or agricultural practices, despite any further change to either the composition of individual foods or the ingredients of manufactured food products, many drug activities remain in the industrialized British diet. At the simplest level, that preprandial shot of Campari or unsweetened vermouth stimulates salivation, gastric juice secretion and liver activity. Aromatic herbs and spices in a meal relax the gastric sphincters and regularize peristalsis in the intestine, promoting better digestion. The inclusion of a dish based on carrot and especially spinach[16] provides a handy combination of both bulking and stimulating laxatives to promote a regular and suitable soft stool, desirable about twelve to twenty-four hours after the meal. The lucky diners who include bitter salad greens like chicorée or raddichio in place of the limp and tasteless glasshouse lettuce of British supermarkets will enjoy similar digestive stimulation. Those with a good fix of crushed garlic in the salad dressing will experience a cholesterol lowering effect, a lowering of raised blood pressure, and a decreased risk of blood clotting; the combined benefit being a lowered chance of dying from a heart attack or stroke as they take their postprandial nap. Any gastronome choosing to enjoy the Turkish habit of handfuls of chopped parsley in a *tabouleh* (rather than the British use of a few leaves used as a discardable garnish) may be pleased to enjoy the subsequent reduced risk of gout since the herb increases excretion of the offending uric acid. Drinks of peppermint tisane or cranberry juice after the meal may reduce the risks of offensive indigestion and flatulence, or of the cystitis that may be secondary to social activity among diners after the meal.

Available drugs in modern WPF

A similar drug heritage can be identified among popular WPF in Britain. Though the notion of people today regularly trawling the hedgerows, river banks and fields for a significant contribution to the daily diet is a mere anachronism, many popular WPF have significant drug value in the modern diet.

The useful drugs in WPF are more interesting than those remaining in foods from modern agriculture or manufacturing activities. The WPF are not intrinsically better for being either natural plants or growing 'naturally'. But they do have a specific medicinal history that is either established from traditional use or is confirmed or explained through recent analysis or experimentation.[17] This history is related to how plant and human evolution has been in parallel. The human diet has evolved over 30–40,000 years.[18] The total metabolic, neurological, anatomical structure and function of the human body has evolved slowly with reliance on the parallel consumption of WPF and other foods. Thus not only is it the body's growth and development but also its response to environmental and pathogen stresses that cause disease and have also developed slowly in parallel.

In contrast, recent dietary manipulation has occurred only over the last 150 years or so. The recent dramatic changes to the diet through agriculture, processing and manufacturing has so transformed our diet that it no longer matches the body's needs for healthy functioning or recovery from disease. This has resulted in a plethora of reports on 'unhealthy eating' and regular Government exhortations for the public to eat more healthily.

In many WPF or diets based on them there is a close approximation to the individual foods humans evolved alongside. Their consumption can be more than an atavistic curiosity but offers scope to learn more about the total function of foods in the healthy human diet.

The table below lists a selection of British WPF that may be gathered in different parts of the country. The medical benefits are listed in most general terms to illustrate the benefits of their inclusion in a habitual diet. Nearly all the listed plants are found in the *materia medica* of practising medical herbalists. Up to 4,000 plants are used medicinally around the world. Not all would be suitable for consumption as food, although many are thus consumed.

Medicinal properties of select British wild plant foods

Common name	Latin name	Medicinal use
Agrimony	*Agrimonia eupatoria*	Antidiarrhoeal
Alexanders	*Smyrnium olusatrum*	Digestive, diuretic
Barberry	*Berberis vulgaris*	Choleretic, laxative
Bilberry	*Vaccinum myrtillus*	Urinary astringent
Bistort	*Polygonum bistorta*	Astringent
Bittercress	*Cardamine hirsuta*	Digestive
Black horehound	*Ballota nigra*	Morning sickness, motion sickness, bitter
Broom	*Cytisus scoparius*	Hypertensive, diuretic
Burdock	*Arctium lappa*	Lymphatic
Carragheen	*Chondrus crispus*	Demulcent, nutritive
Catnip	*Nepeta cataria*	Digestive, colds, flu
Chamomile	*Matricaria recutita*	Bitter, digestive, anti-inflammatory
Chickweed	*Stellaria media*	Antipruritic, wound healer
Chicory	*Chicorium intybus*	Bitter, digestive
Cleavers	*Galium aparine*	Lymphatic, hypoglycaemic
Coltsfoot	*Tussilago farfara*	Colds, catarrh, flu
Cowslip	*Primula veris*	Colds, expectorant
Crab apple	*Malus communis*	Antacid, bulk laxative, gout protector, gall stones
Dandelion	*Taraxacum officinale*	Bitter, diuretic, choleretic
Dog rose	*Rosa cannia*	Antiscorbutic, astringent
Dulse	*Pulmaria palmate*	Nutritive, demulcent
Elder	*Sambucus nigra*	Anticatarrhal, diaphoretic, mild laxative or cathartic
Fennel	*Foeniculum vulgare*	Digestive, laxative
Feverfew	*Tanacetum parthenium*	Antirheumatic, migraines, bitter
Garlic mustard	*Alliaria petiolata*	Digestive, poultice on bites and stings
Good King Henry	*Chenopodium bonus-henricus*	Poultice for boils, good iron source

Ground elder	*Aegopodium podagraria*	Gout
Hawthorn	*Crataegus monogyna*	Hypertension, angina
Hops	*Humulus lupulus*	Bitter, relaxing sedative
Horse chestnut	*Aesculus hippocastanum*	Varicose veins, phlebitis
Horseradish	*Armoracia rusticana*	Circulatory stimulant, chilblains
Juniper berries	*Juniperus communis*	Urinary antiseptic
Lemon balm	*Melissa officinalis*	Relaxant, insomnia
Lime flower	*Tilia europaea*	Relaxant, hypotensive, diaphoretic
Meadowsweet	*Filipendula ulmaria*	Antacid, anti-inflammatory
Milk thistle	*Carduus marianus*	Liver protector
Mints	*Mentha* spp	Antispasmodic digestive, referigerant
Mugwort	*Artemesia vulgaris*	Bitter, menopausal flushes
Nettle	*Urtica dioica*	Hepatic, nutritive
Primrose	*Primula vulgaris*	Colds, expectorant
Raspberry	*Rubus idaeus*	Birth preparator
Salad burnet	*Sanguisorba minor*	Astringent, diuretic
Samphire	*Crithmum maritimum*	Digestive, bulk laxative
Sheep sorrel	*Remex acetosella*	Antiscorbutic, digestive, fungal rashes
Shepherd's purse	*Capsella bursa-pastoris*	Astringent, cystitis, styptic
Sweet Cicely	*Myrrhis odorata*	Digestive, antiseptic on wounds
Thyme	*Thymus serphyllum*	Antiseptic for mouth, lungs, expectorant
Valerian	*Valeriana officinalis*	Tranquillizer, relaxant, antispasmodic
Vervain	*Verbena officinalis*	Bitter relaxant
Watercress	*Nasturtium officinale*	Digestive, antiscorbutic
White horehound	*Marrubium vulgare*	Expectorant, asthma
Wild basil	*Clinopodium vulgare*	Digestive
Wild majoram	*Origanum vulgare*	Sedative, digestive
Wormwood	*Artemisia absinthum*	Bitter
Yellow dock	*Rumex crispus*	Aperient, cholagogue

270

Sources: Robbins (1994); Grieve (1931); Phillips, R., Foy, N., *Herbs* (London: Pan, 1990).

Conclusion

Plant foods from all sources seem to have a wider role in the British diet than the simple 'nutrient' and 'food preference' model of dietetics. The current Government advice on healthy eating centres on the slogan to eat at least 5 portions of fruit and vegetables every day. This represents an interesting shift as it actively seeks to promote healthy body systems not only to encourage adequate nutrition. This is a re-emergence of the Hippocratic aphorism to let medicine be thy food and food be thy medicine.

Pharmagastrology is the study of the interconnections between plant foods and plant medicines. The history of WPF provides insight into a more rational and appropriate understanding of the importance of food to healthy human existence. It encourages the acceptance of multiple dietary roles for foods. The myriad ingredients of plants and their roles in healthy diets come under deeper scrutiny in light of the evolutionary relationships between health and many WPF. It also offers a better understanding of the therapeutic benefits of food and how diets may be better understood as preventers of disease within a wider context of health promotion. Pharmagastrology also invites a deeper appreciation of how the environment, agriculture, the food industry and public information about food and eating all need to be integrated into more comprehensive objectives for policies that influence food and health.

That Sunday stroll to collect a few wild leaves might inspire much more than a delicious lunch.

References and bibliography

1. Mabey, R., *Food for Free* (London: Fontana/Collins, 1972).
2. Mason, L., Brown C., *Traditional Foods of Britain* (Totnes: Prospect Books, 1999.)
3. Grieve, M., *A Modern Herbal* (London: Peregrine books, 1976).
4. Gray, P., 'Edible weeds', in *The Penguin Book of Food and Drink*, ed. Levy, P. (London: Penguin, 1996).
5. Woodward, M., *Gerard's Herbal; the History of Plants* (London: Senate, 1994).
6. Robbins, C., *Introduction to Herbal Medicine* (London: Parallel, 1994), p. 29.
7. Lloyd, G. E. R., *Hippocratic Writings* (London: Pelican, 1978), p. 272.
8. 2 Kings 4:39.
9. Hepper, N. F., *Illustrated Encyclopaedia of Bible Plants* (Leicester: Intervarsity Press, 1992), p. 63.
10. Ibid., p. 130.
11. Scitovsky, T., *The Joyless Economy* (London: Oxford University Press, 1976), pp. 182-190.
12. Lloyd, G. E. R. (1978), pp. 71-2.
13. Huffman, M. A. et al., 'Medicinal plant use by wild chimpanzees: a behavioural adaptation for parasite control?' paper presented to 1992 Amer. Assoc. Adv. Sci. (AAAS).
14. Stockwell, C., *Nature's Pharmacy; a History of Plants and Healing* (London: Century, 1988), p. 77.
15. Ibid., p. 86.
16. Demuth, R., *Green World Cookbook; Recipes from Demuths Restaurant* (Bath: Chupi, 2002), p. 102.
17. Robbins, C. J., *The Household Herbal: a Complete Guide to Plants that Heal* (London: Transworld, 1995).
18. Crawford, M. and Marsh, D., *The Driving Force. Food in Evolution and the Future* (London: Mandarin, 1989), pp. 188-203.

There are No Walls in Eden

William Rubel

> So there is one thought for the field, another for the house. I would have my
> thoughts, like wild apples, to be food for walkers, and will not warrant them
> to be palatable, if tasted in the house.
>
> Henry David Thoreau, *Wild Apples*[1]

There are no walls in Eden. And there are no civilizations without walls. Cain, the
first tiller, committed the first murder, and founded the first city. The walls of civilization are tainted with the cry of the earth – the trauma inherent in the violence of
agriculture that ploughs all before it – and by human blood. The shift from wild foods
to domesticated foods enabled bands of hunter gatherers to transform themselves – or
to be transformed by violent men, like Cain – into the slaves, labourers, artisans, and
visionaries required to create cities of stone, and civilizations with a complex material
culture. The long-term balance between hunters and gatherers and their environment
– idealized in the Garden of Eden – does not exist in societies of tillers. Our own
civilization of tillers has upset the ecological balance of the entire world. In response
to our own actions, and building on our alienation from nature, the rich societies are
increasingly reinterpreting the biblical Eden, a garden in which humans and nature
exist in a symbiotic relationship, into an Eden that is a wilderness in which humans
are by definition an inherently contaminating and destabilizing influence. Rather
than tend the Garden, our new role is to keep our fellow humans out of the wilderness in any role except, grudgingly, as observers. This change in attitude marks the
true historic exile from the Garden of Eden, with significant implications for the
management of wilderness in all parts of the world.

> And the LORD God took the man, and put him into the garden of Eden to
> dress it and to keep it. (Genesis 2.15)

Adam belongs to the Garden into which his Lord has placed him. Adam has a role
within the garden: to tend it. In exchange for his care, he finds sustenance within the
garden. We know from observing the few remaining societies of hunters and gatherers, that they do tend their wilderness – they purposefully set fires to clear land, they
replant parts of plants, they take seeds from one place and put them in another place.[2]
Compared with farmers, and with urbanized populations, hunters and gatherers seem
to be one with their landscape, though, as humans, at least when working as a group,
they stand above all the other animals. Hunters and gatherers are blamed for the

272

extinction of mega-fauna in Australia and North America. Yet, the damage they can do to their environment is limited. Hunters and gatherers are by definition in balance with their environment because they live within a self-regulating system. They move on if food supplies become scarce, and if they don't, there is famine, reducing their burden upon the land from which they gain their sustenance. There are limits to the extent to which hunters and gatherers can alter the ecology of large systems. Hunters and gatherers cannot make a desert from one horizon to another. They cannot drain the Aral sea. If humans still depended on wild foods, the world's climate would not be getting warmer.

> And when the woman saw that the tree was good for food, and that it was pleasant to the eyes, and a tree to be desired to make one wise, she took of the fruit thereof, and did eat, and gave also unto her husband with her; and he did eat. (Genesis 3. 6)[3]

There is a beautiful passage in *Our Mutual Friend* by Charles Dickens in which Lizzie's brother says, 'I used to call the fire at home, her books, for she was always full of fancies... when she sat looking at it.'[4] For the hunter and gatherer, the world around them is their library. Eve knows the fruit of the forbidden tree is good to eat even before she tastes it. The snake says. The wind says. One's neighbour says. One's heart knows.

The authors of Genesis did not provide much information about Adam and Eve's material life before their expulsion from the Garden. We know they didn't make clothing out of skins. It was for their Lord to do that for them once their knowledge of self demanded clothing. But Adam and Eve presumably didn't invent sewing fig leaves at their moment of distress, but rather drew on skills already acquired, which implies they knew how to beat fibre into twine, and how to form a needle. Adam had named the animals, so they will have had their language, their stories, songs, rituals, and their ways of preparing food, and also a particular, personal, identifiable way of making shelters. But even in these enlightened times, we tend to refer to this level of human achievement as culture,[5] rather than civilization.

273

> And unto Adam he said, Because thou hast hearkened unto the voice of thy wife, and hast eaten of the tree, of which I commanded thee, saying, Thou shalt not eat of it: cursed is the ground for thy sake; in sorrow shalt thou eat of it all the days of thy life; Thorns also and thistles shall it bring forth to thee; and thou shalt eat the herb of the field; In the sweat of thy face shalt thou eat bread, till thou return unto the ground; for out of it wast thou taken: for dust thou art, and unto dust shalt thou return. (Genesis 3. 17-19)

Bread was the staple food of the historic biblical period. It was also the staple food throughout most of Europe until comparatively recently, and even today, in English, we 'work for our bread.' And yet, at the core of agriculture's foundation myth – at the source of bread itself – sits a curse. When Cain brings his offering of grains to God, it is rejected. It would take a great deal of effort to make the fruit of the soil that God had just cursed into a viable offering. Perhaps, in the curse against the land – a curse so broad it encompasses the whole enterprise of making bread – we find embedded in the text of Genesis the hunter gatherer's intuitive revulsion against agriculture's inherent violence, and the break from ancient patterns it entailed.

As hunters and gatherers, Adam and Eve worked within the limits of place. If the place failed, they moved on. Farmers don't move on. The farmer stakes out a place on the earth, cuts down the forest, eradicates the field, drains the marsh, demarcates a property line, slices into the earth, kills everything in his path, and then replaces what he has damaged with a monoculture.

The violence inherent in agriculture is implied by our language: three of the most important agricultural implements are associated with violence. The plough: when we plough through something we accomplish our goal in the crudest possible way, with maximum force. The harrow: to harrow is to torment, even torture. The scythe: only the suicide seeks to be cut down by the scythe wielded by the angel of death.

Whether early farmers were slaves is something we don't know. But as slave-farmers are known throughout recorded history – and even recently – the serfs of Russia and the African slaves of America – and as we know that even in America today there are men who are enslaved to pick oranges and sugar cane[6] – it is probably fair to speculate that in the demeaning 'Dust thou art, and unto dust shalt thou return' that closes the curse of Adam's banishment, we find the degradation of the agricultural labourer, if not the slave.

The critique of modern farming practices, including tilling, by green theorists such as Fukuoka Masanobu,[7] Wendell Berry,[8] and Jackson Wes[9] draws on agriculture's violence for its moral force. Modern farming practices, such as using herbicides, breeding crops through the use of genetic engineering, diverting entire rivers for the purposes of irrigation, are merely changes in scale over traditional farming methods – but do not alter the truth that all agriculture is aggressive compared with the hunting gathering idyll represented by the Garden of Eden.

> So he drove out the man; and he placed at the east of the garden of Eden Cherubims, and a flaming sword which turned every way, to keep the way of the tree of life. (Genesis 3. 24)

While the break from depending on wild foods was abrupt and permanent for Adam and Eve, we should assume that they kept in touch with wild foods, that they made forays into the their god's garden to harvest greens, berries, and mushrooms, and also to hunt. Whenever I have spent time with subsistence farmers, whether in Eastern

Europe, Asia, or Africa, there has always been at least some gathering of wild foods.[10] The wild places would also have provided Eve with medicinal herbs with which to heal her family and friends.

In the *Light of August* by William Faulkner, in a passage written in the 1930s, a passage that itself looks back to the 1860s, an abusive husband tells his wife that she can accept no help from neighbours, but must farm her land alone while he goes off to the war. 'God will provide,' he tells her. And she cries out in despair, 'What am I to eat, dandelions and ditch weeds?'[11] What is notable to a modern reader is that from her cry she reveals that she knew dandelions were edible, and that wild pot herbs could be found in ditches. The modern farmer's wife – or the city dweller – would more likely be represented in a novel crying out, 'What am I to eat, air?' Looking out over fields of green most of us see a desert.

In rich countries, and in cities everywhere, there is little knowledge of wild foods. I have noticed that in Europe where gathering wild mushrooms remains a common hobby that the people my age – fifty – tend to know fewer mushroom species than their parents – typically only a few varieties – and their parents harvest many fewer varieties than their parents did. Walking in European forests with friends, I have often been told, 'No, we don't collect that, but our grandparents did.'

There must be many wild foods that were eaten, but for which there is little or no record. I was surprised to find that wild rat – a food I associate with Southeast Asia – was eaten so recently in France that my 1960s-era *Larousse Gastronomique* includes a recipe for rat roasted over the staves of Burgundian wine barrels.[12] From Nabokov's *Pale Fire*, 'Southey liked a roasted rat for supper....'[13]

I do not think it coincidental that as we collectively lose the practice of collecting and eating wild foods – as the Garden of Eden therefore becomes mythic in every sense – that public policy increasingly prohibits gathering in publicly owned lands. There are no open spaces owned by the city, county, or the state in my area – Santa Cruz, California – where one may legally gather greens for a salad, berries for a pie, or mushrooms for a pickle.

> And Adam knew Eve his wife; and she conceived, and bare Cain, and said, I have gotten a man from the LORD. And she again bare his brother Abel. And Abel was a keeper of sheep, but Cain was a tiller of the ground. (Genesis 4. 1-2)

In the Hebrew Bible, history begins with Cain, Eve's first born. He is the first man born a farmer, the first murderer, and the first to exploit the surpluses that farming makes possible to build , and presumably rule, a city. Cain is the mythic father of our civilization. Rather than celebrate agriculture and cities – the very foundation of our material wealth –the Book of Genesis seems to record a darker truth: farming and cities both imply violence – violence against the land, and violence against those who labour, especially violence against those who labour for murderers, like Cain. When Adam and Eve were expelled from the Garden of Eden they were expelled into land that wasn't owned by anybody. The story of Cain is the traumatic story of how the hunters and gatherers lost their land and their freedom – literally and figuratively.

In the Zohar, Cain is identified with impurity and evil.[14] He is of the dark side. The Midrash points out that Cain, Noah, and Uzziah each had an interest in agri-culture, and each came to a bad end, one a murderer, one a drunk, and one a leper.[15] In Midrash stories brought together by Louis Ginzberg, Cain, knowing that he was cursed to the seventh generation, set out to immortalize himself through an ambitious project of city-building.

> This building of cities was a godless deed, for he surrounded them with a wall, forcing his family to stay within.[16]

A murderer, a liar, a cheat, Jewish tradition has it that Cain used every foul means to increase his pleasure, and the wealth of his family.[17] In addition to leading the way in augmenting degrees of inequality within the territories he controlled, he is credited with changing a culture of trustworthiness into one of guile and craftiness: Cain is the mythic author of weights and measures.[18]

To archeologists, Cain's city is the second layer of the ancient city of Jericho. The scale of the first agricultural city represents a complete break with the scale of hunter gatherer settlements. It is six acres, twenty-five times larger than the pre-tiller settle-ment it replaced.[19] Gargantuan by comparison, and complete with a tower and walls to control flooding,[20] it is fair to assume that the social organization that built this city was also very unlike the social organization of hunters and gathers whose community it replaced.

Rousseau, in his essay, *On Human Inequality*, offers a black vision of the shift from hunting and gathering to agriculture and cities, a vision consistent with the Jewish tradition of Cain as a warlord.

> ...work became necessary, and vast forests were transformed into pleasant fields which had to be watered with the sweat of men, and where slavery and misery were soon seen to germinate and flourish with the corns.[21]

From an analysis of human remains we know that the hunters and gatherers who preceded Jericho were healthier than the tillers and labourers who replaced them.[22] Slave or free, the first tillers did not eat as well as they had when roaming the land in search of food.

> If my land cry against me, or that the furrows likewise thereof complain; If I have eaten the fruits thereof without money, or have caused the owners thereof

to lose their life: Let thistles grow instead of wheat, and cockle instead of barley. (Job 31. 38-39)

The farmer cuts into the land. Does the land feel the cut? This passage from Job can be read to imply that the land feels the plough, but that there is a compact between the farmer and the land. The land will accept abuse by the farmer – but only if the farmer approaches the land with honesty. In the Manichean view, as explicated by Bishop Archelaus in the 3rd century CE, everything about farming causes deep harm – including to the soul of the farmer.

Moreover, the reapers who reap ....[are to be] translated into hay, or beans, or barley, or corn, or vegetables, in order that in these forms they, in like manner, may be reaped and cut.[23]

In this Manichean critique of agriculture, bread-making itself is condemned,

And when they are about to eat bread, they offer up prayer first of all, addressing themselves in these terms to the bread: I have neither reaped thee, nor ground thee, nor pressed thee, nor cast thee into the baking-vessel; but another has done these things, and brought thee to me, and I have eaten thee without fault.[24]

The modern American ecology movement is awash in free-floating concerns about the harm we are doing to the world in both a physical and moral sense – and in the harm this harm does us – again – in both a physical and moral sense. The Japanese proponent of 'natural farming', Yoshikazu Kawaguchi, captures these ideas in his self-styled 'online manifesto.' He writes, in part,

Such actions by humans disturb and upset the great harmony of GAIA, and threaten all lives including humans. They devastate the spirit and blur the soul, sickens [sic] the heart, and depletes us of the resistance against illness that harm life, and throw [sic] us into a state of fear. Of course, this is a crisis that is being caused not just by agriculture but all aspects of our human life.[25]

While I doubt any of my readers feel the Manichean concern for the soul of the bread they eat, there are ways in which our concern for the health of the earth brings us to a similar place: a sense that in eating what we eat we may cause harm to the world. Only if the meal we prepare is 100% organic, locally grown, with any meat being grass- and not grain-fed, the fish fished with a line and not a net, and then a variety that is not at any risk, can we sit down to our meal without the ethical burden of having caused some kind of harm as defined by the ecologists – whether that harm is the oil consumed to grow a grain-fed cow, damage to the land or the insect ecology of the countryside, or damage to a particular fish stock. How far we have come from Eden where every bite is a blessing from our Lord, and where we are one with our Garden!

> It might be truly said, that now I worked for my bread. It is a little wonderful, and what I believe few people have thought much upon, viz. the strange multitude of little things necessary in the providing, producing, curing, dressing, making, and finishing this one article of bread.
>
> I, that was reduced to a mere state of nature, found this to my daily discouragement...[26] (*Robinson Crusoe*, Daniel Defoe)

Once Cain built his first city it became impossible to go back. There are many reasons for this – one is that as we tamed the plants and animals we tamed ourselves. We domesticated the fig tree, but the fig tree, through the affection we felt for it, domesticated us. As we enslaved each other we all became enslaved by the promise we found – and that we find – in civilization. While a few of us manage to choose lives that are simpler than those of our immediate family and social group, who drops out altogether to become a hunter and gatherer?

Robinson Crusoe, like Cain[27] – like us – was from the City of Man. He carried walls inside himself. When Robinson Crusoe found himself landed in the Garden of Eden he did not become one with the landscape. His first project was to fortify a dwelling. He then proceeded, through dogged perseverance, to throw himself out of Eden by setting out to make bread – a task that required recreating all the structures of civilization.

Saint Augustine defined Abel as a pilgrim, and thus from the City of God. As a pastoralist, Abel had no need for cities and walls. Had Robinson Crusoe been a pastoralist he would have been able quickly to re-domesticate the goats that were wild on the island, and then he would have been pretty much set. Pastoralists have few possessions, and as with hunters and gatherers, the ecology they depend on is self-regulating.

> And John was clothed with camel's hair, and with a girdle of a skin about his loins; and he did eat locusts and wild honey. (Mark 1:6)

According to the Gospel of Mark, John Baptist put the culture of tilling and the city to his back, clothed himself in the dress of pastoralists, and then walked into the wilderness to sustain himself on wild foods and be closer to his God. Desert locusts (*Schistocerca gregaria*) can often be found in large numbers during the spring in the mountains of Palestine. In the first centuries of the common era locusts were a food associated with the poor.[28] They were boiled, grilled, and brined.[29] It is reasonable to assume that John the Baptist grilled his. Desert locusts are still collected for personal consumption and sale in local markets in the Near East.[30]

Bees fly in a 'beeline' from flowers and sources of water back to their hive.[31] It takes patience to follow bees. I think we should imagine John the Baptist's meditation with his God as being achieved through foraging. While searching for locusts, and while tracing the path of bees, he will have found greens, wild grains, perhaps even trapped small animals, to supplement his meal of poverty and truth.[32] Searching for wild hives, John the Baptist will have been able to align himself with his God on terms similar to those of Adam in the Garden of Eden.

> We obtained one of these handsome birds, which lingered too long upon its perch, and plucked and broiled it here with some other game, to be carried along for our supper.... It is true, it did not seem to be putting this bird to its right use to pluck off its feathers, and extract its entrails, and broil its carcass on the coals; but we heroically persevered, nevertheless, waiting for further information.[33] (Henry D. Thoreau, *A Week on the Concord and Merrimack Rivers*)

In the mid-19th century, Henry Thoreau went with his brother, John, on a canoe trip down the Merrimack river. While they did not eat entirely from the land, wild foods formed a significant part of what they ate, and living off the land was one of the purposes of the trip. But they were living in an increasingly industrial age and could no longer feel entirely comfortable living off the land. Something was changing. Henry felt conflicted about eating the pigeon, and he and his brother felt such revulsion at the sight of a squirrel they caught and skinned that they abandoned the carcass uncooked.

279

The last passenger pigeon died in captivity on 1 September, 1914.[34] At the turn of the 19th century it is estimated that there were more passenger pigeons than all other North American birds combined. The slaughter of the passenger pigeon to the point of extinction – a combination of uncontrolled netting of birds and destruction of habitat[35] – is one of the most egregious examples of the wanton slaughter of a non-human species by humans and is one of the traumas – the slaughter of the bison is another – that underpins the American conservation movement. In Henry Thoreau's argument with himself he expresses an idea that is now explicit in the literature of green organizations, such as the Sierra Club and Earth First. The best use of wild animals and plants is for them to just be.

The Sierra Club's motto, and registered trademark, 'Explore, Enjoy and Protect the Planet!'[36] amounts to a revision of the commandment given Adam to tend the Garden of Eden. The scale is now the planet. In the new vision we stand outside wilderness as protectors, guarding the land from ourselves. We have no agency, at most we observe, and perhaps even that at a distance. 'Protect' is the guiding concept. Wild plants and animals are not our meat. Implicit in the Sierra Club's motto is an absolute prohibition against eating any wild thing from the forest.

WEST GLACIER, MONT. – Rangers at Glacier National Park apprehended two more individuals Wednesday evening, May 12 while in the act of illegally gathering morel mushrooms in the Fish Creek area of the park. No arrests occurred; however, the two men were cited and released.

Pedro-Felipe Gonzalez, 22, of Guatemala (residing in Junction City, Oregon), and Miguel M. Berganza, 19, of Mexico, (also residing in Junction City, Oregon), had just begun to collect morels when rangers made contact with them; therefore, the amount of mushrooms was approximately one pound. Rangers confiscated the morels, the commercial permits, all collection equipment and the subjects' vehicle. All items will be held until court adjudication, which may then include forfeiture of property. (United States Forest Service press release, May 13, 2004.[37])

What horror! What absolute horror! For what crime have these two young men had their livelihood taken away from them? They have lost their morel collecting permit for an adjacent forest, their pocket knives, their packs, and their car! When their case is adjudicated they risk a fine, a jail term, the permanent confiscation of the car, and probably also deportation. What is the crime that warrants this draconian police response? Possession of 225 grams each of morels with a value of at most $3.00? The only crime that could warrant such harsh measures is a crime against the earth in the sense of a heresy.

The press release, in asking the public to turn in other morel collectors, lists seven reasons why morel collecting is dangerous. Here are the first six.

> Potential park impacts from mushroom collecting include disturbance to wildlife species, increased incidence of improper food storage, improper sanitation and/or potential food conditioning of park wildlife, soil impaction and the inadvertent spread of noxious weeds.

Every one of these reasons apply to all visitors to Glacier National Park who walk into the mountains to go backpacking, and most of them apply to every visitor who walks up a trail more than a kilometre or two. All day hikers carry with them some food and water, and toilet paper in case they need to pee or defecate. We can dismiss these reasons as having nothing to do with the police response to morel collectors, as walking in the forest, even off trail, is, as yet, not illegal, much less punishable by the confiscation of ones vehicle.

The scale of western American parks is staggering. To fully appreciate the animus being brought against morel collectors I think it helpful to try to visual the scale of the landscape, and the place of one person, or five-hundred people, and of morels, within it. Glacier National Park is one million acres. There is a large National Forest adjacent to the park – Pedro and Miguel had collecting permits for that adjacent forest.

Morels, like all mushrooms, are fruiting bodies of an underlying fungus. In western North American forests, including those of Montana, morels bloom one year after an ecological catastrophe: a forest fire or clear cutting. Pedro and Miguel were collecting morels where there had been a 130,000 acre fire in the summer of 2003.[38] The next time morels will bloom in large quantity on the spot where Pedro and Miguel were apprehended is in one- to several-hundred years in the future, when the forest has grown back and burned once again.[39]

Why the animus against morel collectors? Why confiscate the men's car at point of contact, rather than issue a warning, and point them back to the adjacent National Forest where they could legally collect. Why include confiscation of the vehicle as a possible penalty for morel collecting? In America, this is the punishment for drug dealers – a major felony offence. Even drunk drivers, people who can be proven by established statistics to have threatened other people's lives, keep their cars. The Forest Service summed up the value of forest mushrooms as follows: 'This process [mushroom bloom and decay] has been taking place for thousands of years and has led to healthy woodland and plant communities.' The Forest Service press release implies two ideas – that there is no place for humans in the wilderness – our very presence is potentially destructive – and that the world is on a knife-edge, and at any moment, even through a tiny action, like collecting mushrooms in a vast wilderness, the balance that has lasted thousands of years could tip, and the healthy forest – or the re-growth of this dead one – could be seriously impaired.

The animus against morel pickers is based on a changing world-view, on the increasing power of the notion that we must protect wild places – but not touch anything within them.

281

> Clearly, the conservation battle is not one of merely protecting outdoor recreation opportunities; neither is it a matter of elitist aesthetics, nor 'wise management and use' of natural resources. It is a battle for life itself, for the continuous flow of evolution. .... It is our decision, ours today, whether Earth continues to be a marvelously living, diverse oasis in the blackness of space, or whether the charismatic mega fauna of the future will consist of Norway rats and cockroaches.[40]

I think we see here a blending of American apocalyptic fundamentalism with environmentalism. And I think this is apocalyptic vision that is beginning to be applied to the management of American parks.

There were no walls in Eden, but until now there was also no wall around Eden. After the expulsion of Adam and Eve it became a quasi-public garden not an unpopulated wilderness. Even the children of Cain visited it often to hunt and gather. They used this food to supplement their farm-based diet. In the new vision, an Eden with people cannot be visualized. It is our duty to the earth – to Gaia – to wall off wild places, and mount guard with armed police. But how can the children of Cain understand wild places when we are no longer gatherers? Drawing on my own experience, I never feel more at one with the forest than when I am walking through the trees feeling the weather, noting the plants, examining the terrain, remembering the same place as it was last year, and as it was as many years before that as I can, in order to compare what I see now with those memories. This is how I find the tree under which I am most likely to find *porcini* for my dinner. Even Saint John the Baptist related to nature through gathering, not just through a stroll in the wilderness. In the United States, it is duck hunters, through their group Ducks Unlimited, who support existing wetlands, and who lobby for expanding wetlands. How are the children of Cain to understand the wilderness – and how to intelligently protect it – how are we to protect our humanness – if we are not allowed to relate to the wilderness as a garden – as humans have been relating to it since we came out of the trees and spread throughout the world. It is important that at least sometimes we be permitted to relate to the natural environment as Adam and Eve did – one of the many animals in nature picking berries for their supper.

Notes

1. Thoreau, Henry David, *Wild Apples* [Etext #4066], http://www.gutenberg.org/dirs/etext03/wldpp10.txt [accessed April 9, 2005].
2. Smith, Bruce D, *The Emergence of Agriculture* (Scientific American Press, New York, 1995), pp. 16-18.
3. All biblical references are to the King James Bible.
4. Dickens, Charles, *Our Mutual Friend* (New York: Penguin Books, 1997) p. 218.
5. A recent *National Geographic News* article on the hunters and gatherers of the Kalahari desert refers to attempts to preserve their 'culture' rather than their 'civilization.' Marshall, Leon 'Bushmen Driven from Ancestral Lands in Botswana' <http://news.nationalgeographic.com/news/2003/04/0416_030416_san2.html > [accessed 9 April 2005].
6. 'Three Florida Men Sentenced in Conspiracy to Detain Workers in Conditions of Involuntary Servitude', <http://www.immigration.com/newsletter1/florida3.html> [accessed 9 April 2005] (par 6 of 13). For more general background see also The U.S. Department of Justice Civil Rights Division website for its Trafficking in Persons and Worker Exploitation Task Force, site < http://www.usdoj.gov/crt/crim/tpwetf.htm > [accessed 9 April 2005] (para. 7).
7. Fukuoka, Masanobu, *The One-Straw Revolution*, trans. Chris Pearce, Tsune Kurosawa, and Larry Korn, preface by Wendell Berry, ed. Larry Corn (Emmaus: Rodale Press, 1978).
8. Berry, Wendell, *The Unsettling of America: Culture & Agriculture* (San Francisco: Sierra Club Books, 1977).
9. Jackson, Wes, *New Roots for Agriculture* (Lincoln and London: University of Nebraska Press, 1980).
10. Patience Gray documented gathering by villagers in Mediterranean Europe in the second half of the 20th century. See Gray, Patience, *Honey from a Weed: Fasting and Feasting in Tuscany, Catalonia, the Cyclades, and Apulia* (New York: Harper & Row, 1987).
11. Faulkner, William, *Light of August* (New York: Vintage International, 1990), p. 467.
12. Montagné, Prosper, *The New Larousse Gastronomique*, ed. Charlotte Turgeon (New York: Crown Publishers, 1977), p. 762.
13. Nabokov, Vladimir, *Pale Fire* (New York: Vintage International, 1989), p. 195.

14. *The Zohar*, trans. and commentary, Daniel C. Matt (California: Stanford UP, 2004), p. 303.

15. *Midrash Rabbah*, trans. by Rabbi Dr. H. Freedman and Maurice Simon, Volume 1 (London: The Soncino Press, 1939), p. 181.

16. Ginzberg, Louis, *The Legends of the Jews*, Vol. 1, 'From creation to Jacob', trans. Henrietta Szold (Baltimore: John Hopkins University Press,1998), p. 115.

17. Ibid., p. 116. On the same page Ginzberg writes: 'The punishment God had ordained for him did not effect any improvement. He sinned in order to secure his own pleasure, though his neighbors suffered injury thereby. He augmented his household substance by rapine and violence; he excited his acquaintances to procure pleasures and spoils by robbery, and he became a great leader of men into wicked courses'.

18. Iibid., pp. 109-115.

19. Smith, op. cit., pp. 2-3. The original settlement was 1 hectare and the next layer 2.5 hectares.

20. Ibid.

21. Rousseau, Jean-Jacques, *A Discourse on Inequality*, trans. Maurice Cranston (New York: Penguin Putnam, 1984), p. 62.

22. Jared,Diamond, *The Worst Mistake in the History of the Human Race*. < http://www.sacredlands. org/jared_diamond_01.htm> [accessed 9 April 2005] (para. 12 of 23).

23. Archelaus, *The Acts of the Disputation with the Heresiarch Manes: Ante-Nicene Fathers*, Volume VI, trans. S. D. F. Salmond, 1871 <http://www.ccel.org/fathers2/ANF-06/anf06-90.htm> [accessed 9 April 2005] (section 9).

24. Ibid.

25. Kawaguchi, Yoshikazu, *Natural Farming and the Path to Life* <http://amana.hp.infoseek.co.jp/ English/kawaguti.html> [accessed 9 April 2005] (para 8 or 17).

26. Daniel Defoe, *Robinson Crusoe* (New York: The Modern Library, 2001), p. 109.

27. St. Augustine, *Concerning the City of God against the Pagans*, trans. Henry Bettenson (London: Penguin Books, 1972), p. 596.

28. Hamel, Gildas H., *Poverty and Charity in Roman Palestine* (Berkeley: University of California Press, 1990), p. 18.

29. Ibid., p. 19.

30. Cressman, Keith, 'Monitoring Desert Locusts in the Middle East: An Overview', *Bulletin Series Yale School of Forestry and Environmental Studies*, 103 (1998) 123-140 (p. 136).

31. *Howe to Find Wild Bees and Get Them* <http://www.bindaree.com.au/newsletters/nldec01.htm> [accessed 9 April 2005].

32. Nothing in the Greek text excludes the possibility that he ate other foods.

33. Thoreau, Henry David, *A Week on the Concord and Merrimack Rivers* < http://www.gutenberg.org/ etext/4232 > [accessed 9 April 2005] (etext number 4232).

34. Ibid.

35. *Passenger Pigeon Extinction: 1914* < http://www.bagheera.com/inthewild/ext_pigeon.htm> [accessed 9 April 2005].

36. <http://www.sierraclub.org > [accessed 9 April 2005].

37. 'Two Commercial Morel Collectors Caught in Glacier National Park': May 13, 2004 < http://www. nps.gov/glac/pphtml/newsdetail12578.html> [accessed 9 April 2005] (para. 1–2). The young men did not show up for their court appearance and so arrest warrants were issued for them. It is a fair assumption that these two men were not in the United States legally. Now that they have failed to appear in court, it is unlikely they could ever legalize their immigration status.

38. This fire burned across two jurisdiction – a national forest adjacent to Glacier National Park, and in the park itself. Fires, such as this one, are usually caused, in part, by the now discredited and abandoned Park Service policy of suppressing all fires. While fire is a 'natural' part of forest health, fires of this size and ferocity are the result of long-standing fire-suppression policies that result in the build up of combustible materials.

39. It is worth keeping in mind, at least to understand the poetry of the place, that Pedro and Miguel were collecting in a blackened forest, in terrain that can be steep, at high altitude, and that the ground they were walking on was covered with a layer of charcoal that crunched with each step. These fires burn so hot that while there are standing trees, there are also many holes in the ground where the fire has burned out the tree, including its roots.

40. *The Problem* < http://www.earthfirstjournal.org/efj/primer/Deep.html> [accessed 9 april 2005] (para. 3 and 7).

The Forest Foodways of the Tribals of India's Bastar District

Colleen Taylor Sen

More than 8% of India's total population, or 84.3 million people, according to the 2001 census, are members of scheduled tribes, also called 'aboriginal tribes' or *adivasis*, Hindi for 'original inhabitants'. They are believed to be descendants of early inhabitants of the subcontinent whose origins are uncertain but over the millennia were pushed back into the forests and hills by invaders, including the Dravidians and the Aryans. One of the oldest and most concentrated tribal regions in India is the district of Bastar in central India, which since the 1930s has been visited and studied by such leading anthropologists as Verrier Elwin, W.V. Grigson and Christoph von Furer-Haimendorf.

More than 350 tribal groups live in every Indian state except Haryana and Punjab. There are two major tribal belts. One extends along the Himalayas from Jammu and Kashmir, Himachal Pradesh, and Uttar Pradesh in the west to the so-called 'seven sisters' – Assam, Tripura, Manipur, Arunchal Pradesh, Mizoram, Meghalaya, and Nagaland in the East. In the last three states more than 85% of the population is tribal. The vast majority of India's tribals (more than 80%) live in the hilly areas of central and western India, where the largest tribes are the 7.4 million Gonds and 5.5 million Bhils. In 2001 two new states were created with significant tribal minorities: Jharkhand, carved out of Bihar, and Chhattisgarh, created from several districts of Madhya Pradesh. Sizable groups of tribals, called Santals, live in Bihar and West Bengal. Smaller groups are found in Tamil Nadu and Kerala, Andhra Pradesh, and Karnataka.

Racially, linguistically, and culturally the tribals are a diverse group. They speak more than a hundred languages belonging to all India's major language families: Dravidian, Indo-European, Austro-Asiatic, and Sino-Tibetan. Even tribals living in the same area may differ substantially from each other in appearance, skin colour, dress, religions, festivals and customs, languages, and foodways.

Indian tribals are granted a special status under the Indian constitution as 'scheduled tribes.' Another protected group constituting around 20% of the total Indian population are 'scheduled castes'. The constitution does not state explicitly how a tribe can be recognized or distinguished from a caste, and the distinction between tribe and caste is often blurred; indeed, according to one anthropologist, 'there exists no satisfactory definition of a tribe anywhere'.[1] Some commonly ascribed attributes of tribes are: geographical isolation; existing as a social formation before the development of or outside of states; political organization under a chief; descent from a common ancestor and affiliation on the basis of kinship; a common language; economic backwardness; and self-sufficiency in economic and cultural life. Many people use the term to refer to any non-Western or indigenous society.

The communities recognized as scheduled tribes are eligible to receive special benefits and to compete for reserved seats in legislatures and educational institutions. The Indian constitution also provides protection against social and economic exploitation. However, this remains a major problem. Tribals have a very high illiteracy rate: 76% for males, 92% for females and are very poor even by the standards of the subcontinent, with 57% living below the poverty line.[2] Malnutrition is rampant and the infant mortality rate very high.

In ancient times, India's aboriginal tribes were food gatherers and primitive hunters. Later many practised shifting cultivation or slash-and-burn farming on the hilly tracts, leaving the plains and broad river valleys to people with ploughs. Land was held in common by the community. Common crops were grain, mainly millets, vegetables, fruits, herbs, and rice. The dense forests that once covered much of the subcontinent provided ample game. In some regions, more advanced agricultural methods were eventually adopted. In the north-east, for example, the Angami Nagas developed sophisticated agricultural and water use practices, including the terrace cultivation of rice, which reduced hunting to a supplementary activity.

Although anthropologists have devoted entire books to such topics as kinship relationships in a south Asian village, they have written relatively little about food, even though most of the vast majority of their subjects' time is spent on food gathering and preparation. However, interest in non-mainstream food appears to growing in India. In 2003 Penguin Books India published *The Essential North-East Cookbook* by a Manipuri author, which describes the cuisines of the tribal peoples of the north-east states and gives recipes.[3] In the fall of 2003 a posh Bombay Hotel offered a buffet dinner that included dishes from the same region.

Nearly twenty years ago I visited the heartland of tribal India: the district of Bastar in Madhya Pradesh. Bastar was at the time the largest district in India in area as well as one of the most sparsely populated; more than 70% of its 2 million people belonged to scheduled tribes. Bastar was at that time off limits to outsiders because of local unrest. However, my husband was working for the government of India during his sabbatical, so we obtained permission to visit the region as well as a car and guide. Today Bastar is open to tourism, though tourist facilities are largely lacking and the official Bastar website warns 'some areas are open to instability, and the whole question of touring tribal districts needs to be approached with acute sensitivity'.[4]

In 1999 Bastar was divided into three districts, the largest of which became part of India's 27th state, Chhattisgarh. The modern district of Bastar has an area of nearly 9000 square kilometres; a population of 1.3 million, 95% of them rural; two towns – Jagdalpur, the capital, with a population of 85,000 and Kodagaon; and 1300 vil-

286

lages. More than 80% of the population over 19 years old is illiterate, the majority of households do not have drinking water or electricity, and infant mortality is high. According to published reports and personal communications, little has changed since our visit but there is hope that now tribals have more political influence conditions will improve.

Bastar's other name is Gondwanaland, the name applied by proponents of the theory of continental drift to one of two hypothetical proto-continents. The distant geological past is visible in enormous outcroppings of ancient rock, which contain vast resources of iron ore, uranium, tin, and other minerals. More than 75% of Bastar is covered with monsoon forests of tropical deciduous trees. The main kinds of forests are sal (*Shorea robusta*), the dominant tree of the region; teak; mixed sal and teak; and bamboo. The north-eastern part of the district is situated on a 2500-foot steep-sided plateau 1200 m above sea level at its highest point. The average annual rainfall is 1540 mm, most of which occurs during the monsoon season (June to September.) The north-western part of the district is covered with hills seamed with valleys and rivers, including the Indravati and its tributaries. Most of the soil is light clay and sand, suitable for raising rice and wet crops. However, deforestation has been continuing.

Bastar is home to many tribes, who speak unrelated languages and do not intermarry. The largest are the Gonds, a term that encompasses several related groups, including the Hill Marias, the Bison Horn Marias and the Murias, all of whom speak different Dravidian dialects. Their origins are unknown. Some scholars claim they are Dravidians who fled into the forests to escape the Aryans in the second millennium BC. Others believe they predate the Dravidians and are related to the Australoid people of the South Pacific. Still others link them to the Mongoloid tribes of north-eastern India. They have lived in Bastar's forests for thousands of years, protected by the rugged terrain against later invaders. The word 'Gond' is derived from a Telugu word meaning 'hill.' Other tribes in Bastar are the Munia, Doria, Dhurva, Bhatar, and Halba, who speak an Indo-European language.

287

Most inhabitants of Bastar live in tiny hamlets in the forests with less than 500 inhabitants. Their huts surrounded by wooden fences are some distance apart and the streets and dwelling places are usually very clean. Sometimes there is a small granary. The impression is one of light and spaciousness, quite different from the typical North Indian village with their narrow alleys and cramped dark houses. All village land is owned collectively.

One reason for the cleanliness is the practice of slash-and-burn farming: Every two or three years the residents move their village to another location to plant their crops. In January the villagers begin clearing trees and underbrush from a tract of forest land near their village. The vegetation dries in the sun for several months, and in May, the hottest month, they set fire to it. The fire smoulders for several weeks; then the workers till the ashes into the soil where they add valuable nutrients. After the first rain, the women plant seeds, using primitive hoes and digging sticks. The most common crops are millets (*Panicum italicum*) and other coarse grains, rice, gourd, cucumber, and tobacco. By November the first grain is ready for consumption. After two or three years, they abandon the plot for new ground. They do not use ploughs or own buffalo, bullocks, or cows. The Muria Gonds who live in the plains tend to be more settled and have started practising sedentary cultivation, especially rice growing.[5]

The diet of the tribals is austere. Staples are a gruel of rice and millet and a dish called *bore*, which is made by fermenting cooked rice overnight and usually eaten for breakfast. This is supplemented by whatever the women can gather in the forest: mangoes, bananas, and other fruits, berries, roots, mushrooms, which thrive in the monsoon season, and tubers including wild tapioca and yams.

Protein consumption is restricted.[6] Milk and milk products are absent from their diet. Wealthier households raise chickens. A source of meat are rats and mice, which are smoked out of the fields after the rice harvest and boiled or roasted. Grubs and insects are also eaten. At one hamlet we visited, an old man was pounding something red in a mortar, which turned out to be a very piquant red ant chutney.

Meat was much more plentiful in the days when Bastar's forests were filled with game, including tigers, panthers, bear, leopards, cheetal (spotted deer), jackal, flying squirrel, wild pigs, barking deer, rabbits, civets, jungle fowl, and bisons.[7] Today the forests are almost empty because of the wholesale slaughter of animals in the past. In a traditional hunt called *porad*, hundreds of tribals would set fire to a long strip of forest and slaughter the animals with spears or poison-tipped arrows when they fled the flames. During our visit, the silence and emptiness of Bastar's forests were eerie: not a bird sang, not a branch rustled. Wandering through the forest we met a hunting party of a dozen young Maria men and their dogs resting in a cool glade next to a water hole. They proudly displayed their day's catch: a single scraggly jungle fowl. They told us they planned to take it back to the village and make a stew so that everyone could enjoy what had become a rare delicacy.

Like most tribes in India, the Gond brew and consume their own alcohol. *Sulfi*, the fermented sap of the sago palm, was readily available for a few rupees a gourdful and became our staple drink in an area where water quality was uncertain. A few minutes after it is tapped, *sulfi* has a delightful tangy dry taste reminiscent of champagne. When it thickens, it packs more of a punch. Gond men, women, and children drank it constantly, and have a saying 'Hell for a Gond is a place where there is no *sulfi*.'

Another alcoholic beverage, *mhowa*, is brewed from the flowers and seeds of the mahua tree (*Madhuca indica*), an ancient plant mentioned in the Vedas. The flowers are placed in a large pot, soaked in water for a couple of days with a change of water, and then boiled. A small pot is placed inside the large pot, so that the vapours from the large pot condense inside. The liquor is decanted through a small pipe. A 19th-century British administrator wrote of *mhowa*, 'The spirit, when well made and mellowed by age, is by no means of despicable quality, resembling in some degree Irish whisky'.[8] In the mid-19th century twenty distilleries near Bombay produced mahua spirit. The Gonds also eat the flowers, sometimes mixed with chickpea flour or parched grains. They crush boiled seeds between two wooden planks or the tree trunks to produce oil for cooking.

The forests also provide products that the tribals sell to outsider traders to purchase necessities such as salt, sugar, oil, and cooking utensils. The most important are tamarind pods; *chironji*, a seed used in Indian sweets; mangoes; cashews; resin; wild cardamoms; honey; leaves used to make leaf plates and *bidi* (Indian cigarette) wrappings; and the cocoons of the tussah silkworm, which feed on sal leaves and produce a heavy silk much valued for saris. Many plants used in Ayurvedic medicine grow in the forests.

Outside one village we met a group of wandering traders from Orissa who were exchanging salt brought from the seashore for an equivalent weight of tamarind. Our guide indignantly pointed out that tamarind sold for twice the price of salt in the open market and branded the traders as exploiters. However, in this case the salt traders were just as poor as the tribals themselves, and had walked hundreds of miles from the seashore and back just as their forefathers had done for centuries, for a profit that barely kept them from the verge of starvation. The government has established cooperatives to supply consumer goods, especially salt, at a fair price but they have not always been successful. They have also formed cooperative societies to buy forest products at a fair price and train the *adivasi* in productive skills.

Festivals in Bastar centre around the forests and harvests. Around two-thirds of the Gonds are animists who worship their own gods and spirits, though elements of Hinduism have been incorporated into their religious beliefs. Most ceremonies for marriages, death anniversaries, and other family events occur in the dry summer months when people are free from agricultural labour. They have five main festivals related to the planting, weeding, harvesting and use of crops, the start of the hunting season, and the date at which certain fruits, flowers, and leaves may be picked for daily use. The dates are chosen by the villages elder and vary by village in the region.

289

While abhorring the tribals' poverty and exploitation, Indian intellectuals have also idealized their life as a sort of Rousseauian paradise. Their social freedom is considerable, especially for unmarried adolescents, and a welcome relief from the caste-ridden strictures of Hindu society. The British anthropologist Verrier Elwyn (who married a tribal woman) rhapsodized over Bastar as a 'Brave New World' where emotions such as jealousy and possessiveness were unknown. India's first Prime Minister Jawaharlal Nehru also eulogized the tribals, writing 'I am not at all sure which is the better way of living. In some respects I am quite certain theirs is better.'[9]

Notes

1. Fuchs, 23.
2. Singh et al.
3. Hauzel,Hoinu. *The Essential North-East Cookbook.*
4. <www.secretindia.net/palace_life_bastar_royal_farm/php>.
5. Some of the varieties grown in Bastar using traditional cultivation practices obtain very high yields. The state of Chhattisgarh is home to more than 20,000 varieties of rice, which scientists are now studying in order to identify strains that are tasty, high-yielding, and hardy. Krishnan and Ghosal, *Rice.*
6. A study of the diet of the Urali, a tribe living in the Travancore Hills in Kerala, which is very similar to that of the Gonds, found it to be nutritionally very inadequate, especially in view of peoples' hard physical labor. Their diet of grains, vegetables, fruits, and small amounts of leafy vegetables provided around 2228 calories a day, 25% less than the recommended amount, and 37 grams of protein, half that consumed by the average Indian and 45% of the recommended amount. Vitamins, iron, and trace minerals were also inadequate. P.N. Sen Gupta, 'Dietaries of Primitive Tribes.'
7. The most famous animal of Bastar and the state animal of Chhattisgarh is conspicuous by its absence: the wild bison (*Bubalus bubalis – B. arnee*), which today lives only in wildlife sanctuaries. It gave its name to the Bison Horn Marias, who wear elaborate head-dresses made from feathers and bison horns during a popular dance.
8. Achaya, *Historical Dictionary*, 137
9. Jawaharlal Nehru, 'The Tribal Folk', in *The Tribal People of India*, p. 2.

Bibliography

Achaya, K. T., *The Food Industries of British India* (Delhi: Oxford Univrsity Press, 1994).
——— , *A Historical Dictionary of Indian Food* (Delhi: Oxford University Press, 2002).
Census of India 2001, http:///www.censusindia.net.
Elwyn, Verrier. *The Tribal World of Verrier Elwin: An Autobiography* (Delhi: Oxford University Press, 1998).
———, *The Muria and Their Ghotul* (London: Oxford University Press, 1947).
Fuchs, Stephen, *The Aboriginal Tribes of India* (London, St. Martin's Press, 1973).
Furer-Haimendorf, Christoph von, *Return to the Naked Nagas* (London: John Murphy, 1976).
Nehru, Jawaharlal, 'The Tribal Folk', in *The Tribal People of India* (New Delhi: Ministry of Information and Broadcasting, Government of India, 1954), pp. 1-7.
Grigson, W. V., *The Maria Gonds of Bastar* (London: Oxford University Press, 1938).
Guha, Ramachandra, *Savaging the Civilized: Verrier Elwin, His Tribals and India* (New Delhi: Oxford University Press, 1999).
Hauzel, Hoihnu, *The Essential North-East Cookbook* (New Delhi: Penguin Books, 2003).
Krishnan, Omkar and Anjali Ghosal, *Rice* (New Delhi: Navdanya, 1995).
National Informatics Center, Chhattisgarh, 'Bastar: The Land of Tribals and Natural Resources,' website http://bastar.nic.in.
Ramnath, Madhu, 'Tropical Deciduous Forests and the Adivasi. Indigenous Tradition as Response to Leaf Fall in Bastar, India', in *Natural Resources Forum* 27 (2003), pp. 304-309.
Sen, Colleen Taylor, *Food Culture in India* (Westport: Greenwood Press, 2004).
Sen Gupta, P. N., 'Dietaries of Primitive Tribes', in *The Tribal People of India* (New Delhi: Ministry of Information and Broadcasting, Government of India, 1954), pp. 91-100.
Singh, Amar Kumar, S.K. Sinha, S.N.Singh, Meera Jawasawal, and M.K. Jabbi, 'The Myth of the Healthy Tribal', in *Global Reproductive Health Forum @ Harvard*, http//www.hsph.harvard.edu/organizations/healtnet/SASIA/forums/Tribals/Tribals/M008.
Thapar, Romila, *Early India: From the Origins to AD 1300* (Berkeley: University of California Press, 2002).

The Fall and Rise of the Wild Turkey

Andrew F. Smith

The wild turkey (*Meleagris gallopavo*) is a large, non-migratory land bird that can fly distances of up to a mile. While they may not be graceful in their flight, wild turkeys have been clocked at speeds of 55 miles per hour. Although they can fly, wild turkeys prefer to use their powerful legs for locomotion, using their wings only to flee danger or to leap at dusk into trees, where they like to roost during the night. They can also float on water, which makes it possible for them to ford wide rivers, such as the Mississippi and the Missouri.

The common turkey originated in North America about 50,000 years ago, but large turkey-like birds have inhabited the continent for a few million years. As their closest living relative is the Asian pheasant, researchers have proposed that the turkey's forebears evolved in Asia or North America from common ancestors, but if so, no intermediate fossils have been located.

Numerous fossils of various turkey species have been unearthed in North America, but only two species survived into historical times: the ocellated turkey (*Agriocharis ocellata*), which is found in Mexico's Yucatán peninsula, Belize and Guatemala; and the common turkey, which ranged throughout much of North America from what is now the Canadian province of Ontario to the area around Veracruz, Mexico. Wild turkeys disappeared from California about 10,000 years ago, perhaps as a result of early human habitation or climatic changes. Geographic isolation created five major subspecies: the Florida wild turkey (*M. g. osceola*), found in the southern half of Florida; Merriam's (*M. g. merriami*), native to the mountain regions of the western United States; the Rio Grande (*M. g. intermedia*), found in the south-central Plains states and north-eastern Mexico; and finally Gould's turkey (*M. g. mexicana*), which is native to north-western Mexico and parts of Arizona and New Mexico. In pre-Columbian times, the range of wild turkeys did not extend into South America or the Caribbean.

Throughout their areas of habitation, wild turkeys have been of great importance to humans since before the dawn of recorded history. Numerous archaeological remains of turkeys have been found throughout North America. In some sites turkey bones ranked second only to deer bones.[1] The Aztecs ate them in great quantities as did many Native Americans. Wild turkeys are easily tamed and at some point during the past two thousand years they were domesticated, probably in more than one location in Mexico and in the American south-west. Domesticated turkeys spread beyond the pre-Columbian range of the wild turkeys, as European explorers found them in the Yucatán peninsula and northern Central America.

Each Native American group developed their own approach to turkeys. Virginian William Byrd observed that some Indians would not boil turkey in the same vessel with 'land animals' for fear of offending 'the Guardian of the Forest'.[2] The Navajo only ate the birds roasted, while others boiled them.[3] Some Indian tribes did not consider the wild turkey enough of a delicacy to warrant the attention of their experienced hunters. The Lipan Apaches ate no other fowl but the wild turkey, while other Native American groups refused to eat any turkey flesh.[4] The Cheyenne eschewed the turkey because they believed it to be a cowardly bird, as it ran away at high speed at the least provocation.[5] The Chiricahua Apaches did not eat the turkey because it ate insects.[6] Turkey eggs, however, were consumed by many Native Americans, and some considered them a delicacy.[7]

Many Indians who did not eat turkeys did value parts of the bird for utilitarian and ceremonial purposes. The feathers adorned clothing and headdresses, and were fashioned into fans. The Hopi used feathers and the bristles from turkey beards to decorate their prayer sticks.[8] The Kiowas and Comanches used turkey feathers on their arrows, and spurs from the birds' legs were used for arrowheads.[9] The Papagoes Indians of the south-west hunted turkeys for their feathers, which were used in religious ceremonies.[10] Turkey bones were made into spoons and awls as well as beads and other decorations. And turkey remains have been found buried along with mortuary offerings.[11]

292

European Contact with the Turkey

European explorers may have encountered turkeys along the Mexican coast prior to 1518, but if they did, no unambiguous references have been found. The first clear reference appears in a description of the Spanish expedition from Cuba led by Juan de Grijalva who explored Yucatán and the Mexican coast in 1518.[12] The following year, Hernan Cortez followed a similar route and landed in Mexico, where the Conquistadores found an abundance of both domesticated and wild turkeys.

The Spanish introduced domesticated turkeys into the Caribbean by 1520 and into Spain shortly thereafter. From Spain, domesticated turkeys were quickly disseminated throughout Western Europe and the Mediterranean, thus making turkey among the first New World food products adopted in the Old World. There are several reasons for its quick entrance into Europe's diet: Turkeys were seen as similar to the prestigious peacock, which had been eaten by the élite since the Middle Ages, but turkey had much better flavour. Turkeys supplied much more meat than did the commonly eaten chicken. As they were easily bred, domesticated turkeys quickly became plentiful throughout Western Europe, and they were enjoyed by all but the poorest people.

How the Turkey Got its Name

In addition to the turkey, Spanish explorers in the New World found many other birds, such as the curassow (*Crax ruba*), crested guan (*Penelope purpurascens*), horned guan (*Oreophasis derbiannus*), and chachalacas (*Ortalis and Penelopina*), all of which were called *pavo*, meaning peacock-like.[13] To make this more confusing, the guinea fowl (*Numida meleagris*), a native of Africa, was also called *pavo*. That Spaniards and subsequently other Europeans linguistically mixed up the turkey, peacock, and the guinea fowl is not at all surprising. All three are large birds, and the males of each species display their tails at mating time. Hence, the Spanish name for turkey is *pavo* (peafowl) or *pavon de las Indias* (peafowl of the Indies). The French called the male *coq d'Inde* (cock of India), which was shortened to *dindon*, and the female *dinde*.

Only English-speaking countries and some former British colonies use the word 'turkey'. Numerous explanations, most of them fanciful, have been offered for the use of this word. Some have proposed that the turkey acquired its name because its call sounds like 'turk, turk', or that it comes from the Hebrew word *tukki*, which means peacock, or that it was a corruption of a Hindu word.[14] Others believe that the bird's name came about because the peculiar gait of the cock resembles 'the proud and Turkish strut'.[15] Still others have proposed that it was named for the 'turkey merchants' who engaged in trade between the Eastern Mediterranean and England, and who frequently stopped off in Spain and may have picked up turkeys before proceeding to England.[16]

As interesting as these explanations may be, the word turkey was used in England prior to the arrival of *Meleagris gallopavo* in Europe. It referred to several birds, the most important of which was the guinea fowl. Guinea fowl had been raised in the ancient Mediterranean, but had not survived in Europe. They were reintroduced into Europe by the Portuguese in the mid-15th century and arrived in England before the common turkey. As guinea fowl were also sold in North Africa, it is not surprising that these birds were called 'turkeys'. As *Meleagris gallopavo* became the dominant bird in England, it retained the name while the other birds were called by other names.

293

Another cause of confusion in nomenclature was the fact that world geography was not well understood in the 16th century, and frequently animals and plants arrived in Europe without their original point of origin being known. Conrad Gesner, a 16th-century Swiss naturalist, was among the first Europeans to describe and illustrate the domesticated turkey. He used the term *gallopavo*, Latin for peacock. He, along with other naturalists of the period, believed that the turkey and the guinea fowl were identical.[17]

By the mid-17th century it was commonly understood that these three birds originated in widely separated locations and were not closely related. So there was no legitimate reason for the 18th-century Swedish botanist, Carl von Linne (more commonly known as Linnaeus), to bestow on the turkey the generic name of *Meleagris*, which had been used in Greco-Roman times for the guinea fowl. For the species name, Linnaeus selected *gallopavo*, which was more appropriate.

Wild Turkeys in North America

European colonists arriving in North America in the early 17th century were already quite familiar with domesticated turkeys. When George Peckham examined Humphrey Gilbert's failed attempt to establish an English colony in Newfoundland in 1583, he made recommendations for what future colonists headed for North America should take with them. On his list were male and female turkeys.[18] Peckham was unaware that wild turkeys twice the size of domesticated ones inhabited Eastern North America.

Adriaen van der Donck, a Dutchman who travelled to New Amsterdam in 1641, reported that wild turkeys were 'large, heavy, fat and fine, weighing from twenty to thirty pounds each, and I have heard of one that weighed thirty-two pounds.'[19] John Lawson, a Londoner who surveyed North Carolina beginning in 1700, told of wild turkeys weighing forty pounds.[20] Virginian William Byrd caught a turkey that weighed thirty-four pounds, and others claimed that some of the birds weighed more than fifty pounds.[21] John Josselyn, who resided in New England in the mid-17th century, dined on a wild turkey that weighed thirty pounds after it had been gutted and cleaned, and said he'd heard of turkeys that weighted forty and even sixty pounds.[22] Yet another source estimated that Maryland turkeys weighed up to sixty-three pounds.[23]

In addition to weighing more, wild turkeys in America were also plentiful. In New England, John Josselyn claimed that in 1645 he saw sixty broods of young turkeys totalling several hundred individuals 'on the side of a Marsh, sunning themselves in a morning betimes'.[24] Adriaen van der Donck reported that wild turkeys were 'found in large flocks, from twenty to forty in a flock'.[25] In 1727 the French Jesuit, Father Sébastien Rasles, wrote that in Illinois, 'We can hardly travel a league without meeting a prodigious multitude of Turkeys, which go in troops, sometimes to the number of 200.'[26] 18th-century English traveller John F. D. Smyth reported that on the upper Ohio River, turkeys were 'without number', and that there were sometimes as many as five thousand in a flock.[27]

In the 19th century, wild turkeys were even more numerous in Texas and Oklahoma. In Frio County, Texas, H. L. Bingham saw in one roost, 'over a thousand turkeys'.[28] Another observer saw flocks containing three thousand turkeys each.[29] Another Texan reported that in ten or twelve acres of dense growth of shrubby trees, 'How many thousands or millions of turkeys there may have been I would not attempt to say.'[30] In Oklahoma, Richard M. Wright saw flocks of turkeys cover the prairie for miles, numbering in the thousands.[31] Many others just reported seeing 'innumerable' or 'countless' turkeys.

The exact number of wild turkeys in America prior to the arrival of Europeans is impossible to know, but based on evidence of the number of the birds in specific areas, turkey specialist Arlie Schorger has conservatively estimated that the wild turkey population at the time of European contact totalled at least ten million birds.[32]

Wild Turkey as Food

Turkeys were eaten in virtually every early European colony on the east coast of North America. Wild turkeys were so numerous along the banks of the James River in Virginia that in 1607 Captain John Smith named the island in the middle of the river 'Turkey Isle'. Two years later, the Indians brought turkeys to Jamestown, which helped stem starvation in that colony.[33] In 1621, William Bradford, first governor of Plimoth Plantation, reported that there 'was a great store of wild turkeys, of which they took many'.[34] William Byrd believed that turkeys were 'a splendid dish, boiled or roasted. The wild ones have commonly a finger's thickness of fat on their back, which one uses for cakes and garden cooking, because it is sweet and far better than the best butter, as I myself have discovered.'[35] In 1797 John Heckewelder, a Moravian evangelist in Ohio, used wild turkey fat as a substitute for butter, and turkey eggs for making dumplings.[36] A pioneer woman in Iowa found turkey eggs more palatable than those of other wild birds.[37]

Several individuals survived on turkeys for long periods of time appear. For instance, in 1773 Joseph and Samuel Martin lived exclusively on boiled turkey for two or three months until their corn crop matured.[38] Through the rural parts of the West wild turkey remained staple foods for some generations. When a family first settled a wilderness area and lacked both grain and vegetables, they called the breasts of wild turkeys and lean venison 'bread', as neither wheat nor corn was available in the wilderness.[39] In Georgia, in the 1830s, 'For bread, they strung up and dried out the 'white' meat of wild turkey breasts, after which they cut it up and beat it into a kind of flour, and kneaded it for bread.'[40]

In addition to providing basic sustenance, wild turkeys were also considered gourmet treats. The French gastronome Jean Anthelme Brillat-Savarin spent two years in exile in the United States after the French Revolution in 1789. He was delighted with the turkey, which he proclaimed was 'certainly one of the most delightful presents which the New World has made to the Old.' He ate wild turkey as well as domestic, writing that wild turkey flesh was 'Darker and with a stronger flavor than that of the domestic bird.' He recorded in his magnum opus, *Physiology of Taste*, that while visiting Hartford, Connecticut, he was invited to hunt on the land of a local farmer, and had the 'good luck' to kill a wild turkey. Back in Hartford, Brillat-Savarin roasted the turkey and wrote that it was 'flattering to the sense of smell, and delicious to the taste. And as the last morsel of it disappeared, there arose from the whole table the words: "Very good! Exceedingly good! Oh! Dear sir, what a glorious bit!"'[41]

Brillat-Savarin was not alone in his devotion to the wild turkey. The American naturalist and ornithologist John James Audubon wrote that it was 'a delicate and highly prized article of food'. It was 'of excellent flavor, being more delicate and juicy than that of the domestic Turkey.'[42] Wild turkey was on the menus of America's best restaurants, such as the City Hotel in New York, and it was often served stuffed with truffles.[43] Gilbert du Montier, better known as the Marquis de Lafayette, appreciated wild turkeys to such an extent that when he visited the United States in 1824–25 he asked John

Hartwell Cocke to send a flock to his estate in France so that he could release them. In gratitude for the shipment, the Marquis sent Cocke a bell for his barn, which still rings on occasion today.[44]

But not everyone agreed with these positive assessments. According to one 19th-century observer, the superior taste of the wild turkey over the domesticated one was created only in the 'imagination'.[45] Others found the flavour of wild turkey very distasteful. There are a few explanations for these negative comments. First, old turkeys, whether domesticated or wild, do not taste as good as young ones. While domesticated turkeys are slaughtered when fairly young, a turkey shot in the wild may be up to ten years old. Second, as wild turkeys disappeared from eastern North America, they were brought to eastern markets from increasingly longer distances away. Prior to refrigeration, turkeys were often weeks old before they reached market. Finally, the taste of a wild turkey depends upon what it eats. For instance, turkeys that feed on bitter chinaberries are inedible.[46]

Turkey recipes have been published in cookbooks since the 16th century, and they were included in most early American cookbooks. As wild turkeys were not available outside North America, all European recipes were for preparing domesticated turkeys. While wild turkeys can generally be prepared in the same manner as domesticated turkeys, there are important differences. Descriptions of roasting or boiling wild turkeys do appear in the general historical literature, but recipes specifically for wild turkeys rarely appeared in 19th-century cookbooks: Marion Harlan includes one in her *Common Sense in the Household* (1871).[47] Marion Cabell Tyree's *Housekeeping in Old Virginia* (1879) included recipes for 'Wild Turkey' and 'A Simpler Way to Prepare Wild Turkey'.[48] Lafcadio Hearn's *La Cuisine Creole* (1885) also contained one for 'Wild Turkey'.[49] A few other recipes appear in cookbooks published through the early 20th century, when they disappear from American cookbooks. This reflects the general lack of wild turkeys in the settled regions where cookbooks were published. By the time cookbooks were published in a region, wild turkeys were fast disappearing.

Decline of the Wild Turkey

The wild turkey was a large bird, and as such, it was much desired, not only for its flesh, but it was also highly prized as a trophy by hunters. In addition, wild turkeys, unlike migratory fowl, remained in the area the year round. The fall and winter were the best seasons to hunt them, and during the coldest months, when other game was not easily found, wild turkeys became a main source of food.

Wild turkeys were also relatively easy to catch. Native Americans used snares and pole traps, which caught one bird at a time.[50] European colonists used hunting dogs to locate and retrieve turkeys, but Adriaen van der Donck reported that 'the greatest number are shot at night from the trees. The turkeys sleep in trees, and frequently in large flocks together. They also usually sleep in the same place every night. When a sleeping place is discovered, then two or three gunners go to the place together at night, when they shoot the fowls, and in such cases frequently bring in a dozen or more.'[51] In 1634, William Wood wrote: 'Such as love Turkye hunting most follow it in winter after a new-fallen Snow, when hee may followe them by their tracks; some haue killed ten or a dozen in half a day; if they can be found towards evening and watch where they perch, if one come about ten or eleven of the clock, he may shoote as often as he will, they will sit.'[52]

In 18th-century Virginia, Robert Beverley wrote that a friend of his had 'invented a great trap, wherein he at times caught many turkeys, and particularly seventeen at one time; but he could not contrive it so as to let others in, after he had entrapped the first flock, until they were taken out.'[53] Wild turkeys were shot, and sometimes whole flocks were driven into log-pen traps.[54] Circular hunts were organized, in which several square miles were surrounded by people who slowly drove the wild turkeys toward a group of hunters. Colonists and early Americans perfected the method and hunts netted hundreds of turkeys.[55]

By the late 17th century, Americans began to recognize that wild turkeys were rapidly disappearing. In 1672, John Josselyn reported that in New England the English and the Indian had 'destroyed the breed, so that 'tis very rare to meet with a wild Turkie in the Woods.'[56] By the 1730s wild turkeys had almost disappeared east of the Connecticut River. They still thrived in upstate New York, eastern Pennsylvania, and most of the South. By the late 18th century, Joseph Doddridge recorded that in Virginia 'wild turkeys, which used to be so abundant as to supply no inconsiderable portion of provision for the first settlers, are now rarely seen.'[57]

The disappearance of the wild turkey from many areas of its original habitat did not diminish the wholesale slaughter of its surviving numbers. The last wild turkey in Connecticut was seen in 1813. Wild turkeys disappeared from Vermont by 1842, New York by 1844, and Massachusetts by 1851. As wild turkeys disappeared from the east coast, they were hunted in western states and sent east frozen by winter weather.[58] As the wild birds became scarcer, they became a prized delicacy, and restaurants occasionally served wild turkeys on special occasions. When Charles Dickens visited the United States in 1842, for instance, he was served 'Roast Wild Turkies Stuffed with Truffles'.[59]

In 1876, the Philadelphia Women's Centennial Committees published *The National Cookery Book*, containing recipes from almost every state and territory. The book explains that in 'western states the wild turkey is still a familiar dish, but it is seldom seen in the cities of the Atlantic coast; here they are only to be obtained in the severe winter weather, when they are brought in a frozen condition many hundreds of miles.'[60] Actually, by this date, wild turkeys had already begun to disappear from many western states as well. They were last seen in Kansas in 1871 and they disappeared from South Dakota by 1875, Ohio in 1880 and in Nebraska the same year. In the following years wild turkeys disappeared from Wisconsin (1881), Michigan (1897), Illinois (1903), Indiana (1906), and Iowa (1907).

So many wild turkeys had been hunted that in 1884 Gaston Fay predicted in *Harper's Weekly* that the wild turkey was soon to become 'as extinct as the dodo'.[61] It appeared as if Fay's forecast was to come true. By the 1920s turkey had virtually disappeared from twenty of thirty-nine states of its original range.[62] Turkeys reached their lowest population in the late 1930s, when they survived only in isolated and inaccessible pockets generally away from humans.[63] Estimates vary as to the number of wild turkeys at that time, but some observers believe that there were as few as 30,000 birds left in the United States.

In many ways, the demise of the wild turkey parallels the slaughter of other North American wildlife. An estimated 60 million buffalo (*Bison bison*) roamed throughout much of eastern North America in pre-Columbian times. During the eighteenth and nineteenth centuries, vast herds of buffalo were killed by hunters and sportsmen. By 1900, the buffalo was nearly extinct. A similar fate confronted wildfowl. Large birds, such as North American cranes and swans, were so prized that they had largely disappeared from the East Coast by 1750. Brants (*Branta bernicla*) had almost disappeared by the 1880s. The canvasback duck (*Aythya valisineria*) became nearly extinct. The passenger pigeon (*Ectopistes migratorius*) numbered an estimated five billion before European contact; they were slaughtered to such an extent that by 1909 only two passenger pigeons remained alive, and five years later the breed was extinct.

The Return of the Wild Turkey

While wild turkeys were rapidly declining, many states passed laws restricting the hunting seasons and regulated the number of turkeys that a hunter could bag during a season. These laws were generally unenforced or ineffective. As many American wildlife species became threatened, Congress passed legislation that was intended to protect wildlife. The Lacey Act of 1905 prevented interstate sale of wildlife. Along with other laws, this prevented the sale of frozen wild turkeys and thus gave some protection to wild turkey flocks. More important was the Pittman-Robertson Act of 1937, which imposed an excise tax on sporting goods and ammunition to pay for the restoration of wildlife. By 1940, Federal Aid in Wildlife Restoration projects began reintroducing wild turkeys into natural habitats.[64] There was yet another important change: during the Depression, many farms were abandoned, and the land reverted to forest, which laid the foundation for comeback of the wild turkey.

With land returning to natural turkey habitats, the main problem was how to capture wild turkeys and re-introduce them to areas devoid of wild turkeys. While many methods were tried, the eventual solution was the cannon net, which propelled a concealed net over flock of turkeys. Initially used to capture waterfowl, it was propelled by black-powder cannons detonated by an operator stationed in a nearby blind. The first wild turkeys known to have been captured this way were taken in South Carolina in 1951. Since then, 'trap and transplant' programmes accelerated. In the 1960s sleep-inducing drugs were used to capture live birds. Computers and solar-powered transmitters with motion sensors have been used to help track wild turkeys.[65]

The results of these restoration efforts have been astounding. From a nadir in the 1930s, wild turkey populations had increased to 500,000 birds in 1959. By 2005, there were an estimate 6.5 million wild turkeys nationwide.[66] Today, wild turkeys occupy more square miles than do any other game birds in North America, and they now inhabit an area far beyond its original ancestral range, including every state (except Alaska), several provinces in Canada, and several countries in Europe.

The return of the wild turkey has also meant the return of hunting. Wild turkey hunting is one of the fastest growing gun sports in the United States. Turkey hunters annually spend more than half a billion dollars on their sport. Likewise, the return of the wild turkey has seen a vast increase in recipes for preparing them, and several cookbooks have been solely dedicated to this purpose, including two books, by Rick Black and A. D. Livingston, both titled *Wild Turkey Cookbook*.[67]

Conclusion

Probably no other game bird has had more of an impact on the peoples of North America than has the wild turkey. The species has directly influenced lifestyles of people living in North America from pre-Columbian times to modern times. Mammalogist A. Remington Kellogg, director of the United States National Museum, claimed that had it not been for the supply of meat from deer and turkeys, the westward expansion of the United States would have been long delayed.[68] Wild turkeys almost disappeared during the early 20th century, but they were among the first wild animals to be successfully reintroduced through the efforts of the government.

299

Notes

1. John W. Aldrich, 'Historical Background', in Oliver H. Hewett, ed., *The Wild Turkey and its Management* (Washington, DC: The Wildlife Society, 1967), p. 6; James Earl Kennamer, Mary Kennamer, and Ron Brenneman, 'History', in James G. Dickson , comp. and ed., *The Wild Turkey; Biology and Management* (Mechanicsburg, PA: Stackpole Books, 1992), p. 9.
2. William Byrd, *Histories of the Dividing Line betwixt Virginia and North Carolina* (Raleigh: North Carolina Historical Commission, 1929), p. 194.
3. Willard W. Hill, *The Agricultural and Hunting Methods of the Navaho Indians* (New Haven: Published for the Department of Anthropology, Yale University, by the Yale University Press, 1938), p. 174.
4. F. M. Buckelew, *The Life of F. M. Buckelew, the Indian Captive* (Bandera, Texas: Hunter's Printing House, 1925), p. 90.
5. H. C. Keeling, 'The Indians: My Experience with the Cheyenne Indians', *Kansas State Historical Society Collections for 1909-1910,* 11 (1910): 308.
6. Morris E. Opler, *An Apache Life-way* (Chicago: The University of Chicago Press, 1941), p. 328.
7. George Henry Loskiel, *History of the Mission of the United Brethren among the Indians in North America* (London: The Brethren's Society for the Furtherance of the Gospel, 1794), p. 91.
8. Leo W. Simmons, ed., *Sun Chief, the Autobiography of a Hopi Indian* (New Haven: Yale University Press, 1942), p. 55.
9. Thomas C. Battey, *The Life and Adventure of a Quaker among the Indians* (Boston: Lee and Shepard; New York: Lee, Shepard and Dillingham, 1875), p. 323.

10. Edward F. Castetter and Ruth M. Underhill, *The Ethnobiology of the Popago Indians* (New York: AMS Press, 1978), pp. 41, 71.

11. A. W. Schorger, *The Wild Turkey; Its History and Domestication* (Norman: University of Oklahoma Press, 1966), p. 363.

12. G. Fernandez Oviedo y Valdés, *Historia General y Natural de las Indias* (Madrid: Impr. de la Real academia de la historia, 1851), Vol. 1, p. 507; Bernal Díaz del Castillo, *Verdadera y notable Relación del Descubrimiento y Conquesta de la Nueva España y Guatemala* vol. 1 (Guatamala: [Tipografía Nacional], 1933), p. 26, both as noted in A. W. Schorger, *The Wild Turkey; Its History and Domestication* (Norman: University of Oklahoma Press, 1966), p. 6.

13. A. W. Schorger, *ut sup.*, 4.

14. Henry E. Davis, *The American Wild Turkey* (Georgetown, SC: Small-Arms Technical Publishing Co., 1949).

15. John Cook Bennett, *The Poultry Book* (Boston: Phillips, Sampson & Company, 1850), p. 106.

16. James C. Clark, ed. and trans., *Codex Mendoza, the Mexican Manuscript Known as the Collection of Mendoza and Preserved in the Bodleian Library, Oxford* Volume 1 (London: Waterlow & Sons, Limited, 1938), p. 58; Reay Tannahill, *Food in History* Rev. ed. (New York: Crown, 1988), p. 211.

17. Conradi Gesneri, *Tigurini medici & philosophiæ professoris in Schola Tigurina, Historiæ animalium...* (Tiguri: Apud Christoph. Froschouerum, 1555), p. 464.

18. 'Sir George Peckham's True Report of the Late Discoueries', Part 2, in Richard Hakluyt, ed., *The Principal Navigations, Voyages, Traffiques and Discoveries of the English Nation* (Edinburgh: E. & G. Goldsmid, 1889), vol. 13, p. 271.

19. Thomas F. O'Donnell, ed., *A Description of the New Netherlands by Adriaen van der Donck* (Syracuse: Syracuse University Press, 1968), p. 50.

20. John Lawson, *The History of Carolina; Containing an Exact Description of the Inlets, Havens, Corn, Fruits, and Other Vegetables of That Country* (London: Printed for W. Taylor and J. Baker, 1714), p. 27.

21. William Byrd [Richmond Croom Beatty and William J. Mulloy, trans., and eds.], *William Byrd's Natural History of Virginia or the Newly Discovered Eden* (Richmond, Virginia: The Dirtz Press, 1940), p. 71.

22. John Josselyn, *New-England Rarities Discovered* (Boston: Massachusetts Historical Society, 1972), p. 8-9.

23. Anonymous, 'Narrative of a Voyage to Maryland, 1705-1706', *American Historical Review* 12 (January 1906): 330-1.

24. John Bakeless, *America as Seen by Its First Explorers; The Eyes of Discovery* (New York: Dover Publications, Inc., 1989), p. 267.

25. Thomas F. O'Donnell, ed., *A Description of the New Netherlands by Adriaen van der Donck* (Syracuse: Syracuse University Press, 1968), p. 50.

26. Letter from Father Sébastien Rasles to his brother, dated October 12, 1723, in Reuben Gold Thwaites, ed., *The Jesuit Relations and Allied Documents: Travels and Explorations of the Jesuit Missionaries in New France, 1610-1791: the Original French, Latin, and Italian Texts, with English Translations and Notes* (Cleveland: The Burrows Brothers, 1900), Vol. 67, p. 169.

27. John F. D. Smyth, *A Tour in the United States of America* (London: For G. Robinson [etc.], 1784), vol. 1, p. 337.

28. H. L. Bingham, 'A Thousand Wild Turkeys', *Forest and Stream* 11 (1878): 410-1.

29. H. H. Lane, 'Oklahoma', in Victor E. Shelford, ed., *Naturalist's Guide to the Americas* (Baltimore: Williams & Wilkins, 1926), p. 496.

30. J. Elgin, 'Christmas Dinner on the Upper Brazos in 1872', *West Texas Historical Association Year Book* 14 (1938): 86.

31. Robert M. Wright, *Dodge City, the Cowboy Capitol and the Great Southwest* (Wichita: Wichita Eagle Press, [1913]).

32. A. W. Schorger, *op. cit.,* p. 61.

33. Karen Ordahl Kupperman, ed., *Captain John Smith: A Select Edition of His Writings* (Chapel Hill: University of North Carolina Press, 1988).

34. William Bradford [Samuel Eliot Morison, ed], *Of Plymouth Plantation 1620-1647* (New York: Alfred A. Knopf, 1952), p. 90.

35. William Byrd [Richmond Croom Beatty and William J. Mulloy, trans., and eds.], *William Byrd's Natural History of Virginia or the Newly Discovered Eden* (Richmond, Virginia: The Dirtz Press, 1940), p. 71.

36. John Heckewelder, 'Notes of Travel... to Gnadenhuetten ... 1797', *Pennsylvania Magazine of History and Biography 10* (1886): 136, 146.

37. Sarah Brewer-Bonebright, *Reminiscences of New Castle, Iowa, 1848* (Des Moines: Historical Department of Iowa, Des Moines,1921), p. 77.

38. S. P. Hildreth, 'Biographical Sketch of Isaac Williams', *American Pioneer 1* (1842): 345.

39. J. H. Jenkins, *Recollections of Early Texas: The Memories of John Holland Jenkins* 3rd ed. (Austin: University of Texas Press, 1958), p. 8.

40. W. A. Covington, *History of Colquitt County* (Spartanburg, S.C.: Reprint Co., 1980), p. 63.

41. Jean-Anthelme Brillat-Savarin, *The Physiology of Taste or Meditations on Transcendental Gastronomy,* translated by M. F. K. Fisher (Washington, D.C.: Counterpoint, 1986), pp. 71, 77-8.

42. John James Audubon, *The Birds of America, from Drawings Made in the United States and Their Territories* (New York: J. J. Audubon; Philadelphia: J. B. Chevalier, 1840-44), vol. 5, p. 42.

43. City Hotel Menu, February 18, 1842, in honor of Charles Dickens, as in Lately Thomas, *Delmonico's: A Century of Splendor* (Boston: Houghton Mifflin Company, 1967), p. 110.

44. Auguste Levasseur [J. D. Godman, trans.], *Lafayette in America in 1824 and 1825* (Philadelphia: Carey and Lea, 1829), pp. 10, 120; C. N. Bement, *The American Poulterer's Companion.* New York: Saxton and Miles, 1845), vol. 2, p. 215.

45. G. Fay, 'The Wild Turkey', *Harper's Weekly* 28 (1884): 848.

46. John. R. Cook, *The Border and the Buffalo: an Untold Story of the Southwest Plains; the Bloody Border of Missouri and Kansas. The Story of the Slaughter of the Buffalo...* (Topeka: Crane & Company, 1907), p. 114.

47. Marion Harlan, *Common Sense in the Household: A Manual of Practical Housewifery* (New York: Charles Scribner's Sons, 1871), p. 179-80.

48. Marion Cabell Tyree, ed., *Housekeeping in Old Virginia. Containing Contributions from Two Hundred and Fifty Ladies in Virginia and Her Sister States* (New York: G. W. Carleton & Co., 1877), p. 92.

49. [Lafcadio Hearn], *La Cuisine Creole; A Collection of Culinary Recipes from Leading Chefs and Noted Creole Housewives, Who Have Made New Orleans Famous for its Cuisine* 2nd edition (New Orleans: F. F. Hansell & Bro., Ltd., 1885), p. 72.

50. Thomas F. O'Donnell, ed., *A Description of the New Netherlands by Adriaen van der Donck* (Syracuse: Syracuse University Press, 1968), p. 50; James Earl Kennamer, Mary Kennamer, and Ron Brenneman, 'History', in James G. Dickson , comp. and ed., *The Wild Turkey; Biology and Management* (Mechanicsburg, PA: Stackpole Books, 1992), p. 12.

51. Thomas F. O'Donnell, ed., *A Description of the New Netherlands by Adriaen van der Donck* (Syracuse: Syracuse University Press, 1968), p. 50.

52. William Wood, *Nevv Englands Prospect; a True, Lively and Experimentall Description of That Part of America Commonly Called Nevv England* (London: Printed by T. Cotes for I. Bellamie, 1634), p. 32.

53. Robert Beverley, *The History of Virginia, in Four Parts ...* (Richmond, Virginia: J. W. Randolph, 1855), p. 256.

54. W. F. Dunaway, *A History of Pennsylvania* (New York: Prentice-Hall, 1948), p. 273; Joseph Doddridge [John S. Ritenour and William T. Lindsey, eds.], *Notes on the Settlement and Indian Wars of the Western Parts of Virginia and Pennsylvania from 1763-1783* (Pittsburgh: np, 1912), p.

88; S. W. Fletcher, Jr., *Pennsylvania Agriculture* (Harrisburg: Pennsylvania Historical and Museum Commission, 1950-55), pp. 409-10.

55. A. W. Schorger, *The Wild Turkey; Its History and Domestication* (Norman: University of Oklahoma Press, 1966), p. 53.

56. John Josselyn, *New-England Rarities Discovered* (London: 1672) Reprint (Boston: Massachusetts Historical Society, 1972), p. 8-9.

57. Joseph Doddridge, *Notes on the Settlement and Indian Wars of the Western Parts of Virginia and Pennsylvania from 1763 to 1783, Inclusive* (Wellsburgh, Va.: Printed at the office of the Gazette, for the author, 1824), p. 105.

58. Thomas F. De Voe, *The Market Assistant* (New York: Hurd and Houghton, 1867), pp. 58-9.

59. City Hotel Menu, February 18, 1842, in honor of Charles Dickens, as in Lately Thomas, *Delmonico's: A Century of Splendor* (Boston: Houghton Mifflin Company, 1967), p. 110.

60. Women's Centennial Committees of the International Exhibition, *National Cookery Book* (Philadelphia: Women's Centennial Executive Committee, 1876), p. 85.

61. Gaston Fay, 'The Wild Turkey', *Harper's Weekly* 28 (1884): 848.

62. Henry S. Mosby and Charles O. Handley, *The Wild Turkey in Virginia: Its Status, Life History and Management* (Richmond, Virginia: Pittman-Robertson Projects, Division of Game Commission of Game and Inland Fisheries, 1943), p. 15; A. W. Schorger, *The Wild Turkey; Its History and Domestication* (Norman: University of Oklahoma Press, 1966), p. 12; John W. Aldrich, 'Historical Background', in Oliver H. Hewett,, ed., *The Wild Turkey and its Management* (Washington DC: The Wildlife Society, 1967), p. 12; James Earl Kennamer, Mary Kennamer, and Ron Brenneman, 'History', in James G. Dickson, comp. and ed., *The Wild Turkey; Biology and Management* (Mechanicsburg, PA: Stackpole Books, 1992), p. 11.

63. Henry S. Mosby, 'The Status of the Wild Turkey in 1974', *Proceedings of the National Wild Turkey Symposium* 3 (1975): 22-6.

64. Harold Titus, 'The Gobbler Gets Attention', *Field and Stream* 45 (December 1940): 26.

65. James Earl Kennamer, Mary Kennamer, and Ron Brenneman, 'History', in James G. Dickson, comp. and ed., *The Wild Turkey; Biology and Management* (Mechanicsburg, PA: Stackpole Books, 1992), p. 14.

66. J. E. Kennamer and M. C. Kennamer, 'Current Status and Distribution of the Wild Turkey',in William M. Healy and Georgette B. Healy, eds, *Proceedings of the Sixth National Wild Turkey Symposium, 26 February-1 March 1990, Charleston, South Carolina sponsored by South Carolina Wildlife and Marine Resources Department, National Wild Turkey Federation, South Carolina Chapter of the National Wild Turkey Federation, and U.S. Forest Service* (Edgefield, S.C.: The Federation, [1990]), pp. 1-12; James Earl Kennamer, Mary Kennamer, and Ron Brenneman, 'History', in James G. Dickson, comp. and ed., *The Wild Turkey; Biology and Management* (Mechanicsburg, PA: Stackpole Books, 1992), p. 16; 'phone interview with Tom Hughs, Biologist, National Wild Turkey Federation, February 8, 2005.

67. A. D. Livingston, *Wild Turkey Cookbook* (Mechanicsburg, PA: Stackpole Books, 1995); Rick Black, *The Wild Turkey Cookbook* (Wever, IA: Black Iron Cookin' Co., 2003).

68. A. H. Carhart, 'Long Rifles and Raw Meat', *Westerners Brand Book Denver* (1945), pp. 171-94, 171.

Really Wild: Britain, Before Agriculture

Colin Spencer

This paper attempts to deal with a land mass which would become Britain and a period when such a transition occurred. From out of those many thousands of years I have chosen three, at the end of the Mesolithic, 7,500–4,000 BC, the earlier marks a settlement in Yorkshire, where there is evidence of the first domestication of the dog, and the last the use of wool. Both surely would be signs of agriculture, but that revolution in human existence, is said to have reached our shores around 3,500 BC. This shows how the great changes in cultural evolution are inevitably very gradual, slow and piecemeal, unlike the forest fire which devastates overnight.

The name Mesolithic has been given to the time between the Palaeolithic and the Neolithic (in Europe roughly 12000 BC–3000 BC) characterized by the appearance of microliths, these are flint tools made from small, sometimes tiny, flakes of flint of astonishing sharpness and efficiency. The microliths in their variety shed interesting light on how the food plants were harvested, then prepared and finally cooked, on how the animals were killed, skinned and butchered, so they are artefacts which reflect in a very personal way on what we ate. They show in my view a high degree of sophistication and technical skill in food gathering and preparation. This is only one reason for my interest in this period.[1]

The area that was to become the British Isles was reoccupied around 10,600 BC, 500 years later than nearby parts of the Continent. It was a period of astonishing climatic changes, which radically changed fauna and flora, hence the food that people consumed changed and grew in this period. The climate reached a warm peak around 11,000 BC (slightly warmer than today) then grew colder again around 9000 BC ending a thousand years later 8000 BC. The changes were caused by the melting of the polar ice caps, similar to what we are experiencing now, except that the polar ice covered a much greater area, it was a huge expanse which embraced the top of what would become these islands.

At the beginning of the Mesolithic the ice would encroach a little one final time; around 11,000 BC it advanced and covered Scotland; there was still a land bridge linking us to the continent, and this gradually became smaller over a few thousand years. In the Boreal – 7,500–5,500 BC – a dry period characterized by cold winters, warm summers and a flora dominated by pines and hazels, the early Mesolithic peoples settled in what would become southern and eastern England, which was still connected by land to the continent, across the Channel to France and across the southern part of the North Sea to the low countries and to Jutland. Just think, one could walk from Yorkshire to Jutland, from Hull to the Dutch archipelago and on to

Esbjerg in Denmark, or in the south walk from Dover to Calais or from Brighton to le Havre, but from thence the Channel began. There is evidence that this land bridge was occupied until 5,800 BC, used for migration of peoples, fauna and flora and for human settlements. Earlier, by 8000 BC the ice had receded once more and agriculture had begun in the Near East, but it was to take another four and a half thousand years before it reached Britain then at last a group of islands.

The land area of Britain was drastically reduced by the rising sea levels which covered the land bridge between us and what would become Scandinavia and then finally filled the Channel and cut Britain off from the continent. But the sea also swept inland along the east and south coast over all the low-lying areas, creating new salt marshes and estuaries, the whole Mesolithic shoreline from Yorkshire to Dorset was flooded and, of course, remains still deep under water, hiding the evidence of many different settlements.

But what could have been these changes that people noticed? The horizon changing from land to sea, the realization that a salt-water marsh was deepening to that of a wide estuary, coracles and log boats could be used when one had waded before. There was less rainfall, strange new trees, shrubs, plants and lichens never seen before, to be cautiously inspected, licked, smelt, tasted and at last chewed. Freshwater lakes filling up with pike, new mammals both large and small, a large island appearing off the south coast and huge estuaries forming, some that were sheltered and would become useful as harbours for trading and fishing boats. To the people living through these changes, though they must have been aware that their land was shrinking – the coast line changing radically on the east and south – they must also have been aware that the food available was becoming more interesting, that new creatures and new plants and fruits brought new flavours, and what is more these flourished in a warmer climate and were thus more accessible. Also, the memory of long, harsh, freezing winters, which necessitated huge stores of dried foods, nuts, fungi, lentils, beans, fruit as well as smoked or wind dried strips of meat and fish, were fading.

We know that Mesolithic communities were on the move, making seasonal migrations to known habitats, they crossed Britain from west to east and back again, they also had settled homesteads. It is interesting to note that architecture came before agriculture. The desire to build a shelter among a small community near an abundant fresh water supply existed some thousands of years before the desire to cultivate the soil next to their homes.[2]

We find Mesolithic sites near coastal waters, fresh water marshes, deltas, estuaries and lagoons of the major rivers. These have far greater edible production than any other zone, partly because of the frost repelling winter warmth of the sea and because valuable minerals are washed down from the highlands. Whole plant communities from shore marginals and floating flora, are directly edible by humankind, while supporting a wealth of mollusc, crustacean, fish, mammal and wildfowl, all benefit from the nutrients washed down from land drainage. The nutritious and easily gathered

Glyceria fluitans, a wild rice-like plant, or clubrush, *Scirpus lacustris*, a type of water chestnut with large tubers, lower stems and seeds which has a productivity higher than maize (*Zea mays*), the water lilies, reeds, water plantain, water gladiolus, water parsnip, water speedwell, marshmallow, marsh samphire, marsh marigold, marsh cress, bog moss, swamp potato. Also growing upon the coast were the edible root ancestors of our beets, kales, turnips, cabbages and parsnips, *Brassicas, Beta, Crambe* and *Echinophora*. Also in the shallows the edible seaweeds: *Zostera, Atriplex, Lathyrus maritimus, Scirpus maritimus*.

At Star Carr – in the Vale of Pickering in north-eastern Yorkshire – occupied around 7,500 BC there was a wide range of mammals to hunt. This site at that time was still at the edge of the northern forests, less than 500 miles from the Norwegian ice-cap. It was situated in the sheltered fringes of the northern pre-Boreal birch forest facing across an exposed ice-locked North Sea, ice that extended to the North Pole. These forests were dense, not allowing much light into them so the plants had to be shade tolerant and tended to be sparse, but at the edge of the forest it was another matter. The Star Carr site was on the banks of a lake. In this setting you would expect meat to be well represented and vegetal foods difficult to find, but the lakeside and marsh plants from evidence of plant remains as in the range cited above, were crucial.

The animal remains at Star Carr have been analyzed and over half of the meat came from wild cattle, followed by elk and deer, with roe deer and wild pig being the third favourite. But smaller animals like pine marten, red fox and beaver were also hunted, almost certainly for their pelts as well as their meat. Considering the lakeside site, the oddest food omission in the Star Carr diet is fish.[3] There are two explanations. Either the lake was still too cold to allow the small prey fish which pike fed on, or the acidity of the peats at Star Carr had destroyed all the fish bones.

The first evidence of herding of sheep by dogs was discovered at Star Carr. This domestication occurred because the dog was used in the hunt to round up wild herds and move them towards the hunters. Dogs are descended from wolves and wolves take their live prey back to the communal lair where it is killed by the leader wolf who takes a few bites, then offers it first to his current bitch before it is thrown to the rest of the pack. Dogs, in the belief that their master/trainer is the top dog, follow the same pattern and round up the kill taking it back to the hunter. Herds of wild animals are at their most vulnerable when they have young to guard, it is then that they flock easily and can form tight clumps when a dog or dogs approach them. The use of dogs in this manner must have been enormously appreciated by early hunters, for it made their main task so much simpler. It has been observed that on hunting excursions, one man with a pack of trained hunting dogs collected three quarters of the meat, and six men without dogs collected one quarter.[4] No wonder the dogs were rewarded with scraps and unwanted bones.

A later Mesolithic site at Morton Tayport in Fife (4,382–4,115 BC) show that there

305

were over forty different species of molluscs eaten, the most common being the cockle (*Cerastoderma edule*); claws of the edible crab were also common among the shells. Of the fish eaten large cod far outnumbered any other, which suggests that they fished by boat in deep water; other fish were haddock, turbot, salmonid and sturgeon, the last were probably caught in shallow water on their way to or from the river mouth. Remains of seabirds were found, the guillemot (*Urua aalge*) being the most common. But they also ate meat and butchering was done on site. By weight the molluscs amounted to one third of the meat consumed.

The most impressive artefacts from the Mesolithic, which gives the greatest insight into their minds and the way they lived, is the huge range of microlithic composite tools for plant gathering, harvesting grasses and digging up roots. There are tools which combine different styles of knife and saw, ones with blades secured in the wood or horn handle which are set obliquely, others with broad trapezes; there are harvesting knives with provision for 5 or 30 microliths, some set into curved antlers like a sickle, others are straight. Then there are the hunting tools, spears, bidents and tridents, barbed fishhooks, shellfish darts, barbed arrowheads and thrusting spears. The great advantage of microlithic tools was that when one of the many tiny blades became blunt, or was chipped or broke it could be replaced with a new one and the weapon or tool was as good as new. Plant fibre was processed to make lines, snares, nets and traps; while water was dammed or diverted to provide temporary traps and storage. There were also smaller tools used for food preparation, for slicing and even for grating: blocks of wood set with microliths with rows of tiny cutting blades or in points, exactly similar to modern graters used today.[5]

Within a family, a lone hunter could be armed with 20 or so barbed arrows each bearing 2 microliths, several fish or bird arrows with 3 sets of barbs going around the top of the arrow and a bident leister for spearing large fish, while the rest of his family, the women and children, might carry several types of harvesting knives and slicing knives, a woven basket to fit over the shoulders for carrying bird and waterfowl eggs, leaves, berries, bulbs, fungi, roots and shoots. Experience would have taught them when to take only one egg from a nest or all of them, knowing which birds would lay more; what berries, bulbs and roots were poisonous or how they must be prepared to eradicate any toxins: whether it would be soaking in water, peeling, chopping or the addition of another substance or herb.

The use of microlithic tools in Post-Glacial woodland and forest regions means more efficient gathering and processing of vegetal foods, this shows an existence where the relationship between early humankind and the earth was extremely close and intimate, indicating a formidable knowledge of edible plants, roots, fruits and nuts, which would have been passed on, both by the practical daily act of gathering and by language, to each generation. The gatherer/hunter/fisher existed in a complex interrelationship with their plant and animal resources. One detects in these thousands of years before agriculture proper, many of the techniques already existed which we associate with it. In some areas the ovicaprids (sheep and goats), cattle, pigs and even hares and rabbits[6] may already have occupied a specially controlled relationship amounting to elementary husbandry. Herd culling where the weak, sick and the wounded animals are easily hunted and killed first would have been inevitable and common practice among hunters for many thousands of years. But there is evidence of control of vegetation by fire, the creation of forest glades which allowed sunlight and space so that different varieties of plants would grow, seed strewing, helping a plant to release its seeds, root reproduction by the cutting up of clumps, a practice easily discovered by accident.

As the ice caps melted and the land mass that would become Europe became warmer, so the Mediterranean plants began to spread northwards. Hazel-nut, apple, pear and other food species were undoubtedly helped by the deliberate fire clearance and encouraged by judicious planting. The nut-bearing beech trees and some edible-root species seem to have made a similarly suspicious preliminary advance into north-western Europe. There is evidence of forest fire-setting in pollen sequences, which opens up the forest canopy allowing grazing and browsing resources for wild deer, cattle and boar, and allows the growth of edible bracken root. Also, the forest glades which grew ever larger and more common, where the edible roots, grasses, seeds, foliage, nuts and fruits now grew in season, would quickly become colonized by the wild pig, the sheep and goats, cattle and deer. It is now known that a diet composed of plant foods, bird eggs, fungi, molluscs, crustacea, fish and herbivores best approaches a high subsistence efficiency; so our ancestors were vigorous and healthy, able to adapt to sudden changes of both climate and habitat, perhaps only seasonally nomadic, beginning to settle. Evidence of homesteads begin at the Star Carr settlement and continue throughout the Mesolithic.

The sea level rose 20 metres between 9,300–7,400 and continued to rise until 5000 BC. Because of this many Mesolithic sites around the coasts of Britain now lie beneath sea level, which is the main reason why this period still remains so infuriatingly obscure. Between 7000 and 5000 BC the Mediterranean invasion at last arrived on these shores and its vegetation established itself: cereal grasses, legumes, wild olive, grape vine, strawberry tree, grass and legume seeds, *Secale dalmaticum*, cistus, myrtle, juniper and evergreen oaks with edible acorns. High yielding hazel-nut trees but most importantly the 'pignolias', pine kernels of the ubiquitous stone pine (*Pinus pinea*) which has one of the highest protein yields of any known nut.

Many herbaceous plants are drought-adapted, including bulbs which can remain dormant for long periods. These include many edible species, *Iris sisyrinchium*, grape hyacinth (*Muscuri racemosum*), orchids, star of Bethlehem (*Ornithogalum umbellatum*), lilies (*Liliaceae*), crocuses (*Irideae*) and, above all, the important wild leek, shallot, garlic, onion family (*Allium* spp.) as well as edible root plants (*Apium, Asphodel, Arum, Carum* spp., *Cyperus esculentis, Pencedarium graveolens* etc.) which were widely distributed and especially abundant in damper mountain valleys, coastal clearings, marsh and swamp edges. Some 200–350 edible species imply that the diet would have been based on pulses/bulbs/grass seeds and nut combinations, balanced by coastal gathering, fishing, fowling and inland hunting of sheep and goats, deer, and aurochs (*Bos primogenius*) – long horns thought to be an ancestor of modern cattle. Within the forest, the tending and caring of the wild food plants could have amounted to simple forest horticulture.

We can glimpse something of the range and diversity of the Mesolithic diet if we consider the seasons. In the temperate regions where there are distinct seasons, plants store up their nutritive energy to tide them over the winter months, once growth is possible again, the plants mobilize these reserves into growing tissues. Humankind thus benefits from using the storage or growing tissue, or by intercepting the food as it passes from one stage to another, hence all types of growing shoots become a delicacy, both tasty and enormously nutritious. Apart from wild asparagus and sea kale, there are the bulbs and rhizomes where the new shoots are at their most nutritious, also fern and nettle shoots when very young and tender are edible, while either become toxic or unpleasant when more mature. Also, the young staminate cones of pines and buds or trees such as lime are a rich source of protein and were all used as food.

In early spring the bulbs of the wild onion (*Allium*) and the rhizomes of Solomon's Seal (*Polygonatum*) appear. The bulbs lie conveniently near the surface, such areas where they are seen to be growing would be bound to be marked, or associative plants observed and taken note of, so peripatetic trawls are unlikely, only necessary when there is a dearth of vegetation. A flour can be made from the rhizomes of bracken (*Pteridium aquilinum*), water plants were much favoured because they are easier to locate, identified then fished up from the mud at the bottom of ponds and lakes. So the tubers of the water-lily (*Nuphar*), arrowhead (*Sagittaria*), and the bulrush (*Schoenoplectus*) were all dried then ground up for flour.

As soon as the frost leaves the ground, tree roots start to take up water, the sap, rich in sugars, starts to flow up the trunks. Birches, lime, aspen, as well as maple, can be tapped for the sap, which is deliciously sweet. But they also yield another source of food, this is the tissue immediately beneath the bark which begins to grow, the new young cells thicken and are rich in proteins and carbohydrates, this new growth is called the cambium, and can be scraped away and became a staple food. (It is still used today available in health shops, called slippery elm from one particular species of elm (*Ulmus rubra*), but in the past elms, poplar, aspen, ash, lime and even pine were used. In Scandinavia a bark bread was made from the tissue.)

As the year progresses the food range available becomes varied and almost infinite. Both wild carrot (*Daucus carota*) and wild parsnip (*Pastinaca sativa*) are frequent plants on the chalk downs of Britain. All types of thistles have edible roots, as well as the base of their flowers being eaten like artichokes (*Carline vulgaris*), while with the Scotch thistle(*Onopordon acanthium*), both the flower base and the stalks can be eaten. In the case of the blesed milk thistle (*Silybum marianum*), the roots, young shoots and flower base were all used. Great burdock (*Arctium majus*) offers its tender stalks, eaten like asparagus, as well as the root, which the Japanese cultivate. At the height of summer there would have been a large range of fruits available.

Hazel-nuts, pine nuts and acorns, with winter roots and rhizomes, were stored for the winter; further foods were kept by drying or pickling in vinegar or honey; meat and fish were wind dried and smoked; butchered meat could be frozen; supplies of molluscs and seaweed remained available through cold months.

The hunting of red deer, roe deer, wild boar and aurochs also provided a constant food source throughout the year. The bones have been found of aurochs, elk, red deer, roe deer, beaver, pine marten, badger, hedgehog, mole, common shrew and the water vole, which were all killed and put to use. Then there were the birds which are mostly marsh species, two of them summer visitors, the crane and the white stork, and there were many species of duck as well as grebes, divers, mergansers and lapwings; the buzzard, the barn owl and the stock dove.

The ungulates and perhaps especially the red deer, were necessary to the Mesolithic economy; they provided horn and bone, pig's tusks and beaver's jaws for tools, teeth and whiskers for decoration, skins for clothing, bedding and for covering huts and boats, the horn was used for carrying and storing liquids, sinews were used as thread, the fat was rendered down for oil and candles.

There was extensive fishing in inland rivers and lakes the fishermen ever watchful for the migratory population of salmon and trout and also the pike in spring and early summer, which congregrate in shallow inland waters in order to spawn. In the lake and river there were the salmonids, eels, pike and perch, as well as the coastal resources of molluscs, crustaceae and seaweeds. There was also the collecting of bird eggs in late spring and capturing of birds on their nests.

Food harvesting and preparation required a microlithic industry. So far thirteen different types of microlith knives have been unearthed, four of those are harvesting knives, two of which are curved like scythes, of these two one has saw teeth and other blades set at an angle. The nine knives are all different, one is exactly the same design as the contemporary Stanley Knife, four have saw blades, others are obviously designed for slicing, some fall into the bean slicer type of sharp flint units 'over which stems, roots and fruits could be quickly drawn in one motion to produce sliced or shredded elements.'[7] If our interpretation of the food preparation tools is correct, then much time was spent in grating, dicing and chopping of fairly hard vegetables, which makes me suspect that these might then have been left to ferment for liquor making. (If they were going to be boiled for a stew they would have been left in large chunks.) We know that at Star Carr there are clues to religious rituals and these clues are found throughout the Mesolithic and beyond continuing down to the Druids. Rituals which involve travelling into the spirit world also involve hallucinogens and the consumption of a strong liquor almost certainly was part of the ceremony.

To sum up, the diet of the Mesolithic people of Britain (population estimated

309

at 50,000 by 7000 BC[8]) was richly varied and abundant. It was extremely healthy nutritionally covering a wide range of wild foods gathered in season from the the local habitat. The people had also created tools of enormous skill for a host of different food preparation tasks which also implies a range of cooking techniques, from roasting, slow pit cooking, over-night ember cooking, boiling, grilling and baking in leaves. These techniques and certainly some of the tools like the flesh hook were still in use throughout the medieval period.

I believe it was in this long period of abundance and technical ingenuity that the characteristic roots of the history of British food began to grow.

Notes

1. Other reasons for my fascination is that it was a time of radical climatic change – like our own – when Britain became isolated from the continent by the sea and when many of our national characteristics were formed, but I have no room to explore this here, though what we eat is a determinant in what we are.
2. Wilson, pp. 1-31.
3. Pryor, p. 83.
4. Simmons, Dimbleby, Grigson, p. 124.
5. Clarke, pp. 454-455.
6. We are told that the Romans brought the rabbit into Britain, but both the rabbit and the mountain hare existed at Boxgrove (near Chichester) in 500,000 BC and were eaten. Like most other small mammals they vanished further south in the Glacials, but then once it became warmer again, they re-colonized the land. What the Romans brought was the farming of rabbits which the Normans reintroduced.
7. Clarke, p. 455.
8. Pryor, p. 103.

Bibliography

Clarke, David, 'Mesolithic Europe:the economic basis', in *Problems in Economic and Social Archaeology*, edited by G. de G. Sieveking, I.H. Longworth and K.E. Wilson (Duckworth, 1976), pp. 454-455.

Pitts, Michael and Roberts, Mark, *Fairweather Eden* (Arrow, 1998).

Pryor, Francis, *Britain BC* (Harper Collins, 2003), p. 83.

Simmons, I.G., Dimbleby, G.W., and Grigson, Caroline, *The Mesolithic: The Environment in British Prehistory*, ed. Simmons, I.G., Tooley, M.J. (Duckworth, 1981), pp 82-124.

Wilson, Peter J., 'Architecture or Agriculture: The Conditions of Human Domestication', paper given for Symposium no 133, *Where the Wild Things Are Now*, March 12-18, 2004, Hacienda del Sol, Tucson, Arizona.

The Artifice of the Hunter: Gathering Ancient Inspiration

Marshall Walker

The category hunter-gatherer has come under critical scrutiny in archaeology and anthropology, not the least for biases inherent in the construction. Hunter-gatherer may be perceived anthropologically as a pejorative term, used to castigate societies as uncivilized. There is also an innate gender bias: that hunters must be men and gatherers necessarily women. Then, too, the categories may seem inflexible when presented with activities that seem to defy their artificial boundary. What about nets? Is trawling, or fowling, with nets, hunting or gathering? The hunter, in particular, is an artificial category – one that may or may not challenge modern notions of gendered activity. But the artifice of the category of hunter is not purely a post-modern academic moot point. In the case of my own research, the later Roman Empire, there is evidence to show that the construction was also clear to the antique mind, which could play on that artifice in representations of Artemis, scenes of the hunter hunted, or spectacles with net-wielding gladiators. As seems especially appropriate for the symposium, that ancient aesthetic is captured in its context in a satiric novel where the artifice of the hunter provides the comic effect of Trimalchio's banquet featuring wild boar.

Biases of a modern construction

Let me begin by addressing some biases that are inherent in hunter-gatherer as a term or definition. It is used to refer to those societies which are subsistence cultures. There are few communities in the world today that fit the bill anthropologically: the Arctic Inuit are one example. In archaeology, hunter-gatherer societies figure in the sphere of prehistoric archaeology. Explaining tangible remains of the most archaic settlements demands some theory of the society that used them. Hunter-gatherer is just such a theory of a social structure. At the beginning of the 20th century W. J. Sollas's theories helped link the archaeological with the anthropological and endowed it with an evolutionary bias. Even while arguing against a strictly Darwinist model of social evolution in favour of change owing to migratory influence, his explanations by analogy tied contemporary subsistence cultures, that he called 'primitive', to prehistoric cultures: 'Modern Eskimos' [sic] to 'Magdalenian Man'.[1] Sollas's use of 'primitive' betrays underlying Darwinist sympathies that societies, such as the Inuit, are essentially inferior to Western society because they are not as evolved. When difficulty arises reconciling the biological theory to cultural development, archaeologists are left trying to explain, or explain away, questions like why evolutionary time is different for cultural and biological development.[2] The term hunter-gatherer still carries with it a trace of that pejorative value judgment. More recently, anthropologists as well as archaeologists have begun to explore the 'prehistory of food', divorcing value-laden theory from subsistence practice by examining the effects that activities like hunting, gathering, cultivating, or other means of food production have had on the landscape.[3] This permits study of any society by means of an essential aspect, that it must obtain food, without necessarily judging it on a teleological scale of advanced versus retarded. In this fashion the activities of hunting and of gathering can be studied fairly as they continue in civilized societies. Of course, the Food Symposium wishes to use this sense when employing the term hunter-gatherer. My paper, like others here, will address the activity in an advanced culture, specifically, the Roman Empire. But the latent evolutionary bias bears repeating as a gentle reminder that the term arrives with 'baggage.'

A more recent construct that intrudes on the term affecting the perception of the activities of hunting and gathering, may well arise from the term's evolutionary association. There is a troublesome gender bias that presumes that all hunters are men, and gatherers therefore must be women. This generalization, fossilized nearly into law, is based on the presupposition that all women are mothers – so busy with breeding that they could not possibly take on any activities of subsistence hunting. Old-fashioned studies of Early Man have been criticized for excluding Woman, which may or not be the case. Nonetheless, feminist critique has persuasively argued and demonstrated that the evolutionary based notions of subsistence cultures where men, and only men, did the hunting, and therefore, men, and only men, made and handled tools are not tenable, neither based on the material remains, nor in comparison to modern subsistence cultures where hunting and gathering account for the main means of food production.[4] Like the evolutionary principles which saturated research in Victorian times, modern scholarship continues to inflect its research with attitudes and prejudices of gendered work, reading the modern cultural divisions backwards into the pre-historical record. Perceiving all women as mothers may have been a dim reflection of the post-World War II society that spawned the theories in those days before feminism when Lee and DeVore's *Man the Hunter* was written, but the reflection of all men as dashing, resourceful hunters was more wishful thinking than mirror on reality.[5] When Dahlberg's *Woman the Gatherer* was put forward as a response in an effort to point to the valuable contribution of women, it did not upset the presumptions of gender bias at the heart of the matter.[6] Despite the best efforts of feminist scholarship, tools, activities or areas of dwellings continue to be pronounced men's or women's even without any proof, based merely on gendered prejudice of modern scholars.[7]

If the roles of hunter and of gatherer have been carefully defined as male for hunters and as female for gatherers, have the activities of each been equally well prescribed? Is there no element of the hunt in tracking down wild vegetal growth to gather? Is it the use of tools that set the hunter and gatherer apart? For, where uncertain fragments

312

of tools remain, there has been a tendency to ascribe both the use and manufacture of tools to men.[8] What about nets? The intended function of a net is for gathering things. The implication therein is that nets belong to the womanly task of gathering. The manufacture of netting is very close to the typically perceived womanly activities of weaving or knitting. The entrenched gender bias that sees each woman as an ever breeding mother restricted by tending her brood, should assign the sedentary task of knotting nets to her. Could that be part of the reason that ephemeral tools such as nets are not often discussed in relation to manly hunting in pre-historic societies? It is not enough to respond that rope and twine are not lasting materials as tooled stone, for even cutting and jabbing instruments had perishable portions that are presumed or recreated by the fantasy of archaeologists.

In the realm of the historic world explored by archaeologists, there is more evidence to work with. Though nets may have disappeared from this record leaving no direct material trace, visual representations and textual evidence provide more to go on. Fishing offers a likely place to begin looking for nets. Fish as food has attracted the attention of scholars of the ancient world,[9] and fish-eating has even been related to the development of a unique political system in classical Athens.[10] However, the activity of fishing, its implements, and its practitioners, have not enjoyed as much attention. Interestingly though, one contemporary Roman text where fishermen feature prominently is the Bible. Two miracles in the Gospels relate to the activity of fishing.[11] In both cases the fishing is being done with nets, and the essential element is that all that the apostles had to do was gather up into their nets the fish that the Lord had provided. The image works as powerfully in the coloured tesserae of Ravenna's 6th-century mosaics as it does in the holy text. May trawling with nets, with or without Christ's help, be counted as gathering fish from the water? As the receptacle for gathered comestibles, nets and netting might be seen as tools of gathering on a par with woven baskets.

As pointed out above, casting aspersions on an extinct society as inferior may be easier in prehistoric archaeology where the record of its material remains stands alone without any written tradition. In such a case a feminist corrective could be exercised on value-laden theory of archaeology that assigns gender distinction where none existed. However, some material remains do attest to gender distinctions, either in daily life or in death where burial goods may differ between men and women. Where material evidence differs for men and women, it must be dealt with. And for historical societies, some written evidence may also report gender differences that must be taken into account. For the Roman Empire, copious written sources, ancient and modern, detail gender differences in many areas of society. Visual material, if it may be taken as evidence of hunting, would seem to confirm that hunting was a masculine activity.

Vir: virtus: virtual hunting
A man's hardiness in the Roman world, as well as the hardness of his body, symbol-

ized the moral uprightness and self-discipline that were the backbone of manly virtue. Virtue was so much associated with free, citizen class men of ancient Rome that the very words for man, *vir*, and *virtus*, were linked in late antique etymology.[12] In the days before he became emperor in the 2nd century, the young aristocrat Marcus Aurelius wrote to his old tutor Fronto, describing a day's hunting, and reporting that even though he did not see the boars that were captured, he nonetheless did daring deeds, including climbing a steep hill, which he was careful to mention.[13] Derring-do was very much the point of hunting in Roman times. It offered the opportunity to display one's manly toughness that was *virtus*, manly virtue. Pictorial images of hunting on objects in a variety of media, metalware, mosaics and etched glass often feature the typical generic hunting scene proclaiming the same virtue in their virtual event. The hero, always male in the depictions, risks life and limb confronting a raging, wild beast, whether he be on horseback like Marcus Aurelius, or on foot. Carefully depicted in contemporary garments, the hunter usually wears the *chlamys*, a cape fastened at the shoulder, and carries a spear or a lance. As Marcus Aurelius' letter shows, participating in the hunt gave expression to a man's virtue even if he was not in on the kill. The important thing was to wield spears against wild creatures, from incredible lions to more plausible wild boar.

Carved stone reliefs from sarcophagi offer some of the best visual representations. Elaborate burial chests are known all over the ancient Mediterranean, but in the second and third centuries after Christ, the Romans took the custom and made it their own. Usually of limestone or marble, sarcophagi sometimes showcase the most lavish stone carving preserved from the Roman empire. The sensational effect of virtuoso carving stands out clearly in two examples from Rome, one preserved in Rome the other in Rheims. Separate commissions for two different individuals use the same stock scene, but finish the lead character with a portrait of the deceased. In both cases, the hunter sits astride a galloping or rearing horse, raising his spear in the moment before he strikes his deadly blow to the ferocious lion. The hectic composition of bodies and flagging drapery help evoke the mêlée. Precisely because the two are so similar, the special care taken in providing the heroic hunter with a portrait face stands out. The codified rhetoric says something specific about the individual. Each one's virtue as a Roman man is highlighted. Fearlessly, he faces a deadly lion, the very embodiment of death – clearly an apt scene for a funeral monument. As the lion was associated directly with the emperor, the sub-text of this general manly hunting valour links the deceased to the *virtus augusti*, the virtue or valour of the emperor.[14] These images cannot inform modern viewers about what hunting looked like exactly, about whether or not there were lions roaming the Apennine hills; nor do they report that hunting was pursued exclusively by men, nor even whether the dead man in question was a hunter or not. Rather they display that not only in their art, but in their minds, ancient Romans perceived the activity as a masculine one. It was an effective means to relate one man's superior hardiness, bravery and daring over other lesser

314

men's, like the collapsed man with the sword below the horse. Therefore it is not an anachronistic bias to read the Roman action of hunting as gendered.

In view of this, the bare-breasted woman stoically appraising the scene beckons the attention of the modern viewer. Dressed in a mix of women's clothes and men's armour, she personifies male virtue, although this stands in direct conflict to the ancient concept of *virtus* as manly, excluding women.[15] On some sarcophagi, this figure even bears a portrait face in order to incorporate the deceased's wife in the same commemoration. However, this is not necessary to explain away the female presence; the contradictory semiotics bothers only the modern mind. The testimony carved in stone affirms that for the Roman sensibility she operated as a reasonable, if not necessary, complement to man's nature. Roman art in this fashion lends credence to a Greek genesis myth of individuals split from an original androgynous sexual nature,[16] so that marriage might represent the reunification of separated gendered aspects of one nature. Whether the female portion of the male soul, or its embodiment in a wife, the feminine occupies a natural place even in the exclusion zone of masculinity. The interpretation of the images is not unlike the carved relief itself: deep and intricate with several different ideas at work at the same time.

Myth plays host and repository to a number of similar harmonious contradictions. As with a female image of *virtus*, some deliberate irony seems to lie in the fact that the deity for that manly pursuit of hunting is a woman: Diana, Artemis, or Phoebe. By whatever name, her fickle control over life and death dwells at the very heart of many representations of mythological themes involving hunting. Diana/Artemis' jealous wrath fell upon the poor hunter, Actaeon, who merely had the misfortune to stumble upon the same watering hole where she was taking her bath. As a penalty for his indiscretion of looking upon her divine nudity – without regard for her careless indecent exposure – Actaeon was transformed into a stag and devoured by his own hounds. The hunter became the hunted.[17] These narratives based on mythological scenes differ from the private vignettes of hunting in the immediately noticeable nudity involved. The Vatican collections hold an example showing Adonis, where in order to underscore his physical beauty, his body is bared in two scenes. Engaged in the hunt, he wears the *chlamys*, but it in no way impedes the perception of his beautifully defined musculature. The other hunters in his party, distinctly less captivating, wear tunics under their cloaks. The other vignette, Adonis's fatal wound being attended to under the nurturing eye of his lover, Venus/Aphrodite, has a remarkably different head. The alteration of a portrait head on the hero's semi-divine body tailors the fixed formula from literature. Mythological sarcophagi offer the opportunity to commemorate individuals through allegorical association with the hero. Further diverging from generic hunting scenes, the fantastical world also permits involvement of women in the hunt directly, as Venus/Aphrodite accompanied Adonis.[18] Or in another case, the only man brave enough to face down the Calydonian boar which Diana/Artemis had sent to ravage the countryside, Meleager, only succeeds because

315

his lover Atalante landed the first blow.[19] And so she is pictured in at least one sarcophagus from Rome. Myth has the capacity to express or explain the way things are, at times by constructing an inversion of the very case under discussion. The artifice of Artemis, her feminine caprice and her vengeful womanly wiles, personifies the manly activity of hunting in the same sort of apposite opposite as the armed woman who represents man's virtue.

Ancient artifice: the spectacle of gender

The same artistic media that offer so many colourful impressions of hunting also report the use of nets in hunting. The nets are not the tools carried by the hunters, who almost universally carry a spear. Vigorous equestrian hunters chase prey, like fowl or deer, into nets manned and manipulated by diminutive figures, as a sarcophagus in Arles shows. By their size, and their less glamorous cape, the hooded *alicula* as opposed to the dashing *chlamys*, these servile figures deliberately claim less attention and importance than the hunters. Yet their participation in the hunting group unquestionably brings nets into the world of hunting rather than gathering, demonstratively a world of men. The intriguing contradiction of the explicit understanding of nets as a manly hunter's tool, and the implicit association of netting as a womanly, woven object may have appealed to the late antique aesthetic. If so, it adds to the aesthetic delight of the spectacle of the ultra-manly figure of the *retiarius*, the gladiator whose traditional stock of weaponry included trident and a net. In a mosaic from Madrid, for example, Kalendio fails to press his advantage after having netted Astyanax. Could there be some subtle humour lodged in the defeat of Kalendio's soft supple net by Astyanax's rigid and persistent armour?

The spectacle of gender did not play itself out only in the arena. Divisions between public and private space in the ancient world did not correlate directly to modern notions.[20] Even the domestic setting of the Roman house provided the site for the transaction of business that today would constitute the public sphere. Gender issues could just as well be staged at the dinner table. The domestic realm should not be understood as a strictly female domain in ancient Rome, but a place with permeable boundaries between public and private, male and female. In Roman houses images were made available to audiences of men and women alike. The *triclinium*, often referred to as the Roman dining-room, was a locus for contemplating artwork. Whether actually reclining at a dinner party, as often imagined, or transacting other business, the people using these rooms often had some of the highest quality work on display to them, either in the room itself, or strategically placed elsewhere in the house that it might be seen, on walls with elaborate fresco paintings, in floor mosaics, or stone carvings.[21] Then, too, the objects they handled might have scenes worked in relief. Subject matter included portraits of Greek dramatists and scenes from their best known works, mythological subjects, as well as generic hunting scenes like the ones examined here: all designed to promote the conversation of the dinner guests.

Paideia is the word used to describe the mutual culture of the elite of the classical world, referring among other things to the classical education that assured that any dinner guest would indeed be conversant on the topics that presented themselves in the surrounding imagery.[22] How did Romans contemplate images? Some indication can be found in contemporary literary sources.

From Philostratus the Elder's writings about pictures in a domestic setting emerges an understanding of the Roman capacity for the abstract, summoning the whole story from a particular detail. Looking at the image of a hunting party on the trail of a fierce wild boar, his imagination runs riot. After a vivid description of the action, both that represented in the image, and that which he imagines happening, Philostratus exclaims, 'How I have been deceived! I was deluded by the painting into thinking that the figures were not painted but were real beings.'[23] Opening with this common trope of suspicion of art as deceitful, Philostratus ends the description with an even more complex twist when he describes members of the hunting party looking upon the heroic youth who hurled the deadly spear, 'gaz[ing] at him as though he were a picture'.[24] In these final lines Philostratus inverts the real/imaginary confusion with which he began, again 'confusing' the image with reality by ascribing the same stupefaction to the people represented. This revelation of the guileful reflection of art, reports that ancient viewers of Roman art appreciated the irony latent in multivalent images. Beyond Philostratus' reflexivity, a modern scholar, Patricia Cox Miller, demonstrated the process of the appreciation of literature and artwork that involved necessary abstraction between different levels – in this case the poetry of Optation that requires the participation of the reader to progress through Latin text, Greek text, switching to images, and back again.[25] Not only reflection on duplicity, but complex relationships of images to text, and images to the space around them, and even to the viewer, constituted levels of depth that ancients traversed with ease and delight. She called this aesthetic of late antiquity, dissonant echoing. In this way ancient Romans could have ruminated on gendered aspects of hunting like the ones raised here, although their thoughts on the matter may have taken drastically different turns from modern feminist ideas.

Petronius' novel *Satyricon*, part-satire, part-comedy of manners, offers a glimpse of this process at work in the 2nd century, even if slightly distorted like a fun-house mirror. The episode of Trimalchio's dinner provides a clue as to how leisured Romans pondered the significance of images over dinner.[26] The social-climbing former-slave throws a party to which the amiable narrator, Encolpius, gets invited. Trimalchio commands entertainment for the evening, calculating everything to impress his guests in this parody of Roman custom, though in the comic hyperbole the plan backfires. The reader, just as the lead character Encolpius, is left with the impression of a pretentious, uneducated oaf.

In Trimalchio's *triclinium* the food itself becomes the object of iconographic dissection. Every one of the thirteen courses of the banquet is a masterpiece of artistry or artifice, or both. Following four courses which are enough to sate Encolpius, the *triclinium* and its furnishings are ensnared in the trappings of the hunt, including barking hounds racing around the table, in preparation for a spectacular dish: whole roasted wild boar. The servant wears an elaborate costume, like a circus exaggeration of the hunter's garb, instead of homespun, his *alicula* is made of silk and spangles. He performs the carving with a hunting knife. As incongruent a sight as a pig in knickers, the roasted boar wears a Phrygian cap. Even Encolpius needs the significance of this detail explained to him. The superficial reason, he is told, is that the boar when presented to last evening's banqueters was refused, thus freed from his fate. But further Trimalchio underscores his own new-won freedom, when he tells a slave to take the cap from the boar's head, put it on, and grants him his freedom. The tertiary level of meaning for the reader would be the incongruous detail that while the boar was a sow, the Phrygian cap was an article of men's apparel, so there is a touch of transvestite irony in the whole distasteful affair.

Of course none of this is real. The dinner party did not happen. Petronius feeds us a gross exaggeration for our delectation, not a slice of life. The pinch of salt that modifies the seeming popularity of hunting portrayed on dinnerware, or in literary dinner parties, comes with the fact that wild meat accounted for less than 18% of the protein diet in ancient Rome.[27] The lavish food that at every turn pretends to be something that it is not occupies such a prominent place in Petronius' novel that its very artificiality must be under attack. The same is true of the gendered constructs served up on the same platter. The comic effect of the scene dwells in the play on the artifice of the hunter, at first by the artificial hunting paraphernalia such as tablecloths painted like nets, with painted attendants holding them. Gender is at play in the comic effect of the mock virility of the servant, feigning manly virtue when his quarry in fact is already dead, stuffed and roasted. But the gendered joke also ridicules the host Trimalchio, as a fat sow of a freedman at the centre of the whole banquet.

The novel itself, far more than Trimalchio, informs modern readers about the advanced ironic sensibility at play in the late antique aesthetic, one quite capable of perceiving the constructed nature of a category like 'hunter' The antique awareness of such artificial constructs generally constitutes the compelling point today. The gendered slur on Trimalchio demonstrates how Romans disparaged effeminate men. It does not challenge the typical gender roles of Roman society; it confirms masculinist gender stereotypes. As artifice in food is under attack, so too, artifice of manhood is under attack. This reveals an antique predilection for critique of socially constructed gender, but one that works to support or endorse the masculinist status quo, rather than seeking to undermine it.

Conclusion

Hunter-gatherer as a description of subsistence societies is fraught with problems. With the caveat of modern biases made clear it is interesting to note that historic societies, too, had their constructs surrounding the term hunter. The Roman Empire, which had a decidedly masculinist view of the hunter, proves to have a very developed and ironic sensibility combining contrasting feminine reverberations with the masculine activity. Petronius uses wild food, domestically cultivated food, and examples of artifice with food to question what he perceives as artifice in society There is something similar in this very civilized conference on wild food. Several contributions here seek to examine society by looking more closely at its relationship to food. My plea has been to look closely as well at the terms we use. Gathering inspiration from antiquity, I ask: what is the artifice in our concept of the hunter?

Notes

1. William Johnson Sollas, *Ancient Hunters and their Modern Representatives* (London: Macmillan, 1915 [1911]).
2. Robert G. Reynolds, 'Why does cultural evolution proceed at a faster rate than biological evolution?', in *Time, Process and Structured Transformation in Archaeology*, Sander van der Leeuw and James McGlade, eds. (London: Routledge, 1997), 269-282.
3. Chris Gosden and Jon Hather, eds., *The Prehistory of Food: Appetites for change* (London: Routledge, 1999).
4. Sarah Milledge Nelson, *Gender in Archaeology: Analyzing Power and Prestige* (Walnut Creek, CA: Alta Mira (Sage), 1997); for tools, see esp. 65-84.
5. Richard B. Lee and Irven DeVore, eds., *Man the Hunter* (Chicago: Aldine, 1968).
6. Frances Dahlberg, *Woman the Gatherer* (New Haven: Yale UP, 1981).
7. Nelson, 1997, as in n. 4, 85-111. Bruce Winterhalder and Eric Alden Smith, *Hunter-Gatherer Foraging Strategies: Ethnographic and Archeological Analyses* (Chicago: University of Chicago Press, 1981) side-step this polemical issue by looking at 'foraging' which includes the efforts of both men and women, but the papers they bring together in their volume deliberately analyze evidence within a strict economic framework that often seems ill-suited to the societies examined.
8. Nelson, 1997, as in n. 4.
9. John Wilkins, David Harvey and Mike Dobson, eds., *Food in Antiquity* (Exeter: University of Exeter Press, 1995).
10. James N. Davidson, *Courtesans and Fishcakes: The Consuming Passions of Classical Athens* (New York: St Martin's Press, 1998 [1997]).
11. Luke, 5:1-11; John, 21:1-14.
12. Mathew Kuefler, *The Manly Eunuch: Masculinity, Gender Ambiguity and Christian Ideology in Late Antiquity* (Chicago: University of Chicago Press, 2001), especially page 21, where he handles Lactantius, *De Opificio Dei*.
13. Fronto, *Epistles*, 4.5.
14. Bernard Andreae, *Die Sarkophage mit Darstellungen aus dem Menschenleben: Die römischen Jagdsarkophage*, ASR I 2 [C. Roberts, ed., *Die antiken Sarkophagreliefs*, Berlin, 1890-] (Berlin: Gebr. Mann, 1980), 135; see also, Paul Zanker and Björn Christian Ewald, eds., *Mit Mythen leben: Die Bilderwerk der römischen Sarkophage* (Munich: Hirmer, 2004), 225-30.
15. Marina Warner, *Monuments and Maidens: The allegory of the female form* (London: Weidenfeld and Nicolson, 1985).

16. Plato, *Symposium*, 189c-193d, even though Plato puts this myth in the mouth of Aristophanes, a cynic who accounts for homosexuality equally naturally as having split from all-female or all-male sexual natures.
17. Ovid, *Metamorphoses*, iii. 198ff.
18. Ovid, *Met.* x. 300f.
19. Ovid, *Met.* viii. 380.
20. Paul Veyne, ed., *A History of Private Life*, vol I: From Pagan Rome to Byzantium, Arthur Goldhammer, trans., (Cambridge: Harvard UP (Belknap Press), 1987 [1985]); on public roles of the élite and public and private aspects of the work world, see especially, pp. 95-138.
21. John R. Clarke, *The Houses of Roman Italy, 100 BC–AD 250: Ritual Space and Decoration* (Berkeley: University of California Press, 1991); see also by Clarke, *Art in the Lives of Ordinary Romans: Visual Representation and Non-elite Viewers in Italy, 100 BC–AD 315* (Berkeley: University of California Press, 2003).
22. Werner Wilhelm Jaeger, *Paideia: The ideals of Greek culture*, Gilbert Highet, trans. (Oxford: Oxford UP, 1986). See also, Henri-Irénée Marrou, *A History of Education in Antiquity*, George Lamb, trans. (London: Sheed and Ward, 1977).
23. Philostratus, *Imagines*, 1:28.
24. Ibid.
25. Patricia Cox Miller, '"Differential Networks": Relics and Other Fragments in Late Antiquity', *Journal of Early Christian Studies*, vol. 6; no. 1 (Spring 1988), 113-138.
26. Petronius, *Satyricon*, 30-79.
27. Michael MacKinnon, *Production and Consumption of Animals in Roman Italy: Integrating the Zooarchaeological and Textual Evidence*, Journal of Roman Archaeology Supplement 54, [Portsmouth, RI,] 2004, 191.

Wild Foods in the Talmud: the Influence of Religious Restrictions on Consumption

*Susan Weingarten**

In his book *Good to Eat: Riddles of Food and Culture*,[1] Marvin Harris attempts to explain the cultural relativism of food ways. What people eat is not just dependent on availability, seasonality, price and taste, but is determined by their culture for reasons not always immediately obvious at first glance. Harris notes the poor diet of lactating women in some cultures where a Western observer might have expected the opposite. He reasons that breast-feeding women immediately after child-birth are unable to contribute to the society's economic efforts, so that there are simply fewer active workers but more demands at this time, and the society is thus unable to add to these women's diet. Thus some foodways can be explained by ecological restraints. The subject of this symposium is 'Wild foods,' and I want to look at how some of the cultural restraints of the *halakhah*, Jewish religious law as laid down in the Talmudic literature (3rd–7th centuries CE),[2] affected the consumption of wild foods by Jews in late antique Palestine and Babylonia. The basic laws about kosher foods are, of course, to be found in the Bible, particularly in Leviticus 11, but I shall not be dealing with the biblical situation, as these laws had undergone considerable additions and developments by late antiquity.[3] Similarly, I will not be concerned with modern religious development of the laws about kosher foods. I shall be using Greek and Latin sources contemporary with the Talmudic sources to try to build up my picture, as well as some modern anthropological material.

Jewish society in late antique Palestine and Babylonia subsisted primarily on agriculture and the raising of domestic animals. Thus the consumption of wild foods was probably marginal in normal times. The use of wild game was severely restricted by the *halakhah*. Wild vegetables, on the other hand, were permitted and seem to have been used all the time but in a small way. They became exceptionally important, however, in the sabbatical year when agricultural lands were supposed to lie fallow. Insects were generally prohibited by the *halakhah*. However, an exception was made for locusts (which are still eaten today, Harris tells us, in all the 65 countries they invade from Mauritania to Pakistan).[4] This, then, is an example of the opposite: permission to eat otherwise restricted foods. This paper will thus concentrate on hunting, wild vegetables and locusts as examples of how the *halakhah* defined what was good to eat for the Jews of late antique Palestine and Babylonia.

Hunting

The *halakhah* makes it a principle to cause as little pain as possible to animals. It is forbidden to eat a 'limb torn from a living animal,'[5] or an animal which had been injured. This restriction effectively meant a ban on hunting, for an animal had to be captured whole and uninjured and then slaughtered in what was seen as the quickest possible way, by slitting the throat. So hunting with dogs which catch the wild animal and hold it with their teeth would not be allowed, as the animal would be injured. Schwartz, in his article 'Dogs in ancient Jewish rural society,'[6] confirms this: there are many mentions of dogs as guard dogs or sheep dogs in the Talmudic literature, but not one mention of hunting dogs. And it is clear from Graeco-Roman literature and art that dogs were used in hunting in late antiquity – many mosaics from all over the Roman empire, including Palestine, show dogs holding their prey. Bows and arrows or stones from sling-shots were similarly out. The only forms of hunting allowed, then, would be chasing animals into an enclosure. There is indeed evidence of this – there were enclosures called *bivar*, probably from the Latin vivarium,[7] where domestic animals were raised until they could be slaughtered There is some evidence that there were sometimes serendipitous accidents which resulted in trapping whole live wild animals: there is a discussion of a case where a deer happens to come into a house on the Sabbath: do the Sabbath laws allow one to close the door on it to keep it for the next day?[8] Sometimes such wild animals would have been kept in the *bivar*, but it is not clear how widespread this phenomenon was. In any case, many wild animals would not be kosher for eating – deer and wild goats were probably all that were allowed.

But trapping birds was another matter. If bird-lime was used, this was allowed, as only the feathers would be caught and the bird itself would usually not be damaged. There is evidence from the Talmudic literature that birds were trapped in this way.[9] The Syro-African rift valley, down which the Jordan flows into the Dead Sea, is a route for massive bird migrations in spring and autumn – more birds pass this corridor than any other part of the world.[10] Many of them come down to water and rest in the swamps north of the Sea of Galilee so this would be ideal for trappers. Numbers 12.31-34 records the quails miraculously provided for the children of Israel in the wilderness of Sinai.[11] Quails still come and sit, exhausted, on the sands of Sinai at migrating season, and there are accounts of Bedouin bringing them live in cages to be sold in the markets of Jerusalem in the first half of the last century.[12] I see no reason why things should have been much different in antiquity.

I shall not be discussing fish here, although they undoubtedly come under the category of 'wild foods.'

In general, we can imagine that a settled society with domesticated livestock would have had little need for the relatively small additions that could be made to the diet by hunting. These halakhic restrictions thus survived. Such was not always the case – when the rabbis who laid down the *halakhah* went too far, the laity would

322

protest. This is recorded in the Talmudic sources: such laws were defined as 'law which the community could not bear,'[13] and the rabbis would give in. This was the case, for example, when the rabbis wished to prevent too much social contact between Jews and pagans, and forbade Jews to eat not only food that had some connection with pagan cult and rituals, but also their ordinary produce, including their oil. This ban was eventually rescinded as untenable. The rules finally decided for eating food that had belonged to a pagan stated that cooked food was forbidden, but raw food allowed. In other words, if we look at this in the terms of Levi-Strauss, where the raw is the primitive and the cooked the civilized, this is effectively a rejection of the civilization of the pagan.

Wild vegetables

Usually there were no restrictions on the eating of vegetables, as long as the tithe for the priests was taken. But the Bible[14] laid down rules for a seventh, sabbatical year when the land was to lie fallow and not be cultivated. Anything which grew by itself on previously tended land was to be made free for all. The restrictions of the sabbatical year often tended to impose great hardships on the population, especially in years with bad harvests or heavy taxation by the non-Jewish authorities. During the empire-wide economic crises of the 3rd century it looks as if many people had little or nothing to eat in the sabbatical year. Since these laws came from the Bible itself it was much more difficult to cancel them than the merely rabbinical prohibitions we saw above, and the Talmudic literature records all sorts of attempts by the rabbis to ease their plight. It was only the 'Land of Israel' which had to lie fallow in the seventh year: produce from abroad was allowed. So the rabbis were actually forced to re-define the borders of the 'Land of Israel' in order to help people find food: cities which had a majority of pagan population were redefined as being outside the 'Land of Israel' and their produce was thus permitted, and food was also imported from Syria.[15] One village synagogue just outside Scythopolis, a city with a pagan majority, had the permitted and forbidden places and foods inscribed on the floor on a mosaic.[16] The restrictions related to cultivated food, but vegetables which grew wild were permitted.

323

Probably wild vegetables were used always by the poor in order to supplement their diet. However, the amount they were used is impossible to quantify and assess.[17] But it is clear that in the sabbatical year much of the population came to be dependent to some extent on these wild growths. There is a whole tractate of the Jerusalem Talmud devoted to the subject of the sabbatical year, with much discussion of wild foods. Here, as in the earlier Mishnah and Tosefta as well, there are a great number of instances where wild and cultivated varieties of the same plant are carefully distinguished from each other, which shows us something of the importance of the wild plants in the diet in the sabbatical year.[18] One partial list of them includes: *pegam* (rue), wild shoots of *yarbizon* (goosefoot), *halaglogot* (purslane), hill-*cusbar* (coriander), celery which grows by streams, meadow *gargir* (rocket); the aftergrowths of mustard.[19] The description of many of the plants by place of growth – hill, meadow, stream – certainly defines them as wild. But some of the names in the list exemplify the problems of dealing with food in the talmudic literature. It is not always possible to identify for certain names of plants, especially wild plants, with the plants which actually grow in the Middle-East today.[20] The identification of *pegam* as rue is reasonably clear – rue was *peganon* in Greek and a well-known culinary herb in Apicius. Pliny tells us it could be cultivated but was better if stolen.[21] *Cusbar*, coriander is familiar from the Aramaic translations of the Bible and has parallels in Akkadian, Syriac and Arabic. Mustard is probably white mustard, *brassica alba*, still one of the common wild plants in present-day Israel. But other identifications are often based on educated guesses by the Hungarian scholar Immanuel Löw who wrote *Die Flora der Juden* at the turn of the 19th and 20th centuries. As far as I know he never visited Palestine or Babylonia.[22] There is also a certain amount of evidence of wild foods in contemporary Christian literature about the diet of the monks of the Judaean Desert, although this may not necessarily be good evidence for the diet of ordinary people in Palestine.[23]

Yet another biblical restriction connected with agriculture was the ban on growing two different kinds of crops together. Various crops are singled out for discussion, and one part of the Mishnah which deals with this, Kilayim [two kinds], discusses what kinds of vegetables are allowed to grow together with the vines in a vineyard. Transgression of this ban meant that the vines were not to be used, – so the rabbis are careful to distinguish between what are seen as deliberately sown crops, and thus forbidden, and wild growths, which are permitted. So we learn that thistles (*qotzim*) are allowed, – i.e. they are seen as wild growths, but artichokes (*qinras*) are not allowed – they are seen as cultivated rather than wild growths.[24] We will return to thistles and artichokes later, but meanwhile we will note that Patience Gray in her delightful *Honey from a Weed*[25] describes a little girl in Tuscany collecting edible weeds from her father's vineyard, which she divided into two categories: cooking and salad. On Naxos, Gray tells us, women and children gathered wild chicory, wild mustard, milk thistles and the blessed thistle and others. The wild chicory was eaten boiled with olive oil and a few drops of wine vinegar.

Wild and cultivated chicory appear in the Talmudic literature as well: *olesh*, pl. *olshin* are distinguished from field *olshin*, but they are considered the same 'kind' and allowed to be grown together. Even more helpfully, Greek names are given in the Jerusalem Talmud Kilayim[26] to help identify them, and by the way inform us that they are eaten raw: *entubin* from the Greek *entubon*, wild chicory or endive, is mentioned and identified by the Hebrew for chicory, *olshin Olshin*, the JT continues, are also known as *troximon*, from the Greek general word for vegetables eaten raw, (and *troximon*, another Talmudic source tells us, tastes sweet at first, then bitter[27]). Finally, JT Kilayim makes it clear that wild chicory is called *oltin* in Aramaic. Cultivated chicory is *Cichorium endivia* (the Babylonian Talmud actually tells us that *olshin* are *handevei*),[28] while the wild variety common now in Israel is *Cichorium pumilum*.[29] Claudine Dauphin, writing of the diet of the monks of Syria and Palestine in antiquity, suggests that the monks set themselves apart from the rural population by eating green vegetables raw, for 'neither the city dwellers nor the rural population ever ate any food raw except at times of famine.'[30] This does not seem to be supported by the Talmudic material.

Having seen the relatively clear evidence here about wild and cultivated chicory (or endives), I want to look now at the much more complex class of edible prickly thistles in the Talmudic sources.

'They that sit at the gate talk of me.' (Ps 69.13) This [said Rabbi Abbahu] refers to the nations of the world who sit in theatres and circuses. They then take a camel into their theatres, put their clothes upon it and ask one another 'Why is it in mourning?' to which they reply 'The Jews observe the laws of the sabbatical year and have no vegetables so they eat this camel's thorns and that is why it is in mourning...'[31]

Here Midrash Lamentations, which deals mostly with the destruction of the Second Temple, the Bar Kokhba Revolt, and the Roman persecutions which followed, is describing the state of the Jews as a subject people in their own land, now ruled by mocking Romans who laugh at them for being unable to eat the produce of their land in the sabbatical year and being reduced to animal food, in this case thorns, *hohim*. (Mishnah Shevi'it, when dealing with the wild foods permitted for food in the seventh year actually defines *hohim* together with *dardarim* as animal, as distinct from human, food.[32]) It is not clear exactly what plants '*hohim*' refers to – the word means literally thorns or prickles and there are a number of prickly plants which grow wild in Palestine which can be used for food.[33] One suggestion is the thistle called *Scolymus hispanicus*. In some cases the prickly stem can be peeled and the inside eaten, in others the part of the stem below ground can be eaten and in other cases the flower-head with its overlapping scales. I am presuming that plants which grow wild in the country today will be the same as those which grew wild in antiquity, though this may not always be the case.

There is a discussion of edible prickly plants in another Palestinian midrash, commenting on the verse in Genesis which describes Adam's curse: having been thrown out of the Garden of Eden he is condemned to less desirable food: 'Thorns [*qotz*] also and thistles [*dardar*] shall it [the land] bring forth to thee.'[34]

This clearly implies edible, if not necessarily pleasant food, so the Midrash then explains: '*Qotz* thorns are *qinras* artichokes and *dardarim* thistles are '*akavit* ?cardoons.' However, in case we think our troubles of identification are over, the Midrash continues:

Some reverse this: Thorn is *'akavit* ?cardoon and thistle is *qinras* artichoke. This is because [the Hebrew word for thistle], *dardar*, is so-called because it consists of rows [Hebrew: *dar*] above rows [of overlapping leaves like scales].

Artichokes are one of the few vegetables that can indeed be identified, as their name *qinras* comes from the Greek *Kynara*, although it is still difficult to know whether the artichoke proper is meant here, or the very similar cardoon. The classical authors, however, were quite clear that there were a number of edible thistles which grew wild, and that the artichoke is a cultivated variety of these. There are no details I could find in the Talmudic sources of how they ate wild thistles, but we do find details in the 2nd-century CE Greek court doctor Galen who tells us how 'country people' prepared wild thistles, eating them when 'newly emerged from ground and before the leaves produce thorns,' dipped in *garum*[35] and vinegar when raw, or with oil when boiled. He names the golden and spindle thistle as edible. Galen also notes that the artichoke was prepared in the same way and describes it as 'overvalued.' This might be because of what he saw as its negative health properties, for he calls it unwholesome, especially when hard and woody, and says it has bitter juice. Thus it is preferable to boil artichokes and add coriander if eating it with oil and *garum*, although this is unnecessary if it is fried in a pan.

However Galen's objections to artichokes may possibly be an echo of the attitude we find in Pliny[36] in a discussion of the extraordinary profitability of the cultivated artichoke (to which we will return later). Pliny also disapproves of the artichoke: man, he says, turns monstrosities of the earth, things all four-footed animals shrink from, (presumably the wild thistles) into objects of gluttony. He is also indignant about the enormous prices charged for artichokes, and their import to Rome from as far away as Carthage and Cordoba. This long-range trade is possible because the artichokes are 'preserved in honey diluted with vinegar with the addition of laser root (asafoetida) and cumin'. Pliny then adds, again with a note of disdain: 'so there should be no day without thistles (for dinner)'.

This picture in the classical literature of artichokes as food for the rich and upper classes is confirmed by the Talmudic literature. Artichokes were certainly seen as food for the nobles of Rome in the following source, which is a commentary on the biblical description in the book of Esther of the King of Persia's week-long feast: 'Bar Yohania made a feast for the notables of Rome ... What was missing? Only the artichoke.'[37]

Talmudic sources also record that artichokes were sent long distances to be eaten by the famous and very wealthy Rabbi Judah the Prince: 'Bonius sent Rabbi [Judah] a measure of artichokes from Nawsah, and Rabbi [Judah] estimated it at two hundred and seventeen eggs.'[38]

The eggs here, as often in the Talmudic literature, are a measure of volume. Nawsah probably refers to a settlement on an island in the river Euphrates outside Babylonia.[39] It was a long way from Galilee where Rabbi Judah lived, so presumably some sort of measures to preserve the artichokes like those mentioned by Pliny above must have been used.

Unlike the Graeco-Roman sources, there is no moral condemnation of artichokes as being symbols of excessively expensive consumption or monstrous because of their lowly origins. The rabbis of the Talmud tend to appreciate good food and see feasting as desirable, rather than to be condemned. Perhaps it is the difference between the haves and the have-nots – Pliny as a Roman aristocrat can afford to condemn luxury eating; most of the rabbis, as poor people themselves, can only desire. Even the unusually wealthy Rabbi Judah the Prince himself, when looking back nostalgically for the now legendary time when the Temple still stood, represents his longing for it in terms of desire for the wonderful foods that would have been available in that now mythological time.[40]

One of the reasons for the desirability of artichokes as food may also have been the effort needed to prepare them – an effort usually only available to the rich – the poor would have had no time for this. But one time when the poorer people would have had time would be on a festival when ordinary work was not allowed, but the work of cooking was permitted, as it contributed to the enjoyment of the festival. Thus it is specifically stated that while general cutting of vegetables was not allowed (in case people actually went and cut them down in the fields on the festival) trimming artichokes and 'akavit was allowed, as this was part of the preparation needed for cooking these vegetables: '[On a festival] they do not cut vegetables with shears but they do trim the qinras artichoke and the 'akavit ?cardoon.'[41] The word translated here as cardoon is 'akavit, or 'akubit which we saw earlier together with the qinras, artichoke as the identification of the edible prickly thorns and thistles, kotz and dardar. Cardoon, however, is just a guess. There have been various modern attempts to identify these names with prickly plants that grow wild in the area – Feliks has suggested an edible variety of Carthamus, the safflower, on the basis of a Talmudic source which identifies dardara with qurtemei de-hohim, Carthamus of the thorns.[42] (This seems to have been used as ancient Viagra.[43]) Nowadays there are wild varieties in semi-desert areas of Israel. However, elsewhere he identifies dardar with the Centaurea thistle, since a 9th-century commentator writes that it is called kangar in Babylonia, and has thorns on it which may be peeled off and the inside eaten.[44] However, Babylonian sources may not be familiar with the somewhat different flora of Palestine.

One of the sources above identified 'aqav or 'aqub with dardar, (although it then proposed a different identification). However, another midrash separates the 'aqub from the dardar, and appears to use them both as symbols of any sort of prickly plants.

Rabbi El'azar b Simon took Elijah the Prophet on his back and bore him up mountains and down valleys, through fields of [a]kuvin and fields of dardarin....[45]

327

However, the context is a sort of myth or dream sequence of suffering and bearing a burden so it is hard to know if we can deduce any real identifications from it. What does seem generally clear is that the consumption of wild prickly plants was seen by many as one of the less pleasant aspects of the observance of the sabbatical year.[46]

Locusts

The list of kosher and non-kosher animals in Leviticus 11:20 forbids the eating of all sorts of insects. The only exception made is for four different kinds of locusts and grasshoppers: 'locust, bald locust, beetle, grasshopper.' Three of the species are difficult to identify, but some Jewish communities have an unbroken tradition that the Hebrew *hagav*, which the Authorized Version translates 'grasshopper,' refers to the desert locust, *Schistocerca gregaria*. This locust is endemic in small numbers within a wide band of countries from Mauritania to Pakistan, but when climatic conditions are right begins to multiply. Swarms of millions of locusts borne on the wind then eat every available bit of vegetation – locusts were one of the ten plagues of Egypt in the book of Exodus and are mentioned as catastrophic in other biblical books as well. A locust invasion can still mean famine in our times and the United Nations FAO keeps a permanent locust watch.[47] In the ancient world, destruction of crops would have meant famine and death for people relying on agriculture. Thus it is clear that effectively permitting the eating of locusts, unlike other insects, would have meant preventing the population from dying of starvation.

328

There are records of eating locusts as far back as the second millennium BCE – ancient Sumerian documents record a sauce based on locusts perhaps like the Graeco-Roman *garum* They called it *siqqu*.[48] Pictures of locusts borne on skewers appear in a carved relief from Nineveh, showing them carried into Sennacherib's feast (8th century BCE).

Although locusts were famine food, they were considered good to eat in the Talmudic literature. This is clear from a midrash which discusses the taste of the 'mess of pottage' for which Esau sold his birthright to Jacob. The pottage, the midrash tells us, had the taste of all the good that is prepared for the righteous in the time to come.

> 'But what did he actually give you to eat?' he demanded. 'I do not know,' he replied, 'but I tasted in it the taste of bread, the taste of meat, the taste of fish, the taste of locusts and the taste of all the good things in the world.'[49]

It is clear that locusts here are included with good sustaining food – unlike fruit and vegetables! It is also seen here as a class of food by itself, separate from the rest.

Locusts were and still are eaten boiled or roasted over coals or toasted on a spit or fried. In the time of the Talmud they were also preserved and possibly fermented with salt like the Sumerian *siqqu* or the Graeco-Roman *garum* – the Talmud talks of both a sauce of fish and a sauce of locusts.[50] A *midrash* shows that people reacted to a locust invasion by collecting them and pickling them in barrels and jars. The *midrash* is discussing the biblical account of the ten plagues sent by God on the Egyptians, and comes to the plague of locusts:

> What is the meaning of there remained not one locust? (Exodus 10:19). Rabbi Yohanan said: 'When the locusts first came the Egyptians rejoiced and said: 'Let us gather them and fill barrels with them.' Then did God say: Wretches! Will you rejoice with the plagues I have brought upon you? Immediately the Lord turned an exceeding strong wind, this is the westerly wind which took up the locusts. What is the meaning of there remained not one locust? Even those which had been pickled in their pots and barrels took wing and fled.'[51]

During times of invasion it was easy to catch locusts from the swarms of millions, but at other times it was not so easy. A source which discusses whether they may be caught on the Sabbath says they can be caught at the time of dew but not in the heat of mid-day, except when they are swarming.[52] Locusts, being cold-blooded, can be easily caught in the cool dawn, which is when the Yemenite Jews used to collect them. Talmudic and Greek sources note locusts could be smoked out or roasted by burning vegetation. The Greek authors Strabo and Diodorus Siculus have descriptions of a people who were called the Akridophagoi, literally the locust-eaters.[53] They are part of a list of all sorts of semi-mythological peoples living at the fringes of the inhabited world along the coasts of Africa. These people lived only on locusts which they obtained by setting light to forests, and smoking and roasting them. But apparently setting fire to vegetation and roasting or smoking the locusts was an accepted method of catching locusts to eat. As we noted above, one of the things forbidden to Jews was food cooked by a pagan. Thus the Babylonian Talmud tractate dealing with pagans, discusses a pagan who set fire to a marsh, and whether Jews are allowed to eat the roast locusts resulting from such an act.[54] The discussion turns on whether the roasting of the locusts was intentional, or whether it was an unintended consequence of the pagan's act. This, then, would seem to imply that getting locusts by setting fire to vegetation as seen in the classical sources was a normal method of obtaining them.

Locusts were clearly sold in the markets, because the Babylonian Talmud says they should not be bought from pagan vendors.[55] This was because the pagans were liable to sprinkle them with wine, and wine of pagans, although not considered 'cooked' was forbidden in case it had been used for pagan religious rituals. Locusts are also mentioned together with preserved vegetables including capers, and as being sold from ships.[56] This presumably means that there was some sort of trade in them, local or even international. Their wings were removed with a knife before eating, like the scales of a fish.[57] Strabo's Akridophagoi also ground up dried locusts and made cakes of the locust flour. There is evidence of baked locust cakes from 19th-century Yemenite Jews as well.[58]

Thus it is clear that in antiquity locusts were eaten roasted or smoked, pickled and salted, and sprinkled with wine, and that a fermented and/or salty sauce were made from them. They were eaten when there was nothing else, but were seen as a desirable food. Yemenite Jews, almost the only Jews to preserve the tradition of locust-eating to the present day, still see locusts as desirable, with a taste like walnuts and almonds. Not everyone would agree. The 18th-century traveller von Rosenhof[59] reports that locusts boiled in salt water smell like shrimps, but taste 'repellant and repugnant'. He and his companions spat them out or vomited 'just as if they had taken a drug for vomiting'. On the other hand the explorer David Livingstone reported that they tasted 'like caviar'.[60]

We began this paper with the comments of Harris on what people found 'good to eat'. He suggests, when it comes to insects, that most Western people find them disgusting because we do not eat them, rather than that we do not eat them because we find them disgusting. I wonder if the reports of the taste of locusts are similarly influenced less by the actual taste rather than by the cultural attitudes of those eating them. Perhaps we can reverse Harris: Jews did not eat locusts because they were good to eat: they found them good to eat because they ate them.

Notes

* I am grateful to Dr Yuval Shahar for his help with this paper.
1. Marvin Harris, *Good to Eat: Riddles of Food and Culture* (London, 1986, repr. Prospect Heights, 1998).
2. For a brief explanation of the Talmudic literature, see my paper 'Nuts for the children: the evidence of the Talmudic literature', *Proceedings Oxford Symposium on Food and Cookery 2004*, (forthcoming). .
3. For an interesting analysis of Leviticus: Mary Douglas, *Leviticus as Literature* (Oxford, 1999); for an analysis of the restrictions on eating meat together with milk (which he dates to the period of the Mishnah and the Talmud): David Kraemer, 'Jewish Eating Practices in the Early Rabbinic Age', paper given at the Society for Biblical Literature Conference, Denver, Colorado, November, 2001 to be published in idem, 'Jewish Eating Practices' (forthcoming).
4. Harris op.cit. p. 170.
5. see eg. Tosefta Avodah Zarah viii 6; Babylonian Talmud [BT] Sanhedrin 59a and many more.
6. J. Schwartz, 'Dogs in ancient rural Jewish society', in A. M. Maeir, S. Dar, Z. Safrai (eds), *The Rural Landscape of Ancient Israel* (Oxford, BAR 2003), pp. 127-36.
7. See eg. Mishnah Shabbat xiii 5 and parallels.
8. Ibid.
9. Mishnah Kelim xxiii 5 mentions nets, snares, bird-traps, a bird basket, and bird cage. Mishnah Shabbat viii 4 also mentions a *shavshevet* which is interpreted by a 10th-century dictionary as lime-twigs. .
10. 'Bird migration in the eastern Hemisphere', *National Geographic* Maps, (Washington D. C., April, 2004): 'The Dead Sea Valley hosts the world's largest confluence of avian migrants, as many as a billion birds exhausted ... from flights ... refuel near the Red Sea.'

11. Cf. D. C. Lewis, E. S. Metallinos-Katsaras, L. E. Grivetti, 'Coturnism: human poisoning by European migratory quail', *Journal of Cultural Geography* 7 (1987), 51-6 (*non vidi*).

12. M. Kislev, 'Hunting edible birds as an economic activity', in S. Dar (ed.), *New Research on the Ancient Agriculture and Economy of the Land of Israel* (Ramat Gan, 1992, in Hebrew), pp. 52-9.

13. BTAvodah Zarah 36a.

14. Leviticus 25: 2-5; ibid., 20-22.

15. The Jerusalem Talmud [JT] Demai ii, 22c lists the pagan towns exempted by Rabbi Judah the Prince in the 3rd century.

16. For a useful summary of the inscription and an English translation: J. Sussman 'The inscription in the Synagogue at Rehob', in L. I. Levine (ed.), *Ancient Synagogues Revealed* (Jerusalem, 1981), 146-53.

17. K. L. Pearson, 'Nutrition and the early-medieval diet', *Speculum* 72 (1997), 1-32 esp pp. 13-14 'Wild greens were doubtless consumed, as they still are today in peasant communities throughout Europe. The nutritional value of most wild plants has not, as yet, been adequately studied, so that any analysis of their significance in the diet remains purely speculative.'

18. Tosefta Nedarim iii, 6.

19. Mishnah Sheviit ix 1: the identifications here are from H. Danby's translation of the Mishnah (Oxford, 1933). Other identifications by Y. Feliks, commentary on *Talmud Yerushalmi*, Tractate Shevi'it vol. I , (Jerusalem, 20002, in Hebrew) include *yarbizon* = *Amaranthus* based on the Arabic name; *gargir* = either *Eruca sativa* or *Diplotaxis erucoides*, or *Nasturtium officinale*. Of these, *eruca sativa* was grown as a garden herb by the Greeks and Romans: A. Dalby, *Food in the Ancient World from A to Z* (London, 2003), sv rocket.

20. J. M. Frayn, *Subsistence Farming in Roman Italy* (London, 1979), 57-72; J.M. Frayn, 'Wild and cultivated Plants', *Journal of Roman Studies* 65 (1975), 32-9, notes the difficulty of distinguishing wild and cultivated plants, partly because the categories of the Greek and Romans were not always same as our own. She suggests that there seem to have been three types of wild plant which can be differentiated: 'those which grow outside the bounds of cultivation or fallow land or pasture; those found on pasture-land; those growing in fallow fields.'

21. Pliny, *Natural History* 19.123.

22. I. Löw *Die Flora der Juden* I-IV(Vienna, 1924). It should be noted that a large number of his educated guesses were right.

23. On the diet of monks see Y. Hirschfeld, *The Judean Desert Monasteries in the Byzantine Period* (New Haven/London, 1992), 89; C. Dauphin, 'Plenty or just enough? The diet of the rural and urban masses of Byzantine Palestine', *Bulletin of the Anglo-Israel Archaeological Society* 17 (1999), 39-65.

24. Mishnah Kilayim v 8.

25. P. Gray, *Honey from a Weed: Fasting and Feasting in Tuscany, Catalonia, the Cyclades and Apulia* (NY, 1986, repr. Totnes, 1997).

26. JT Kilayim i, 27a.

27. JTPesahim ii. 29c.

28. BTPesahim 39a.

29. N. Feinbrun-Dothan, *Flora Palaestina* vol. III (Jerusalem, 1966) = *Cichorium pumilum Jacq.* no. 690. p. 408: to be found in fields, road-side and waste places all over. Löw (above n. 22), p. 415f,.

30. C. Dauphin (art. cit. above, n. 23), 39-65 esp. p. 48.

31. Lamentations Rabbah Proem 17 (ed Buber 7b).

32. Mishnah Shevi'it vii,2.

33. Y. Feliks, commentary *Tractate Shevi'it* vol. I (above, n. 19), p. 380.

34. Genesis Rabbah 20,10, on Genesis 3, 17-18. Interestingly, the Septuagint translation of this verse has *akantha* here, the same word as the Greek NT uses for Jesus' crown of thorns in Mark 15,17 and John 19,2.

35. *Garum*, the famous Graeco-Roman salty fermented fish sauce, used widely as a condiment; see eg.

331

A. Dalby, op. cit. sv *garum*; R.I. Curtis, *Garum and Salsamenta: Production and Commerce of Materia Medica* (Leiden, 1991); M. Grant, *Roman Cookery* (London, 1999).

36. Pliny, *Natural History* 19,8,43*152f.

37. S. Klein in his article 'Bar-Yohannis from Sepphoris at Rome', BJPES 7 (1940), 47-51 (in Hebrew), thought that this may be the first reference to the famous Roman Jewish artichoke dish *carciofi alla giudia* (for a recipe see E. Servi Machlin, *The Classic Cuisine of the Italian Jews* [NY, 1981, 1993], pp. 180-1); see also I. Löw, op.cit, vol. I, p. 409. Unfortunately there is no proof of this charming suggestion, since, as we have seen, artichokes seem to have been famously popular among the Roman pagan nobility.

38. BT Eruvin 83a. .

39. For the identification of Nawsah see Aharon Oppenheimer, *Babylonia Judaica in the Talmudic Period* (Wiesbaden, 1983), pp. 266-7.

40. See on this S. Weingarten, 'Magiros, nahtom and women at home: cooks in the Talmud', *Journal of Jewish Studies* (forthcoming).

41. Tosefta Betzah [Yom Tov] iii,19 and cf BTBetzah 34a.

42. Y. Feliks, commentary *Tractate Shevi'it*, vol. II (above, n. 19), pp. 106-7.

43. BT Gittin 70a; R. Johanan said, 'This is just what restored to me my youthful [sexual] vigour.'

44. BT Gittin 70a; Löw, op. cit., vol. I, 406f. *Dardar* is identified with the class of thistles which includes *Centaurea iberica* by Feliks in his commentary to *Tractate Shevi'it* (above, n.19), vol. I, p. 379.

45. Pirqei de Rav Kahana 197.5.

46. It is clear that wild plants sometimes tasted worse than their cultivated counterparts: Felix notes the fact that wild arum, loof, eaten in the seventh year, tastes more unpleasant than cultivated arum, even after cooking: Y. Feliks, commentary *Tractate Shevi'it* vol. I (above, n.19), p.318-19.

47. www.FAO.org/NEWS/GLOBAL/LOCUSTS?LOCFAQ.htm .

48. *The Assyrian Dictionary* (Chicago, 1992), part III, v. 17, pp. 99-100: *siqqu: garum* – a brine or sauce made of fish, crustaceans or grasshoppers. One of the words denoting locusts in the Talmudic literature is *saqi* or *saqah*, qv. eg. BT:Ta'anit 6a. It is interesting to note that the FAO website (above) shows a Swazi recipe for roast locust called *Sikonyane*.

49. Midrash Genesis Rabbah 67.2.

50. Fish sauce: *tsir dagim*; locust sauce *tsir hagavim*.

51. Midrash Exodus Rabbah xiii, 7.

52. Tosefta Shabbat xii 5 and parallels.

53. Strabo, 16.4.12; Diodorus Siculus, 3.29.1.

54. BTAvodah Zarah 38a.

55. BTAvodah Zarah 40b.

56. loc.cit.

57. Tosefta Uqtsin ii,16.

58. Z. Amar, *The Locust in Jewish tradition* (Ramat Gan, 2004, in Hebrew), p. 43.

59. Roesel von Rosenhof, *Insecten-belustigungen* (Dutch ed. 1779), vol. 2 para 37 pp. 297f, quoted by F.S. Bodenheimer, *Insects as Human Food* (The Hague 1951), p. 46. Bodenheimer has many more different accounts of the taste of locusts, hardly any two the same.

60. D. & C. Livingstone, *Narrative of an Expedition to the Zambesi and its Tributaries and of the Discovery of the Lakes Shirwa and Nyassa, 1858-1864* (London, 1865), pp. 374-5.

Recipe for a Bacchanal

Carolin C. Young

Have your summer picnics become humdrum? Are your family barbecues stultifyingly dull? Why not liven up your outdoor feast with a potent splash of pagan ritual? Instead of firing up the grill, celebrate nature at an unfettered Bacchanal!

The complete mysteries cannot be revealed to the uninitiated. However, the following instructions should suffice to guide the novice through the basic elements of these ancient rites. Before reading further, disbelievers must be strongly cautioned. Do not be deceived by Bacchus' indulgent, carefree demeanour. Although the god of wine and fertility, called Dionysus by the Greeks, keeps company with Laughter and Revel, his revenge upon those who scoff at his divinity is ruthless. Witness King Pentheus torn to pieces by his own mother and aunts in a Bacchic frenzy; the Maeonian fisherman turned into dolphins; and the daughters of Minyas transformed as bats.[1]

Even those sympathetic to the deity should proceed with care. Without warning, the joyous Bacchanal can become unrelentingly brutal. Impassioned celebrants in ancient Rome hunted down those who refused to submit to their whims; flung them into dark caverns; then tortured, and sometimes even killed, their victims.[2] Often, the bodies were never recovered – carried off by the wrath of the god, it was said.

Rome's more reserved citizenry grew so frightened by the unruly festival that the Senate outlawed it in 186 BC. Bacchus, however, merely laughed at this mortal attempt to stamp out his most divine and bestial feast. Although legally banned, the celebration continued to flourish in the murky darkness of the forest and of the night, where the god, sometimes called Dendrites 'he of the trees', reigns supreme.

There are safer, gentler ceremonies than the Bacchanal at which to venerate the wine god. Rural Dionysia honour him with a carnivalesque parade of a large, erect phallus, baskets of fruit and bread, jars of water and wine, and much song and dance. The more urbane city Dionysia culminate with a competition to determine the best authors of comedy and tragedy. And Roman Liberalia, a procession of wine and *liba* (hot cakes coated with warm honey), enjoyed official sanction long after the raucous Bacchanals had been prohibited.[3] These festivals, which invite unruly Bacchus into domesticated territories, thereby render him less threatening, perhaps in the hope that he (and his followers) will respect the elemental rules of hospitality.

But for those who dare to step outside the safe borders of society to meet and honour Dionysus in his chosen realm, a reward awaits. At the Bacchanal, where human law dares not curb the heady powers of the god, who was also called Liber 'the free one,' Eleutherios 'the liberator,' and Lyaeus 'he who releases,' unfettered frenzy can wholly overtake you.

Guiding Principles

Although a liberal affair by definition, the Bacchanal, nevertheless, demands adherence to a few governing rules. Most importantly, wildness, both literal and metaphoric, must be cultivated at every turn. This is why it is not only imperative not only to drink large quantities of wine, but also to do so out of doors – preferably in a shady, wooded grove untouched by civilization or, like the celebrants in Euripides' *Bacchae*, under fir trees on an open cliff.[4] It is also desirable (although optional) to have a lake, brook, or river nearby. The most Bacchanalian of locations is next to a river that flows with wine, rather than water, such as the one that Philostratus describes on the mythical island of Andros.[5]

You may, if you follow Roman, rather than Greek, custom, have your Bacchanal in any season you like. As the rites spread from Greece into Sicily, and then further north, their frequency increased steadily. The feast, originally held once biennially, then occurred three times per year; and, at its popular height in ancient Rome, as often as five times per month.[6] However, at whichever date you choose, your Bacchanal *must* take place at night.[7]

Many claim that the orgiastic qualities of the earliest Bacchanals were largely exaggerated.[8] These events, restricted to women only, were, however, rather dull; and, held, as they were, in the dead of winter, on the icy summit of Mount Parnassus, extremely uncomfortable.[9] It is far more pleasurable, and thereby pleasing to the god, to, like the Romans, embrace the debauched reputation of the proceedings.

Choose your guest list carefully. You will need a good quantity of well-oiled young nymphs. Virgins are unnecessary and even undesirable for such a purpose. Although occasionally tolerated, extra virgins should be saved for Arcadia.

In Euripides' *Bacchae*, wise old Teiresias argued:

> Dionysus will not compel women to act foolishly where sex is concerned. Rather, such folly lies in their own nature. [...] Remember: even in ecstatic worship a chaste woman will not be corrupted.[10]

She may, however, in such an atmosphere, be forced into desperate acts in order to preserve her virtue. While attending a Bacchanal, the virginal nymph Lotis only escaped the embrace of lecherous Silenus by turning into a flowering tree. This myth exemplifies the fact that a prude is a nuisance to look after under such circumstances and is best advised to worship a more suitable deity such as Diana.

In order to guarantee that your fellow celebrants have the desired beauty, stamina and requisitely dissipated bent of mind, you may also wish to uphold the Bacchic rule implemented in 188 BC, which banned those older than twenty years of age from participating in the rites. (No minimum age applied. The Roman consul Postumius complained, 'If you knew at what ages the males are initiated, you would feel not only pity but also shame for them.')[11]

Alternately, you may invite any and all to join in. Venerable Teiresias defiantly boasted:

> Will someone say that in preparing to dance with my head crowned with ivy I show no respect for my old age? No, for the god had not distinguished young from old where dancing is concerned: he wants to receive joint honour from everyone and to be magnified without exception.[12]

Bacchus places no limits on sex, age, class, or weight (heftier nymphs should consult instructions for the 'Bacchanal à la Rubens'). As classicist E.R. Dodds noted, in contrast to the aristocratic god Apollo – patron of poets, philosophers and athletes – Dionysus is the people's god, worshipped by slaves and women, and for whom even a country bumpkin might dance a jig.[13]

Character is another matter. 'The feast of grape-crowned Bacchus' described by Ovid was not attended by all the gods, but rather, only those who served him:

> And whoever is not hostile to play,
> Namely Pans and young satyrs all ready for sex
> And goddesses who haunt streams and lone acres.
> Old Silenus came, too, on a sway-backed donkey,
> And the red-groined terror of timid birds. [Priapus]
> ...Naiads were there, some with hair flowing uncombed,
> Others with locks artfully coiffured.[14]

This mixture of deities provides an exemplary guest list to imitate.

Attendees should wear fawnskins, which may be ornamented with strands of white wool.[15] If fawnskins are not available, nudity is always appropriate. Or, you may wear tunics. If the latter are chosen, these should be revealingly torn, hitched, or shifted (also see notes on the 'Bacchanal alla Tiziano').[16] Feet must be bare in order to inflame desire.[17] Hair should be long and dishevelled.

Assemble the following ingredients

Wine – as much as you can afford. You need not, however, spring for aged vintages. A young, light wine has the characteristics of the god it honours.
Grape Clusters – include tendrils and vines wherever possible. Have excess for decorative use and, if possible, a life-size bed of grapes.
Figs – several baskets. Bacchus favours this most lusciously sexual of fruits.
One or More Live Goats – goats became Dionysus' special enemy because they nibbled on his vines.[18] In spite of this, he sometimes transformed himself into one. At other moments, he appeared as a bull, which for this reason may be

added or substituted for the goat. Either way, your beast must be alive and have horns (like Bacchus himself).

Milk – as an infant, poor Bacchus was cut into pieces by Titans and boiled in it.[19] Nevertheless, this did not succeed in putting him off the stuff so it always appears at his feast.[20]

Honey – Liber discovered it while returning from India. [21]

Fennel Stalks, Long– one per participant. These are precious to the god from his youth in Nysa.

Ivy –you can't have too much because 'Bacchus loves the ivy most'. As a young boy, the nymphs of Nysa, who guarded him, screened his crib with it.[22]

Pine Cones – one per participant. Pine is sacred to the god.

Pine Branches –– ditto.

Optional:

Fruit and other Picnic Foods – add as desired. However, intricate recipes that require elaborate preparation should be avoided because they detract from the untamed, bestial nature of the event. Moreover, a limited menu will maximize the effect of the wine, whose intoxicating power is essential to achieve the desired state of Bacchic ecstasy.

Spices – especially cinnamon and saffron. Bacchus brought these, as well as the scents of frankincense and myrrh, back from his conquest of Persia and India. (See variation for a 'Bacchanal à l'indienne').

Bryony with its Berries.[23]

Oak Leaves and Branches.

Flowers – 'Bacchus,' Ovid reminds us, 'loves flowers. Bacchus' pleasure in the wreath/Can be known from the Ariadne star.' [24]

Snakes.

Special Equipment:

Cymbals.

Pipes.

Drums – another name for Dionysus is Bromios 'the roaring god'. He instructs his Bacchants to 'take up the drums that are native to Phrygia, drums invented by Mother Rhea and by me,' and make a loud din.[25]

Wooden Phalli – keep in a box until the ritual begins (best not to scare the neighbours). These sacred objects, symbols of male fertility and sexual appetites, also commemorate the wooden phallus set upon Promsymnos' tomb with which Bacchus allowed himself to be taken as a woman to honour his debt for gaining directions to cross into and out of the underworld.[26]

String.

Before you begin:

1. Fatten your goat and groom his coat until it gleams. As an extra flourish, you may drape him with garlands and/or gild his horns.

2. Form your pine branches into torches. Lace with sulphur and charcoal.[27] You should have as many as you can carry since Bacchus was especially fond of torchlight.

3. Wrap each fennel stalk with ivy and attach a pine cone at its tip. This is your *thyrsus* or Bacchic wand. If you wave this properly during the rites, you should be able to conjure up magically the necessary wine, milk, and honey listed in the ingredients above. One witness reported:

> Someone took a thyrsus and struck it against a cliff, and out leapt a dewy spring of water. Another struck her fennel wand into the ground, and the god at that spot put forth a fountain of wine. All who desired a drink of milk dug with their fingertips into the ground and the white liquid bubbled up. From their ivy-covered thyrsi dripped streams of honey.[28]

This technique is difficult for the beginner to master. Therefore, it is advisable to bring along an adequate supply of these key items until you get the hang of it.

4. Make an ivy and grape-leaf wreath for each participant. Intersperse pine cones, oak branches, bryony, and flowers as desired.

5. Make festive garlands to match.

6. Use the string to hang the wooden phalli in the surrounding trees.

Note: When Bacchanalian rites first arrived on the Italian peninsula, initiates abstained from sexual intercourse for ten days prior to the festival.[29] On the tenth day, a solemn meal was served, followed by a purification by water before the mysteries. This practice came to be viewed as unduly restrictive (not to mention highly impracticable when the feast was held five times per month) so it was dropped. If the Romans didn't bother, why should you?

Instructions

1. After sunset, light your torches, bang drums, crash cymbals, and toot pipes as you march into the woods. The music should be loud, unrestrained, and continue throughout the proceedings. This will engender a state of general confusion, which helps to guard the mystery from the uninitiated and to conjure frenzy amongst its participants.

2. Once you arrive at your chosen clearing burn incense.

3. Call the god by all his names:

The Loud One, the Deliverer from Sorrow,
Son of Thunder, The Twice-Born, The Indian,
The Offspring of Two Mothers, God of the Wine-Press,
The Night-hallooed, and all the other names
Known in the towns of Greece.[30]

4. Wave your *thyrsus* over the ground.
5. Pour a libation to the gods. (If your *thyrsus* has not made wine spurt from the ground use your reserve supply.)
6. Sing hymns to Bacchus, who was also called 'Dithyrambos'. (The original dithyramb was an ecstatic, passionate choral hymn dedicated to Dionysus.)
7. Drink heartily.
8. Rip the flesh from the living goat (or other beast) and eat. If necessary, the goat may be slain. However, the meat must be eaten raw. There should be much tearing of flesh and dripping of blood. Communion wafers or bread, although symbolically analogous, may not be substituted. Paganism is not for the faint of heart.

    The exact method for performing this ritual has never been adequately recorded, perhaps because one must be heavily intoxicated before commencing it. We may, from this fact, infer that if you can still remember to follow instructions or to describe what you are doing you are not drunk enough to move on to this portion of the ritual. Go back to the previous step until you can't read this.

9. Wash down with liberal quantities of wine, as much as you can manage (after all, both liberal and libation take their name from their inventor, Liber.)[31] If you have conveniently situated yourself near a lake or trickling brook, you may dilute the wine with water, but only sparingly.[32]
10. Let snakes sacred to the god lick your face clean.[33] Bloodied hands may be washed in clear waters, if handy.
11. Sing and dance around the goat with abandon.[34]
12. Make wild cries and shouts. Allow convulsions to overtake you. Pronounce oracles.[35] Succumb to the agonized ecstasy, the rebirth through dismemberment, and the miracle of ingesting the divine flesh and blood of the god. If you have surrendered yourself fully, this will be less awkward than it might seem. If you find yourself hesitating, go back to step 9.
13. Race to the nearest river or lake with your hair flying wildly behind you and plunge your torch into the water. If you have primed it sufficiently with sulphur and charcoal it should still be flaming when you raise it back in the air.[36]
14. Choose your partner and head for the trees; or, like Ovid's gods, recline on grass-lined couches.[37]
15. From this point on, there are no rules.

Variation for a 'Bacchanal à l'indienne'

Only a few minor alterations are necessary in order to transform the classical Bacchanal into an homage to the mythological conqueror of India and Persia. In addition to the goat, you will need a menagerie of exotic animals – preferably leopards, tigers, and bejewelled elephants. (Note: these are for show. Do not slaughter them.)

Because the triumphant god returned home from his exotic travels with rich spices including cinnamon and the heady scents of frankincense and myrrh use these as much as possible in your feast.[38] Saffron should also be employed liberally for added colour and flavour.

The resulting festival should closely resemble the torch-lit rites performed in the jungles of south-eastern Sri Lanka for the Kataragama Skanda, identified with the Tamil hill god Murukan, whom worshippers believe arrived from overseas on a stone raft.[39] Let your feast be:

> Harmonious with the dances wild
> Of frenzied maids by the Red-god stirred
> The flutes do pipe the lyres do twang
> The drums roll loud and the tabors sound.[40]

Variation for a 'Bacchanal alla Tiziano'

For a Bacchanal suffused with 16th-century, Venetian languor consult Titian's resplendent paintings for Duke Alfonso d'Este's *camerino d'alabastro* in Ferrara.[41]

339

Instead of fennel stalks, make your Bacchic wands with 'branches wound about with tendrils of vines,' as seen in Titian's *Bacchanal of the Andrians* (*ca.* 1523–4) and *The Worship of Venus* (1520), both at the Prado, in Madrid. These *thyrsi* resulted from a mis-translation in the edition of Philostratus' text that inspired the paintings. Unlikely to miraculously produce wine, they are, however, very pretty.[42]

For a tasty Renaissance addition to the menu, include exotic game birds, such as the guinea fowl perched in the tree of *The Andrians*. For cooking suggestions, consult Cristoforo di Messisbugo's 1549 *Banchetti, compozioni di vivande e apparecchio generale*.[43] The book provides menus and recipes from the Este family's grand outdoor banquets as well as suggestions for how best to incorporate sugar sculptures of Bacchus at your feast. Dosso Dossi's *Bacchanal*, now at the National Gallery, London and which may likely have been part of the original *camerino* series, also suggests sweet melons as an appropriately depraved treat.[44] Adherents to humoral dietary theory should, however, avoid these with the utmost care.

Never, at a 'Bacchanal alla Tiziano', serve wine in plastic cups; use your best stemware and porcelain. Place your fruit in imported Chinese porcelain bowls, as seen in Bellini and Titian's *Feast of the Gods* (1514–29), now at the National Gallery, Washington, D. C.; or serve wine in a *cristallo* pitcher as shown in *The Andrians*. Although an inhabitant of wooded groves and hills, Bacchus loved anything that was luxurious and sensuous. (So did Duke Alfonso. The rare enamelled glass pitcher shown in the painting is quite possibly modelled on a piece in the Este collection, which Titian accompanied the duke's agent to Murano to commission, and which he also possibly designed.[45])

Dress some of your guests in sumptuous fabrics, such as those worn by the two gallant couples seen in *The Andrians*, and two of the women in *The Worship of Venus*.[46] Expensive jewellery with a slightly Eastern bent, such as the dangling earrings seen on the dancing maenad in *The Andrians*, is also appropriate. The pair depicted simultaneously illustrate cutting-edge fashion (they became extremely popular in Venice just after Titian painted the picture) and bespeak Bacchus' exotic travels to the East.[47]

Unlike the American Superbowl, the Bacchanal encourages 'wardrobe malfunctions'. This is especially true at the 'Bacchanal alla Tiziano'. X-rays reveal that when Titian reworked Bellini's *Feast of the Gods*, he raised the nymph Lotis' right leg into a more suggestive pose.[48] He also bared her breasts, as well as those of the Goddess Ceres and loosened the standing nymph's hairdo into long, flowing tresses.

In spite of such artful dishevelment, it remains imperative at such an occasion to 'present so exquisite a combination of modesty and ease,' that you appear to have 'stepped out of the pages of Castiglione's *Cortegiano*.'[49] The two Venetian-garbed maidens in *The Andrians* exemplify the required demeanour.

Sing: 'Who drinks and does not drink again does not know what drinking is,' the words clearly inscribed in the music fragment in foreground of Titian's *Andrians*. The notes are for four voices and may be read up or down, backward or forward, but should rise or fall by a whole tone with each repetition.[50] According to Edward Lowinsky, this *canon per tonos*, composed by Adriaan Willaert, who served in Alfonso's court, was such an unusual form that it was not repeated for a hundred years.

In addition, you may wish to bring along your dog or other pets. As *Bacchus and Ariadne* (1520-3), now at the National Gallery, London, shows, these can be useful at chasing any impish little satyrs whose antics get carried away.

Although too young to take part in the sexual frolics, scampering toddlers enacting the roles of Cupid and putti augment the atmosphere of general disarray. For example, they can casually wee on nymphs and rivers, as seen in *The Andrians*; or kiss, wrestle, and dance, as demonstrated in *The Worship of Venus*.

(Lest you, like King Pentheus, complain that Bacchanalian revelry honours Aphrodite, mother of Cupid, more than the god of wine, remember Ovid's words: 'Venus in the wine/is fire within fire!'[51] To honour wine without love is merely banal, not Bacchic. And, as the poet states, 'There [at banquets] flushed Love has often clasped the horns of reclining/Bacchus in a seductive embrace.'[52])

Baroque Bacchanals:

If you wish to add a heavy dose of opulence and excess to your Bacchanal, look to the Baroque, an era which embraced the wine god more enthusiastically than any since the

Roman Senate banned the celebration. Among the myriad painters who lent their creative genius to the theme, Nicolas Poussin and Peter Paul Rubens stand out. Inspired directly by Titian, both made the subject their own. If you are unsure about which method you prefer, W. Hazlitt provides a helpful comparison of the two:

> Rubens' Satyrs and Bacchantes have a more jovial and voluptuous aspect, are more drunk with pleasure, more full of animal spirits and riotous impulses; they laugh and bound along… but those of Poussin have more of the intellectual abstractions of the same class, with bodies less pampered, but with minds more secretly depraved.[53]

Variation for a 'Bacchanal à la Rubens'

Those with gelatinously rippling flesh take heart. In Rubens' eye, hefty thighs, an enormous belly, and undulating cellulite evidence consistent, rather than occasional, devotion to the wine god. This aesthetic is best demonstrated in his Bacchanalia (c. 1615) at the Pushkin Museum, which shows that all participants must have substantial flab in order to most fully glory in and pay tribute to Dionysus.

Variation for a 'Bacchanal à la Poussin'

No matter how wild, the 'Bacchanal à la Poussin' requires participants not only to maintain an elevated, classical demeanour, but also chromatic and geometric balance. Therefore, this should be considered 'Advanced Bacchanalia' and only undertaken after simpler forms of the feast have been mastered.

To begin, first imitate Poussin's version of *The Andrians*, also called *The Great Bacchanal with Woman Playing a Lute* (*ca.* 1627-8), now at the Louvre. Loosely classicizing wraps and togas in saturated hues of red, yellow and blue should be worn. Obviously, you will also need a lute instead of cymbals and drums. This instrumental change advantageously slows the pace, which makes it easier for the group to practice how to keep its compositional equilibrium.

Advanced Bacchants may then attempt Poussin's *Bacchanalian Revel Before a Herm of Pan* (*ca.* 1636), *The Triumph of Pan* (1636) (both at the National Gallery, London), or *The Triumph of Bacchus* (known through a copy at the Nelson Gallery-Atkins Museum, Kansas City). Following these examples, while dancing at a whirlwind pace, keep the previously mentioned balance of symmetry and hue. Simultaneously, you should also squeeze clusters of grapes into the bowls of scampering children or pour wine from a classical ewer.

Do not, however, skip the goat sacrifice. If you have an extra goat, mount it and ride it with your desired partner; then embrace and pose suggestively. This is prohibitively difficult to do while holding the *thyrsus* – so drop it on the ground beside you (decorously).

For a Baroque flourish, place statues of Pan or Priapus, generously garlanded with flowers, into your wooded grove. These may be painted the traditional red of male fertility images by boiling ivy stems and mixing with urine.[54] Cornucopias of flowers and fruit may also be held or generously scattered. Masks, tambourines, and horns can be tossed about as well.

Variation for a Bacchanal à la Velasquez

The Spanish painter Diego Velazquez' *Bacchanal* is the easiest of all to re-enact: simply head for the woods with a good quantity of wine; offer a toast to the donor of this magnificent gift; then, imbibe heavily.

Velazquez demonstrates that one may dispense with the *thyrsus*, the goat, and even the frenzied maenads. In *The Drinkers* (1629), now at the Prado, a group of rustic, peasant labourers sit at the edge of a forest drinking boisterously, perhaps to celebrate the new vintage. They wear drably coloured, rough-hewn clothes suitable for the fields and carry only simple earthenware and tumblers. However, the gusto with which they enjoy Bacchus' gift summons the deity before them. Dionysus, attended by a beautiful, young satyr, crowns one of his worshippers with an ivy wreath. Perhaps, if you are sincere enough in your prayer, or liberal enough with your consumption, Bacchus will arrive to bless you, too.

342

Select Bibliography

Colantuono, Anthony, '*Dies Alcyoniai*: The Invention of Bellini's *Feast of the Gods*', in *The Art Bulletin*, LXXIII no. 2 (June 1991), pp. 237-56.

Dalby, Andrew, *Bacchus: A Biography* (London: The British Museum Press, 2003).

Dictionary of Subjects and Symbols in Art, ed. by James Hall, rev. edn (New York: Harper & Row, 1979).

Dodds, E. R., *The Greeks and the Irrational* (Berkeley: University of California Press, 1951).

Euripides, *Bacchae, Iphigenia at Aulis, Rhesus*, ed. and trans. by David Kovacs (Cambridge, MA: Harvard University Press, 2002).

Fehl, Philip, 'The Worship of Bacchus and Venus in Bellini and Titian's Bacchanals for Alfonso d'Este' in *Studies in the History of Art*, VI (1974), pp. 37-95.

Harrigan, Patrick, 'Dionysus and Kataragama: Parallel Mystery Cults,' in *The Journal of the Institute of Asian Studies*, XIV no. 2 (March 1997), pp. 1-28.

Holberton, Paul, 'The choice of texts for the Camerino pictures,' in *Bacchanals by Titian and Rubens. Papers given at a symposium in Nationalmuseum, Stockholm, March 18-19, 1987*, ed. by Görel Cavalli-Björkman (Stockholm: Nationalmuseum, 1987), pp. 57-66.

Livy, 'Rome and the Mediterranean': Books XXXI–XLV of the *History of Rome from its Foundation*, trans. by Henry Bettenson (Harmondsworth: Penguin, 1976).

Lowinsky, Edward E., 'Music in Titian's *Bacchanal of the Andrians*: Origin and History of the *Canon per Tonos*,' in *Titian: His World and His Legacy*, ed. by David Rosand (New York: Columbia University Press, 1982).

Messisbugo, Cristoforo di, *Libro novo nel qual s'insegna a' far d'ogni sorte di vivande secondo la diversità de' i tempi così di carne come di pesce* (Facsimile reprint of Venice: 1557 edn., Bologna: Arnaldo Forni, 1982).

A New English Dictionary on Historical Principles, ed. by James A. Murray, I, pt. 2. B. (Oxford: Clarendon Press, 1888), pp 607-608.

Nilsson, Marin P., *Greek Folk Religion* (Philadelphia: University of Pennsylvania Press, 1998).

Ovid, *The Erotic Poems: The Amores, The Art of Love, Cures for Love, On Facial Treatment for Women*, trans. and ed. by Peter Green (London: Penguin Books, 1982).

——, *Metamorphoses*, trans. by Rolfe Humphries (Bloomington: Indiana University Press, 1983).

——, *Fasti*, trans. and ed. by A. J. Boyle and R. D. Woodard (London: Penguin, 2000).

Pailler, Jean-Marie, *Bacchanalia: La répression de 186 av. J.-C. à Rome et en Italie* (Rome: École Française de Rome, 1988).

Poussin, Nicolas, *Poussin, Sacraments and Bacchanals: Paintings and Drawings on Sacred and Profane Themes by Nicolas Poussin 1594-1665* (cat. to the exh. held Edinburgh: National Gallery Scotland, 16 Oct.-13 Dec. 1981).

Schmitz, Leonhard, 'Dionysia,' in *A Dictionary of Greek and Roman Antiquities*, ed. by William Smith (London: John Murray, 1875), pp. 413-14.

Titian, ed. by David Jaffé (London: National Gallery, 2003).

Wind, Edgar, *Pagan Mysteries in the Renaissance*, new ed. (London: Faber and Faber, 1967).

Young, Carolin C., *Apples of Gold in Settings of Silver: Stories of Dinner as a Work of Art* (New York: Simon & Schuster, 2002).

Notes

1. Euripides; Ovid *Met.* III.693-733; *Met.* III.584-692; *Met.* IV.389-413.
2. Livy XXXIX.14 The decree, known as the *Senatus consultum de Bacchinalibus*, was also inscribed on a bronze tablet now in Vienna.
3. Ovid *Fasti* III.733, III.762.
4. Euripides, p. 15.
5. Philostratus *Imagines* I.xxv in Fehl, p. 91.
6. Livy XXXIX.
7. Euripides, p. 57.
8. Livy XXXIX; Euripides, pp. 77-9.
9. Dodds, p. 271.
10. Euripides, p. 39.
11. Livy XXXIX.14.
12. Euripides, p. 31.
13. Dodds, p. 76.
14. *Fasti* I.395-400, I.405-6.
15. Euripides, p. 21.
16. *Fasti* I.406-410.
17. Ibid. I.410-13.
18. Ibid. I.352-60.
19. Dalby, p. 42.
20. Euripides, p. 23. The messenger who spied upon the rites reported that the ground ran with milk and the nectar of bees.
21. *Fasti* III.739-60.
22. Ibid. III.767-9.
23. Euripides, p. 21.
24. *Fasti* V.345-6.
25. Euripides, p. 17.
26. Dalby, pp. 111-17, 127-8.
27. Livy XXXIX.8.
28. Euripides,, p. 79.

29. Livy xxxix.8.
30. *Met.* IV.15-20.
31. *Fasti* III.733, III.778.
32. *Fasti* I.404.
33. Euripides,, p. 83.
34. This ritual is the origin of the word tragedy from the Greek *tragodia* or 'song around the goat.' Comedy, likewise, owes its origins to Bacchus. Its name is derived from the *komos*, or drunken parade of the City Dionysia.
35. Livy XXXIX.
36. Ibid.
37. *Fasti* I.402.
38. Ibid. III.729-31, *Met.* IV.393-4.
39. Harrigan pp. 1-2.
40. Ancient Tamil poem dedicated to Murukan in Harrigan.
41. The subjects were chosen not by Titian, but by Mario Equicola, a humanist secretary in the service of the duke's sister Isabella d'Este in Mantua. For inspiration, he turned to a new Italian translation of Philostratus' *Imagines*, which describes fictive paintings (*ekphraseis*) in an imaginary gallery in Naples, as well as more widely known texts such as Ovid's *Metamorphoses* and *Fasti*. Other artists – Dosso Dossi, Raphael, Fra Bartolomeo, and Bellini – were hired for the project long before Titian. However, with Raphael preoccupied in Rome and the deaths of Fra Bartolomeo and Bellini, Titian made the series his own – even going so far as to 'fix' Bellini's Feast of the Gods. The theme of Dionysian revelry was one that Titian, no stranger to Venetian pleasures, understood first hand. A guest who later supped in his Venetian garden described the event as a 'Bacchanalian feast'. See Young, pp. 41-63.
42. Moscus trans. of Philostratus, *Imagines*, produced for Isabella d'Este and borrowed by Duke Alfonso d'Este, trans. into English by Fehl, p. 92.
43. The facsimile of the later 1557 edition in the bibliography uses a different title.
44. Fehl, p. 51.
45. Ibid, p. 76.
46. Fehl has made the suggestion that the mythical creatures attending are invisible spirits surrounding a bacchanalian picnic shared by two young couples, making music, p. 75.
47. Jaffé, 108.
48. Fehl, p. 43.
49. Ibid, p. 75.
50. Lowinsky, pp. 198-202.
51. Euripides, p. 31; Ovid, *The Art of Love* 143-4.
52. *The Art of Love* 133-4.
53. Hazlitt 'On a landscape of Nicholas Poussin,' (London: 1821-2) in *Poussin*, p. 117.
54. Hugh Brigstocke in *Poussin*, p. 44.